ORIENTAL, BLACK, AND WHITE

Sketches from the Crystal Palace Pantomime: CINDERELLA

ORIENTAL, BLACK, AND WHITE

THE FORMATION OF RACIAL HABITS
IN AMERICAN THEATER

Josephine Lee

THE UNIVERSITY OF NORTH CAROLINA PRESS

Chapel Hill

© 2022 The University of North Carolina Press

All rights reserved

Designed by Jamison Cockerham
Set in Scala and Golden Hills
by codeMantra

Manufactured in the United States of America

The University of North Carolina Press has been a member
of the Green Press Initiative since 2003.

Complete Library of Congress Cataloging-in-Publication Data
is available at https://lccn.loc.gov/2022010529.
ISBN 978-1-4696-6961-8 (cloth: alk. paper)
ISBN 978-1-4696-6962-5 (pbk.: alk. paper)
ISBN 978-1-4696-6963-2 (ebook)

This book is freely available in an open access edition thanks to TOME
(Toward an Open Monograph Ecosystem)—a collaboration of the Association
of American Universities, the Association of University Presses, and the
Association of Research Libraries—and the generous support of University of
Minnesota Libraries. Learn more at the TOME website, openmonographs.org.

Contents

List of Illustrations vii

Acknowledgments ix

INTRODUCTION Oriental, Black, and White 1

1
The Racial Refashioning of *Aladdin*
21

2
The Lesser Roles of Ira Aldridge
44

3
Blackface Minstrelsy's Japanese Turns
60

4
The Tricky Servant in Blackface and Yellowface
79

5
The Chinese Laundry Sketch
100

v

6

"Maybe Now and Then a Chinaman": African American
Impersonators and Chinese Specialties
118

7

Divas and Dancers: Oriental Femininity and
African American Performance
137

8

Oriental Frolics and Racial Uplift in the
Early African American Musical
165

9

Pleasure Domes and Journeys Home: *In Dahomey,
Abyssinia, The Children of the Sun*, and *Shuffle Along*
191

10

Fantasy Islands: Staging the Philippines, 1900–1914
224

CONCLUSION Racial Puzzles, Chop Suey, and
Juanita Long Hall in *Flower Drum Song* 253

Notes 271

Selected Bibliography 313

Index 327

Illustrations

Harold Nicholas and Fayard Nicholas in *Tin Pan Alley*
6

Walter Crane, "New Lamps for Old Ones"
28

Walter Crane, "He Found That He Had Fallen
Back Lifeless upon the Couch"
29

"'Aladdin,' at the Lyceum"
37

Joseph Grimaldi as Kazrac in *Aladdin, Or, The Wonderful Lamp*
39

"Character Sketches from 'Aladdin' at Drury-
Lane, and 'Cinderella' at the Crystal Palace"
40

The Virginia Mummy
53

Thomas Dilward, or "Japanese Tommy"
66

"Natural Mistakes," published in *Harper's Weekly*
67

Harry Fiddler and Reuben Shelton
129

"Fiddler and Shelton: Those Two Clever Boys"
135

Main cast of the 1865 Paris Opera premiere of
Giacomo Meyerbeer's opera *L'Africaine*
144

Anna Madah Hyers in the role of Urlina
in *Urlina, The African Princess*
145

Sheet music for "The Oriental Coon" by Ed. Rogers
152

Aida Overton Walker
156

"John W. Isham's Oriental America:
40 Minutes of Grand Opera" lithograph
177

"John W. Isham's Oriental America: The Manhattan
Club, Grand Hunting Chorus" lithograph
179

"John W. Isham's Oriental America: Fantaisies d'Orient" lithograph
181

Sheet music for "The Wedding of the Chinee and the Coon"
189

Noble Sissle and chorus from *Shuffle Along*
217

Juanita Long Hall and ensemble in *Flower Drum Song*
265

Acknowledgments

A project of this size necessarily involves too many people to acknowledge properly, but I will do what I can. I owe great thanks to those who helped to edit and produce this book at the University of North Carolina Press, including Lucas Church, Mary Carley Caviness, Julie Bush, and Lindsay Starr. A special thanks to Dylan White, whose kindness, enthusiasm, and energy for this project buoyed me up whenever I got bogged down. I received a generous fellowship for my research from the National Endowment for the Humanities; any views, findings, conclusions, or recommendations expressed herein do not necessarily reflect those of the NEH. The College of Liberal Arts and the Department of English at the University of Minnesota also provided much-appreciated support for my research. I am grateful for the support of John Coleman, Jane Blocker, and Andrew Elfenbein in providing institutional resources to focus on this project. I also wish to thank Frances Spaulding and Alexandra Brown for their help in preparing my application for the NEH Fellowship as well as Kate McCready and Emma Molls for their assistance with the TOME award.

In May 2018 I was fortunate enough to participate in a "Library Sprint" with the University of Minnesota Libraries. The incredible team of Ben Wiggins, Cecily Marcus, Deborah Ultan, Yao Chen, Nancy Herther, Marguerite Ragnow, and Dorothy Berry devoted considerable time, effort, and expertise in order to help me access materials that would completely transform this project. Mark Horowitz at the Library of Congress, John Calhoun at the New York Public Library for the Performing Arts, and Matthew Wittmann at the Harvard Theatre Collection also provided valuable assistance and advice from afar.

Each of my chapters builds on the painstaking and admirable work and wisdom of fellow scholars as well as fans of theater history, as can be seen in the many names listed in the notes. In particular, Mari Yoshihara and Dave Roediger expressed their unwavering support for my scholarship and for this project; Robin Bernstein and Stephanie Batiste patiently made their way through an early draft; and anonymous readers provided excellent advice on behalf of the University of North Carolina Press. The ever-amazing Esther Kim Lee offered meticulous and inspiring suggestions that helped this book take its final shape. I am also indebted to Krystyn Moon once again for sharing her vast store of archival knowledge as well as her enthusiasm for scholarship in the history of the performing arts.

Many friends, colleagues, and students sustained me through the writing process with food for thought (and actual food), and I am grateful for their interest and encouragement. Last, but certainly not least, I am indebted to my family members far and near. My husband, Kevin Kinneavy, and sons, Julian and Dylan Lee Kinneavy, deserve lots of applause for their patience and encouragement. It has been a joy and a gift to be able to work on this project with you cheering me on at each and every step of the way.

Acknowledgments

ORIENTAL, BLACK, AND WHITE

Introduction

ORIENTAL, BLACK, AND WHITE

On November 2, 2000, a post appeared on the forum the Mudcat Café, an online space dedicated to discussion of British and American folk music, requesting help in identifying the words to a song, "My Castle on the Nile," which the user remembered singing "at Girl Scout camp."[1] Subsequent replies provided different versions of the lyrics as well as information about various recordings. Other posts readily identified the song's origins: composed by John Rosamond Johnson, with lyrics by James Weldon Johnson and Bob Cole for the 1900 musical *Sons of Ham*, the song was used in one of several African American musicals that starred the comedy team of Bert Williams and George Walker and was later incorporated into *In Dahomey*, another Williams and Walker musical, first produced in 1902.

For those familiar with the contributions of Williams and Walker to the history of American musical theater, the lyrics of "My Castle on the Nile" easily conjure up Williams's familiar sad-sack stage persona, an impoverished and comic figure who muses on current misfortunes and longs for an alternative way of life.

Dere ain't no use in try'n to rise up in de social scale,
Less you kin trace yo' name back to de flood.
You got to have ancestral halls an' den you mus'nt fail,
To prove dere's indigo mixed in yo' blood.
I done foun' out dat I come down from ole chief Bungaboo
My great-gran'-daddy was his great gran' chile.

An' so I'm gwin'ter sail away across de waters blue,
To occupy my castle on de Nile.
In my Castle on de river Nile
I am gwinter live in elegant style
Inlaid diamonds on the flo'
A Baboon butler at my do'
When I wed dat princess Anna Mazoo
Den my blood will change from red to blue
Entertaining royalty all the while
In my Castle on the Nile.[2]

However, as indicated on the Mudcat Café, "My Castle on the Nile" was not always performed by African American singers. For instance, it was recorded by the baritone Arthur Francis Collins, billed as the "King of the Ragtime Singers," who sang songs using the personae of black characters so frequently that publicity by Edison Phonograph took pains to ensure that he was not mistakenly seen as a "Negro."[3] Like other popular songs written by Cole and J. Rosamond Johnson (for instance, their 1902 hit "Under the Bamboo Tree"),[4] "My Castle on the Nile" had many encores in professional and amateur settings, probably with most of its singers unaware of the song's origins on the early African American musical stage.[5]

"My Castle on the Nile" can be read as yet another instance of the many complicated and unequal racial interactions enacted through American theater and music. Its words emphasize the black-white dimensions of a long and troubled history of expression, exchange, impersonation, and appropriation. Denied the blue blood of European elitism, the dialect-speaking character at its center sets his version of royal ancestry in Egypt. His naming of the "river Nile" reflects a popular interpretation of the Old Testament in which African Americans were seen as the descendants of Ham, cursed by Ham's father, Noah, and relegated to slavery. Interestingly enough, this emphasis on black lineage is not the only kind of racial reference in the song. The lyrics of "My Castle on the Nile" point to tropes not only associated with blackness but also defined by orientalism, imagining a diamond-encrusted castle in a faraway land, foreign status and leisure, and marriage to the princess "Anna Mazoo." These oriental allusions allow the central character to voice discontent with hierarchies based on descent ("indigo mixed in yo' blood") and longing for alternative spaces of social power. They also enhance the comic exaggeration of the song, exposing the ludicrous nature of a fantasy done up in "elegant style" as exotic adventure and luxury are translated into the baser terms of stereotypical blackness: descent from "ole chief Bungaboo," a "Baboon butler" and a monkey valet, and hunger for chickens (ostriches) that grow "six feet tall."

Thus the lyrics of "My Castle on the Nile" exemplify how the caricatures of blackface minstrelsy and "coon songs" are often interwoven with other kinds of racial fantasy. Its oriental tropes draw upon a long cultural history in which the lands, peoples, and cultures of Asia, the Middle East, and northern and eastern Africa are depicted in colorful, imprecise, and often amalgamated ways. Orientalism's rich lands, cruel despots, quaint locals, exotic maidens, and opportunities for adventure and profit became staples of European and British literary and artistic presentation, suggesting how, as Edward Said described, "European culture gained in strength and identify by setting itself off against the Orient as a sort of surrogate and even underground self."[6] Written in 1797, Samuel Taylor Coleridge's poetic fragment "Kubla Khan; or, A Vision in a Dream" illustrates this well, with its descriptions of a powerful Mongol ruler ("In Xanadu did Kubla Khan / A stately pleasure dome decree"), marvelous places and edifices ("a miracle of rare device / A sunny pleasure-dome with caves of ice!"), savage desire ("woman wailing for her demon lover!"), and a nubile muse who inspires the poet to new heights of artistry ("It was an Abyssinian maid, / And on her dulcimer she played, / Singing of Mount Abora").[7] From the seventeenth century on, British and Continental theater rendered similar spectacles, albeit less famously, on the stage.[8]

As Esther Kim Lee has documented, yellowface and brownface performances of oriental characters on the American stage have deep roots in British and Continental theater practice.[9] By the time "My Castle on the Nile" was written, orientalism had become a familiar staple of American theater. The song's exaggerations emphasize the pointedly fictive nature of these fantasies, with the imagined settings and inhabitants of the Orient prized for their spectacular appearance rather than their representational authenticity or psychological depth. During the mid-nineteenth century, theatrical parodies mocked both orientalist fashion and those foolish enough to fall prey to its allure. Adaptations of Jacques Offenbach's 1855 *Ba-ta-clan*, produced in London and New York as George Alex Lingard's *Ching Chow Hi*, revealed its "Chinese" emperor, princess, and other characters to be French (or English or American) expatriates in disguise.[10] European, British, and American playwrights alike borrowed devices from Molière's 1670 "comédie-ballet" *Le Bourgeois Gentilhomme*, in which the social pretensions of the foolish Monsieur Jourdain lead him to promise his daughter to a

"Turkish prince." Unsurprisingly, Molière's oriental noble turns out to be Cléonte, a French suitor dressed in elaborate costume and speaking gibberish. Molière includes several scenes of cross-racial impersonation; M. Jourdain is easily deceived by Cléonte's disguise and allows himself to be dressed in a ridiculous outfit and turban, after which the others pretend to induct him into foreign royalty and then humiliate him. In the United States as well as abroad, many playwrights readily copied Molière's oriental devices and stage situations. For instance, Willard Spenser's 1882 operetta, *The Little Tycoon*, features General Knickerbocker, a man infatuated with things Japanese, who promises his daughter in marriage to the "Great Tycoon of Japan." The so-called Tycoon is of course not Japanese at all but the hero Alvin in disguise, who captivates the General with his fluent mock Japanese.

ALVIN (TYCOON). Yum yum boerum-jorum; ki-yi ki-yi! Sangar
   sangaree. Pongo-congo-ongo-wongo belladonna nux vomica,
   ki-yi.
GEN. KNICKERBOCKER. Pure Japanese! What a divine accent! What a
   glorious language! We shall all be speaking it yet.[11]

Many works thus lampooned orientalism as a form of pretense, staging scenes in which cross-racial performance served as an easy comic ruse. Scenes of patent inauthenticity helped to couple satiric humor with the allure of lavish spectacle, rendering the theatrical Orient as a complete fabrication and justifying how little effort should be made to represent real people or their culture accurately or fairly.

This brand of theatrical orientalism often found itself sharing the stage with other kinds of racial impersonation, notably blackface minstrelsy. Nineteenth-century minstrel troupes were quick to capitalize on the success of oriental-themed productions, such as Carcross and Dixey's Minstrels' "new Chinese burlesque" of Offenbach's *Ba-ta-clan*; *Ching-Chung-Hi; or, Burlingame's Teacady* in 1869 at the Eleventh Street Theatre in Philadelphia;[12] and Kelly and Leon's Minstrels' burlesque *Ba-ta-clan* in 1870–78, with scenery and costumes "among the richest ever seen in a minstrel hall."[13] *The Little Tycoon* also generated *Little Fly Coon*, a parody by McNish, Johnson, and Slavin's Minstrels that in 1887 was "rewarded with two weeks of good business."[14]

African American as well as white performers were regularly included in these visions of the Orient as, to use Edward Said's memorable phrase, "the stage on which the whole East is confined."[15] As "My Castle on the Nile" demonstrates, African American writers, composers, and performers drew on a common theatrical vocabulary that portrayed both black and oriental races as inherently different from white characters. Orientalism became a notable feature in many milestones of African American theater history: the groundbreaking performances of individuals such as Ira Aldridge, Billy Kersands, the sisters Anna Madah Hyers and Emma Louise Hyers, Sissieretta Jones, and Aida Overton Walker, or significant "firsts" such as John W. Isham's *Oriental America*, Bob Cole and Billy Johnson's *A Trip to Coontown*, and musicals starring Williams and Walker. In between were many less obvious instances in which black and oriental figuration intersected on the American stage. These moments of interracial performance were neither accidental nor novel. Rather, they were part of ongoing patterns of representation that allowed both white and African American performers to take on both blackface and oriental roles. As this book will show, these interracial encounters highlighted how American theater's racial representations could move beyond the binary oppositions of "black" and "white" performance.

Much of the historical record of these theatrical encounters have been lost, but certain theatrical habits of cross-racial performance and juxtaposition remain captured in cinematic nostalgia. One example appears in the 1940 movie musical *Tin Pan Alley*, directed by Walter Lang. Starring Alice Faye and Betty Grable as a pair of singing sisters, the film pays homage to the early twentieth-century American vaudeville stage and dreams of show business success. The sisters' rise to fame is marked by a star turn in an extended song and dance number, "The Sheik of Araby," toward the end of the movie. One of several cross-racial performances featured in *Tin Pan Alley*, this oriental number both contrasts with and compounds the comic and erotic racial meanings expressed through earlier moments of blackface minstrelsy and Hawaiian hula-inspired numbers. "The Sheik of Araby" sequence is anchored by the plump, turbaned Sheik (Billy Gilbert) who eats grapes and lounges amidst his harem (a bevy of white chorus girls in revealing costumes). The ensemble is entertained by a dark-skinned female dancer (credited only with the stage name "Princess Vanessa Ammon") wearing an elaborate headdress who poses seductively to the exotic sounds of tinkling bells and flutes. Her feature as an oriental slave girl is followed by an impressively acrobatic tap dance sequence by brothers Harold Nicholas and Fayard Nicholas, wearing feathered turbans and loincloths and little else.

They in turn are followed by Faye and Grable, who perform a tap dance and identify themselves as two of the many wives of the so-called Sheik. Despite their midriff-baring oriental costumes and their joyful musical

Harold Nicholas and Fayard Nicholas in *Tin Pan Alley* (1940).
Author's collection.

declarations of devotion to their "Baghdad daddy," the pale skin and blonde hair of Faye and Grable emphasize their whiteness. The sisterly duo then join with the Sheik to perform a version of the song "The Sheik of Araby," a musical tribute to Rudolph Valentino's starring role in the 1921 silent film *The Sheik*.[16]

"The Sheik of Araby" number in *Tin Pan Alley* makes no pretenses to originality or innovation in terms of its oriental effects; despite its scandalously revealing costumes, the harem scene and oriental dancers are staged

Introduction

as conventional and even predictable theatrical tropes. The Sheik's yawning demeanor signals a state of bored familiarity, at least until his interest is finally piqued by the star turns of Faye and Grable. But in retrospect, the most memorable aspects of "The Sheik of Araby" number are not these appearances by white celebrities but those of African American dancers such as the now-forgotten "Princess Vanessa Ammon" and the Nicholas brothers, whose roles as servile eunuchs are quickly belied by their incomparable athleticism, musicality, and style. By 1940, the brothers were well-known for their superlative dance performances, despite often being relegated to the "specialty act" rather than allowed the star billing they so clearly deserved. Their appearance in *Tin Pan Alley* functions both as a record of their incredible talents and as cinematic nostalgia for a past theatrical moment, as 1940s cinema reenacts—and in doing so, reinvigorates—the earlier joys of vaudeville entertainment. It also establishes how the integration of the African American performer and black character within the oriental scene was a standard part of these earlier theatrical pleasures. *Tin Pan Alley* operates both as a nostalgic look at an earlier moment in theatrical history and as a marker of what might seem to be a puzzling and incongruous juxtaposition of racial types and actors. In doing so, it sets the stage for our investigation of how intermingling the tropes of blackness and orientalism came to be an ingrained aspect of theatrical practice.

This book has several objectives. One is to underscore the importance of orientalism as an important foundation for American theater, something that has already been emphasized in a number of recent works of scholarship.[17] Another is to show how African American as well as white performers, like "Princess Vanessa Ammon" and the Nicholas brothers, made significant use of theatrical orientalism and how these performances register an intriguing and less well-known aspect of nineteenth- and early twentieth-century theatrical genres such as blackface minstrelsy, vaudeville, or musical comedy. Third, the book looks at how black and oriental figuration intersected in ways suggestive of interracial relationships sometimes hidden or erased by the rigidity of racial classifications. Since "black" and "oriental" are often framed as inherently oppositional and conflicting characteristics, qualities, and subject positions, this book reflects on what it might mean if racial subjects and objects belonging to these two categories were seen as being in close proximity or even imagined as interchangeable.

In order to move toward these objectives, each chapter examines a series of texts and images that shed light on past theatrical productions, such as playscripts, scores, stories about actors, and reviews. However, the larger aims of this project move away from trying to reconstruct the experience of live performance from existing archival records or describing a particular artistic movement or stage practice. Instead, the book uses theatrical examples to illuminate a broader cultural history and to reflect upon the impact of theater—especially its capacity to revive and reproduce characterization, behavior, interaction, and spectacle—on everyday life offstage. Two introductory concepts might be helpful to consider at this point: how theatrical enactments helped to establish distinctive "racial habits" both on and off the stage through the construction of characters and cross-racial interactions, and how performances that were marked as black and oriental shared the spaces of nineteenth- and early twentieth-century American theater.

ON THE PERSISTENCE OF RACIAL HABITS

I kept repeating mechanically those well-drilled and firmly established "tricks" of the part—the mechanical signs of an absence of genuine feeling. In some places, I tried to be as nervous and excited as possible, and for that reason performed a series of quick movements; in others I tried to appear naive and technically reproduced the gait and the typical gestures of the part—the external result of a feeling that was dead. I copied naïveté, but I was not naive; I walked with quick, short steps, and so on. I exaggerated more or less skilfully [sic], I imitated the external manifestations of feelings and actions, but at the same time I did not experience any feelings or any real need for action. As the performances went on, I acquired the mechanical habit of going through the once and for all established gymnastic exercises, which were firmly fixed as my stage habits by my muscular memory, which is so strong with actors.[18]

Biographer David Magarshack recalls how the influential theater practitioner and acting teacher Konstantin Stanislavski addressed the onstage "habits"—repeated actions, gestures, and expressions ingrained in the actor's technique—that prevented a much more psychologically complex approach to acting. According to Stanislavski, these exaggerated gestures and mannerisms, copied and passed down among generations of actors, inhibited and thwarted attempts at more realistic characterization. Though Stanislavski was not talking specifically about race, his description highlights how theatrical performance encompasses both racial ideology and enactment in reducing human complexity to the repetition of stage type.

8   *Introduction*

As Eddie Glaude suggests, the "biases, stereotypes, and the history of racism in this country" produce their own set of habits that undergird everyday racial inequalities and oppression.[19] This persistent reincarnation of racial stereotypes is regularly demonstrated in today's news, as photographs capture politicians and celebrities in embarrassing costumes, designer items bear the telltale influence of racial caricature, and instances of cross-racial casting and whitewashing come under fire. Stereotypes exist not only as the strange relics of a racist past but as a set of constantly reanimated enactments. Nineteenth- and early twentieth-century American theater served as both the point of origination for many of these character types and as one of the most important cultural practices that helped ingrain racial fantasy into conventional perspective. As performed live in the theater, racial stereotypes are not just distorted images misrepresenting real people but also experiences convincing live audiences of their reality and authenticity. Whether humorous, melodramatic, romantic, heroic, or ridiculous, theatrical characters serve as the models for enacting and perceiving racial Others.

The repetitive and ingrained nature of racial habits, even when produced in the fictional space of the stage, touch on what sociologist Pierre Bourdieu has called *habitus*, the real-life "system of dispositions, that is of permanent manners of being, seeing, and acting and thinking."[20] Bourdieu's formulation captures the mindless repetition of everyday actions and interactions, the "intentionless invention of regulated improvisation."[21] Harvey Young has elegantly adapted Bourdieu's *habitus* to describe how African Americans must negotiate "an *idea* of the black body [that] has been and continues to be projected across actual physical bodies" through a "slippage of abstraction into material" that creates "an embodied experience of blackness . . . tantamount to imprisonment."[22] For Young, "habitus allows us to think about the black body as a construct built by the sedimentation of similar experiences, critical memories, and enactments. It enables us to see that black bodies can be different—variably situated within society and equipped with opposing habiti—but can at the same time be read from a common perspective."[23]

In her examination of racism as "habitual," philosopher Helen Ngo emphasizes the ethical responsibility to think of racial habit not only as the "sedimentation" of unconscious behaviors but as "active and ongoing" processes. Racial habits are "*held*—not merely acquired."[24] Studying theater provides a unique opportunity, then, to examine the general formation, usage, and mobilization of racial habits; it also helps us think about what is unique to the actor's presentation of racialized beings and relationships and why performers *hold* onto as well as adapt and challenge certain conventions of performing race. Theatrical performance generally presumes an actor's special ability and privilege to move in between characterizations and thus enact (if not feel) multiple *habiti*. However, with regard to race in casting, the American stage has a checkered past. Nowhere is this more clear than in the genre of blackface minstrelsy, which blended infectious music, captivating dance, and rollicking humor with cross-racial mockery. In 1843, the Virginia Minstrels famously performed in New York City the first full evening of what they billed as the "oddities, peculiarities, eccentricities, and comicalities of that Sable Genus of Humanity."[25] These white minstrels were seen as representing the "sports and pastimes of the Virginia Colored Race, through medium of Songs, Refrains, and Ditties as sung by Southern Slaves,"[26] and their successors used blackface to demonstrate the many "curiosities" and "eccentricities" of enslaved Africans and the hard-and-fast distinctions presumed between black and white bodies. Minstrelsy's racial habits were influenced by ideologies of racism that, as St. Claire Drake has suggested, justified slavery as a system in which "the slave owner was expected to differ in physical type from the slave."[27] In addition to demonstrating black inferiority, displays of the "Sable Genus" also promised elements of the exotic and foreign. As Robert Toll has noted, early minstrelsy promised to satisfy white northern curiosity about blacks "at a time when slavery was becoming a major national controversy." Northerners "believed or wanted to believe that black slaves differed greatly from free, white Americans," and thus minstrels catered to assumptions about black "peculiarities," with minstrels describing themselves as "Ethiopian Delineators" and "Congo Melodists" and titling their acts "Virginia Jungle Dance," "Nubian Jungle Dance," "African Fling," or "African Sailor's Hornpipe."[28]

Blackface minstrelsy's popularity helped codify which theatrical roles became predictable and familiar not only for white actors but also for African Americans. As Toll notes, African Americans had appeared in musical and dance entertainments since the colonial period but were mainly confined to minstrelsy's racial caricatures.[29] One notable exception was the African Grove Theatre, formed in 1821 by William Alexander Brown and James Hewlett, in which performances of Shakespeare and other heroic works were explicitly directed toward audiences comprising "Ladies and Gentlemen of Color." As Marvin McAllister has described, these performances were part of a tradition of African Americans playing whiteface or stage European roles that has "operated for centuries just beneath America's representational radar."[30] Much more visible in American theater history were the significant numbers of African American performers who joined in the more lucrative touring black and integrated minstrel troupes from the 1850s on. Their performance often offered "authentic" depictions of plantation slavery and preserved the blackface roles popularized by white minstrels. For instance, in 1878 the notable actor and comedian Sam Lucas became the first African American actor in commercial theater to play Uncle Tom in the popular *Uncle Tom's Cabin*, a role that remained significant for him throughout his career.

Just as the many peoples of Africa, the West Indies, and the Caribbean were collapsed into caricatures of the "Sable Genus," so did a vast geographical and cultural amalgamation make up the fictive Orient on the American stage. Theatrical orientalism imagined barbaric heathens and despotic luxury in the Ottoman Empire, the profit of Silk Road trade, alluring commodities from China and Japan, and colonial power over exotic islands in the Pacific. Obvious geographical and cultural differences were often collapsed in favor of a familiar set of racial habits associating the Orient with opulent excess, despotic power, magical objects, and fantasy. In 1847, the Ravel family, a troupe of visiting French acrobats and dancers, staged a New York performance of *Kim-Ka! or the Misfortunes of Ventilator* featuring a "splendid Chinese tent, supported by richly carved columns," as well as "porphyr baths" and "a magnificent pavilion" set against a "picturesque garden on the margin of a silvery lake."[31] Events include a sumptuous grand court procession that is interrupted by the spectacular entrance of a fiery balloon, announcing the arrival of the French aeronaut Ventillateur. Ventillateur hides in a pavilion decorated with life-size nodding-head statues of Chinese mandarins; after some comic business in which Ventillateur pretends to be a statue, the emperor Kim-Ka orders him imprisoned. He is ultimately released and allowed to marry the beautiful Princess Lei after a humorous dispute over having his head shaved (presumably to emulate Qing dynasty practices of wearing a queue). The Emperor then calls for the finale, a grand divertissement with "a grand display of Chinese fireworks." The version of China depicted in *Kim-Ka!* is a fantasyland that did not demand seriousness or accuracy; French performers easily played Chinese subjects as well as the heroic Ventillateur, and in the end Ventillateur becomes "Chinese" through the simple act of shaving his head.

As John Kuo Wei Tchen has detailed, American elites from colonial times onward adopted the "tasteful display of passionately coveted things from the 'Orient' and the 'Indies'" that "distinguished one moneyed space from the other."[32] In nineteenth-century America this association of the Orient with patrician tastes shifted toward the more commercial display of oriental goods, motifs, and even people, as staged for a more middle-class public. The 1834 New York exhibition of Afong Moy, billed as the "Chinese Lady," singled her "astonishing little feet" for special attention; similar fascination followed "Miss Pwan-Yekoo, the Chinese Belle" in the "Living Chinese Family" display in impresario Phineas Taylor Barnum's "Chinese Museum," which opened in 1850; she was described as "so pretty, so arch, so lively, and so graceful" and her "minute feet" as "wondrous!"[33] The "Siamese twins" Chang and Eng Bunker were brought to the United States from Thailand in 1829 by Robert Hunter, a British merchant. They toured the United States and England with great success, contracting with the Barnum to appear at the American Museum in 1860 and then again in 1868 at George Wood's museum at Broadway and Thirtieth Street.[34] Associations of oriental cultures with extraordinary physicality, supernatural powers, or erotic sensuality were also seen in the immense popularity of visiting Chinese, Japanese, "Arab," or "Hindoo" acrobats and magicians or of "oriental dances" performed by women of North Africa and the Middle East, such as the famed "Little Egypt" at the 1893 World's Columbian Exposition.

In terms of numbers and commercial value, these performers could not compete with the widespread success of white and African American impersonators, whose portrayals, though less authentic, still served to fuel and satisfy much of the popular demand for oriental curiosities and fantasies. That black and oriental representation came together so frequently on the American stage is perhaps unsurprising, given that the habits of both were so deeply ingrained into theater practice in America. As the quest for novelty drove commercial theater in particular toward variation and diversion, black and oriental settings, characters, themes, songs, and stage objects were served to theatergoers alongside one another, and sometimes as part of the same evening's entertainment. Thus American theatrical production created regular opportunities for active encounters and closer proximity among producers, performers, and spectators, who for at least some time would share the same dramatic spaces.

THE SHARED SPACES OF BLACK AND
ORIENTAL REPRESENTATION

After January 1, 1849, 539 Broadway in New York City became the "Chinese Assembly Rooms" and the location of John Peters Jr.'s "Great Chinese Museum." This venue was later managed after April 22, 1850, by P. T. Barnum, who replaced Peters's name with his own and added a "Chinese family" as well as "a huge and magnificent assemblage of 'curiosities' from China" that for its time was the largest outside of Asia.[35] After profiting handsomely from the three-month success of these displays, Barnum closed his museum sometime between July 23 and August 15, 1850.[36] But the theatrical function of the "Chinese Assembly Rooms" continued, this time with blackface and other less pointedly oriental curiosities. Later remade into the Broadway Casino (also Buckley's Music Hall and the Melodeon) after September 1, 1853,[37] the building served as the home of minstrelsy, burlesque, variety, and other entertainments until it was destroyed by fire in 1868.[38]

In 1882, another Casino Theatre was built at 1404 Broadway at West Thirty-Ninth Street, with the distinction of being the first theater in New York to be lit entirely by electricity; it had the added attraction of New York's first roof garden in 1890. Like its predecessor, the second Casino Theatre also conspicuously displayed spectacular oriental-themed effects and productions. An ambitious structure of brick and terracotta, it was considered by some to be "the best example of Moorish architecture in the city."[39] Its successful productions included the 1900 New York production of the 1899 London hit *Florodora*, whose first act is set in a fictional island in the Philippines,[40] and the 1902 New York production of George Dance and Howard Talbot's successful London hit *A Chinese Honeymoon*. The Casino also became an important venue for early African American musical theater. On September 21, 1896, the Victor Herbert operetta *The Gold Bug*, which featured Bert Williams and George Walker, also premiered at the Casino.[41] On July 4, 1898, Will Marion Cook and Paul Laurence Dunbar's one-act musical *Clorindy; or, The Origin of the Cake Walk* was performed as an afterpiece to Casino manager Edward E. Price's *Summer Nights* at the roof garden at the Casino, making it the first musical with an all–African American cast to be performed at a Broadway house.

By the early twentieth century, an amalgamation of racial performances had become typical fare for New York theatergoers. For instance, during the summer of 1907, the second Casino (now one of several theaters managed by Sam S. Shubert and Lee Shubert) produced *Fascinating Flora*, a vehicle for the actress Adele Ritchie, who had previously appeared in *A Chinese Honeymoon*. Other productions that summer included George M. Cohan's *The Honeymooners* at the Aerial Garden, Oscar Wilde's *Lady Windermere's Fan* at Keith and Proctor's Harlem Opera House, and a new comic opera, *The Alaskan*, opening mid-August at the Knickerbocker Theatre. *The Alaskan* promised novelty and "local color" by bringing in twelve sled dogs from Alaska as well as "choruses of Esquimau girls, Nome show girls, miners, prospectors, and feminine visitors to Nome."[42] The chanteuse Eugenie

Fougère, performing at Hammerstein's Roof Garden, was lauded for her cakewalks and performance of popular "coon songs" as well as for her revealing costumes and risqué demeanor.[43] Sharing the featured billing with Mlle. Fougère was "Shekla," the "Hindoo Conjurer," who was described by his manager Willie Hammerstein (son of impresario Oscar Hammerstein I and father of famous lyricist Oscar Hammerstein II) as "a Hindoo whom we discovered in a minor music hall of London."[44] There was also a rare entertainer of Chinese descent, singer Lee Tung Foo, described as "the Chinese baritone," appearing on the vaudeville bill at Keith and Proctor's Twenty-Third Street Theatre.[45] Two all–African American musicals also had productions in New York: Bob Cole, J. Rosamond Johnson, and James Weldon Johnson's *The Shoo-Fly Regiment* came to the Grand Opera House in early June and the Bijou in early August, while the Chicago-based Pekin Theater Company's production of *Captain Rufus* was performed mid-August at Hurtig and Seamon's Music Hall.[46]

Representations of blackness in American theater, whether as seen in the popular practice of minstrel blackface or in the breakthrough performances of African Americans, are often thought of as existing worlds away from the dramatization of the lavish and foreign Orient. But as these examples show, the collusion (or collision) of these two kinds of racial performance took place in multiple instances. The remainder of this book demonstrates how black and oriental representations and cross-racial enactments were joined in many different productions and genres, from wordless pantomimes to the banter of vaudeville, from the lighthearted song and dance of musical theater to the arias of tragic opera. Looking at the intersection of black and oriental performance allows us to revisit American theatrical entertainment at a formative stage as well as to take stock of how its signature tropes and characterizations sometimes affirmed and at other times challenged one another. The performers and productions examined here were most assuredly never intended to inspire prolonged deliberation on racial matters; they employed cross-racial impersonation and fantasy to elicit laughter, tears, wonder, applause, and profit. But in retrospect their histories also can be understood as part of a broader multiracial ideology, an "imaginative geography," that, as Edward Said reflected, is "less a fact of nature than it is a fact of human production."[47]

OVERTURE

This book examines a plethora of examples: key plays, performers, and productions that reveal the deep and sustained imbrication of black and oriental representation in American theater history. That these examples involve multiple circumstances, theatrical styles, and frames of reference means that each of the following chapters necessarily changes in focus and argument. Several chapters emphasize the production history of a single story, such as *Aladdin*, or consider the career of a particular actor; others comment on the characterizations, themes, and other devices included in different plays and productions. Nonetheless, there are some consistencies among them. The first three chapters demonstrate how American theater associated orientalism with opulence, exoticism, and deception. Later chapters mark how such resonances persist, even as in the second half of the nineteenth century the initial attractions of the theatrical Orient with its lavish settings and quaint inhabitants were supplanted by much more abject figures of immigrant "Chinamen." The book also asserts the legacy of nineteenth- and early twentieth-century theater practice by African Americans, whose work left as much of an impact on American theater history as did that of their white counterparts. Each chapter thus contemplates the ways in which performances of orientalism by African Americans may have been different from those enacted by white performers. However subtle, such differences suggest that character types are not just resurrected but also modified by various performers; this allows for the possibility that racial habits can have not only iterative but also combinatorial properties that change both their immediate effects and long-term significance.

The first part of this book includes a heavy dose of British and European theater, acknowledging the extent to which people, productions, and theatrical practices have regularly moved from Britain and the Continent to the United States and back again. Chapter 1 begins by looking at British and American versions of *Aladdin*, probably the earliest and most enduring of the works that include both black and oriental characters. First appearing on the London stage with John O'Keeffe's 1788 harlequinade *Aladin; or, The Wonderful Lamp*, the story of *Aladdin* remains alive and kicking in the theater as well as in film and popular culture. Early *Aladdins* provide insight into how spectacles of oriental magic and adventure might be juxtaposed with images of black servitude and villainy through the presence of black slaves and an "African" magician.

Nineteenth-century stage *Aladdins* featured the character Kazrac, a mute servant who directly connects the figure of the Chinese slave with the minstrel caricature of the enslaved African. The Kazrac role was clearly informed by the racial identities of those who played him, and among the many who did so was the renowned African American actor Ira Aldridge. Chapter 2 looks at several of Aldridge's comic characterizations: Kazrac in *Aladdin*; Mungo, a popular black slave character from Isaac John Bickerstaff and Charles Dibdin's 1768 operatic afterpiece *The Padlock*; and Ginger Blue in the farce *The Virginia Mummy*, a character first popularized in 1835 by the blackface minstrel Thomas Dartmouth ("T.D.") Rice. While Aldridge was more famous for his playing of Shakespeare's Othello and other heroic roles, chapter 2 contemplates how these "lesser" roles, which comment on oriental as well as black representation, must affect any assessment of Aldridge's successful career in Great Britain and Europe.

Chapter 3 focuses on two distinctive examples of how American black-face minstrelsy capitalized on the "Japan craze," the interest in Japanese arts, crafts, and culture following the 1853 "opening" of Japan to the West by Commodore Perry. The African American minstrel Thomas Dilward adopted the stage name "Japanese Tommy," cultivating the elitist and fem-inized aspects of orientalism in service of a stage persona that moved away from the masculine and competitive physicality often associated with min-strelsy. Walter Ben Hare's *Abbu San of Old Japan* (1916), an amateur play written for an all-female cast that juxtaposes Japanese characters with a blackface "Mammy" type, also speaks to minstrelsy's popularity for female performers. Probably written for student performance, Hare's play high-lights the tensions between the adventuresome spirit and cosmopolitan nature of the liberated white New Woman performer and the exotic Japanese and the familiar comic blackface roles that she might play.

While American theater retained its interest in the foreign and patri-cian aspects of the Orient, another type of oriental figure grew increasingly familiar in the second half of the nineteenth century. At once comic and menacing, the figure of the Chinese immigrant laborer was quite different from the quaint inhabitants of fantastical lands or valuable ornamental objects that had previously come to life on the American stage. Julia H. Lee has pointed out how this characterization, as promoted through both political debates and works of literature, articulated anxieties about race, American national identity, and labor that showed the interplay between the fantasies of the "Negro Problem" and the "Yellow Peril."[48] Chapter 4 shows how such tensions are made part of melodramas such as James McCloskey's *Across the Continent* (1870) and Bret Harte and Mark Twain's *Ah Sin* (1877), where comic Chinese immigrant characters are specifically contrasted with the figures of the black servants. Chapter 5 examines how the ubiquitous "Chinese laundry sketch" in vaudeville revealed a continuing pattern of hos-tility and suspicion toward Chinese immigrant men. In these sketches, the laundryman's incomprehensible language and dubious business practices arouse the ire of customers and lead to trouble with the law. Played both by white actors and by African American performers, Chinese laundryman characters were pictured as in competition with both white and African American labor. Chapter 5 also suggests how the relentless repetition of this stereotype—a pigtailed and barely intelligible figure who eats strange food and tries to swindle his customers—takes a different turn when adopted by African American performers in sketches featuring a "Chinaman" paired with a "coon" figure.

Ira Aldridge and Thomas Dilward were some of the earliest African American performers to employ oriental characterization as part of their repertoire, but they were far from alone. The second half of the book documents the increasing involvement of African Americans in oriental roles. Chapter 6 surveys how African American impersonators such as Tom Brown, Harry Fiddler, Sam Cook, George Catlin, and Frank Walker specialized in vaudeville acts featuring Chinese immigrant characters. Chapter 7 focuses on how African American women used orientalism to add new dimensions to their leading roles in musical theater and dance. Anna Madah Hyers, Sissieretta Jones, Aida Overton Walker, and others strategically employed the association of the oriental female with erotic attraction, sexual availability, and acquiescence to masculine power, even while their public images maintained the decorum expected of proper African American femininity.

Chapters 6 and 7 emphasize how cross-racial performance became a way for African American performers to expand their range of available roles as they negotiated not only the continued popular demand for blackface minstrel caricature but also the expectation that they serve as role models for racial respectability and progress. Orientalism presented certain expressive possibilities but also required that African American performers negotiate the fine lines between respectable display and extravagant or sensual excess that defined these shows. Chapter 8 illustrates how these constraints continue to impact the writers, composers, managers, and performers of early all–African American musicals. The exotic attractions of the oriental harem were both hinted at and carefully contained within Sam T. Jack's 1890 *Creole Burlesque Show*, whereas a much more cultured and patrician version of orientalism is front and center in John W. Isham's 1896 *Oriental America*. In contrast, Bob Cole and Billy Johnson's 1897 *A Trip to Coontown* employs oriental elements not only to add novelty and sex appeal but also to satirize black racial progress and its connection to wealth and reputation.

The final chapters considers the possibility of new relationships between blackness and orientalism in African American musicals of the early twentieth century. Here orientalism not only served to enlarge the range of theatrical expression, characterization, spectacle, and theme but also created the opportunity to comment on African American social mobility, pan-Africanism, and interracial intimacy. Chapter 9 looks at four musicals—the Bert Williams and George Walker vehicles *In Dahomey* (1902) and *Abyssinia* (1906), Salem Tutt Whitney and J. Homer Tutt's *The Children of the Sun* (1919), and Noble Sissle and Eubie Blake's *Shuffle Along* (1921)—that use seemingly standard oriental fare: comic Chinese immigrants, nubile chorines, and exotic settings. But just as these shows repurposed the blackface stereotypes of minstrelsy, so did they rework the terms of stage orientalism to suit their own needs. A similar modification of racial habit operates in the trio of African American musicals—Bob Cole, James Weldon Johnson, and J. Rosamond Johnson's *The Shoo-Fly Regiment* (1906), the Pekin Company's *Captain Rufus* (1907), and the Black Patti Troubadours' *Captain Jasper* (1913)—at the center of chapter 10. As compared with white-produced plays about the wars in the Philippines, these works show more ambivalent attitudes about race and imperialism even while they celebrate black military heroism during the Spanish-American and Philippine-American Wars.

These chapters on vaudeville and early African American musicals offer insight into the vexed relationship between African American performers and the oriental characters that they impersonated onstage. The conclusion explores further the possibility of affinity between African Americans and Chinese immigrants as it might have been developed through the close proximity of both the stage and the Chinese restaurant. The book ends with a look at the career of Lily "Pontop" Yuen, a dancer and comedian of African American and Chinese descent, as well as at Juanita Long Hall's performances as Madam Liang in the 1958 Broadway musical *Flower Drum Song*.

Most of the examples given here were written and performed prior to the New Negro Movement and the 1925 founding of the Krigwa Players Little Negro Theatre (named for the Crisis Guild of Writers and Artists) by W. E. B. Du Bois and Regina Anderson. In 1922, Alain Locke would call for the necessary cultivation of both the "Negro actor" and the "negro drama" in "the protected housing of the art-theatre flower"; only then, he writes, could both flourish "to the utmost perfection of the species." Much more could of course be written about how this new "negro drama" as well as later instances of musical theater juxtaposed black and oriental representations and further complicated their conjoined meanings. But these chapters should be enough to demonstrate that even within what Locke called "the demands and standards of the market-place" and "the exploitation and ruthlessness of the commercial theatre,"[49] there was some opportunity for a complex articulation of cross-racial identification and affiliation.

A NOTE ON TERMINOLOGY

Unfortunately, this research at times requires the reproduction of racial slurs as well as other offensive and damaging speech and descriptions; whenever possible, I have tried to place such examples within the confines of their historical usage. Aside from direct quotations, I generally use the terms "black" and "oriental" to describe theatrical characters and other racial representations. When referring to actual people, I use racial and ethnic designators such as "African American" or "Chinese immigrant," even while acknowledging that these designators do not capture fully the identities of those they describe. The performer Bert Williams, for instance, was born in the Bahamas and would have been referred to in his own time as "Negro" rather than the more contemporary terms "African American" or "Black." With some exceptions, such as in chapter 9, I do not make broad use of the terms "Afro-orientalism," "Afro-Asian," or "Black orientalism," since most scholars use these terms to refer to forms of interracial political solidarity or concerted intellectual engagement between African Americans and Asians or Asian Americans.[50] Interracial affinities have long been significant to African Americans such as W. E. B. Du Bois, who in his *Souls of Black Folk* commented that "the problem of the twentieth century is the problem of the color-line,—the relation of the darker to the lighter races of men in Asia and Africa, in America and the islands of the sea."[51] Du Bois saw particular connections to India and the Middle East as places of shared roots as well as common cause in anticolonialism. In the June 1919 issue of *The Crisis*, he wrote that "the sympathy of Black America must of necessity go out to colored India and colored Egypt": "Their forefathers were ancient friends, cousins, blood-brothers, in the hoary ages of antiquity. The blood of yellow and white hordes has diluted the ancient black blood of India, but her eldest Buddha still sits black, with kinky hair; the Negro who laid the founding stones of Egypt and furnished some of her mightiest thinkers, builders and leaders has mingled his blood with the invader on so vast a scale that the modern Egyptian mulatto hardly remembers his descent. But we are all one—we the Despised and Oppressed, the 'niggers' of England and America."[52]

But although they bear intriguing resonances with these reflections on the affinities among peoples of African, Asian, and Middle Eastern descent, the theatrical examples addressed in this book often lack both radical intention and profundity. The connections between black and oriental representation in the commercial theater thus seem substantially different from any "Afro-oriental" affinity and more akin to what Bill Mullen deems a "secret history" of orientalist "cultural fetishism" than to sustained alliance.[53] At the same time, these theatrical moments do reveal, as Julia H. Lee has written, how "Asian American and African American identities are mutually constituted"[54] and urge us to consider the possibility of value in as well as limits to these interracial connections.

1

THE RACIAL REFASHIONING
OF *Aladdin*

Despite criticism for having a white director (Guy Ritchie) and using extras in brownface makeup, the 2019 live-action version of Walt Disney Studio's *Aladdin* was a box office success. The film prominently featured actors of Middle Eastern and South Asian descent such as Mena Massoud (Aladdin), Naomi Scott (Princess Jasmine), Marwan Kenzari (Jafar), Navid Negahban (Sultan), and Nasim Pedrad (Jasmine's handmaid Dalia) as well as the African American actor Will Smith as the Genie. Other aspects of the live-action film, however, were not so new; it largely replicated the settings, plotline, and songs of Disney's 1992 animated *Aladdin*. Musing on its unexpected popularity, *Screenrant* writer Kayleigh Donaldson concluded that for Disney, "nostalgia sells,"[1] referencing a widespread fondness for the 1992 *Aladdin*, whose colorfully animated scenes—a bustling marketplace, a splendid royal palace, and a magical Cave of Wonders—as well as memorable soundtrack made the centuries-old tale of *Aladdin* popular again. Directed by Ron Clements and John Musker, the animated *Aladdin* not only was one of Disney's highest-grossing movies but also inspired numerous television and theatrical adaptations.

With an all-white creative team and nearly all of its characters and singers voiced by white actors,[2] Disney's 1992 *Aladdin* also inspired considerable debates about its orientalism. The fictional kingdom of Agrabah, presumably located near the River Jordan, is described in the opening song "Arabian Nights" as "a land from a faraway place / where the caravan camels roam," with the additional (and later excised) comment that it's "barbaric, but hey, it's home."[3] The 1992 *Aladdin* also features a host of stock characters memorably described by Jack Shaheen as "dastardly villains and harem maidens."[4] An equally interesting but less controversial aspect of the film is how it evokes blackness in several of its characterizations. The film's opening sequence introduces the story as beginning "on a dark night, where a dark man waits with a dark purpose." Disney's "dark man," the villainous magician Jafar, is not explicitly identified as a black character. However, Jafar does appear at times to have darker skin than the other characters; he also wears red and black clothing, transforms himself into a black cobra, and is ultimately trapped in a black lamp. However, Disney's 1992 *Aladdin* does not associate blackness wholly with villainy. Even though the sympathetic character of the Genie is colored blue, the composer Alan Mencken suggested that he had envisioned this character as "black, a hipster" figure such as Fats Waller.[5] The white actor Robin Williams improvised the Genie's banter to include multiple references to African American entertainers and music. The Genie also openly laments his enslavement within the lamp (describing his dilemma as "phenomenal cosmic powers, itty-bitty living space") and expresses a desire for freedom that echoes civil rights struggles, most obviously when the Genie celebrates his emancipation from the lamp with a jubilant appropriation of Dr. Martin Luther King's line "Free at last."

As rendered by Disney, *Aladdin* uses both negative and positives references to blackness to enhance the story's oriental motifs. Agrabah's exotic world is marked by outmoded and despotic forms of governance. The film parallels the Genie's enslavement with black racial oppression and the plight of Princess Jasmine, who longs to escape the confines of the palace and her arranged marriage, with contemporary feminist struggles against patriarchy. The happy ending celebrates the success of the poor but virtuous Aladdin as well as an imagined conclusion to both patriarchal oppression and racialized servitude. Like its storyline, *Aladdin*'s mixed racial motifs did not originate with Disney's 1992 film. From the eighteenth through the early twentieth century, the story of *Aladdin* has fascinated audiences not only with displays of wealth, magic, and romance but also with the staging of black as well as oriental characters. This chapter traces a much older set of *Aladdin* productions that have been largely forgotten in favor of Disney's "whole new world" yet whose racial habits still linger in contemporary retellings of the *Aladdin* story. These begin with a 1788 staging of John O'Keeffe's pantomime *Aladin; or, The Wonderful Lamp* at London's Covent Garden and, on the other side of the Atlantic, a New York performance of *Aladdin; or,*

The Racial Refashioning of Aladdin

The Wonderful Lamp on October 25, 1816.[6] Early *Aladdins* intertwined black and oriental representation, juxtaposing depictions of Chinese splendor and magical objects with the demonstrated villainy of an "African" magician and the exploits of slaves played in yellowface and blackface. *Aladdin's* lasting popularity suggests not only the continued viability of these racialized figures but also their careful adaptation to suit changing times.

The production history of *Aladdin* presents a foundational case study in which the two kinds of racial habits defined as blackface and orientalism come together in direct contact. In the many different renditions of this story, blackface roles such as the evil magician and the abject slave are placed within a recognizably oriental tale of adventure, despotic power, spectacular luxury and wealth, and magic. That blackface performance and orientalist characterization have worked so well together in various versions of *Aladdin* shows the extent to which different racial habits are compatible and mutually reinforce presumptions about the superiority of whiteness and the inferiority of both black and oriental characters. That the *Aladdin* story remains so popular suggests the continued hold of these racial habits in American popular culture, even as ingrained stereotypes are no longer only played by white actors but now inhabited by a multiracial cast.

MAGICAL OBJECTS AND THE ORIENTAL MARKETPLACE

"The Story of Aladdin: Or, the Wonderful Lamp" first appeared in French between 1704 and 1717 in Antoine Galland's translations of *One Thousand and One Nights* along with other popular stories such as "Ali Baba" or "Sinbad"; these tales, often called in English the *Arabian Nights*, were subsequently translated into multiple languages and published in many countries, with the earliest English versions in 1706–8.[7] As Marina Warner has commented, the fascination with *One Thousand and One Nights* displayed Europe's "disruptive incredulous bedazzlement" with Middle Eastern and Asian cultures.[8] It is unclear whether the *Aladdin* story ever existed in Arabic, although as Arafat Razzaque has described, the story may well have been told to Galland by Anṭūn Yūsuf Ḥannā Diyāb, a translator and merchant from Aleppo, Syria.[9] Galland's translated version takes place in an imaginary locale in China[10] but names characters as "good Musselmen," describes the kingdom as ruled by a sultan and a vizier, and gives characters Arabic names such as Ala-ʻu-ʻd-Din (or "exaltation of the Faith"), Badroulboudour or Badroulbadour (Badr al-Budur, or "Full moon of full moons") for the princess, and Mustapha for Aladdin's deceased father.[11]

Theatrical *Aladdins* in Britain and the United States continued to reproduce this cultural slippage, though most early stage versions were set in China. Ross Forman has suggested how in Victorian Britain, these fantastical spectacles of China foregrounded "ornament and adornment, pageantry and display," giving viewers "a sense of mastery over a conceptually imperialized space of China."[12] A similar fascination no doubt influenced the 1816 American production of the *Grand Melo Dramatic Romance Called Aladdin; or, The Wonderful Lamp* at the Philadelphia Theatre, whose stage directions call for "Mountains and Waterfalls" spanned by "Chinese Bridges," over which a "Grand Procession" passes.[13] The story of Aladdin also suggested the fascination with oriental fantasies around the Silk Road and its opportunities for adventure, trade, and profit. Little surprise, then, that theatrical versions of *Aladdin* evoked not just the imperial survey of lands but also the marketplace of oriental goods and commodities, such as textiles, embroidery, jewelry, Japanese lacquer, "willow plate" china, and tea. John O'Keeffe's 1788 *Aladin; or, The Wonderful Lamp* evokes both travel and commerce. The magic lamp is described as hidden "twixt two mountains high and steep / In a vally [*sic*] dark and deep" somewhere in "Arabia's spicy vales." The scene then shifts to comic characterizations of London craftsmen, providing songs for a potter who makes mugs for the "Jemmy Cheapside Buck" or "Fleet-Street Miss" and coachmaker "Tom Axle" with his "shop in Long-Acres."[14] The potter directly comments on the competition between Chinese and English-made porcelain and reminds the audience to purchase the domestic product rather than the foreign import.

> And why abroad our money fling
> To please the fickle Fair?
> No more China, China bring,
> Here's English China-ware.[15]

Later versions of *Aladdin* similarly blended references to oriental goods into elaborate scenes of consumption or more casual comic references, including satirical names for characters such as Aladdin's mother, the Widow Twankay, named for a popular brand of cheap tea. An 1874 Christmas staging by Edward Litt Leman Blanchard at Drury Lane dispensed with the typical opening of the story (a dramatic monologue by the villainous magician); instead, Blanchard staged a market street with whimsical signs such as "*Shod-Hi, Late Mustafa, clothing mart and general outfitting warehouse,*" "*Chow Chow Canton Dining Rooms—bird's-nest soup always ready—original house for puppy pies,*" and "*O Mi, dealer in curiosities.*"[16] American versions of

The Racial Refashioning of Aladdin

Aladdin readily followed suit. An advertisement for *Aladdin; or, the Wonderful Lamp* at Barnum's American Museum emphasized its vast array of Chinese objects: "With over 100 performers in the different parts, with real Chinese Dresses, real Chinese Banners, real Chinese Lanterns, &c, imported expressly for this Establishment from Canton, and to be presented in a style of the MOST LAVISH MAGNIFICENCE."[17]

As Susan Nance has indicated, in the United States the *Arabian Nights* stories inspired "a tradition of extravagant and sumptuous creativity" that "provided unparalleled depictions of luxury, ease, and magical self-transformation in robust language that closely matched the promise of consumer capitalism as it developed between 1790 and 1935."[18] The tale of *Aladdin* had a particular connection to this craze for oriental goods, with a story centering around a hero who, through a chance encounter and a magic lamp, becomes fabulously rich and marries a princess. Objects with magical powers—especially oriental ones—promised to help ordinary people circumvent social hierarchies of wealth, power, and status. But while oriental consumption was front and center, it was not the only kind of racial spectacle used in the *Aladdin* story. Theatrical *Aladdins* also staged blackness in ways that both enhanced and altered these oriental effects.

"A DARK MAN WAITS WITH A DARK PURPOSE": BLACKFACE AND *ALADDIN*

Early dramatizations of the *Aladdin* story consistently borrowed from Galland's designation that the unnamed magician comes from Africa. After the magician imprisons Aladdin in the cave, Galland's narrator comments that "this Action of the *African* Magician's plainly shew'd him to be neither *Aladdin*'s Uncle, nor *Mustapha* the Taylor's Brother, but a true *African*, as he was," and then adds that "*Africa* is a Country that delights the most in Magick of any place in the whole World."[19] After the magician steals the lamp, he magically transports Aladdin's palace to Africa and threatens to rape the princess, further solidifying the connection between his true racial identity and dark purpose.

British nineteenth-century theatrical versions vary in their presentation of the magician's blackness. Neither the cast list for John O'Keeffe's Covent Garden *Aladin* (1788) nor the playbill for an 1826 Drury Lane production of *Aladdin* (set in Persia) identifies this character as "African."[20] Stage directions and plotline often make little racial distinction between the magician and the Chinese characters. The magician is easily able to pass himself off as Aladdin's uncle, as Aladdin and his widowed mother overlook his lack of resemblance to Aladdin's deceased father and embrace him as a wealthy relation, and at no point is a cross-racial transformation ever signaled. However, the magician's "African" roots were by no means forgotten even for the audiences of some of these productions. In the opening scene of Blanchard's 1874 Drury Lane *Aladdin*, Abanazar the magician, played by Fred Vokes, simply *"throws off travelling hat for skull cap with ornamental appendages, shows himself in Chinese suit."*[21] The *Illustrated Sporting and Dramatic News* notes that "Fred is the 'African magician'" but that "'he has no wool on the top of his head in the place where the wool ought to grow,' but has a wondrously elastic pigtail, and otherwise represents 'John Chinaman.'"[22] This review contrasts the "wondrously elastic pigtail" of "John Chinaman" with the perhaps more typical blackface minstrel wig through a reference to Stephen Foster's 1848 minstrel song "Old Uncle Ned."[23]

While Vokes may not have worn blackface for his magician role, others readily adopted blackface makeup and caricature in playing the villainous magician. In J. Wilton Jones's 1880 Christmas pantomime *Aladdin and the Wonderful Lamp; or, Harlequin and the Fairies of the Jewel Cavern*, the King greets Abanazar's appearance with "Surely I know that face—that eagle eye— / that curling forehead blackened up with dye!"[24] The satiric wordplay of Henry J. Byron's 1861 burlesque *Aladdin or, The Wonderful Scamp!* referenced both fashionable Chinese commodities (the Vizier's son, Aladdin's romantic rival, is named "Pekoe") and popular minstrel characterizations of black children as "pickaninnies" as the Emperor recalls Princess Badroulboudour once taking her "grand toys" to play outside "with small plebian boys."

> Much to her parent's horror, in the street,
> Returning with such face and hands and feet!
> Mud an inch deep; it made your father shudder,
> And had the same effect upon your *mudder*.
> For tomboy tricks, there was, I'd bet a guinea,
> Not all in Pekin, such a *Pekin-ninny*.[25]

Byron's burlesque uses similar wordplay to conflate Abanazar's unwanted sexual advances with the repulsive nature of his blackness.

> ABAN. (L.) Look down upon a lover, my adored,
>   Whose unsusceptible young heart you've floored;
>   Oblige him with a smile, one, trifling snigger, —
>   Don't look so precious black upon this nigger.

PRINCESS. (R.) Nigger! apply that term you truly can, sir,
　　You are indeed a wicked *negromancer*.
ABAN. That word, when properly pronounced, my dear,
　　Is *nec*-romancer—neck—below the ear,
　　To hint, miss, I forbear; but if too daring—
　　You'll find I'm in another way *for-bearing*.[26]

This interplay between *Aladdin*'s Chinese characters and the "African" magician played up the contrast between the fashionable commodities and patrician tastes of orientalism and the inferiority and evil associated with blackness, as seen in a striking set of 1901 illustrations by Walter Crane for the story. In "New Lamps for Old Ones," the magician passes himself off as a Jewish merchant (also identified as such in popular versions of the *Aladdin* story) in a yellow robe and conical hat; his dark skin, thick red lips, and large and clumsy appearance distinguish him from the quaint Chinese figures around him.

In the illustration "He Found That He Had Fallen Back Lifeless upon the Couch," the figures of Aladdin and the Princess, positioned delicately in front of an oriental screen, hover over the body of the magician, whose black hands and face and kinky hair again show his racial difference from the Chinese characters. A turbaned black figure in the background hints at both a spatial and physical similarity between the magician and the "African" servant. This contrast between delicate chinoiserie and reviled blackness suggests even more of a theatrical opportunity for the actor in the star role of the magician. This role would allow the performer to showcase his skills at a host of roles, transforming himself from "African" magician to impersonate Aladdin's long-lost uncle, and then in some versions disguising as the "Jewish merchant" in order to obtain the lamp.

BLACK ENSLAVEMENT AND ORIENTAL EXCESS

British holiday entertainment regularly adopted popular songs, characters, and comic routines from blackface minstrelsy to please audiences desiring novelty along with their nostalgia. Theatrical versions of *Aladdin* were no exception. J. Wilton Jones's 1880 Christmas pantomime *Aladdin* includes a song, "Massas Sent a Jellygram," identified as "Mohawk's Christmas Number" by the Mohawk Minstrels. In Jones's afterpiece, the characters reappear first for the "*Feast of Lanterns set in a 'Chinese Landscape' (Willow pattern)*" with the King then calling for a minstrel-style semicircle with "Let's tell the tale in Christy Minstrel fashion."[27] For theater historian Michael Booth,

Walter Crane, "New Lamps for Old Ones" (1901).
The Miriam and Ira D. Wallach Division of Art,
Prints and Photographs, New York Public Library.

Walter Crane, "He Found That He Had Fallen Back
Lifeless upon the Couch" (1901).
The Miriam and Ira D. Wallach Division of Art,
Prints and Photographs, New York Public Library.

E. L. Blanchard's pantomimes can be distinguished from others by their avoidance of puns and emphasis on a graceful and elevated style; by his final version of *Aladdin* in 1885, Blanchard grumbled "about the gags of music-hall comedians" in his productions.[28] However, even Blanchard actively employed the common devices of blackface comedy in his 1874 Drury Lane *Aladdin*, with a scene at the popular Ramsgate resort including "*a lot of* NIGGERS *[who] now come with* PUNCH *as the time-keeper*" who sing, then "*walk around, do a few steps, and then collect money from crowd, who all applaud,*" and another in a toy warehouse with a mechanical *"nigger"* that *"assumes all kinds of grotesque positions."*[29]

In America, *Aladdin* was less a standard part of holiday pantomime tradition but just as popular a theatrical entertainment. From the 1840s through the 1870s, American productions of *Aladdin* were featured in skits and one-acts in variety acts, burlesque, and vaudeville, many offering black caricature as well as oriental spectacle. Unsurprisingly, American versions of *Aladdin* were often produced by blackface minstrel companies. A version of *Aladdin or the Wonderful Lamp, the Grand Chinese Spectacle* by composer Thomas Comer and playwright Silas Steele at the Boston Museum in 1847 inspired burlesques by C. A. Becker that same year and then a decade later by the minstrel troupe Buckley's Serenaders.[30] Buckley's May 1857 *Aladdin* was described in *Porter's Spirit of the Times* as produced at "great expense, and in gorgeous style [as] a new grand burlesque extravaganza," with performers "appear[ing] in Tartaric complexions" rather than in their usual blackface.[31] As in Britain, U.S. productions of *Aladdin* regularly included blackface sketches or musical numbers. For instance, in the 1895 Broadway production of *Aladdin Jr.; or A Tale of a Wonderful Lamp,* Princess Badroul-badour sang Hattie Starr's "Little Alabama Coon" with the refrain

> Go to sleep my little picaninny,
> Brer' Fox'll catch you if yo' don't
> Slumber on de bosom of yo' ole Mammy Jinny
> Mammy's gwine to swat yo' if you won't.[32]

The story of Aladdin also was performed by African Americans. A June 1897 edition of the Indianapolis-based African American newspaper *The Freeman* commented that minstrel impresario Frank Dumont was "busy rewriting" the touring all-black *Darkest America* and that "the third act will be entirely taken up with the opera of 'Aladdin.'"[33] Through the first decades of the twentieth century, regular reports of *Aladdin* as staged by African American professional and amateur casts in children's theater, marionette shows, circuses, and dance revues appeared in other African American periodicals such as the *New York Age,* the *Washington Tribune,* and *People's Voice.* For instance, in April 1929, the *New York Age* reported the start of a regular Saturday morning children's theater offering as part of the New Negro Art Theatre, with *Aladdin* projected as one of the offerings, alongside *Cinderella* and *Water Babies,* to be produced with a semiprofessional cast.[34]

Few records of any African American performances of *Aladdin* remain, and none suggest that there were any major differences between these

The Racial Refashioning of Aladdin

productions and those performed by white actors. The name "Aladdin" was regularly used in advertising in African American newspapers for products such as an Aladdin "turban" (headscarf), vacuums, tea pots, (unsurprisingly) lamps, and even a twenty-eight-day "Aladdin Cruise," starting in January 1925, to the Panama Canal, South America, Cuba, Puerto Rico, Jamaica, Barbados, Martinique, Trinidad, the Virgin Islands, and the Bermudas, as advertised in the *New York Age*.[35] This reaffirms Nance's argument that the *Arabian Nights* tales functioned to promote "the romantic promise of magical self-transformation, repose, and contentment to be found in the market" and to endorse "hedonistic consumption" for Americans regardless of racial identity.[36] However, one notable newspaper article indicated that, at least for some African Americans, the story of *Aladdin* meant more than a marketing ploy. A 1931 issue of the *New York Age* commented on a front-page story from the *Cleveland Guide* (described as "Ohio's Leading Negro Weekly") about a public school production of "Aladdin's Court." The article related that out of the 135 characters depicted in the drama, the "only part given Negro children were those of slaves fanning a white prince," and that upon learning of this, "some Negro children walked out." The supervisor, a Miss Kirkpatrick, subsequently responded that "the colored children should feel honored to take the part of slaves." The incident inspired this reflection from the *New York Age*:

> Exactly why the colored children should feel honored to take the part of slaves is not explained, especially as their only action was to fan a white prince. The complexion of the prince seems a little anachronistic for a drama of so Oriental a character as that suggested by the title of "Aladdin's Court." But perhaps the sarcastic supervisor never learned that in the countries of the Orient the princes are more than likely to be of a complexion other than white. If she had paid any attention to the photogravure section of the Sunday papers, she would have found pictures of several Eastern potentates whose complexion more nearly approximated that of the Negro school children than that of the whites.

The article continued by affirming that "color is not always a badge of slavery" and noting that there were "serfs and thralls and villains of the twelfth and thirteenth centuries" who were "Anglo-Saxon slaves," as well as the original white settlers in the Americas who were sent "as criminals or as bound servants." It concluded that "slavery is a condition that has been forced upon many conquered races by their conquerors, whether the subject race was white or black."[37]

This *New York Age* article eloquently illustrated how the casting even of a school production of *Aladdin* had the power to affirm or challenge existing hierarchies of racial representation and servitude. It also signaled the appeal of a plot in which a commoner, by dint of good fortune and a particular lamp, would be able to ascend to riches and power. This aspect of the tale was not lost to African American writers and performers who repeatedly made reference to the *Aladdin* story in their musicals; as later chapters in this book will show, a number of early African American musicals such as the Bert Williams vehicle *Mr. Lode of Koal* (1909) and Eubie Blake and Noble Sissle's *Shuffle Along* (1921) would refer to *Aladdin* in describing the fantasies of black characters dreaming of wealth and power.

But the *New York Age* article also pointed out a much more troubling aspect of the *Aladdin* story: its reliance on spectacles of slavery. In addition to imagining the villain as "African," many versions of *Aladdin* emphasized the presence of slave characters who were identified as black. In Galland's translation of the story, the Sultan demands that Aladdin produce "forty Basons [*sic*] of Massy Gold, full of the same Things [jewels] you have already made me a Present of, and carried by the like Number of Black Slaves, who shall be led by as many young and handsome white Slaves, all dres'd magnificently."[38] Galland describes how consequently, with the help of the genii of the ring and the lamp, Aladdin stages a parade of these slaves through the streets, which become "crowded with Spectators, who ran to see so extraordinary and noble a Sight." Other slave processions follow when the Princess "set forwards for *Aladdin*'s Palace, with his mother on her left Hand, follow'd by a hundred Women Slaves, dress'd in a surprizing Magnificence."[39]

While Galland describes slave pageants consisting of both white and black men as well as women of indeterminate race, only the black male slaves appear in the theatrical versions of *Aladdin*. In two early nineteenth-century productions, one staged at Philadelphia's Chestnut Street Theatre in 1835 and the other in the 1850s at the Boston Theatre, Aladdin rides "*in a costly Chinese palanquin, supported by four brilliantly dressed Ethiops.*"[40] Blanchard's 1874 version calls for Princess Badroulbadour to enter "*in palanquin, borne by black slaves.*"[41] Similar images are evoked even in productions of *Aladdin* that relied on parody rather than pageantry. In an 1855 burlesque by John Robert O'Neill titled *Aladdin, or The Wonderful Lamp: A Piece of Oriental Extravaganze in One Act*, the popular tune "I Dreamt I Dwelt in Marble Halls" (borrowed from the 1843 opera *The Bohemian Girl*) was adapted for Princess So-Loveli with a new opening: "I've dream'd when I dwelt in marble halls / With black slaves and muffs at my side."[42]

Thus, even while the *Aladdin* story allows for magical instances of social mobility, it maintains hierarchies based on race and color. Galland describes the Princess as "the most lovely beautiful brown Woman in the World" and pictures Aladdin's transformation as a process of whitening through the magic of the bath: "After he had pass'd through several Degrees of Heat, he got out, but quite a different Man from what he was before. His Skin was clear white and red, and his Body lightsome and easy, and when he return'd into the Hall, found, instead of his own, a noble Habit, the Magnificence of which very much surprized him."[43] Thus from its origins, the story of *Aladdin* associated dark skin with not only evil magic but also natural servility.

It is not difficult to see how these lavish spectacles of black enslavement enhanced *Aladdin*'s displays of oriental wealth and power. But even when the pageant of black slaves did not appear, even the most stripped-down *Aladdin* included at least one enslaved figure, the Genie of the lamp. Some versions of *Aladdin* included yet another slave character, the mute figure of Kazrac. As these characters became the center of comic attention and heroic action in the story, their servitude was presented as an inescapable feature of the oriental kingdoms they inhabited.

CHIN-CHIN; OR A MODERN ALADDIN

The Genie of the lamp emerges as a potent comic characterization in Broadway's 1914 *Chin-Chin; or A Modern Aladdin*, written by James O'Dea, Anne Caldwell, and R. H. Burnside with music by Ivan Caryll. The production was a vehicle for the popular duo of Dave Montgomery and Fred Stone, who had previously received Broadway acclaim in 1903 as the Scarecrow and the Tin Man in *The Wizard of Oz*, adapted from Frank L. Baum's stories with music by Paul Tietjens and A. Baldwin Sloane. According to the New Orleans *Times-Picayune*, *Chin-Chin* "adhere[d] more or less faithfully to the Arabian Nights story" but is "up to date"[44] in turning the Princess and her father into wealthy Americans traveling in China. *Chin-Chin*'s more "modern" take on *Aladdin* also involved doubling up the role of the Genie as "Chin Hop Lo" and "Chin Hop Hi," played respectively by Montgomery and Stone.

Chin-Chin begins in the oriental marketplace, as Montgomery and Stone were first displayed "as graven images in a Chinese toy bazaar,"[45] and in their opening song, "Chinese Honeymoon," they identify themselves as

Slaves of young Aladdin's lamp
Our present master is a scamp

Old Abanazar we must mind,
Until that magic lamp we find.

Subsequent verses move away from the Chinese characterizations of earlier *Aladdins*. Chin Hop Lo and Chin Hop Hi sing about a wedding attended by "Slant-eyes Masons, Elks and Eagles," in which the entertainers are the "Chinese Tenor" named "So Long," who sings "sweetly with his wife, 'Sing Song,'" and their sons "In Key," "Oh Gee Ah Mee," and "Low Hi See." The bridal couple also receive wedding gifts described as "weird and strange," including

A dozen flat irons and a range
An ironing board, some starch and soap,
A ringer and a pulley rope.

Chinese characters are no longer far-away and magical inhabitants of foreign lands but appear as immigrant laundrymen, members of fraternal organizations, and even vaudeville entertainers. But even though these incarnations of Chinese characters appear more modern, they are still pictured within a "weird and strange" array of entertainments in the play. *Chin-Chin's* efforts were clearly directed at comic escapism, a predictable move given that its Broadway premiere was only a few months after the start of the First World War. To that end, it included a variety of fast-paced specialty acts and musical numbers, many of them centered on the comic antics of Montgomery and Stone, who were known for their clowning and mimicry. A playbill for a production of *Chin-Chin* at the Illinois Theatre in March 1916 listed the duo as playing not only Chin Hop Hi and Chin Hop Lo but also the Widow Twankay, French gendarmes, Ignace Paderewski, a would-be bareback rider "Mlle. Falloffski," a ventriloquist, and a "coolie" (the last perhaps a return to Chinese characterization).[46]

Chinese acts were only one aspect of Montgomery and Stone's performances and apparently did not entail much effort at authenticity on their part. One of their songs was "Go Gat Sig Gong-Jue" (presumably meaning "The High Cost of Living"), which was reported to have been written in English by librettist Anne Caldwell and James O'Dea and then translated by a Chinese man living in Washington, DC.[47] In his autobiography, Fred Stone recalls little of the song's meaning, only that "the curtain had Chinese characters all over it and Dave and I sang a Chinese song about a mile long that we had had a lot of trouble memorizing." He does tell the story of how one night during the show he saw in one of the theater boxes "some distinguished

Chinese gentlemen who were carefully looking over the Chinese symbols on the curtain." Finally after the performance he and Montgomery asked the men what the symbols on the drop were and were told with a laugh that "it's just a laundry list" that reads "'One, two, three, four, if, but.' That's all."[48]

Chin-Chin's references to blackness were equally superficial. No black-face roles were specified for the show, but Montgomery and Stone did end the first act with "Ragtime Temple Bells," a song that tells the story of "a great big Yankee black Jack Tar" who "on the coast of China one fine day, / Cut his sticks and ran a-way." The former slave then gets a job as a janitor in "a heathen temple" and retunes the bells in ragtime syncopation, which causes its Chinese listeners to dance uncontrollably: "Ev'ry chink goes just as dippy / As a coon from Mis-sis-sip-pi."[49] The lyrics do suggest an intriguing situation in which a black American sailor liberates himself and finds a more satisfying life in China and even hints at the interesting prospect of hybrid forms of black-Chinese music and dance as the Chinese "heathen knave" who hears the syncopated bells starts "doing the Turkey trot." However, it is highly unlikely that either this song or other numbers in *Chin-Chin* ever escaped racial caricature.

It is not hard to see the direct connections between *Chin-Chin*'s facile use of yellowface and the heavy influence of blackface stereotypes in American show business. Stone and Montgomery began their professional careers in minstrel companies and teamed up when both were performing with Haverly's Minstrels. The doubling of the Genie role in *Chin-Chin* recalls the many versions of *Uncle Tom's Cabin* in which the leading roles were played by two actors; in fact, Stone made his theatrical debut as Topsy in a double version of *Uncle Tom*.[50] Whether appearing in Chinese character or singing a ragtime tune, the cross-racial impersonations of Montgomery and Stone in *Chin-Chin* suggested strong similarities to the modes of acting in blackface minstrelsy. David Roediger has observed that "genius" for white minstrels in blackface was "to be able to both display and reject the 'natural self,' to be able to take on blackness convincingly and to take off blackness convincingly."[51] This profound idea sheds light on a comment made by one reviewer of *Chin-Chin* on Broadway that "[Chin Hop] Hi and [Chin Hop] Lo's ultimate reward was to be turned white."[52] This remark underscores how the white identities of Montgomery and Stone enabled their many impersonations and undergirded their theatrical success. Gerald Bordman writes of the comic duo, "For the rest of their career they played similar roles in similar shows, taking what bygone times would have turned into pantomime and making it into a unique musical comedy genre. Time and again their offerings were to prove the major success of the season; and while they had a few imitators they had not rivals."[53]

Chin-Chin was hardly exceptional either in reviving the oriental fantasy of *Aladdin* or in including a coon song amid its other show numbers. But casting Montgomery and Stone as Chin Hop Hi and Chin Hop Lo did allow the "slaves of the lamp" to dominate the stage and set up a precedent for other comic versions of the Genie, including the acclaimed performance of Robin Williams in Disney's 1992 animated musical. Williams's pointedly "black" and "hipster" version of this character in turn encouraged the casting of African American actors in *Aladdin*. While the 1992 Disney film *Aladdin* and its television spin-offs continued to feature white actors as the Genie, the 2011 Seattle and 2014 Broadway versions of *Aladdin* cast James Monroe Iglehart (who won a Tony Award for the role); touring versions of the musical and other theatrical entertainments based on Disney's version, as well as the 2019 live-action film with Will Smith, have regularly presented African American actors in this role.[54]

However, Disney's Genie was also not the first time a prominent role in *Aladdin* was played by an African American actor. Throughout the nineteenth century, stage versions of *Aladdin* also featured the character of Kazrac, who was played briefly by the notable African American actor Ira Aldridge in 1834. The next chapter will consider Aldridge's playing of Kazrac along with some of other "lesser" roles that Aldridge played. But first, a final section will explore how this character moves from a minor role to center stage.

THE SILENT CAPERS OF KAZRAC

A drawing of an 1844 *Aladdin; or The Wonderful Lamp* burlesque by Albert Smith and Charles Kenne at London's Lyceum shows Aladdin's carriage drawn by women dressed as fairies and flanked by rows of men in "Chinese" hats and mustaches.[55] A lone blackface figure scampers behind the carriage. This figure was likely that of Kazrac (sometimes spelled "Kasrac" or "Kasrack"), a mute slave who begins in the service of the evil African magician and then switches his allegiance to Aladdin. Kazrac is mentioned as early as Charles Farley's 1813 Covent Garden *Aladdin*[56] and continued through the century as a leading role in many British and American productions. While only the magician's lackey, in some productions Kazrac occupies more of the action than the titular hero. Unlike the secondary female characters such as Aladdin's mother, the Widow, or the brave handmaid Zobyad, Kazrac

The Racial Refashioning of Aladdin

"'Aladdin,' at the Lyceum." *Illustrated London News*, August 17, 1844.

demonstrates singular physical abilities in clowning and heroic action. It is likely that his character was given these opportunities because of the traditional cross-gender casting of Aladdin, a role that in early versions was often played by female actresses.

The script of one version of *Aladdin*, produced in 1835 at Philadelphia's Chestnut Street Theatre, shows the dramatic potential of the Kazrac role. In the opening, a fearful scene ensues as the magician Abenazac admonishes Kazrac to obey him: "Fear not, unworthy slave; remember, when I freed thee from the hands of that Tartarian horde, whose enmity had of thy speech bereft thee, thou did'st engage thyself to be the partner of my vent'rous fate," and Kazrac mutely *"implies consent."* This version of *Aladdin* gives a significant measure of agency as well as emotion to this slave character. Though he is compelled to obey Abenazac, Kazrac seizes every opportunity to rebel, refusing to get the lamp for him and trying to warn Aladdin of Abenazac's evil intentions. After Aladdin retrieves the lamp but refuses to give it to Abenazac, Kazrac tries to aid him but is also thrown into the cave, leading Aladdin to lament their shared fates: "Oh, Aladdin, Aladdin! and art thou never to see the light of heaven again? And thou, too, poor, dumb, faithful Kazrac, must suffer for thy love of me!" It is Kazrac who instructs Aladdin to rub the lamp and who entertains the audience as they escape: "Kazrac, *all joy, dances about, and gathers some fruit [jewels]; and the scene closes as he goes up the steps."* Through gesture and action, Kazrac expresses a range of emotions but also provides comic relief and heroic support. In act 2, Aladdin hides by the Royal Baths to see the Princess, and stage directions indicate that "KAZRAC [is] also there in a comic situation." The two voyeuristically observe the women, including a *"number of Female Slaves dancing,"* after which Aladdin's rival, the Vizier's son Azack, tries to seize the Princess. Aladdin and Karzac both intervene: "KAZRAC *encounters, overcomes, and forces* AZACK *off,*" while "ALADDIN *receives the Princess, swooning in his arms, the alarm raised.*"

Perhaps the most interesting moment of this version of the Kazrac role is in the final scenes after Abenazac steals the lamp from a sleeping Kazrac. Abenazac then transports the Princess and Aladdin's palace to Africa, while Aladdin and Kazrac pursue him. In the ensuing confrontation, Kazrac defends Aladdin and is instrumental in Abenazac's final defeat. In Galland's translation of *Aladdin*, it is Aladdin and the Princess who poison the magician, but in this theatrical production, Kazrac provides the thrilling finale. Abenazac "*runs to* ALADDIN, *dashes him to the ground, draws his dagger, and is about to stab him, when* KAZRAC *catches his arm, wrests dagger from him, and stabs him—he falls—*KAZRAC *holds him down with one hand, while with the other he pulls out the wonderful lamp from* ABENAZAC'S *bosom, and laughs.*" After Kazrac's excited moment of vengeance, the Princess is embraced by her father and "*supported by* ALADDIN *on his knees,*" while his mother is shown "*weeping, with her arms around* ALADDIN'S *neck.*" Kazrac, in contrast, is shown "*in ecstacies [sic]*" as "*the curtain falls slowly, amid flourish and shouts.*"[57]

The many expressive moments given to Kazrac in the 1835 Philadelphia *Aladdin* also appear in other theatrical versions of *Aladdin*. In Blanchard's 1874 version at Drury Lane, Kazrac's part in the ending is less gleefully murderous; he does not kill the magician Abanazar, who is instead punished by drinking a magic potion that forces him into a frantic dance. Still, Kazrac is important to the rest of Blanchard's dramatization, guiding Aladdin to use the power of the magic ring and humorously spying on the Princess when she goes to the baths, which causes even the villain Abanazar to chide him: "Kazrac, you are peeping. Fie, it's very naughty!"[58] This blend of hilarity and heroism suggests the distinctive attractions of this role, which was played to great acclaim by many notable comic actors, perhaps most famously by Joseph Grimaldi in Charles Farley's 1813 Covent Garden *Aladdin; or, The Wonderful Lamp.*[59]

Famed for his amusing stage business, Grimaldi undoubtedly influenced a number of later productions. For instance, his famous scenes of hilarious gluttony might have inspired a scene in the 1835 Philadelphia production in which Aladdin, the Widow, and Kazrac consume an elaborate feast: "*They uncover the dishes, and they all eat voraciously.*"[60] Blanchard's 1874 London version also contains similar stage directions that note, "*Business with Kazrac, which brings all to front of stage,*" after which Aladdin comments, "You, really, Kazrac, shouldn't eat so fast."[61] Dance, gesture, and movement

The Racial Refashioning of Aladdin

Joseph Grimaldi as Kazrac in *Aladdin; or, The Wonderful Lamp*.
Portrait by William Appleton (between 1820 and 1860).
Billy Rose Theatre Collection, New York Public Library.

"Character Sketches from 'Aladdin' at Drury-Lane,
and 'Cinderella' at the Crystal Palace."
Illustrated London News, January 16, 1886.

were all crucial to this speechless role. In 1878 a version of *Aladdin and His Wonderful Lamp or The Flying Palace and Big Ben of Westminster*, performed at the Royal Aquarium Theatre in Westminster, featured an elaborate aquatic transformation scene with sea nymphs and anemones. Despite this spectacle, "the loudest applause was received by Paul Martinetti as the magician's slave Kazrac for his 'fantastic dancing' and 'remarkable pantomime powers.'"[62] Blanchard included versions of Kazrac in several versions of *Aladdin*. According to the London *Times*, his 1865 production at the Royal English Opera featured the well-known actor W. H. Payne as Abanazar, "a semi-serious grotesque," and his brother, Fred Payne Jr., as Kazrac, a "hyper-comic grotesque individuality." Both actors were thought to be "infinitely diverting."[63] In Blanchard's 1885 Drury Lane version, Charles Lauri as Kazrac performed what *Punch* deemed "a marvelous dance."[64] Lauri's reputation for physical mimicry gives some indication of what he brought to the role. Known as the "Garrick of Animal Mimes" for playing cats, dogs, monkeys, and kangaroos, he also played blackface roles such as Friday in *Robinson Crusoe*.[65] The London newspaper the *Era* found his particular talents underutilized in the 1885 Blanchard *Aladdin*, which was devoted to spectacular effects: "Charles Lauri was wasted as Kazrac, being given no opportunities for his agile capers,"[66] but the *Illustrated London News* included a memorable drawing of Lauri as the "Slave of the Ring."[67]

The cast list for a 1816 production of *Aladdin* at the Philadelphia Theatre describes Kazrac as the magician Abanazar's "Chinese slave."[68] In this and subsequent editions of *Aladdin*, neither the stage directions nor costume descriptions indicate that he was dressed any differently from other "Chinese" characters. William Appleton's illustration of Joseph Grimaldi as Kazrac shows him with a long moustache and wearing colorful layered attire of loose trousers, blue shirt, red coat, and tasseled hat, with a sword in each hand. A mid-nineteenth-century Boston production dresses Kazrac in *"white Chinese trousers, with blue binding—fly and cap—black shoes,"* while the *"black Slaves, carrying Aladdin's presents,"* wear *"white tunics and trousers, black arms and leggings—brass bracelets, collars and breastbands."*[69] In J. Wilton Jones's 1880 version, he is identified as *"Kazrac, a heathen Chinee."*[70] In a production of *Aladdin* during the 1863–64 season of Mrs. John Wood's Olympic Theatre, Kazrac would be played by Charles T. Parsloe Jr., who, as we shall see in chapter 4, would later win fame for his comic Chinese immigrant roles. Parsloe played Kazrac wearing a "coolie hat," loose coat and trousers, and long mustache.[71] But though depicted as a Chinese rather than a black slave, Kazrac's parodic posturing connects him to the many comic caricatures of black slaves and servants in blackface minstrelsy as well as to the pantomime tradition of the black-masked Harlequin. The actor Charles Burke, for instance, took on this role in 1890 wearing a harlequin costume and a long queue.[72] In the 1895 Broadway production of *Aladdin Jr.; or A Tale of a Wonderful Lamp*, the comic role of "Abanazer's apprentice," played by John J. Burke, was named "Crambo," suggesting a hybrid combination of the familiar blackface caricature of Sambo with the Kazrac role.[73]

Like that of the Genie and other slaves, the service of Kazrac remained an unquestioned part of the Aladdin story. In the 1835 Philadelphia *Aladdin*, a dialogue between two unnamed "citizens" suggests the broader impact of Aladdin's wealth and generosity.

> FIRST CITIZEN. Well, this is a rare youth—something like a Prince; here have I lived these forty years, under the very nose of the court as were, and never was taken the least notice of before.
> SECOND CITIZEN. To be sure. When the ceremony was over, how the black slaves did shower the gold; by the long beard of the great Fo Hun, I got twenty pieces in the scramble.[74]

These two characters then sing a gleeful song that compares how under the knavish Vizier, the "nobles meaned and the people groaned / Subdued by abject slavery," while with Aladdin's accession to power, "blithe and gay we pass the day. / And every face looks cheerily." Yet despite the celebration of this song, their commentary suggests that only some benefit from Aladdin's rise in fortunes. While a citizen might receive "twenty pieces" of gold, it is the "black slaves" who must distribute this wealth without benefiting from it. Aladdin's rise from poverty to power contrasts with the conspicuous enslavement of those characters who remain in (sometimes literally) supporting roles.

Kazrac is one of those unfortunate characters. Despite his supplying much of the muscle as well as the comic fun, his presence in *Aladdin* is as easily forgotten as that of the unnamed black slaves, valued only for what they carry. His popularity waned in the twentieth century, and there is little mention of this character in reviews after 1900. But in closing this survey of theatrical *Aladdins*, we might also see Kazrac as providing one of the more interesting connections between these earlier transatlantic musical entertainments and Disney's animated musical film over a century later. Disney's 1992 *Aladdin* has only one main Genie character. However, the movie does multiply the number of sidekicks who accompany the villain and the hero through the story. The mute Kazrac has become Abu, Aladdin's beloved and beleaguered monkey companion. Devoid of speech, Abu's highly expressive face and body add comedy and pathos to the story as he aids in acts of theft, demonstrates unwavering loyalty to Aladdin, and helps to rescue Princess Jasmine. Like Kazrac, he is the center of comedy as well as the workhorse, as his body is memorably transmogrified by the fast-talking Genie to provide whatever form of labor might be necessary.

But in the 1992 animated *Aladdin*, Abu is not alone in his function as a loyal servant or as a racialized figure. Disney provides another character who provides Aladdin with help in the form of an oriental commodity, a magic carpet. There is also a devious parrot, Iago (voiced by Gilbert Gottfried), who serves Jafar throughout the movie. If the mute Abu retains some of the uncomfortable racial associations linking monkeys to black stereotypes (as is suggested by critics of Disney's 1967 animated version of *The Jungle Book*), Jafar's avian accomplice seems to depart from the stock caricatures of both oriental and black characters. Yet at the same time, his name clearly recalls the unscrupulous villain who goads Shakespeare's "tragic Moor" Othello into murdering his wife. The surly and sarcastic bird not only provides comic relief but also reminds us that Jafar is ever the "dark man" in pursuit of a "dark purpose." Race and servitude are once again entangled in these secondary characters as Iago's name, however faintly, echoes the "African" origins of the magic so central to *Aladdin*'s oriental tale. Thus Disney's revivals of this very old story do more than just preserve the vestiges of intertwined black and oriental representations; their animation, live action, and other devices of movie magic also give these racial habits new traction.

2

THE LESSER ROLES OF
IRA ALDRIDGE

After his appearances with William Alexander Brown and James Hewlett's African Grove Theatre Company in New York in the early 1820s, Ira Aldridge spent the rest of his acting career touring the UK and Europe. He made his London debut as Oroonoko in *The Revolt of Surinam; or, a Slave's Revenge* (an adaptation of Thomas Southerne's *Oroonoko, The Royal Slave*, based on Aphra Behn's novel)[1] and was renowned for other heroic black characters, most famously Shakespeare's Othello, a role he played throughout his career until his death in 1867. In 1863, the French poet, novelist, and critic Théophile Gautier saw him perform Othello in St. Petersburg, Russia. Gautier expected to see a fiery and wild performance in the style of actor Edmund Kean ("une manière énergique, désordonnée, fougueuse, un peu barbare et sauvage"). However, according to Gautier, Aldridge played his Othello scenes, even the final smothering of Desdemona, in a restrained and classical manner ("un jeu sage, réglé, classique, majestueux") that was reminiscent of the intellectual and refined Shakespearean William Macready. Gautier commented that this great "Negro tragedian" took on this approach "doubtless to appear as civilized as a white." But Aldridge's "magnificent" entrance that evening left a particular impression on Gautier that exemplified more than white civility: "He was Othello himself as created by Shakespeare, with his eyes half closed as though dazzled by an African sun, his nonchalant oriental attitude, and that casual Negro manner that no European can imitate."[2]

Gautier's description of Aldridge's "oriental" calmness combined with "Negro" relaxation places the famous actor's rendition of Othello within the tradition of "tawny" Othellos in lighter makeup and exotic costumes, as performed by mid-nineteenth-century actors such as Edmund Kean in the UK and Edwin Forrest on the American stage.[3] Within this slate of performers, Ira Aldridge makes for a particularly intriguing example of how "oriental" refinement helped to refute assumptions of innate savagery and barbarism in black characters. As Myra Lynn Stephenson has pointed out, illustrations of Aldridge as Othello portray him "wearing a Venetian cap and mantle rather than a turban and flowing robes" but with "adornments such as a curved sword, drop earrings, and several arm bands [that] give these representations a faintly Oriental cast."[4]

Such descriptions suggest that Aldridge was thoroughly familiar with the racial habits of theatrical orientalism and used them to inform the costume and delivery of his most famous tragic roles. But Aldridge's deployment of orientalism went well beyond his Shakespearean performances. This chapter moves away from Aldridge's better-known heroic roles to examine instead his comic portrayals of the slave Mungo in the 1768 operatic afterpiece *The Padlock* and the black waiter Ginger Blue in the 1835 farce *The Virginia Mummy*, a character first made famous by blackface minstrel T. D. Rice. While much less refined, these stereotypical roles illuminate important dimensions of Aldridge's emblematic career and how he incorporated both black comic typecasting and oriental motifs—sometimes separately, sometimes in tandem—in his repertoire.

First, we look briefly at his performances of Kazrac, the mute Chinese slave character featured in many nineteenth-century productions of *Aladdin*. Aldridge played Kazrac on tour in Ireland in 1834, in a production staged by actor-manager Frank Seymour, who played the African magician, here called Abenzac.[5] The production drew praise from the *Cork Evening Herald*: "This Grand Eastern Spectacle . . . absolutely electrified the audience, whose approbation was testified by loud and reiterated bursts of acclamation."[6] Aldridge drew special praise for his playing of Kazrac: "Our opinion of the talents of the African Roscius is heightened, as we continue to witness his versatility in performing various characters. His conception of character is perfect and his acting which in an European would be more than respectable, is in an African truly wonderful."[7] Aldridge's Kazrac was likely the only time he ever played a Chinese character. But his casting shows the frequency with which he played cross-racial roles throughout his career. In addition to his performances as Shakespeare's Macbeth, Shylock, and King Richard III,

Aldridge also played a myriad of what biographer Bernth Lindfors describes as "other white, off-white, and tan characters" such as "an Eskimo chief, a Javanese husband, an Afghan military leader, a Dominican prince, a Spanish moor, [and] the ghostly apparition of a Dutch sea captain," thus adding "a wide range of interesting foreigners and strangers" to his repertoire.[8]

That orientalism informed a number of these roles can be seen in a vivid description of Aldridge in the largely nonspeaking role of Caesar, servant to the pirate Blackbeard, for a benefit performance of John Cartwright Cross's nautical pantomime *Black Beard the Pirate; or, The Captive Princess* (1798) in Alnwick, Northumberland, on January 30, 1843. Aldridge played a devoted servant who was heavily featured in the extravagant displays of sentiment and heroics.

> Caesar, the faithful accomplice of the dastardly Blackbeard, assists in
> the capture of a Turkish vessel and keeps watch over two prisoners
> taken on board—a Mogul prince and princess. Blackbeard instantly
> falls in love with the princess, preferring her to his wife, Orra, and
> threatening to kill Orra if she should interfere with his courtship of
> the beautiful captive. When he later discovers Orra attempting to
> murder her rival, he stabs his wife to death, and Caesar carries her
> body away. Caesar also protects Blackbeard from an assault by the
> Mogul prince, whom he drives away with a sword. The pirate ship
> is then attacked by a British war vessel, and rather than surrender,
> Blackbeard orders Caesar to blow up his ship. Caesar advances to-
> ward the powder magazine with a lighted match but is slain before
> he can reach it. In the furious battle that follows, Blackbeard is killed
> and thrown overboard.[9]

The real Blackbeard (Edward Teach or Edward Thatch, ca. 1680–1718) prof-ited from the bustling mercantile and slave routes between Britain, Europe, the West Indies, and the North American colonies. Yet this theatrical pan-tomime highlights less the struggles incurred by British and European colonization than the imagined conflict between Blackbeard and a "Turkish vessel" with Mogul captives. Much like *Aladdin*'s Kazrac, Caesar's loyal black servitude is fully demonstrated in this tale of piracy, despotic power, and slavery on the high seas.

In both *Aladdin* and *Black Beard*, oriental settings gave slave roles such as Kazrac and Caesar an exotic cast and also shifted depictions of slavery to the realm of fantasy, further away from direct commentary on British and American involvement with the slave trade. Theatrical orientalism also

The Lesser Roles of Ira Aldridge

allowed Aldridge to demonstrate his considerable range of acting skills by playing not only high tragedy and melodramatic pathos but also comedy. While there is no indication that Aldridge ever played either *Aladdin*'s Kazrac or *Black Beard*'s Caesar again, two other regular roles suggest a similar versatility. These were the slave Mungo in Isaac John Bickerstaff and Charles Dibdin's *The Padlock* and the waiter Ginger Blue from the farce *The Virginia Mummy*, who, like Kazrac, became popular for their foolery and displays of appetite and dissipation. Through including these humorous characterizations, usually played in tandem with more heroic scenes, Aldridge consistently received acclaim for his dramatic range. For instance, on tour through Scotland in 1839 Aldridge was praised for his presentations of high tragedy as Othello and as the vengeful Moorish prince Zanga in Edward Young's 1721 play *The Revenge*: "In his graceful 'strut,' his bold and dignified appearance, his self-possession, and excellent elocution, the audience at once recognize the man of genius and education." The same reviewer also noted Aldridge's appearances as Mungo and Ginger Blue in condensed versions of *The Padlock* and *The Virginia Mummy*, commending his performances as "a specific for ennui" and the "most potent *anti*-fogmatics in this proverbially gloomy month."[10] In addition to showing Aldridge's talents as a comic actor, these roles also demonstrated the ways that oriental elements could provide an added complexity to black stereotypes. While still adhering to the demands of racial exaggeration, Aldridge's execution of both Mungo and Ginger Blue demonstrated how the skilled actor might alter, however subtly, the presentation of one racial habit by contrasting it with another.

ALDRIDGE AS MUNGO

While much has been said of the influence of American blackface minstrelsy on transatlantic theater, many early nineteenth-century depictions of black slaves were probably influenced less by Jim Crow than by the West Indian slave character Mungo, who appeared in the operatic afterpiece *The Padlock*, written by Isaac John Bickerstaff with music by Charles Dibdin. Adapted from Miguel de Cervantes's *El celoso extremeño*, *The Padlock* debuted in 1768 at London's Drury Lane with Dibdin as Mungo and had its American debut at Philadelphia's Southwark Theatre in 1769. The play was enormously popular; according to theater manager Charles Durang, in Philadelphia it was "performed several times almost every season from its debut to 1800."[11] Dibdin even named one of his sons Charles Isaac Mungo Dibdin.[12] Though *The Padlock*'s setting was originally in Salamanca, Spain,

American versions were quick to seize upon the play's relationship between Don Diego and his slave Mungo as connected to American slavery. In the Philadelphia production, Lewis Hallam Jr. modeled Mungo's speech on that of black American slaves; in his 1832 *History of the American Theatre*, William Dunlap commented that "Mr. Hallam was unrivalled to his death, giving the Mungo with a truth derived from study of the Negro slave character, which Dibdin the writer could not have conceived."[13]

In *The Padlock*, the wealthy and elderly Don Diego has placed an enormous lock on his house in order to keep Leonora, his young ward and intended wife, away from the outside world. The noble Leandro can see his beloved Leonora only by impersonating a lame musician-beggar and befriending Don Diego's slave Mungo. Mungo directly challenges Don Diego's patriarchal authority, helping his young mistress escape the attentions of her guardian and find love with Leandro. Mungo is depicted somewhat sympathetically; he is generous in aiding Leandro and speaks out against Don Diego's mistreatment. But he is far from heroic. Speaking in heavy dialect and comically inebriated in act 2, the greedy, uncultured, and foolish figure of Mungo became, as Jenna Gibbs describes, a "ubiquitous icon of blackness in prose, theater, and print." Gibbs notes that by the late eighteenth century, "Mungo" was "a synonym for an African slave," and images of black slaves were often "accompanied by lines from his song 'Mungo here, Mungo dere, / Mungo every where / Me wish to de Lord I was dead.'"[14] British abolitionists used Mungo's complaints about Diego's unreasonable demands and physical abuse to highlight the plight of slaves, and his distinctive dialect and use of malapropisms were copied by American playwrights such as John Leacock and John Murdock for their own black slave characters.

Mungo was a regular offering in Aldridge's repertoire and was performed in tandem with tragic characters. As biographers Herbert Marshall and Mildred Stock write, Mungo was "the one role, apart from Othello, that he played the whole of his life, without a break, and he never failed to bring the house down."[15] On tour in Ireland in the mid-1930s, Aldridge received acclaim for outperforming the other actors in the same company: "In the after piece, Mr. Aldridge, as Mungo, called forth the loudest applause: his personification of the double-faced rouguish [sic] African was excellent." This *Kilkenny Moderator* review continued thus: "We can imagine nothing superior to his drollery and the perfect manner in which he identified himself with the character; the best proof of which was the continued roar of laughter in which he kept the house till the close of the piece, and which nothing but high genius could have excited under such unfavorable circumstances; the music being of the most wretched description, in addition to which the other performers had their parts but very imperfectly."[16]

Reviews of Aldridge focused on the comic nature of his gullible and at times intoxicated Mungo. He played Mungo's drunken scene quite convincingly, as a reviewer of his 1843 performance in Haverfordwest in Wales concluded: "We have never witnessed a better representation of a man in a state of inebriety. The stupid look and greasy skin, the up-turned eyes, the disposition to quarrel, and the frequent mistakes were each and all true to the life." The review urged audiences to "by all means go and witness his Mungo in *The Padlock*—hear him sing his *nigger* melodies, accompanying himself on the guitar, his 'Sich a gittin up stairs,' 'Jim Crow,' and if this is not sufficient to dispel care and banish grief, we will turn physician for once, and prescribe a perpetual cold bath for the patient, as thinking it to be an uncurable case."[17] Descriptions such as this emphasized Aldridge's use of popular minstrel songs as well as the drunken foolishness to which his Mungo was reduced. However, in contemplating Aldridge's performance of this role, it is important to keep in mind that *The Padlock* also allows Mungo to demonstrate the capacity for sympathy and rebellion as well as folly. Interesting enough, *The Padlock* infuses these dimension of Mungo's character, as well as the disguise of the hero Leandro, with pointed references to oriental enslavement and deception.

The oriental underpinnings of *The Padlock* are rendered through Leandro's pretense to have been the victim of "Turkish" slavery in order to win Mungo's trust and sympathy. Leandro describes one of his musical numbers as "a song I learn'd in Barbary when I was a slave among the Moors," introducing it with a story of "a cruel and malicious Turk, who was called Heli Abdallah Mahomet Scah." Leandro enraptures Mungo with his tale of this "wicked Turk" and his "fair Christian slave named Jezabel." When Jezabel does not consent to the Turk's "beastly desires," Leandro intones, "he draws out his sabre, and is going to cut off her head." Leandro then segues into song: "Here's what he says to her (*sings and plays*). Now you shall hear the slave's answer (*sings and plays again*). Now you shall hear how the wicked Turk, being greatly enraged, is again going to cut off the fair slave's head (*sings and plays again*)." [18] Leandro's story resembles a tale that, according to Rana Kabbani, was popular in sixteenth- and seventeenth-century European travel writing: a Turkish sultan falls in love with a slave girl, only to behead her in front of his courtiers once he realizes he has been neglecting his state duties.[19] Leandro further tries to persuade Mungo by making the fictional slave girl into a "fair Christian" and her death a punishment for resisting unwanted sexual advances. The story does the trick, and once Mungo lets the disguised Lean-dro into Don Diego's house, Leandro further embellishes the tale by giving Mungo and the lascivious nursemaid Ursula more fictional fodder: how he was once captured by a "Barbary Corsair" and taken to Sallee (the Moroccan port of Salli, now part of Rabat), then sold as a slave to an "infidel Turk" who "had fifty-three wives, and one hundred and twelve concubines."[20]

Leandro's oriental stories rely on the popular European imaginings of white slavery, North African piracy, and despotic oriental rule.[21] Tales of white Christians held captive to the "infidel" as well as of polygamy and sexual slavery in harems had long been associated with what Edward Said has described as the "peril" of the Ottoman Empire, which until the end of the seventeenth century "lurked alongside Europe to represent for the whole of Christian civilization a constant danger, and in time European civilization incorporated that peril and its lore, its great events, figures, virtues, and vices, as something woven into the fabric of life."[22] Kabbani has pointed out how nineteenth-century European paintings depicted oriental men traffick-ing in female slaves, projecting onto them innate brutality and lascivious desires and suggesting a fundamental distinction between Eastern and Western masculinity.[23] In a broader context, *The Padlock*'s references to sto-ries of oriental enslavement seem to comment on the despotic Don Diego's excesses of power over Leonora, Mungo, and others in his household. How-ever, that Leandro tells them in ways that are both patently deceptive and comically manipulative also suggests a familiar lesson about the duplicitous nature of oriental fantasy. Mungo's fascination illustrates how a black slave can be easily deceived by the tales of Turkish enslavement he sees as akin to his own. Mungo is quite undone by his foolish decision to let Leandro into the house; even as Leandro and Leonora are united in the end, he remains in slavery and suffers a final beating from Don Diego.

But however Mungo is seen as foolish, in these scenes of sympathetic identification he nonetheless displays a generosity and charity that contrasts with both Don Diego's tyranny and Leandro's clever self-interest. Leandro's oriental tales also inspire Mungo's desire for rebellion, as he contemplate how they might join together toward emancipation:

We dance and we sing,
Till we make a house ring,
And, tied in his garters, old Massa may swing.[24]

While Mungo's drunken acts of rebellion are quickly put down, such moments seem to echo, albeit comically, Aldridge's more heroic slave roles.

Another of Aldridge's regular performances was as the "royal slave" Oroonoko, a tragedy that fueled abolitionist sentiment in Britain. One playbill for *The Revolt of Surinam* described it as "a most faithful Portrait of the horrors that arise out of that dreadful traffic, which it is the proudest boast of Britain to use her best efforts towards suppressing," and stated that Aldridge's performance "must receive an immense portion of additional interest from being supported in its principal character by a *Man of Colour* and one of the very race whose wrongs it professes to record."[25]

Thus Leandro's oriental deceptions not only further his courtship of the fair Leonora but also prompt Mungo's imaginings of cross-racial alliance and revolt. Aldridge's performance might well have highlighted these more rebellious dimensions of Mungo as well as his temporary state of inebriation. Marshall and Stock's biography of Aldridge argue that he inserted comic songs into his act not only to capitalize on his audience's delight in blackface minstrelsy but also to protest slavery's horrors. For instance, Aldridge included his own renditions of "Possum Up a Gum Tree," a song popularized in England by Charles Mathews's *A Trip to America* (1824). The English actor Mathews parodied a black tragedian from New York's African Grove Theatre spouting out famous lines from *Hamlet* and *Richard III* in conjunction with a rendition of "Possum Up a Gum Tree," and his version of the song depicted an opossum who gets pulled from a tree by a racoon; the racoon in turn is then tricked by a "cunning nigger" who gets the opossum in the end. Aldridge's lyrics, in contrast, also highlighted the abuse of black slaves.

> Massa send we Negro Boy
> Board a ship, board a ship,
> There we work and cry, "Ye hoy"
> Cowskin whip, cowskin whip,
> Negro he work all de day,
> Night get groggy, night get groggy,
> But if Negro he go play
> Massa floggy, Massa floggy,
> Possum up a Gum Tree, etc.[26]

This version of "Possum Up a Gum Tree" clearly reinforces why Mungo, who is frequently beaten onstage, has good reason to hope that "Massa may swing." Aldridge regularly performed this song in conjunction with plays expressing abolitionist sentiments, among them Thomas Morton's 1816 musical drama *The Slave; or, the Blessings of Liberty.*

The oriental elements in *The Padlock* also suggest multiple and contrasting juxtapositions of Aldridge's comic roles with his most famous part, Shakespeare's Othello. Leandro's tale of enslavement by an "infidel Turk" plays off Mungo's sympathies to win access to his beloved, a device that clearly resonates with Othello's account of winning Desdemona through telling his own story "of being taken by the insolent foe and sold to slavery." In both roles, the common enemy is imagined as the Ottoman Empire, whose enslavement of both black and white characters defines its barbarism. Othello's final climactic speech in act 5, scene 2 projects his self-loathing onto the oriental enemy, describing his punishment of "a malignant and turbaned Turk" before stabbing himself. Though the comic *The Padlock* and the tragic *Othello* have very different outcomes, in both black characters act in response not only to their treatment by white characters but also to a larger orientalist imagination in which non-Christian Others are depicted as barbaric enemies fit for punishment, or as potential allies, or perhaps both in turn.

ALDRIDGE AS GINGER BLUE

That an arrangement of *The Virginia Mummy*, labeled "A Negro Farce" and credited to C[harles] White, was published as number 315 by the London publisher John Dicks shows the concurrent popularity of "Negro farces" and oriental curiosities in the mid-nineteenth century.[27] The cover image pictures the main characters at the climax of the play. On one side is the romantic lead, Captain Rifle, along with Lucy, his love interest. Rifle is dressed in a "*Persian*" disguise (an elaborate coat and feathered hat) that he wears in order to ingratiate himself with Dr. Galen, Lucy's guardian. At the center is Rifle's gift to Dr. Galen of an oriental mummy, as impersonated by the black waiter Ginger Blue. On the other side are an Irish servant, O'Leary, and a painter, Charles. In this scene, Dr. Galen force-feeds Ginger Blue what he thinks is his "Compound extract of Live-for-ever" that can reanimate the dead. Dark-faced and gingerly stepping out of his sarcophagus, Ginger Blue's wide-eyed figure presents a striking contrast to the slumped figure of the white-faced mummy next to him.

This edition of the play, published in the late nineteenth-century series of "Dick's Standard Plays" for a popular readership and amateur performance, is among several published and manuscript versions of *The Virginia Mummy*.[28] Notably, Dick's Standard Plays lists as part of its dramatis personae those who performed "at the Surrey Theatre in 1847," and among

The Lesser Roles of Ira Aldridge

Cover illustration for *The Virginia Mummy*, Dicks' Standard Plays.

them, Ira Aldridge as Ginger Blue. This edition makes no mention of the well-known blackface minstrel T. D. Rice, who has been credited with having premiered the role in 1835 in Mobile, Alabama. Rice performed in blackface as Ginger Blue regularly through his career, including performances in the UK; however, "Dick's Standard Plays" does not list him as the author, nor does it mention other previous productions of *The Virginia Mummy*, such as those by Christy's Minstrels.

For the purposes of this edition, Aldridge's performances in the leading role of *The Virginia Mummy* eclipsed those of white minstrel impersonators. Like the role of Mungo, the part of Ginger Blue showed Aldridge's ability to command the stage as a comic actor. But Ginger Blue allowed for an even more complex set of cross-racial interactions to take place in the shifts between the black character and the figure of the oriental mummy. If *The Virginia Mummy* reinforced distinctions between the degraded states of blackness and the elitism of orientalism, the role of Ginger Blue—a comic tour de force for Aldridge—also highlighted how black characters and black actors could take part in and profit from, rather than be deceived by, orientalist impersonation.

The Virginia Mummy was based on William Bayle Bernard's The Mummy, a play first performed by London's Adelphi Company in 1833 that remained popular on the nineteenth century stage.[29] Bernard's play does not use blackface. Rather, the romantic lead, Captain Canter, pays an impoverished white character, Toby Tramp, to impersonate a mummy and pretends to be an "Eastern traveler that has brought over the veritable frame of King Cheopa" in order to gain access to Fanny, the daughter of Mandragon, an avid collector of curiosities. Both mummy plays satirize the popularity of Egyptian antiquities, which had attracted much attention in Britain in the 1820s and 1830s; the British Museum, for instance, prominently featured mummies and coffins in a new display in 1838. However, The Mummy also draws on well-established plots and themes, borrowing directly from Molière's Le Bourgeois Gentilhomme as well as other theatrical mockeries of oriental fashion. In William Wycherley's 1675 comedy The Country Wife, multiple sexual affairs take place in a room offstage under the guise of female characters "toiling and moiling for the prettiest piece of china,"[30] and Bernard's The Mummy uses a similar double entrendre when Mandragon sends his daughter out with the disguised Captain Canter: "By the bye, she has a great curiosity on all oriental subjects, and I have made bold to promise that you would gratify her" (Bernard 11).

The worship of the mummy by Mandragon in The Mummy and by Dr. Galen in The Virginia Mummy follows the common association of the Orient with fetishized objects and erotic excess. In The Mummy, the Irish servant Larry Bathershin calls Mandragon "one of the most degrading species of Infatuators." When challenged by the painter Theophilus Pole with "Do you impunge his taste? his love for every thing that's rare?," Bathershin retorts, "It's not rare, it's over done" (Bernard 7). The Virginia Mummy likewise mocks Galen's obsessive desire to get his hands on "the mortal remains of Egypt and China" (White 3). In both plays, the infatuation of white characters with oriental objects leads to deviant fantasies of physical intimacy and necrophilia. The mummy not only is prized for its rare and royal origins but also inspires the desire for physical interaction. Though Mandragon addresses the mummy with reverence, saying, "Form of the mighty Pharoah [sic], I approach thee with due awe," he quickly moves into closer contact, noting that "the flesh quite soft, the organs all entire" (Bernard 11). However, this contact turns to the threat of dismemberment: "His bones are as soft as muscle, his flesh would cut like cheese—or I might try a third experiment, which involves a still more curious theory—bore through his skill, and see if he has a brain." The painter Theophilus gleefully imagines not only taking apart the mummy's dead body but also capturing its pain should they revive it: "Should signs of vitality display themselves, we'll bind him to a plank—hand and leg immovable, then as he writhes and yells, and his eyes glare open with the spasm, I'll catch the grand expression, and throw it upon canvas" (Bernard 12).

Both *The Mummy* and *The Virginia Mummy* use the comic enactment of the mummy to create an effective contrast between the inert oriental mummy and the enormously vital character who impersonates him. Toby Tramp is an enthusiastic but inept actor who describes his debut in *Richard II*: "The hit was tremendous—before I reached the hit scenes my acting was so affecting, half the people were obliged to go out" (Bernard 4). Ginger Blue is a much more reluctant performer who demands considerable compensation for playing the mummy. However Toby Tramp and Ginger Blue ultimately fail in playing the mummy, their roles require considerable acting ability in moving quickly between impersonations of the dead mummy and the boisterous characters who play them. Toby Tramp (played in the 1833 Adelphi production by the famed comic actor John Reeve) launches into Shakespearean parody as well as explosively reanimates the mummy, bursting his head through his own portrait. The role of Ginger Blue in *The Virginia Mummy* adds still another dimension to the actor's transformation by layering a set of contrasting racial typologies onto the debased tramp and his oriental disguise.

At times, Ginger Blue's impersonation suggests a racial likeness between the black character and the oriental mummy he plays. W. T. Lhamon has suggested that the play connects the word "mummify" with the Arabic *mummiya*, meaning "bitumen or pitch," commenting that "mummies looked like characters daubed in burnt cork and like characters smeared with tar."[31] However, within the world of the play the parallels between debased blackness and oriental value are also questioned. The Irish domestic O'Leary exclaims, "And is that what you call a mummy? It looks for all the world like a smoked hog" and fears being left "alone wid this black looking mummy" (White 6). The painter Charles remarks on the mummy's "prodigious height" and wonders "if his race were all that colour" (White 7). If oriental disguises are seen as transparently fraudulent and easily discarded, the mask of blackness is suggested to be an indelible trait for Ginger Blue.

Comparison of the roles of Toby Tramp and Ginger Blue reveal strong differences between the abilities of white and black actors to play the mummy. Toby Tramp in Bernard's *The Mummy* revels in his drunken claims to be "King Pharoah in all his glory" (Bernard 18). In contrast, *The Virginia Mummy* contains an extended comic dialogue between Charles and Ginger Blue stressing the enormous divide between fantasies of oriental nobility and blackface types. When Charles enthuses that the mummy "no doubt . . . was some great personage, and stood very high in his native country," Ginger Blue undercuts this dignified image with "When I was up de tree, arter de possum" (White 7). If Charles pictures the mummy as formerly an artist who "handled the brush," Ginger Blue corrects this to "de whitewash-brush," and in addressing speculation that the mummy was a musician, Ginger Blue asserts, "Jist gib me de banjo, dat's all" (White 7).

While Toby Tramp fancies himself a "Master of Arts" (Bernard 4), *The Virginia Mummy* limits Ginger Blue's willingness and ability to impersonate the oriental mummy. The white hero of *The Virginia Mummy* can easily manage the superficial disguise of oriental impersonation. Captain Rifle's pretense to be an Egyptian is aided by his suntanned skin: "I am afraid Lucy will scarcely know me—for a two years' campaign on our western frontier changes a man's complexion as a chameleon does its color" (White 2). His disguise clearly takes little effort other than donning an undistinguished "*Persian suit*," of which O'Leary remarks, "He's got a hat on like a washerwoman," and Charles adds, "And an overcoat like a short gown" (White 6). In contrast, Ginger Blue, while elaborately decked out in bandages and headdress as the mummy, is still inadequate to his assigned task of oriental impersonation. Ginger Blue's comic lapses emphasize the inadequacies of black characters both in comprehending and in impersonating the more patrician forms of orientalism. His performance is marked by repeated lapses in form, as he has difficulty following instructions to "be silent as death" and to "try to remember that mummies are dead and never eat" (White 5). Despite Rifle's coaching on the basics of embalmed inaction, Ginger Blue cannot help but give way to his appetites, stealing Dr. Galen's sugar, eating his breakfast, drinking his whiskey, and biting his servant's finger.

But again, while the play makes clear the limitations of black characters to transcend their grossly racialized bodies, it also allows the actors playing them to demonstrate their considerable skills at comic timing, physical ability, and stamina as well as mimicry. *The Virginia Mummy* ends with Ginger Blue's embrace of his role as he offers his body up to future audiences as a racially amalgamated novelty: "And should any ob de faculty hab occasion for a libe mummy again, dey hab only to call on Ginger Blue; when dey'll find him ready dried, smoked, and painted, to sarbe himself up at de shortest notice" (White 8). T. D. Rice and other white actors in this role emphasized their skills at cross-racial impersonation both in the blackface role of Ginger Blue and as the oriental mummy he plays. As David Roediger has suggested, blackface minstrels were "the first self-consciously *white* entertainers in the world," whose "simple physical disguise—and elaborate cultural disguise—of blacking up served to emphasize that those on stage were really white and that whiteness really mattered."[32] Particular lines of dialogue in *The Virginia Mummy* draw attention to the privilege of wearing blackface makeup over having black skin. In the version of *The Virginia Mummy* attributed to T. D. Rice by W. T. Lhamon, Rifle says that he will decorate Ginger like a mummy, "white, black, green, blue, and a variety of colors," and Ginger responds with, "Massa, put plenty of turpentine wid de white paint so it won't rub off. I like to make 'em believe I'm a white man, too."[33]

Aldridge's playing of Ginger Blue may have entailed some subtle yet telling alterations to the dialogue of *The Virginia Mummy*. In the version published by Dick's Standard Plays, the line "I like to make 'em believe I'm a white man, too" disappears, and Ginger Blue's preceding line is altered to the more ambiguous "Put in lots of glue so de white paint won't rub off?" (White 5). There are a number of other differences between Rice's script and the published adaptation presumably used by Aldridge. Dick's Standard Plays does not include an exchange between Galen and Ginger Blue that accentuates the difference between the presumably high status of the mummy and the lowly Ginger Blue, while in Rice's script Dr. Galen muses that the mummy's lips "perhaps did seal the nuptial kiss to some fair Princess, chaste and fair as the lily beams of Bright Aurora," and Ginger responds, "De only Prince he kiss was old Aggs, and she's as black as the debbil" (Lhamon 174–75). Yet whether these lines may have been changed or excised as a particular response to Ira Aldridge's appearance in *The Virginia Mummy* is uncertain, since the rest of the play, including the numerous deprecations of blackness by Ginger Blue himself, remains unchanged. Various versions of the script suggest that for Aldridge as well as white actors, playing the character of Ginger Blue may have entailed using blackface makeup layered over with the mummy's wrappings. Both Rice's script and the version by White include a line uttered by Charles when he first touches the disguised Ginger: "How soft and moist the flesh is, and quite warm. How confoundedly it smells of shoe blacking" (Lhamon 172; White 7).

Might Aldridge have improvised other original stage business and more opportunities for the character of Ginger Blue that don't appear in the published versions of *The Virginia Mummy*? Reviews suggest no particular evidence for such innovations. Aldridge, like Rice, included familiar minstrel songs as well as retained the overall racial typecasting of Ginger Blue. In January 1841, on a tour of northern counties of England, he performed at the Theatre Royal in Preston with a reviewer noting "a condensed version of *Othello* and a complete performance of *The Egyptian* [i.e., *Virginian*] Mummy, into which he inserted the songs 'Jim Crow' and 'Lubly Rosa,' accompanying himself on the guitar into the latter."[34] Lindfors cites playbills that describe Aldridge in the role as "an independent Nigger Head waiter, always absent when wanted, yet mindful of his perquisites, remarkably familiar, bursting with fun & laughter, very industrious (by deputy,) but receives all gratuities in person, a most accomodating [sic] appetite, & his love of money induces [him] to become a mummy."[35]

At the same time, reviews also consistently affirm that Aldridge's performances belied any notion of his having limitations, racial or otherwise, as an actor. On tour in Derby, England, his Ginger Blue was deemed "a rare specimen of racy humour," one that "kept the risible faculties of his auditors in full exercise, to the end of the afterpiece."[36] On tour in the Midlands region of Ireland, an 1839 performance as Ginger Blue "kept the house in roars of laughter."[37] Aldridge was praised by the *Doncaster Chronicle* for an 1841 performance in South Yorkshire county, England: "As Ginger-blue, the avaricious, pompous and ragged-head waiter . . . he was inimitable."[38] In one memorable instance in 1845, he performed the role in Derby, England, in tandem with a version of *Othello*. Both plays were missing key actresses, and one eyewitness wrote, "The performance appeared rather peculiar, inasmuch as Desdemona and Emilia were conspicuous by their absence, and even *The Virginia Mummy* was acted without the aid of a lady!" However, the account went on to say that "*The Virginian* [sic] *Mummy*, however, restored good temper to the audience, for Mr. Aldridge was a genuine comedian, and the vagaries of Ginger Blue kept the audience in roars of laughter and sent everybody away satisfied."[39] In 1839, an Irish reviewer concluded of Aldridge that "'tis no trifling degree of eulogy to say, that in '*Ginger Blue*,' the *Virginia Mummy*, he is fully equal to RICE."[40]

If the plot of *The Virginia Mummy* implied the inability of a black character to enact an oriental role, Ira Aldridge's highly acclaimed performances as Ginger Blue and other characters challenged this very assumption. The

London *Era* praised Aldridge's skills in both tragic and comic performance during the fall of 1846: "The versatility of Garrick himself, who played Richard and Abel Drugger, Macbeth and Jerry Sneak on the same night, appears at any rate to attach to the African Roscius, who in the evening achieves his Othello or his Zanga, with his Mungo and his Ginger Blue. The sock and the buskin appear, by provincial criticism, to fit him equally; the tear or the horse-laugh being alike at his command."[41] An 1858 essay, "Mr. Aldridge, the African Tragedian," published in the *Illustrated London News* emphasized these skills at both genres as well:

> As both a tragic and a comic actor, Mr. Aldridge's talents are undeniably great. In tragedy he has a solemn intensity of style, bursting occasionally to a blaze of fierce invective or passionate declamation, while the dark shades of his face become doubly sombre in their thoughtful aspect; a nightlike gloom is spread over them, and an expression more terrible than paler lineaments can readily assume. In farce he is exceedingly amusing; the ebony becomes polished; the coal emits sparks. His face is the faithful index of his mind; and, as there is not a darker frown than his, there is not a broader grin. The ecstasy of his long, shrill note in "Opossum Up a Gum Tree" can only be equaled by the agony of his cry of despair over the body of Desdemona.[42]

These comments proclaimed Aldridge's versatility and talents as an actor, just as much as his 1825 renditions of Othello and Oroonoko surprised those skeptics who expected his performance to be, as one London reviewer stated, "a mere burlesque on acting, by some sooty child of ignorance."[43] In fact, his stints in these comic roles might have showcased his transformative skills even more. As Felicity Nussbaum writes, "Whiteness is portrayed as fundamental and permanent while blackness is ornamental and temporary until a black actor takes the stage, and the white spectator freshly confronts the fictive nature of race while attaching blackness to a real body."[44] While Aldridge has elicited critical praise for taking on more dignified and serious roles, his performances of racial caricature in the comic roles of Mungo, Ginger Blue, and Kazrac ran a much greater risk of audiences conflating his identity with those of the foolish and servile characters he played. That he could remain visible as the skilled actor rather than as the natural incarnation of these lesser roles reinforces the unique nature of his abilities and artistic achievement.

3

BLACKFACE MINSTRELSY'S
JAPANESE TURNS

As previous chapters have suggested, the distinctive racial habits promoted by blackface minstrelsy—racial impersonation, black caricature, and plantation nostalgia—reached far beyond the borders of the United States. Both before and after the U.S. Civil War, minstrel performers had eager audiences in England and other parts of Europe. In her study of *Uncle Tom's Cabin*, Sarah Meers comments, "Minstrelsy was from its earliest incarnations a transatlantic phenomenon."[1] Blackface entered into British pantomime and harlequinade through the characterizations of Jim Crow and other minstrel types as well as via popular musical numbers. The American minstrel actor Thomas Dartmouth (T. D.) Rice received great acclaim in London performances playing in *Bone Squash Diavolo* at the Surrey Theatre and appearing in William Leman Rede's play *Flight to America* at the Adelphi, both in 1836.[2] Rice was followed by a host of Jim Crow imitators who appeared in holiday pantomimes that same year, including in *Cowardy, Cowardy, Custard; or, Harlequin Jim Crow and the Magic Mustard Pot* (Adelphi), *Harlequin and George Barnwell* (Covent Garden), and *Harlequin and Old Gammer Gurton* (Drury Lane).[3] Michael Pickering has detailed how American companies such as Dan Emmett's Virginia Minstrels toured successfully in Britain in the 1840s, inspiring British minstrel troupes to create their own shows.[4] Characters such as Friday in pantomime versions of *Robinson*

Crusoe (beginning with R. B. Sheridan's version at London's Drury Lane in 1781) also wore the mask of minstrel blackface.[5]

Minstrel performance also had its transpacific dimensions, beginning with the events following Commodore Matthew Perry's 1853 forcible "opening" of Japan, where diplomatic exchanges included a blackface minstrel show staged by American sailors for Japanese officials. These events were subsequently satirized by Christy's Minstrels in a skit featuring characters named "Simnobudgenokamia," "More Hoecakeawake Moonshee," and "Princess Ko-ket."[6] While never entirely displacing the black caricatures that had defined the minstrel show, in the later nineteenth century elements reflecting the larger public interest in Japan increasingly became part of the minstrel stage. According to Robert Toll, when the Imperial Japanese Acrobats toured in 1865 and 1867, at least eight major U.S. companies included acts with titles such as "The Flying Black Japs."[7] While touring London in 1867, Christy's Minstrels performed a musical number played on a "Japanese Fiddle" as well as added a "Chinese Dance," and an undated program for the London-based Mohawk Minstrels lists a "New Original and Japaneasy Absurdity," by Harry Hunter and Edward Forman, "Come Let Us Be Jappy Together."[8] A number of minstrel shows were inspired by the 1885 success of W. S. Gilbert and Arthur Sullivan's *The Mikado*; these included Thatcher, Primrose, and West's *The Mick-ah-do* and *The Black Mikado* and parodies by Haverly's, McIntyre and Heath's, and Carncross's Minstrels.[9]

As Mari Yoshihara has described, the widespread American interest in Japanese arts, crafts, and decor as well as artistic, literary, and theatrical representations of Japan was part of larger orientalist traditions either embracing Asian cultures as "seductive, aesthetic, refined culture" or rejecting them as "foreign, premodern, Other."[10] Minstrelsy incorporated both traditions, using acrobats and "Japaneasy" comic absurdities as well as more refined characterizations, settings, and themes influenced by Japanese styles. In 1900, the *Freeman* described how the setting for "Big Minstrel Festival" of the Richards and Pringle's and Rosco and Holland's minstrel troupes had a "Japanese finish, and was gorgeously handsome."[11] Rosco and Holland's part of the show opened with the curtain rising "on a darkened stage which gradually lightens and reveals 'The Oriental Terrace,' and the opening number, 'Ragtime in the Orient.'"[12]

Such elements highlighted not only the ubiquity of the "Japan craze" but also the shifting form and direction of the minstrel show as it increasingly moved from music hall and saloon venues into more respectable venues and even elite theater spaces. As Toll has suggested, earlier blackface minstrel production "offered antebellum Americans an irresistible entertainment package" with "no characterization to develop, no plot to evolve, no musical score, no set speeches, no subsidiary dialogue—indeed no fixed script at all. Each act—song, dance, joke, or skit—was a self-contained performance that strived to be a highlight of the show. This flexible structure meant that even with the repetition of the traditional three-part minstrel show form, minstrelsy could adapt to the tastes of their specific audience while the show was in process."[13] This adaptation was particularly marked after the Civil War as minstrel shows expanded in size and diversified in theme. As Stephanie Dunson has noted, minstrel songs became popular not only in the music hall but also in the parlors of middle-class homes. This shifted the nature of these performances away from raucous entertainments primarily by and for working-class white men, with "the blackened guise becoming a corporeal playground for the performance and project of myriad improprieties and social indiscretions." Minstrelsy instead began to enter into entertainment and domestic spaces in which "women marked the standard and standing, where 'performers' were familial, where pantomime was oddly partnered with propriety."[14]

This movement toward performing in domestic spaces and for white female spectators provided additional incentives for minstrel performance to incorporate the more patrician aspects of the Japan craze. As Yoshihara has documented, white women were perhaps the most avid consumers of Japanese-themed imports and entertainments, purchasing Japanese artwork and decorative objects, emulating Gilbert and Sullivan's *The Mikado* and Giacomo Puccini's *Madama Butterfly*, and participating in cross-racial masquerades.[15] Blending blackface minstrel tropes with pointedly Japanese elements underscored minstrelsy's shift from comic rowdiness to refinement, from lowly and humble to more exotic and decorative characters, and from masculine to feminine tastes. This chapter examines two striking instances of how minstrel performance was juxtaposed with Japanese themes and characterizations. The first is in the career of Thomas Dilward, one of only two African Americans hired by white-dominated minstrel companies prior to the Civil War. Dilward took on the stage name "Japanese Tommy," suggesting the cultivation of an endearing and diminutive oriental persona that enhanced his appeal as a minstrel performer. The second is a 1916 play, Walter Ben Hare's *Abbu San of Old Japan*, whose all-female amateur cast makes a very different kind of connection between playing Japanese and minstrel blackface. In Hare's play, "Old Japan" becomes a space for white female performers to play not only Japanese characters but also a stereotypical Mammy figure. Emphasizing the contrast between nostalgic blackface and fashionable yellowface, *Abbu San of Old Japan* shows how different kinds of racial impersonation can provide equally respectable outlets for white female energy and excess. While these two examples illustrate very different contexts and actors, both suggest how the entrenched racial habits of traditional minstrelsy could be effectively modified in order to appeal to broader audiences and to profit from the novelty of the Japan craze.

THE MANY FACES OF JAPANESE TOMMY

Thomas Dilward (also spelled "Dilworth," "Dilverd," or "Dilwerd") began as a professional minstrel in 1853 with Christy's Minstrels and worked with many integrated companies, including Dan Bryant's, Wood's, Morris Brothers', and Kelly and Leon's Minstrels. He also played with all-black troupes such as Charles B. Hicks's Original and Only Georgia Minstrels Slave Troupe.[16] Dilward made appearances around the world, including an 1870 tour of Ireland and other parts of Great Britain with Sam Hague's Great American Slave Troupe.[17] His was a relatively long career, as evidenced by his billing in the UK touring shows of Hiscock and Hayman's Australian Federal Minstrels, who visited at the Free Trade Hall in Manchester from October 11, 1880, until the spring of 1881. In 1882, the *New York Times* commented that he sued a Brooklyn restauranteur for being "refused a meal, for which he had the money to pay," for $5,000 in damages under the Civil Rights Act of 1875.[18] Dilward's 1887 funeral notice described him as "a popular songster and a contortionist" who "appeared in both male and female parts." Despite his relatively long career in minstrelsy, at his funeral it was reported that "but few friends were present."[19]

Dilward played the violin, sang, danced, and appeared in sketches,[20] but it was perhaps his height that made him a theatrical curiosity. The white minstrel producer Edward Le Roy Price described "Thomas Dilverd" as "a colored man, whose height of 37 inches made him a valuable acquisition to the many companies he was associated with; he was not dependent on this for his success, for he was a good comedian, and played male and female roles equally as well."[21] Harry Reynolds's 1928 *Minstrel Memories* reminisced that Dilward was a "quaint coloured dwarf" who performed with Sam Hague's Georgia Minstrel Troupe, driving a one-horse trap in a pageant.[22] Dilward was billed as "African Dwarf Tommy" and "The African 'Tom Thumb,'" no doubt capitalizing on the popular appearances of Charles

Sherwood Stratton as "General Tom Thumb" in carnival and stage entertainments under P. T. Barnum's management.

It is not certain to what extent Dilward cultivated any identifiably Japanese aspects to his acts. A selection of songs published in 1871 as *Japanese Tommy's Songster: Containing a Selection of the Most Popular Melodies of the Day* contains no references to Japan in the lyrics.[23] Neither photographs nor reviews indicate any particular affinity for Japanese dress or characterization, and apart from his name, there are only a few oriental references in his stage material. In 1884, he is recorded to have appeared with George W. Harding, the stage manager for the Boston Dime Museum and dialect comedian and vocalist, to present the skit "Fun in a Chinese Laundry."[24] Dilward is credited by John Russell Bartlett's *Dictionary of Americanisms* with introducing the phrase "hunky-dory" from "the name of a street, or a bazaar, in Yeddo"[25] (Edo or Tokyo), though no further indication of actual linguistic connections with Japan have been found.

Dilward's act seems to have consisted mainly of acts common on the minstrel stage. Reynolds's *Minstrel Memories* includes a rare photograph of him onstage during a UK tour dressed in a Hussar's uniform and carrying what is either a broom (a prop that Dale Cockrell suggests was used to define performance spaces in blackface minstrelsy as well as mummer plays) or a brush.[26] The brush might have signaled Dilward's singing of "Uncle Snow," a number identified "As Sung and Danced by JAPANESE TOMMY, at Christy's Opera House, Brooklyn," in an 1863 collection from Christy's Minstrels, *Christy's New Songster and Black Joker*. Sung in dialect, the lyrics mocks its character's pretensions and exposes his humble status. "Uncle Snow" identifies himself as "an artist wid de brush by profession" but reveals that his "art" is simply menial labor: "I'm de greatest white washer in all creation." He then boasts, "I'm a goin' down to Washington, / To try and get a job to whitewash all de black deeds ob dis nation."[27] However, the second verse further deflates his posturing.

'Bout ninety years ago, oh, it's to dis town I cum,
    Oh, den I was a clever little feller;
Oh, I saved a dime or two,
    And I'd hab you all to know,
I set up whitewash bisness in a cellar.

Another photograph of Dilward, a studio portrait from 1866, shows him elaborately outfitted in a fashionable dress with a broad hoop skirt, ruffled sleeves, white gloves, and a beribboned bonnet.[28] Dilward performed with a number of minstrel troupes in which white female impersonators such as George Christy or "The Only Leon" (Patrick Francis Glassey) had made black female "wench" or prima donna figures a standard part of minstrel performances. These cross-gender performances, common in all-male minstrel troupes, entailed racial mockery: the supposed incongruity of the black male body playing the delicate and proper demeanor of upper-class white femininity. However, it also allowed for the performer to show his skills at imitation as well as singing and dancing, confirming Price's assessment that Dilward "played male and female roles equally as well."

A different studio portrait taken of Dilward between 1855 and 1865 shows a carefully groomed and genial man neatly dressed in a suit and bow tie. Like portraits taken of white minstrels, this photograph registers the evolution of minstrelsy in the later nineteenth century into a more genteel entertainment geared toward middle- and upper-class women as much as working-class men. As Stephanie Dunson has pointed out, by the mid-nineteenth century, minstrel songs and characters had become not just part of more respectable theaters but also part of the intimate entertainments of white middle-class society. Sheet music covers displayed images of "upstanding, well-groomed white performers" alongside "the grotesque black characters they portrayed."[29] This refined image of Dilward would have had a similar function, adding Dilward to the ranks of those who distanced themselves from the comically debased black types that they played onstage.

Dilward's adoption of the stage name "Japanese Tommy," though perhaps not fully determining the nature of his stage acts, suggests an additional oriental dimension to this genteel image. Dilward joined Christy's Minstrels in 1853, the year that Commodore Perry opened Japan to American trade. It is likely that Dilward was capitalizing on both the general interest in U.S.-Japan relations and the specific social success of another "Japanese Tommy": Tateishi Onojirō Noriyuko, a member of the first Japanese embassy to the United States in 1860. A teenager traveling with his interpreter uncle, Onojirō became a minor celebrity during his visit to the United States.[30] He was nicknamed "Tommy" after his childhood name, Tamehachi, and was called "a darling fellow" and a "Japanese prince" by U.S. newspapers.[31] Onojirō attracted immense attention from the press and was particularly noted as popular with white society women. The *New York Tribune* reported that "bevies of maidens gaze beneficently upon him all day,"[32] and one reporter for the *New York Times* remarked that upon his return voyage, "when not studying or guzzling he writes soul-touching love-letters to his sweethearts in America—lying in the most polished manner to all of

Thomas Dilward, or "Japanese Tommy" (between 1855 and 1865).
Brady-Handy Photograph Collection, Prints and
Photographs Division, Library of Congress.

NATURAL MISTAKES.

GENTLEMAN. "Hi! Here, you Nigger, come here!"
COLORED GENTLEMAN. "Nigger!—no Nigger, Sar; me Japanese, Sar!"

TOMMY (a little how-come-you-so). "One of dem (hic) is my Hat me know; but me be (hic) if me can tell which him is."

"Natural Mistakes," published in *Harper's Weekly*, June 30, 1860.
Prints and Photographs Division, Library of Congress.

them, and signing himself 'Your lovely TOMMY.'"[33] The gregarious teenager even inspired a musical number, the "Tommy Polka" (1860) by German immigrant C. Grobe, with the following lyrics:

Wives and maids by scores are flocking
Round that charming, little man,
Known as Tommy, witty Tommy,
Yellow Tommy, from Japan.[34]

Onojirō's popularity, particularly with women, clearly was the subject of racial mockery as well as curiosity. In general, the Japanese, while greeted as curiosities and sometimes as foreign dignitaries, were also reviled as non-white. This derision can be seen in a parodic cartoon, "Natural Mistakes," published in a June 1860 edition of *Harper's Weekly* that directly compares a rebellious African American waiter—who refuses to be designated "n——" and instead claims to be Japanese—with a drunken version of a Japanese noble.[35]

Yet the interest in Onojirō (and other Japanese people and objects perceived as "charming" and "little") may well have also made him an inspiration for Dilward's act, which was clearly popular among white audiences. Using his short stature to style himself as the diminutive and witty "Japanese Tommy" allowed Dilward an association with elite society's curiosity about Japan. With the increasing numbers of African American performers in integrated minstrel troupes, being "Japanese" would have allowed Dilward to distinguish himself even more as a character specialty. A March 15, 1869, playbill for a performance at the Theatre Royal on King Street in Bristol, UK, has as its headline "The Great American Slave Troupe and Japanese Tommy"; Dilward as "Japanese" stands out from the rest of the cast, which included the very different curiosity of "16 real negros from the plantations of America."[36] A 1914 retrospective on minstrelsy by Frank Dumont reminisced that "from time to time dwarfs have appeared with the troupes and excited attention, notably Japanese Tommy, a colored dwarf, who was quite funny as a 'prima donna,' and in the 'Essence of Old Virginny'"; Dumont noted that "Bryant's Minstrels had another dwarf, called 'Little Mac.'"[37]

African American men, already stigmatized by race, would have been regarded as even more deficient for having short stature. The "What is it?" attraction at P. T. Barnum's American Museum exhibited performers such as William Henry Johnson, an African American dwarf, as the missing link between human and animal.[38] Both Johnson and versions of "Japanese Tommy" were put on public display but for markedly different reasons. Notably, in 1860 the American Museum advertised the attraction of both Johnson and a wax figure of Onojirō. Johnson was billed as "THE LIVING 'WHAT IS IT?' OR MAN-MONKEY, the most interesting, amusing, and wonderful creature known," a description followed by additional notice of the "life-like Wax Figure of the famous TOMMY, OF THE JAPANESE EMBASSY, With the identical suit of Clothes worn by him here, and an autograph letter to Mayor Leland, to whom he presented the suit."[39] An 1861 account in *Wilkes' Spirit of the Times* also makes a comparison between Johnson as Barnum's "Living 'What Is It?'" and a "Japanese Tommy," this time an appearance by Dilward with Bryant's Minstrels rather than a wax figure of Onojirō. Importantly, this comparison renders both of these as curiosities but also suggests a distinction between Johnson playing the "man-monkey" and Dilward playing Japanese Tommy: "There was also at the Bryants' the 'Japanese Tommy; or What is it?' some three feet six inches in height, and as great a puzzle for physiologists as the 'What is it?' at Barnum's. We sat with open mouth and dubious soul while gazing at this nondescript. We marveled at how he was made, and questioned in our minds as to what theatrical manufacturer had begotten him. Whoever it is, he has turned out an unmistakably well finished article, and such a one as admirably answers the purpose of those who engage him."[40] Instead of being taken for the "missing link" between beast and human, Dilward as "Japanese Tommy" is pronounced to be more like the wax figure of Onojirō, "an unmistakably well finished article."

JUBA, DILWARD, AND MINSTRELSY'S GENDERED DOMAINS

To appreciate Dilward's oriental stage name even more fully, we might consider how his Japanese-themed performance, especially in its appeal to white feminine society, challenged what William Mahar has called "the nearly exclusive male domain of the minstrel show."[41] Scholarship on early minstrelsy has focused on its definition in terms of working-class masculine identity, exchange, and competition. For instance, Eric Lott's groundbreaking study *Love and Theft* emphasizes the symbolic and literal dimensions of minstrelsy's black-white male relations as a "social unconscious" enacted through "an affair of male bodies where racial conflict and cultural exchange are negotiated between men"[42] and in which the figure of the black male body expresses "bold swagger, irrepressible desire, sheer bodily display."[43] Such terms have heavily influenced perceptions of the man thought to be the first African American minstrel. Sometimes identified as William Henry Lane[44] and at other times "Master Juba" or "Boz's Juba" (following a description by Charles Dickens in his 1842 *American Notes*), Juba is thought to have been born either in 1825 or 1830 and to have begun his career in New York's Five Points neighborhood.[45] He traveled to London in 1846 and 1848 with the Ethiopian Serenaders as the only African American performing in an otherwise all-white minstrel company and died in his twenties, an early death probably related to his relentless working conditions.

Juba elicited extraordinary praise for his performances, especially his dancing skills. A description in the *Manchester Guardian* registers his relative youth, less-than-imposing build, and a somewhat quiet demeanor: "He is apparently about eighteen years of age; about 5 feet 3 inches in height; of slender make, yet possessing great muscular activity. His head is very small, and his countenance, when at rest, has a rather mild, sedate, and far from unpleasing expression."[46] Nonetheless, descriptions of his performances in both the United States and Great Britain not only stress extraordinary artistry and athleticism but also imagine him as a powerfully masculine figure dominating the minstrel stage. For instance, Juba's fame was enhanced through participation in a series of highly publicized competitions with John Diamond, sometimes called the "greatest white minstrel dancer,"[47] who issued a set of challenges to "any person in the world to trial of skill at

Negro dancing, in all its varieties, for a wager of from $200.00–$1000.00."
According to Mark Knowles, Juba and Diamond's dance-off was eagerly
anticipated, with Juba winning all but one of the matches.[48]

Charles Dickens's often-cited description of Juba's New York performance in 1842 details the spectacle: "Five or six couples come upon the
floor, marshalled by a lively young negro, who is the wit of the assembly, and
the greatest dancer known. He never leaves off making queer faces, and is
the delight of all the rest, who grin from ear to ear incessantly." When the
energy in the room begins to lag ("Every gentleman sets as long as he likes
to the opposite lady, and the opposite lady to him, and all are so long about
it that the sport begins to languish"), Juba is portrayed as saving the show.

> Suddenly the lively hero dashes in to the rescue. Instantly the fiddler
> grins, and goes at it tooth and nail; there is new energy in the tam-
> bourine; new laughter in the dancers; new brightness in the very can-
> dles. Single shuffle, double shuffle, cut and cross-cut; snapping his
> fingers, rolling his eyes, turning in his knees, presenting the backs
> of his legs in front, spinning about on his toes and heels like nothing
> but the man's fingers on the tambourine; dancing with two legs, two
> right legs, two wooden legs, two wire legs, two spring legs—all sorts
> of legs and no legs—what is this to him?

When the dance is concluded, Juba is pictured as a victorious champion,
laughing and basking in applause: "And in what walk of life, or dance of
life, does man ever get such stimulating applause as thunders about him,
when, having danced his partner off her feet, and himself too, he finishes
by leaping gloriously on the bar-counter, and calling for something to drink,
with the chuckle of a million of counterfeit Jim Crows, in one inimitable
sound!"[49] Dickens portrays Juba as dominating the floor and his partner (a
white male blackface performer in female dress), authoritatively calling for
drink, and having a distinctive "chuckle" that suggests his manly bravado.

Demonstrations of exceptional control and power were the hallmarks of
Master Juba's career. His recognition as the "father" of a uniquely American form of tap dancing registers his importance to what was seen as
minstrelsy's working-class and masculine ethos.[50] This hypermasculine
image was asserted even as Juba, like Dilward, at times appeared in "wench"
roles. The *Manchester Guardian* describes how, at a performance in 1848,
Juba appeared as "Lucy Long, in character," wearing an elaborate and feminine costume: "With a most bewitching bonnet and veil, a *very* pink dress,
beflounced to the waist, lace-fringed trousers of the most spotless purity,

Blackface Minstrelsy's Japanese Turns

and red leather boots,—the ensemble completed by the green parasol and white cambric pocket handkerchief,—Master Juba certainly looked the black demoiselle of the first ton to the greatest advantage."[51]

Eric Lott has suggested how minstrel songs such as "Miss Lucy Long" projected onto grotesque black female figures worries about infantilization, emasculation, and even castration.[52] The lyrics of "Miss Lucy Long" stress these caricatures of unappealing femininity as well as the use of blackface makeup: her teeth "is grinnin' / Just like an ear ob corn" and "look like tobacco pipes"; she has skin "as bright as soot," and she is "a lubly creature, Tho' her mouth is rather wide." Juba's performance of the song might well have accentuated the parodic distance between the female character of Lucy Long and the minstrel man playing her. However, he is also described as convincingly feminine even in this clearly exaggerated role, setting off a degree of confusion with his ability to impersonate the "black demoiselle." It seems significant, then, that Juba's act as Lucy Long was followed by a series of dances in male costume that restored attention to his powerful choreography. The *Manchester Guardian* continues: "The highland fling, the sailor's hornpipe, and other European dances, seemed to have been laid under contribution, and intermixed with a number of steps which we may call 'Juba's own,' for surely their like was never before seen for grotesque agility, not altogether unmixed with grace." The threat of Juba's believably feminine performance as Lucy Long is mitigated by noting a "grotesque agility" that returned Juba to the rough and ready minstrel realm. The *Manchester Guardian* further restores Juba to manliness by commenting that "many were the handkerchiefs employed to conceal the smothered laughter of their fair owners."[53] This remark projects onto his dancing body the ability to elicit erotic desire from female audience members, a comment that contemporary scholar Stephen Johnson embellishes by speculating that "the minstrels were 'hot'; perhaps Juba was hotter."[54]

Looking at these decidedly masculine framings of Juba's career and reception emphasizes the distinctive place that Thomas Dilward's billing as "Japanese Tommy" occupied in the world of minstrel performance. If, as Eric Lott has suggested, "to put on the cultural forms of 'blackness' was to engage in a complex affair of manly mimicry,"[55] Dilward's yellowface suggests very different aims, resonating with feminine desire for oriental celebrities such as Onojirō and with the commodity fetishism of Japanese arts and decorative goods. Sianne Ngai notes that the idea of "cuteness" first emerged as "a common term of evaluation and formally recognizable style" in an increasingly industrial nineteenth-century United States, as concurrent with the "ideological consolidation of the middle-class home as a feminized space supposedly organized primarily around commodities and consumption." According to Ngai, cuteness revolved "around the desire for an ever more intimate, ever more sensuous relation to objects already regarded as familiar and unthreatening." Perhaps the appeal of Dilward's act was similarly "an eroticization of powerlessness, evoking tenderness for 'small things' but also, sometimes, a desire to belittle or diminish them further."[56] This seems borne out in an undated description of Dilward as "The Celebrated Ethiopian Comedian": a "talented little comedian" with "a fund of natural humor" who was "an excellent vocalist and dancer"; the comment stated that these qualities, "combined with his exceedingly short stature and great activity, made him at once a favorite and pet of the public."[57]

In a period in which the people of Japan were seen as novel curiosities, Dilward's "Japanese Tommy" suggested an exotic, marvelous, and cute object rather than the more standard minstrel fare. On July 4, 1860, the *New York Times* described how festivities included a presentation at Laura Keene's Theatre of *Tycoon; or Young America in Japan*. The characters of this comic burlesque included "Young Coon" ("a relative of old Zip Coon, and nephew of Tycoon") in addition to a comic figure perhaps inspired by versions of *Aladdin*: "Koniac," described as "a third-class spirit—i.e. a djinn. Addicted to power, a sort of bottle imp—in fact, a regular Japanese bohemian."[58] Another account in the *Times* disparaged the "Japanese characters" of this burlesque as "chiefly Chinese in Roman dresses, talking strong Bowery."[59] This account also mentioned that this was one of several fashionable Japan-themed amusements:

> Matinées are the order of the day, two at both the Bowerys, at George Christy's, at Bryants and at the Palace Gardens. Here "versatile performers" and "talented *danseuses*" will diversify the hours of patriotic emotion with comic pantomime and grand "Japanese ballets," led by "Little Tommy." Japan has dropped a little into the sere and yellow leaf, perhaps, for the natives, but for the "strangers from the provinces" the land of blacking may still have charms, and we desire that "all such" may understand that the Japan of their dreams will be on exhibition to-night at Miss Laura Keene's Theatre.[60]

"Little Tommy" evidently fit right in with this array of racially amalgamated pastimes, relocating the appeal of the minstrel act not in displays of masculine power but rather in people and objects marked as decorative, feminized, and diminutive. Dilward's Japanese turn thus moved away from the rigid terms that defined other minstrel men and helped reframe his performance to suit the fashion of the times.

In the introduction to *The Witmark Amateur Minstrel Guide and Burnt Cork Encyclopedia*, white minstrel performer and manager Frank Dumont declared that "minstrelsy is the one American form of amusement, purely our own, and it has lived and thrived even though the plantation darkey, who first gave it a character, has departed."[61] Dumont's 1899 book suggested themes for amateur minstrel shows that would reflect changing entertainment demands, including a "Congress of All Nations," in which an international set of characters, arranged in a traditional minstrel semicircle, all sit under an enormous American flag bearing the image and title of "Admiral Dewey." The interlocutor is "Uncle Sam," flanked by "a Frenchman, Spaniard, German, Chinaman and Kaffir" on the left and an "Englishman, Russian, Turk, Esquimaux and Indian" on the left. The end men include "an Irishman and a Scotchman" with tambourines and "a negro and a Japanese" on bones.[62] This idea may well have been inspired by the 1890s "All Nations" minstrel shows staged by William S. Cleveland's troupe, billed as the "Colossal Colored Carnival Minstrels." Cleveland's integrated company included "thirty-three whites, twenty-seven blacks, eleven Arabs and ten Japs," distinguished by the display of "the company, entire . . . on the stage at one time, not separate or distinct," with the *New York Clipper* commenting in 1895, "This is the only company that gives this performance."[63]

Despite Dumont's reflection on the departure of the "plantation darkey," a significant number of standard blackface characterizations and minstrel songs remain in his *Encyclopedia*. The "Chinaman," "Kaffir," and "Japanese" characters in the "Congress of All Nations" and two oriental-themed songs are also mentioned. The first of these is "Yung Go Wap," performed by "the Jap" character in "Congress of All Nations";[64] the other "Oriental Novelty" is Hattie Starr's "Two Little Japanese Dolls," which Dumont specifies for a seemingly unrelated sketch, "Our Girl Graduates."[65] While the former song assumes a white man as one of the many international figures under the watchful eye of Admiral Dewey, the latter draws attention to the performance of orientalism by white female amateur minstrels.

In her examination of guides for amateur minstrel production in community organizations, fraternal orders, schools, and businesses, Barbara Schulman has detailed how such instructional manuals emphasized the careful disciplining of white bodies and libidinal energies into the polished professionalism of the minstrel show and highlighted blackface minstrelsy's shift into respectable, middle-class amateur entertainment.[66] While most of these manuals were aimed at male performers, Dumont's *Encyclopedia* acknowledged the active presence of women performing in minstrel blackface. According to Robert Toll and Annemarie Bean, while female minstrels were relatively novel in the early days, all-female companies such as Madame Rentz's Female Minstrels were formed as early as 1870, and women were participating fully in professional minstrel shows by the 1890s.[67] Dumont's *Encyclopedia* states that "it is quite the fad for ladies to 'black up' and give a minstrel show" and offers "valuable suggestions" geared "to the ladies in their minstrel efforts," such as wearing black gloves rather than black makeup on the hands. Dumont also supplies several "suitable sketches, monologues and burlesques wherein ladies appear."[68]

The musical selections for "Our Girl Graduates" include titles such as "Honey Little Black Boy Dan," "I Won't Play Second Fiddle to No Yaller Gal," "Mammy," and "My High Stepping Lady" (described as a "Swell Coon Song, introducing Cake Walk") in addition to the yellowface number "Two Little Japanese Dolls." While the subject of Starr's "Two Little Japanese Dolls" is a doomed romance between two dolls,[69] its title echoes a much more lighthearted number from Gilbert and Sullivan's *The Mikado*, "Three Little Maids," a song that places into memorable harmony an quaint trio of Japanese schoolgirls released from the strictures of "a ladies' seminary." Its flirtatious energy as well as vibrant harmony made "Three Little Maids" especially appealing to the many white female performers who appeared as *The Mikado*'s Yum-Yum, Peep-Bo, and Pitti-Sing. These "Japanese" numbers suggested a careful refinement of minstrel performance and a shift away from the erotic and wayward energies of earlier female black caricatures such as the irresponsible and irrepressible Topsy of *Uncle Tom's Cabin*. While Dumont's related sketch "Our Girls at School" depicts mayhem in the all-female classroom, "Our Girl Graduates" is accompanied by a drawing of female performers in caps and gowns, and without blackface, in an orderly minstrel semicircle.[70] Taken together, Dumont's "Our Girls at School" and "Our Girl Graduates" suggest how unruly schoolgirls might be managed both by strict education and by the structure of the minstrel show.

Mari Yoshihara writes that through participation in the "Japan craze," middle-class white women could be turned into "agents of the culture of Orientalism without their having to physically travel to the Orient," as this "consumption and material culture offered women a cultural, educational, and liberating experience akin to the grand tour of the world which their wealthy male counterparts undertook."[71] This idea also informed a 1916 play, *Abbu San of Old Japan: Comedy-Drama in Two Acts for Fifteen Girls*,[72] written by Walter Ben Hare, a prolific yet largely forgotten playwright (and meteorologist) who would later publish, like Frank Dumont, a guide for amateur blackface minstrelsy, his *Minstrel Encyclopedia* (1921). Written for an all-female cast, Hare's *Abbu San of Old Japan* fuses songs from Gilbert and Sullivan's *The Mikado* with a predictably picturesque Japanese setting and characters. The plotline, involving court intrigue, romantic rivalry, and heroic rescue, was clearly suited to production at an all-female school.[73] The play echoed other Japanese- and Chinese-themed student productions popular in the 1890s and after, along with Asian-inspired *tableaux vivants* and costume parties.[74] What makes *Abbu San of Old Japan* distinctive is its inclusion of a blackface Mammy figure among its many yellowface characters, a figure who presents yet another possibility for young white female performers to contrast new adventures in Japan with old versions of plantation nostalgia.

The play moves through a romantic tale of disguises, abductions, and happy resolutions involving the exalted Princess Abbu San, her rivalry with her relative Lady Yu-Giri, and the evil machinations of the ambitious Duchess Fuji-No. Delivered in heightened language, the intrigues of the plot are punctuated by multiple songs lifted out of Gilbert and Sullivan's *The Mikado*. Like *The Mikado*, *Abbu San of Old Japan* emphasizes the allure of exotic oriental femininity and the fascination with ornamental objects, scenes, and costumes. The play calls mainly for a cast of women dressed in kimonos wearing elaborate wigs and eye makeup; Hare's carefully detailed instructions for the latter read, "*Surround the eyelashes with two fine line penciled black, continuing outward and curving slightly upward, meeting just beyond the corner of the eyes*" (Hare 5–6). The second act's chrysanthemum festival provides the opportunity for Gilbert and Sullivan hits such as "The Flowers That Bloom in the Spring," as sung by "*eighteen (or fewer, if desired) maidens*" (Hare 31) dressed in rose, yellow, and white kimonos and carrying matching chrysanthemums, and "Three Little Maids" staged in the style of the Savoy Theatre, as "*ABBU, MATSUKA and KIKU advance from rear with short teetering steps, fans spread under chins*" (Hare 44). Japanese decorative objects are central to the plot, as Ohano, the wife of a bandit chief who is hired in a plot to abduct Princess Abbu San, poses as a peddler selling "excellent carvings in honorable ivory. Beautiful butterflies and fans. Embroideries and laces of wondrous texture" (Hare 42).

Hare includes a varied array of female roles, including refined court ladies and quaint village maids, the disreputable Ohano, the conniving Duchess Fuji-No, and Okuku, a "porter woman" who has "the strength of three
men." Okuku, the "worthy giantess porter," wears masculine trousers and
"conical straw hats covered with dried grass" of the male porters and is singled
out as different from the more delicate Japanese court ladies by her physical appearance as well as occupation. Descriptions of her offstage actions
suggest extraordinary strength and prowess: "Even now hath she separated
two fighting coolies. She strikes one in the middle with honorable pole. He
doubles up like human jackknife. Now he slinks away. See, she attacks the
other. He runs after his companion. And now she is calmly filling the flower
vases. Ah, what a woman!" (Hare 38, 35).

Okuku becomes the object of admiration for a white American character,
Miss Henrietta Dash, who declares her to be a model for her newspaper
story "on the new woman of Japan" (Hare 35). Henrietta exemplifies the
adventuresome spirit of the liberated "New Woman" who finds inspiration
in travel in Japan, having "written six articles for the Richmond *Sun* on the
Manners and Customs of the Japanese" (Hare 18). What makes *Abbu San
of Old Japan* more than yet another dramatization of white female fascination with Japanese culture is Henrietta's black servant, Aunt Paradise.
Abbu San of Old Japan is certainly not the first time in which references to
blackface minstrelsy enter into a faux-Japanese setting; for instance, Gilbert and Sullivan's *The Mikado* gives several nods to blackface minstrelsy.[75]
But in *Abbu San of Old Japan*, Aunt Paradise establishes a more sustained
contrast between the refined and decorative world of Japan and a black female character who is embodied in grossly physical ways. Aunt Paradise is
described in stage directions as a *"Black Mammy from 'Ole Virginny'"* who
"should be very stout" and dressed in *"black face and gloves. Woolly wig. Black
and white check calico dress. Red vest. Alpine hat with red quill."* She enters the
play *"much exhausted, puffing and blowing, [and] fanning herself vigorously"*
(Hare 6, 16). Grotesque and emasculating fantasies of excessive appetite
and girth had already been long associated with minstrel caricatures of black
femininity.[76] These figured substantially into the stereotype of the Mammy,
a characterization popularized by minstrel songs and advertising campaigns
such as the R. T. Davis trademark "Aunt Jemima," first brought to life by
Nancy Green at the 1893 World's Columbian Exposition in Chicago.[77] As
Isabel Wilkerson has pointed out, Mammy's rotund and cheerful demeanor
and her association with bounteous amounts of food belied the realities of
enslavement, under which "most black women were thin, gaunt even, due

to the meager rations provided them."[78] Aunt Paradise typifies this fleshly excess, expressing disdain for Japanese delicacies and constantly ravenous for "stewed chicken giblets" and large quantities of other humble fare:

AUNT P. Lawsy, Miss 'Retta, I don't like dis yere place *a*-tall. Dis colored lady sure wishes she were back in ole Virginny. She sure does.

HENRIETTA. The idea, Aunt Paradise! Why, home was never like this.

AUNT P. No'm, home ain't nuffin' like dis, and I'se mightly glad and thankful dat it hain't. Don't hab no knives ner forkses, but ebrybody has to eat wif a couple little sticks. And what does dey eat? Answer me dat? What does dey eat? I'se et so much rice and tea dat I'se black in the face. And some ob dere mixings. Lawd only knows what *is* in 'em. I jes' has to shet ma eyes and take 'em on faith. I'd gib 'leven thousand dollars for about fifteen slices of ole Virginny peanut-fed ham wif sugared yams on de side. (Hare 17)

Aunt Paradise's jovial commentary and physical humor recall the roles of minstrel end man as well as emphasize her lack of decorum in stark contrast with Japanese politesse. When Princess Abbu tells Henrietta, "Your conversation gives me much pleasure. Glad am I that you condescend to set dainty food on unworthy floor," Aunt Paradise immediately shows her *"very large shoes"* and comically interjects: "Dainty foot! Dat's me" (Hare 20). When Henrietta tells her that she will be presented at court, she tells her, "De last time I was presented at court, de judge gib ma sister's husband's oldest offspring about sixty days on de rock-pile," and says, "I don't like dat word court. I's jest naturally suspicious ob anything dat sounds like a policeman" (Hare 18). Aunt Paradise constantly interrupts the overall fantasy of "Old Japan" with the familiar stuff of American blackface minstrel comedy, with repetitions of longing for her home in "ole Virginny" referencing the familiar blackface tunes "Carry Me Back to Old Virginia" (by Edwin Pearce Christy of Christy's Minstrels) and "Essence of Ole Virginia" (the trademark dance of Billy Kersands). Her lines also satirize the fascination of white Americans with Japanese customs and commodities. Henrietta declares that in Japan, "the people are so charming, so naive," but Aunt Paradise disparages Japanese dress: "Looks to me like dey all runnin' round dressed in nightgowns." She is likewise disoriented by Japanese customs: "Dey jes' sits like a toad on de floor—and dat certainly ain't dignified. Why every time I sets down in Japan, I jes' naturally loses ma jurisprudence" (Hare 18).

Abbu San of Old Japan allowed its young white female performers to enact a multiracial as well as varied cast of characters, both to demonstrate charming and strange Japanese customs and to offer evidence of female strength and authority. For instance, the stage manager Masago establishes her control at the play's opening by informing the audience, "I tell you when to laugh, I tell you when to weep, I tell you when to applaud" (Hare 7). Whether as the adventuresome Henrietta, the powerful Okuku, or the noble Abbu San, these dramatic portrayals stress the liberating potential for young white women to enact as well as explore "Old Japan" through acts of yellowface impersonation. The notable exception, of course, is in the role of Aunt Paradise, a character seen as fixed in a humorously abject state even at the curtain call; when she is hailed by Masago as "the venerated black!" she only repeats her plaintive cry, "Say, when is we all goin' back to ole Virginny?" (Hare 53–54).

The play further accentuates Aunt Paradise's limitations by making her the only character in the play to register negative racial feelings toward both black and Japanese. When Kiku, one of the Japanese maids of honor to the Princess, welcomes her as an "honorable black lady" to the imperial court, Aunt Paradise retorts, "Lookee yere, gal, I wants it distinctly understood dat I ain't black. No, ma'am! I'se jes' only a highly seasoned mahogany—dat's all" (Hare 19). In contrast to Henrietta's open-minded fascination with Japanese culture and the Japanese characters' salutation of both black and white "honorable" ladies, Aunt Paradise is rigidly tied to plantation nostalgia and to segregationist thinking. She laments how being in Japan unsettles her sense of security in firm racial distinctions between black and white: "Think ob it. Me, a 'spectable colored lady ob de Baptist persuasion, ridin' 'round in a big baby-carriage, pulled by one of dese yere no-count Japanese mulattoes. I don't like yaller folks nohow. I likes 'em white, and I likes 'em black; but dis yere yaller nebber did appeal to ma sense ob de beautiful" (Hare 17).

By displacing both anti-Japanese and antiblack racism onto Aunt Paradise, the play heightens the distance between old-fashioned racial suspicions and the worldliness associated with white females who consume Japanese culture. Unlike the curious Henrietta, Aunt Paradise is portrayed as trapped within the limitations of old racial perspectives as well as by nostalgia for her plantation home. Thus *Abbu San of Old Japan* broadens the gap between the white New Woman who revels in the freedom of exploration and performance in "Old Japan" and the black character who is still trapped in the Mammy role. The play imagines orientalism as giving white women a more liberated sense of self and an expanded internationalism but nonetheless still uses blackface caricature as a homing device for Japanese adventure.

4

THE TRICKY SERVANT IN BLACKFACE AND YELLOWFACE

Beginning in the 1850s, the figure of "John Chinaman" began appearing in blackface minstrel songs, comedy skits, and stump speeches. As Robert Toll has detailed, minstrel portrayals of Chinese male immigrants sported queues and loose-fitting trousers and tunics, spoke in nonsense words, and ate dogs, cats, mice, and rats. Minstrels performed "Burlesque Chinese Dances" and nonsensical songs with such lyrics as "Ching ring, chow wow, ricken chicken, a chew / Chinaman loves big bow wow and little puppies too."[1] These characterizations were substantively different from the exotic curiosities and magical beings that had previously represented the theatrical Orient, instead presenting Chinese immigrant men as bumbling domestic servants, unintelligible laundrymen, or cunning villains. In the 1870s, Chinese immigrant characters also proliferated in a variety of other theatrical genres such as melodrama. Whether pictured as amusing misfits or invasive foreigners, these stereotypes were used alongside other ethnic types to provide comic relief and local color. For instance, in Bret Harte's frontier melodrama *Two Men of Sandy Bar*, first performed in 1876, the laundryman Hop Sing makes a brief but memorable appearance alongside a Mexican character to help reveal a main character's secret identity.

> CONCHO [*impatiently*]. Well! you saw him?
> HOP SING. Me see him.

CONCHO. And you recognized him?

HOP SING. No shabe likoquize.

CONCHO [*furiously*]. You know him, eh? *Carramba!* You *knew* him.

HOP SING [*slowly and sententiously*]. Me shabe man you callee Diego. Me shabbee Led gulchee call Sandy. Me shabbee man Poker Float callee Alexandlee Molton. Allee same, John! Allee same!²

These characterizations also registered larger concerns about the increasing numbers of Chinese immigrants and their role in the American labor force and national body. As Robert Lee has noted, Chinese immigrant men, seen as competitors during the California gold rush, were increasingly perceived as threats to white working-class male labor, "a source of pollution" whose very presence constituted "a boundary crisis."³ Songs such as "National Miner," sung to the air of the blackface minstrel song "Massa's in de Cold Cold Ground," emphasizes white labor competition with Chinese miners.

> Here we're working like a swarm of bees,
> Scarcely making enough to live,
> And two hundred thousand Chinese
> Are taking home the gold we ought to have.⁴

Minstrel acts also satirized marriages between Chinese men and Irish women, reflecting fears of interracial unions that might threaten the status of working-class whites and immigrant Irish.⁵

These anxieties about Chinese immigration were closely tied to tensions around race, labor, and slavery. In the early nineteenth century, male Chinese immigrants had been considered as potential substitutes for freed African slaves on plantations in the Caribbean and in the United States. But even those who advocated for the continuation of the slave trade opposed "coolie" labor, with planters arguing that the presence of Chinese labor in the Caribbean was a sign of the "utter decay" and total collapse of the "natural order."⁶ As Lisa Lowe suggests, "The Chinese were instrumentally used in this political discourse as a *figure*, a fantasy of 'free' yet racialized and coerced labor, at a time when the possession of body, work, life, and death was foreclosed to the enslaved and the indentured alike."⁷ This figuration entered into post-emancipation debates in the United States as well. Moon-Ho Jung writes that Chinese coolies were seen as a "coerced and submissive labor force by anti- and proslavery forces alike" and "came to embody slavery in the age of emancipation."⁸ After emancipation, African

The Tricky Servant in Blackface and Yellowface

Americans and Chinese immigrants were both employed as low-wage workers whose servility could be in some ways excused by their presumed racial inferiority. As Caroline Yang has indicated, "Antiblack racism was recalibrated, not dismantled, through the non-Black Chinese worker figures in U.S. literature after emancipation."[9]

Just as the situation of the Chinese immigrant worker was conditioned by concerns about slavery, so were theatrical depictions of Chinese immigrants in the United States colored by familiar portrayals of black servitude. Unsurprisingly, Chinese immigrant characters regularly shared the stage with popular black stereotypes, with white actors playing both kinds of roles. Depictions of black and Chinese immigrant characters also were undergirded by the same logic that linked racial status with perceived fitness for menial labor. In his book *Iron Cages*, Ronald Takaki describes how at a formative stage of nation building in the new republic, white constructions of national identity promoted "rational, ascetic, and self-governing individuals" and projected negative qualities such as the lack of discipline and luxurious excess onto enslaved African Americans, Indigenous peoples, and Mexican or Asian immigrants. Thus these racialized subjects were simultaneously incorporated as part of the workforce and rejected from citizenship and power in the new nation.[10]

This book emphasizes the distinctive formation of the racial habits of blackface and orientalism on the nineteenth-century American stage. But it is important to acknowledge that although they are often configured as quintessentially American stereotypes, the comic minstrel figures of Jim Crow and John Chinaman were also informed by theatrical conventions that were in place well before the racial habits of minstrelsy and melodrama in the United States. Minstrelsy's black fools and Chinese immigrant servants— along with earlier characterizations of Mungo in *The Padlock* or Kazrac in *Aladdin*—bore a marked resemblance to the stock types of classical Greek and Roman comedy and their later progeny, the *zanni* of sixteenth-century Italian commedia dell'arte. The *servus callidus* (tricky servant) of classical comedy was known for his displays of gluttony and florid language. In the drama of Plautus, for example, clever slaves bragged, pontificated, and gave their masters advice on love and fortune; they also addressed the audience directly, made wisecracks, mixed Greek with Latin phrases, and launched into tirades.[11] In the commedia, servant characters' antics and appetites were again popularly featured in the *zanni* (from which the word "zany" derives), who appeared alongside or sometimes interchangeably with the more famous roles of Scapin, Scaramouche, Pedrolino, Arlecchino (Harlequin), and Pulcinella (Punch). Like the *servus callidus*, the *zanni* were ignorant, discontented, and impoverished, seen as the lowest part of the social hierarchy and often subjected to beatings and other forms of abuse.

Both tricky servants and *zanni* did the dirty work and bore the brunt of onstage chaos in theater, providing important bits of stage business with florid speeches, comical gestures (*lazzi*), and acrobatics. Sianne Ngai has identified how the *zanni* portrayed "a temporary, itinerant worker in a household" who was relegated to specific kinds of "unproductive" and certainly unheroic labor in domestic service or menial work.[12] In addition to exhibiting their baser natures through gluttony, drunkenness, brawling, or lust, these characters provided theatrical fun through demonstrations of physical labor and punishment that often showed them bumbling through various onstage tasks and beaten by their masters. One term from the commedia tradition still in broad usage is "slapstick," which referred to wooden devices once used to create audible sound effects without undue pain to the actors. Thus the comedy performed by the tricky servant made evident the unrewarding, degraded, and often futile nature of service labor as well as the perils of its failure.

It is not hard to see how these classical and commedia characterizations informed later depictions of foolish, irrational, and degenerate black characters, whose actions on the stage demonstrated their inability to accomplish even the menial tasks to which they were assigned. *The Padlock* presents one example as the slave Mungo enters with "*a Hamper of Provisions on his Back*" and curses his master Don Diego for "sending me always here and dere for something to make me tire like a mule." He makes clear that he suffers cruel abuse from Don Diego ("You lick me every day with your rattan"), only to incur another beating when he reminds Don Diego of his service:

MUNGO. You know, Massa, me very good servant.
DIEGO. Then you will go on.
MUNGO. And ought to be use kine—
DIEGO. If you utter another syllable—
MUNGO. And I'm sure, Massa—
DIEGO. Take that—Now will you listen to me?[13]

Like their predecessors Mungo and Kazrac, later nineteenth-century black and Chinese immigrant characters appeared on American stages in the form of these comic tricky servants. Robert Hornback has noted the roots of American blackface minstrel types in much earlier traditions of European performance that depicted black characters as childlike, irrational,

The Tricky Servant in Blackface and Yellowface

savage, degraded, and foolish; for Hornback, minstrel dialect, a "verbal mixture of childish pretensions and linguistic estrangement," might well have come from "the blackface *Langue harlequine,* a comically inept literary black dialect" that proved "infinitely malleable in later traditions."[14] The misadventures and punishments of abject Chinese immigrants, whose exaggerated appearance and distinctive singsong language likewise marked their racial inferiority, also provided moments of slapstick and comic stage business.

Yet despite these similarities, the figure of John Chinaman was not always a ready substitute for Jim Crow. Rather, a marked uneasiness can be seen in the theatrical shift from blackface to yellowface characters. The remainder of this chapter will detail several examples of how the ebullient figure of the tricky servant and the humorous mayhem around him were used to distinguish between the fitness of black servants and Chinese immigrant workers for service labor. These include a minstrel sketch, "Chinese Servants," published in William Courtright's guide for amateur minstrelsy, *The Complete Minstrel Guide* (1901), and two earlier melodramas, James Mc-Closkey's 1870 *Across the Continent* (likely the first full-length play including an immigrant Chinese character) and Bret Harte and Mark Twain's 1877 *Ah Sin.* In each of these works, Chinese immigrant laborers demonstrated not only their social inferiority and inability to carry out their duties properly but also other qualities—including cunning self-interest—that made them even more threatening to white masters than their black counterparts. Thus this newer comic figure of the Chinese male immigrant seemed to offset as well as place into relief some of the ways in which black servitude had become a dominant theatrical habit.

CHINESE SERVANTS IN BLACKFACE FORM

The sketch "Chinese Servants" appears amid the other offerings for jokes, stump speeches, musical numbers, and sketches in William Courtright's *The Complete Minstrel Guide,* most of which call for white amusement at black failure (such as the sketch "The Nigger Store-Keeper," depicting a store owner overwhelmed by his unruly customers).[15] The plot of "Chinese Servants" involves two unemployed black characters, Joe Garvey and Jim Jackson, who are told by the white director Hiram Out that there are jobs only for Chinese immigrants. The comic banter provides an opportunity to show their impudence as well as to voice their resentment against Chinese workers.

JACK. We are looking for a job.

HI. We've got no use for niggers.

JACK AND GAR. Who's niggers?

HI. Well, colored men then.

GAR. We ain't colored.

HI. What are you, if you are not?

JACK. No, sir, we're not colored, we were born this way.

HI. Well, we've got no use for you, there's only calls for Chinamen.

GAR. See, that's what I told you, no chance for an American citizen.

    (Courtright 109)

Chinese characters do not actually appear in "Chinese Servants"; rather, they are impersonated by the black characters Garvey and Jackson as played by amateur white actors in blackface. Each actor is directed to wear first a *"negro wig"* and then add to this blackface disguise a *"crown of light colored hats with a black braid sewed in the back for the queue or tail"* (Courtright 107) in order to pass for Chinese. After Hiram suggests that Garvey and Jackson impersonate Chinese men, the pair put on Chinese costumes and *"imitate swinging walk of Chinaman, both making fun of the others appearance"* in what is clearly a mockery of both black and Chinese characters. While "Chinese Servants" stresses the white employer's stated preference for Chinese immigrants over African Americans, both groups are paralleled in moments of black ignorance and Chinese unintelligibility. Garvey and Jackson's tortured attempts to read the words on the sign "Intelligence Office" turn into equally unfortunate attempts to learn "Chinese" from Hiram.

HI. Now, you must have a Chinese name. [*To Garvey.*] Your name
    will be One Lung.

JACK. I will be One Liver.

GAR. One Lung and One Liver.

HI. No, your name is Fat Choy.

JACK. Oh, I'm going to quit.

GAR. No, come on, you can be the cook.

HI. You can't talk Chinese. I will give you something to say. Now, you
    say to everything that's asked. [*To Garvey.*] Cow Sing Whoop La.

GAR. Who ever heard of a cow singing whoop la?

HI. And you say, Hung Wa No Sabe. [*To Jack.*]

GAR. Cow Sing Whoop La.

JACK. Hung Wa No Sabe. (Courtright 110)

The Tricky Servant in Blackface and Yellowface

When Garvey and Jackson take on their new jobs as "Chinese" servants to a white couple, Mr. and Mrs. Smithers, they quickly lose control over the domestic situation. The two argue over money, get drunk, and blunder attempts to feed and quiet the children. Finally these "Chinese servants" wind up falling on the babies (made of cloth heads sewn on bladders), who explode as the parents reenter. The scene ends with Mrs. Smithers fainting in the arms of her husband. This chaotic scenario establishes the incompetence of the two blackface characters as well as questions the wisdom of hiring the Chinese servants. The comic layering of blackface and yellowface roles highlights how the incompetence of black domestic service, as translated into Chinese form, soon turns into horrific accident.

While insisting that both black and Chinese workers are potentially dangerous, the sketch also satirizes the leisured status of white characters. Courtright's "Chinese Servants" targets the reversal of gender roles in Mr. Smithers's hiring of "a couple of Chinamen" (Courtright 111) so that his wife can attend her club meeting rather than carry out her motherly duties. The sketch mocks Mrs. Smithers's abdication of her domestic responsibilities as well as her refusal of her husband's offer of Irish, Dutch, French, Swedish, Japanese, Hungarian, Italian, or Austrian servants over Chinese. This pins the blame for the chaos in the nursery not only on the failures of the servants but also on the domineering white wife. As Heidi Kim suggests, the Chinese immigrant man was often typecast as feminine not only in his appearance and dress but also in his employment in "women's work." Yet when employed as household servant or laundryman, the Chinese immigrant did not seemingly compete with white men in the workplace. Thus his race helped him negotiate both racial scapegoating and gender politics, acting "as a barrier that made the gender-bending more acceptable and prevented this employment from threatening white masculinity."[16] The presence of the Chinese immigrant man in the domestic space, at close proximity to white women and children, was considered potentially dangerous; however, as Robert Lee has suggested, it also "saved True Womanhood from the physical demands of the secular cult of cleanliness" and "assign[ed] supervisory and management roles to women."[17] "Chinese Servants" thus obviously demonstrates the catastrophic outcome when the wrong kind of domestic help is hired but also more subtly questions whether this help is needed in the first place.

Like many other theatrical works, Courtright's "Chinese Servants" sketch made clear that both African Americans and Chinese immigrants were expected to justify their place in the national body through performing whatever forms of manual labor or domestic service were needed by white society. While Mrs. Smithers makes the wrong choice in hiring Chinese immigrant labor, Garvey and Jackson have no options other than racial impersonation and menial servitude. Their inability to do the tasks to which they are assigned expresses not only assumptions of intrinsic racial inferiority but a deeper anxiety about substituting Chinese for black labor in America. At the same time, in Courtright's fantasy of workers, racial substitution, and slapstick chaos, Chinese immigrants figure prominently but never actually appear; by the time Courtright's amateur minstrel guide was published in 1901, exclusion laws barring entry, citizenship, land and property ownership, and education to Chinese had already been in place for nearly two decades. Thus it is also illuminating to compare the compressed hostility of this compact sketch with the more ambiguous racial ridicule presented in two plays written prior to the 1882 Chinese Exclusion Act: James McCloskey's *Across the Continent* and Bret Harte and Mark Twain's *Ah Sin*. Both are full-length works in which the figures of Chinese immigrants, Very Tart and Ah Sin, have a much more active role. When these plays were first produced, Chinese immigrant characters were still relative newcomers to the theatrical stage; nonetheless, their perceived connections to tricky servants in blackface lend their comic turns a predictable familiarity.

CAESAR AUGUSTUS AND VERY TART
IN *ACROSS THE CONTINENT*

Across the Continent; or, Scenes from New York Life and the Pacific Railroad was originally written by actor-manager James McCloskey.[18] After its first unsuccessful run, McCloskey sold the play to actor Oliver Doud Byron. Byron's revision opened its first successful New York production at Mrs. Conway's Park Theatre on November 28, 1870, with Byron himself playing one of the leads, Joe Ferris; it subsequently ran for ten consecutive seasons. Each of the four acts of *Across the Continent*'s melodramatic plot imagines a different kind of threat to the white American family at its center. The first three acts of the play take place in the unsavory Five Points neighborhood in New York. Act 1 depicts the Constance family, broken by alcoholism and hunger, and the cruel saloonkeeper John Adderly, who profits from their distress. The evils of alcohol (a preoccupation that McCloskey would continue later in works such as the 1872 drama *The Fatal Glass*) are highlighted: Constance is seen suffering delirium tremens while his long-suffering wife goes off into the snow to beg for food for her starving children. When both the father and the mother die, the children are adopted by Thomas Goodwin, a kind merchant. Act 2 takes place twenty years later, as Goodwin's adopted son Tom and his intrepid friend Ferris (known as "the Ferret" for his ability to find useful things) encounter John Adderly's son (also called Adderly, played by the same actor) in a seedy bar, where they witness his despicable actions as well as the dangerous behavior of other patrons. This scene, as Kenneth Cerniglia has suggested, harbors a "potpourri of American ethnic stereotypes," all of them unscrupulous.[19] For instance, the murderous Italian immigrant Giovanni exploits several "Street Arabs" (girls kidnapped from Italy) and kills his own brother onstage. Act 3 sees the younger Adderly scheming to get Goodwin's fortune through marrying his adopted daughter, Louise; his plans are foiled in an elaborate series of turns, and he is exposed as a villain. In the final act, Adderly, who has escaped from prison, allies with a band of Indians to attack the Goodwin family, who has just arrived on the Union Pacific Railroad.

If alcohol, undesirable immigrants, and savage Natives successively endanger the lives of the Goodwin family and their friend Ferris, it is John Adderly and his son who are ultimately responsible. The younger Adderly puts into motion Giovanni's murder of his brother as well as stirs up Chief Black Cloud's anger and urges him to take revenge on the "white race" for taking away Indian lands. Adderly's villainy is clearly associated with racial contamination. Early in act 2, Tom describes him as "a dark sort of a person," to which Joe Ferris inquires, "Not colored, I hope?," and Tom clarifies "No, I mean his actions" (McCloskey 80). In the final act, he declares that he has become one of the tribe of the "red-skinned devils" (McCloskey 111–12) in attacking the Goodwin party. If Giovanni and Chief Black Cloud threaten brutality and violence, Adderly serves as the white mastermind behind each of the dangers they pose; for instance, Ferris explains Adderly's cutting of the telegraph wire as "positive proof that white men are directing the Indian's movements," since "no Indian would have been cunning enough to cut that wire" (McCloskey 112).

Across the Continent's melodramatic dangers, many of them in racial form, are offset by moments of comic relief provided by two black and Chinese characters: Caesar Augustus,[20] the foolish black servant to the Goodwin family, and the Chinese immigrant Very Tart. Like Caesar, Very Tart operates in the service of the virtuous white Goodwin party and is regarded with indulgence and amusement. Very Tart's appearance at the opening of act 4, set at a Union Pacific Railroad station, epitomizes the westward movement of the Goodwin family and their symbolic settlement of the frontier. Yet unlike Chief Black Cloud, Very Tart presents a puzzle upon his first appearance.

> AUNT S. What in the world is *that?*
> JOE. Well, we haven't named it yet.
> AUNT S. Well, it looks exactly like a Chinese firecracker.
> CHI[NAMAN]. Me no firecracker, me skyrocket. (*Sits on box, and gets his finger pinched in lid.*) Oh, oh, oh. (*Joe points to show him he's sitting on the lid.*)
> JOE. See. (*Chinaman gets up. Joe shows him the end-pieces on the box. Chinaman sits again and grins.*) (McCloskey 106)

Though different in appearance and behavior, both Caesar and Very Tart demonstrate racial inferiority through their problematic service to the Goodwin family as well as their repeatedly failed attempts to behave as the white characters do. Caesar, who has joined "an amateur dramatic society," punctuates his lines with misquotations of Shakespeare. His acting attempts recall the many nineteenth-century blackface minstrel parodies that, as Hornback has noted, incongruously juxtaposed Shakespeare verse with "Negro English" in "an absurd amalgamation of extremes: eloquence and ineloquence, the beautiful and the grotesque, the high and the low."[21] In act 3, Caesar is seen not only butchering Shakespearean lines but being constantly distracted from his domestic duties, so much so that Louise worries that "I'm afraid we shall have to discharge him" (McCloskey 97). Just as Caesar misremembers his Shakespeare, so do Very Tart's actions emphasize his imperfect imitation of civilized customs, language, and work.

> JOE. Come here, Tart. (*To others.*) Watch me telephone to China. (*Takes Tart's cue.*) Hello, Tart!
> CHI[NAMAN]. Hello!
> JOE. You're crazy.
> CHI[NAMAN]. Me, too. (*Joe turns away laughing.*) Now me talkee. (*Takes end of cue.*) Hello—hello—hello. (*Jerks his cue, disgusted, jumps on box.*) (McCloskey 107)

The laundryman Very Tart is also inept in his domestic duties; when Johnnie O'Dwyer, friend to Joe Ferris, asks Very Tart why he uses starch when washing his socks, he replies, "Me no putee starchee sockee. Me putee sockee starchee" (McCloskey 110).

But while they provide only a modicum of domestic help to the Goodwin party, Caesar and Very Tart add racial significance to the play's overall vision of American development and westward expansion. Prominently featuring new technologies such as the railroad and telegraph, *Across the Continent* also marks dramatic changes to the legal status of African Americans. When in act 4 Caesar is asked to count the numbers of people who have just arrived, he includes himself as a "respectable gentleman." When told that "we don't count niggers out here," Caesar retorts, "Well, I guess you counted 'em last election just the same" (McCloskey 111), acknowledging the recent ratification of the Fifteenth Amendment.[22] *Across the Continent* registers another moment of national change in the increasing number of Chinese immigrants. Though similar comic characterizations of Chinese immigrants had appeared since the 1850s on the minstrel stage, Very Tart's appearance in a full-length play helped initiate what would become an even more widespread theatrical type.

The popularity of comic Chinese immigrant characters was greatly enhanced by the publication of Bret Harte's poem, "Plain Language from Truthful James" in *Overland Monthly* magazine in September 1870. The role of Very Tart does not appear in the character list for either the November 1870 production of *Across the Continent* at Mrs. Conway's Park Theatre or at the subsequent Niblo's Garden production the following year, so it seems likely that the comic presentation might have been added or expanded in later productions to capitalize on the immense popularity of Harte's poem. Harte's poem depicts Ah Sin, a Chinese immigrant character who is discovered cheating at cards, an association of Chinese immigrants with gambling that probably inspired the wry remark from Very Tart that caps off Caesar's count of the Goodwin party.

> CAE[SAR]. Well, dar's de old man and de young man, de two young ladies, and de old woman. Two dogs, a Thomas cat, Big and Little Casino. . . .
> CHI[NAMAN]. Fullee hand. (McCloskey 111)

The synopsis for the 1871 Niblo's Garden production suggests additional unpublished moments that give Very Tart a significant role in the ending of the play as well as a comic function.[23] These additional episodes include the device of "Opium in the Indian's Whiskey" preceding the battle with the Indians, which leads to a plot twist: after "Ferret and His Party [are] Overpowered," there are episodes titled "The Drowsy Indians" and "Opium Has the

Desired Effect." These events are inserted before the final rescue sequence, suggesting that the Chinese immigrant character—and the opium with which he is inevitably associated—helps to subdue the attacking Indians.

However, neither Very Tart nor Caesar are given heroic qualities. When the Goodwins and their friends do battle in the final scenes, they enlist both Caesar and Very Tart in their defense. As Johnnie helps Caesar and Very Tart arm themselves, both insist that they are as prepared as the white men.

> JOHN. How are you heeled?
> CAE[SAR]. How is any nigger heeled? Got a razor.
> JOHN (*to the Chinaman*). You—are you heeled?
> CHI[NAMAN]. Allee samee Melican man. (McCloskey 111)

Though armed on behalf of the Goodwin party, their actions in the heat of battle are comically contrary. Caesar's bravado turns into Falstaffian cowardice; mistaken for Chief Black Cloud by Very Tart, he falls on his knees in terror. Later, he disguises himself by putting on a "*Rip Van Winkle wig*" and "*whitewashing*" his face (McCloskey 112), setting up a slapstick scene in which an Indian character tries to scalp him, only to pull off the wig.

Just as they fail in domestic service, these characters also prove themselves inadequate in war, opting for self-preservation rather than defending the white characters. Very Tart decides that he would rather not fight like a white man: "Melican man like fightee. Chinaman like sleepee in box" (McCloskey 112). But his racial inferiority and social deviance is established much earlier. After the elderly and lovelorn Aunt Susannah drinks from a bottle of liquor, Very Tart exclaims, "Ah ha—Melican woman like jig water. Me likee, too," and then imitates her: "*Takes bottle out of her hand and drinks. Offers it back several times, but fools her and drinks himself, talking Chinese all the time, and keeps this up till the bottle is empty.*" He then makes advances toward her:

> CHI[NAMAN]. Me makee mashee. (*Sits beside her.*) Ah, there my
>   size—me stealee you. (*Tries to put his arm around her. She jumps
>   quickly—he falls, then chases her.*)
> JOE. Here—what is the matter, Tart?
> CHI[NAMAN]. (*Joe comes forward with Tom.*) Melican woman fightee.
>   (McCloskey 107)

In the heat of battle and while Caesar has to be rescued from the Natives, Very Tart instead pursues revenge on Aunt Susannah: "*Aunt Susannah*

The Tricky Servant in Blackface and Yellowface

comes out of station in nightgown and exits hurriedly L.1.E. Chinaman opens box and shoots at her as she runs off. She returns and runs out R.3.E. Chinaman fires another shot and goes out after her. Caesar enters L.2. followed by Indian who catches him, as Johnnie enters L.3., and grabs Indian. All exit" (McCloskey 114). These farcical moments suggests that both the black servant and the Chinese immigrant are ill-suited to carry out the business of the white characters who employ them. They also emphasize the distinction between the armed and dangerous Very Tart and Caesar insofar as the former presents an added lascivious threat to white womanhood.

Like their classical and commedia forebears, Caesar and Very Tart function as tricky servants who, despite their efforts, cannot emulate the artistry or manners of their presumed betters. Even though they might steal the show with funny business and even win sympathy from audiences, their stories are not at the center of these plays they inhabited. While some theatrical classics made versions of the *servus callidus*—such as Plautus's Pseudolus, Molière's Scapin, or Beaumarchais's Figaro—into heroes, most just used them as the butt of jokes. McCloskey's *Across the Continent* is no different in this respect. Whether it is the Goodwins and Joe "the Ferret" or the "dark" Adderly who prevails, the lot of these black and Chinese tricky servants does not improve.

AH SIN'S MINSTREL ENTERPRISE

Rosemary Bank has estimated that at least nine dozen frontier melodramas were professionally performed between 1800 and 1870, with 500–700 more between 1870 and 1917; the last third of the nineteenth century was the pinnacle of frontier melodrama's popularity.[24] Roger Hall finds that in "the late nineteenth century, approximately five to ten percent of all touring productions in the United States were plays about the frontier. Many of those plays gained enormous popularity, packing theatres in all the major cities, and some toured for as many as ten, twenty, or even thirty seasons."[25] Among these, works such as Joaquin Miller's *The Danites in the Sierras* (1877), Bartley Theodore Campbell's *My Partner* (1879), and George H. Jessop's *Gentleman from Nevada* (1880) regularly included Chinese immigrants alongside a host of other ethnic and racial types, as suggested in the *New York Evening Post's* 1881 description of the frontier melodrama as an "abundance of miners in flannel shirts" with "the inevitable Chinaman."[26] The most sustained of these Chinese immigrant roles was the titular character in Bret Harte and Mark Twain's *Ah Sin*.

As in *Across the Continent*, *Ah Sin*'s Chinese immigrant character is both infantile and cunning, a mixture of qualities that followed the lead of Bret Harte's poem "Plain Language from Truthful James," later retitled "The Heathen Chinee."[27] As described by the narrator, "Truthful James," Ah Sin is described as having a "pensive and childlike" and "bland" smile. Underneath that outwardly innocent expression, however, the "heathen" Ah Sin has "dark" ways and demonstrates his wily and "peculiar" nature in a game of euchre played against the narrator and another white character, Bill Nye. This popular characterization provided the inspiration for *Ah Sin*, which, while ostensibly coauthored by Harte and Twain, had by its final version (at least according to Twain) "hardly a footprint of Harte in it."[28]

The play blends a satire of western mining life with a comedy of manners. *Ah Sin* opens with a mining rivalry between the villain Broderick, a wealthy but uncultured man, and the more genteel York (whom Broderick calls "the gentleman capitalist, the dandy scientist").[29] The two engage with Plunkett, an old miner who makes up colorful fantasies of his youthful exploits and has given up on his claim, not knowing that it is about to yield a fortune in gold. The intrigue over Plunkett's claim deepens as Broderick schemes to win it through playing Plunkett in a card game. After Ah Sin rigs the game so that his friend Plunkett wins, Broderick attacks Plunkett and throws him off a cliff. Ah Sin is the sole witness to the crime and steals Broderick's bloody jacket as evidence, swapping it for another when Broderick tries to bribe him into silence. Integrated with this plotline is a romance between York and Miss Tempest, the daughter of a wealthy judge from San Francisco. Realizing that York has mistaken her for Plunkett's daughter, Miss Tempest and her mother continue the ruse so that she can secure York's affections, even coaxing the actual daughter and mother Plunkett into changing roles. These comic impersonations underscore the social divide between eastern gentility and the lawlessness of western mining life. The latter is characterized by wild excesses, whether in the tall tales of Plunkett or in the violent attempts by the miners to lynch each of those accused of murder: first Ah Sin, then York, and finally Broderick.

While no black characters appear in *Ah Sin*, the influence of blackface minstrelsy is evident, especially in the stage business of the Chinese immigrant character Ah Sin. While Ah Sin begins the play as a laundryman, whose constant utterance of "You wantee washee-washee?" defines his encounters with other characters, he later is employed as a personal servant by York, who wants to get more information on the missing Plunkett. His role thus suggests what happens when the "heathen Chinee" takes over

The Tricky Servant in Blackface and Yellowface

the domestic services of black characters and how this already racialized servitude plays differently in Chinese form.

Ah Sin's turn as York's servant is marked by repeatedly unsuccessful attempts at serving polite society. He tells the audience, "May be me mighty poor servant—don't know how. Well, me watchee-watchee—do everything see Mellican man do—pretty soon me learnee" (*Ah Sin* 58). This earnest attempt by Ah Sin at imitating white American manners spurs a later scene in which Mrs. Tempest tries to teach him how to set a proper table: "*Mrs. T. lifts it up—holds it a minute to let him see, then lets it fall. Ah Sin lifts leaf—holds it a minute then lets it slam down,*" and "*she tries to spread [the tablecloth], it flies out of her hands and lights beyond the table on the floor—Ah Sin exactly imitates this performance and grins at his success*" (*Ah Sin* 71–72). Ah Sin is not the only character who tries to imitate high society; the rustic Mrs. Plunkett, for instance, also pretends to be the society matron Mrs. Tempest, which results in mangled attempts at polite speech, such as "The mutuality of your pleasure in meeting *us*, could not be more mutual than the mutualness of our pleasure in meeting *you*" (*Ah Sin* 80). Yet Mrs. Plunkett's mode of imitation is fundamentally different from Ah Sin's racial mimicry. Her excessive verbosity contrasts with Ah Sin's unintelligibility, and her pretense ultimately leads to success, unlike Ah Sin, who shows himself to be inept at domestic chores in filling the salad dressing cruets with kerosene and castor oil. Mrs. Tempest declares that "this mental vacuum is a Chinaman to the marrow in one thing—the monkey faculty of imitating" and calls Ah Sin a "poor dumb animal, with his tail on top of his head instead of where it ought to be" (*Ah Sin* 72). Ah Sin's acts of imitation highlight the distance between white society and the Chinese immigrant and mock both the complicated rules of high society and the uncivilized character who is unable to fulfill them.

While the play *Ah Sin* was neither critically nor commercially successful, the character of Ah Sin as played by Charles T. Parsloe Jr. was praised for his innovation. In the *San Francisco Daily Evening Bulletin*, Mary Clemmer writes that the play was bogged down by "struggling puns and laborious jokes" but that its title character was especially memorable.

> As I watched it slowly unfold last evening, I asked, what is its object, and concluded that its crowning purpose was to display "Ah Sin." It was written for him—a new type of man in the American fabric, political and social—a creature at once shy and sly, reticent and talkative, cunning and amiable, weak, yet powerful, subtle as air, acute as quicksilver—a servant, a pariah, a thief, yet child of the oldest

civilization on our earth—nothing short of absolute genius can depict him as he is, and he who can will outrank in special personali-
ties Raymond or Joe Jefferson. When Joe Jefferson first played "Rip
Van Winkle," he was not the Rip *par excellence* of to-day. He grew
by time, and added many silent, subtle touches to fill perfectly the
character. So we seemed to see last night in Charles Parseloe [*sic*],
the clown, and promise of the perfect Heathen Chinee. Then why
not give us more *Ah Sin* and less of the bungling story; less cumber-
some, coarse people; less vulgarity and more keen wits?[30]

Wearing a queue attached to a skullcap, Parsloe sported a gap between his
teeth that suited what Mark Twain called "the true Mongrel look" of the
character Ah Sin.[31] Parsloe had already made his appearance in the role of
Hop Sing in Harte's *Two Men of Sandy Bar* and later would reproduce this
type of character in playing Washee Washee in Miller's *The Danites in the
Sierras*, Wing Lee in Campbell's *My Partner*, and similar figures in Bill Nye's
The Cadi (1891) and J. Cheever Goodwin's *Evangeline* (1896).[32] By the time
he appeared as Wing Lee in *My Partner*, he had earned the praise of the *New
York Mirror*: "In Chinese roles Mr. Parsloe is inimitable."[33]

Twain himself assessed Parsloe's performance as Ah Sin as authentic:
"Whoever sees Mr. Parsloe in this character sees as good and natural and
consistent a Chinaman as he can see in San Francisco."[34] The Washington
correspondent for the *St. Louis Globe-Democrat* also praised Parsloe as Ah
Sin, who "comes on [as] the most complete Mongolian ever born outside
the Celestial Kingdom."[35] The *New York Times* wrote that "Mr. Parsloe's
Chinaman could scarcely be excelled in truthfulness to nature and freedom
from caricature."[36] The *New York Herald* called Parsloe "the life of the play"
and said that "he has the merit of being always funny and never vulgar, and
his imitation of the Chinaman is natural and free from extravagance or buf-
foonery."[37] But other reviews quickly pointed out that the play drew on stock
characterizations rather than actual Chinese immigrant life. For the *New
York Sun*, Ah Sin was represented as "a lying, stealing, motiveless, merry-
andrew, intent only on 'washee, washee,' and a sort of Humpty-Dumpty
ubiquity" that "fails to give any illustration of Chinese character whatever,
and presents us with an American burlesque."[38] The New York *Spirit of the
Times* commented that "if Mark Twain supposes for one moment that this
character, as enacted, is a correct portraiture of the Chinaman, he is mistaken. It is a reflection of the American burlesque of the Chinaman. Nothing
more." The *Spirit of the Times* review continued:

The Tricky Servant in Blackface and Yellowface

It is not intended to be true or to be typical—only to be funny, and Mr. Parsloe knows very well how to be funny without being correct. In the first place, he does not use the language of the imported Asiatic. It is the language that the Western humorists impute to him, when they would be intelligently funny at his expense. In the second place, he does not make himself up like the Chinese. His is not the Mongol face, or demeanor, only the Chinaman's dress, and one or two of his antics. It is a Bowery boy in a short gown, grinning, and mixing the dialect of Washington Market with the business of Tony Pastor's.[39]

Ah Sin offered Parsloe the most sustained version of what would become his most popular character type. Yet his characterization drew not on direct observation of Chinese immigrants but on already established comic formulas, including those of minstrel blackface. Jacqueline Romeo notes that Parsloe's first teacher was his father, an English actor who "excelled at sagacious ape and comic dancing roles in pantomimes," such as in *Jack Robinson and His Monkey*, "the Dumb Negro" in *Tuckitomba, or, the Obi Sorceress*, and the role of "Caesar, 'a whitewashing nigger,'" in *New Years Gambols*, a ballet pantomime that called for a "nigger dance."[40] Like his father, Parsloe played "ape" roles in pantomime, including the title role of *Pongo!; or, the Mischievous Ape*, and cross-racial roles, including the Chinese "Kasrack, the mute slave" in *Aladdin*.[41] According to Parsloe's 1898 obituary, he was a member of an unspecified minstrel company in the 1855–56 season "and being a good banjo player made a success in this line."[42] Five years before his first Chinese role as Hop Sing, he was featured in "plantation songs and dances" during a "levee scene" in the 1871 frontier melodrama by T. B. De Walden and Edward Spencer, *Kit, The Arkansas Traveler*, a song and dance number criticized by the *New York Times* as "the embodiment of the impertinent, vulgar, noisy, and wholly improbably negro."[43]

In the role of Ah Sin, Parsloe's skills at minstrel song and dance were showcased in a brief interlude in act 3, in which York offers to entertain the female characters with a "novelty," saying that "my Chinaman is always meddling around the shows and picking up something or other, and he mimics everything he sees there." After some monetary encouragement from York, Ah Sin announces, "Me singee littee songee" (*Ah Sin* 82). Though not stated explicitly, Ah Sin's "littee songee" could well have been "The Chinee Laundryman," as sung by the San Francisco Minstrels (a favorite of Twain's).[44] In the 1870s, a regular part of the group's repertoire was

"The Chinee Laundryman," in which a Chinese immigrant figure sings in a characteristic dialect.

> Me workee all day in Chinee laundry
> For "Ching Chow," dat's his name;
> Me catchee all de rats in de markey
> Makee pot-pie all-a-same. (*gong*)
> All-a-same (*gong*) all-a-same (*gong*).
> Me soon become a cit'zen
> And votee just like me please
> By'm by me gettee a good jobbee
> To workee on de police! (*gong*)
> Police! (*gong*) Muchee clubee! (*gong*).[45]

While the Chinese figure expressed his aspiration to become an American citizen, the chorus affirms his innate cultural differences through his inability to endure American music: he says, "No like brass band, / Makee very sick" and directs the "Mellican man" to listen to his "littee song" played with "a chi-nee fiddle, and a shang-hai gong."[46]

Despite his presumed inability to mimic society manners, the character Ah Sin does demonstrate the ability to pick up objects, literally as well as figuratively. Ah Sin's magical production of the *"gorgeous costume, and odds and ends of dramatic properties"* that he has "picked up" (*Ah Sin* 82) at the theaters in San Francisco, underscores his constant thievery throughout the play. His main prop is a bag into which he gathers and then reveals an endless series of items, a comic device that proved not only an opportunity for Parsloe's "antics" but a racial characteristic defining Chinese character. Twain was well aware that Ah Sin would act as an effective representation of all Chinese immigrants rather than as an individualized portrait of one. He even justified the play in these terms: "The whole purpose of the piece is to afford an opportunity for the illustration of this character. The Chinaman is going to become a very frequent spectacle all over America by and by, and a difficult political problem, too. Therefore, it seems well enough to let the public study him a little on the stage beforehand."[47] His portrayal of Ah Sin as an inveterate thief, therefore, marked the Chinaman's presumably questionable nature, a premise that was called out by one astute *New York Sun* reviewer: "*Ah Sin* steals everything he can lay his hands upon. Does Mark Twain mean to tell us that this is characteristic of the Mongolian race, or will he acknowledge in his next speech that it is simply funny?"[48]

The Tricky Servant in Blackface and Yellowface

While seen as a loyal friend to Plunkett and ultimately useful to York, Ah Sin constantly reaffirms his own self-interest by turning each of his labors—constant acts of theft, offering to do "washee," serving York, wangling a high price for Broderick's bloody jacket, or singing a "littee songee"—into money-making enterprises. Although all the characters have pecuniary motives, money is highlighted above all other motivations for Ah Sin; moreover, this individual brand of greed is suggested to be consistent with the Chinese immigrant's uncertain claim on American resources. While like the white miners, Ah Sin wants to strike it rich, he notably resorts to raiding other mines rather than having his own claim: "Onee, twoee, fivee, 'levene, eighte holee, muchee holee, no goldee (*takes up pick and commences to dig in Brod's claim*)—too muchee workee no good for Chinaman. (*picks up a piece of gold and comes down stage jabbering Chinese*) Come back tonightee, catchee plenty goldee, mally Ilish girl, go back to China. Allee same" (*Ah Sin* 46).

Though perhaps unintentionally, Bret Harte's poem "Plain Language from Truthful James" had already ingrained the assumption that the Chinese immigrant was inherently untrustworthy. In Harte's poem, Ah Sin is not the only character who cheats; he models his card game on tactics learned from white men such as Bill Nye, with a sleeve "stuffed full of aces and bowers / And the same with intent to deceive." However, the poem does give Ah Sin, with his "childlike" demeanor, Chinese long sleeves, and waxed fingernails, a racial advantage at pretense. After Ah Sin duplicates the "right bower" dealt to the narrator, the others realize that they have been taken in. This leads Nye to exclaim, "We are ruined by Chinese cheap labor," and to resort to racial violence: "And he went for that heathen Chinee." As Gary Scharnhorst has noted, the widespread allusions to the poem suggest that rather than acting as "an ironic indictment of anti-Chinese sentiment," Harte's poem too often "seemed to license that sentiment," with "predominantly white, middle-class readers" identifying "not with the 'heathen' Ah Sin but with his presumed racial superior, Bill Nye, the ostensible victim of his trickery."[49]

Scholars have pointed out that Twain as well as Harte felt a measure of sympathy for the increasingly targeted Chinese immigrants.[50] The play makes clear that the murderous fervor that drove anti-Chinese views and legislation could hurt virtuous white characters as well. The animosity directed against Chinese immigrants in Harte's poem is seen in the miners' threats to hang Ah Sin at the end of act 2: "*They all make a dive for Ah Sin, who scrambles between their legs and upsetting one or two of them—jumps on the table, seizes flat iron and shrieking and gibbering Chinese"* (*Ah Sin* 69). York too is threatened with lawless violence when at the end of act 3 (ironically subtitled "Border Justice") he is accused of Plunkett's murder. While he expresses the hope that Ah Sin might vouch for him, he is reminded that he now faces the consequences of racist state laws prohibiting testimony by Asians (as well as by African Americans and American Indians) against white defendants.

> YORK (*amazedly*). But at least, Ah Sin here, knows that I—
> AH SIN. Chinaman evidence no goodee.
> YORK (*excitedly*). At least, I must know the authority by which I am arrested?
> FERGUSON (*gravely*). Certainly; by order of the highest authority in the land—Judge Lynch! (*Ah Sin* 83)

Yet like Harte's poem, *Ah Sin* marks Ah Sin with moral ambiguity even while satirizing the pervasive anti-Chinese sentiment and mob mentality of most of the miners. While the villain Broderick vilifies Ah Sin by calling him "you moral cancer, you unsolvable political problem" (*Ah Sin* 46), the hero York confirms, "His face is as unintelligible as a tea chest" (*Ah Sin* 57).

Imagined as a free agent, sojourner, and thief rather than a trustworthy servant, Ah Sin's service to York and other white Americans presents a new level of uncertainty. As Yusha Pan has detailed, Ah Sin not only performs funny business but also comments on the deception and folly of the white characters, thus showing that "his level of intelligence is above those arrogant, white characters who are contemptuous of him."[51] For instance, he trenchantly points out the hypocrisy of anti-Chinese sentiment when he mistakenly believes Plunkett to be a polygamist: "Plunkee got 2 wifee—Mellican man no likee Chinaman hab 2 wifee—Chinaman no likee wifee sell wifee—poor wifee got no home—Mellican man no likee wifee, lun away, let poor wifee starve—Mellican man too muchee—clivilized" (*Ah Sin* 63). However, as Pan comments, the play also highlights how Ah Sin's inveterate thievery, gibberish, and physical comedy turn into "a yellowface minstrel show" that might fuel anti-Chinese sentiment.[52] Ah Sin's clever commentary acts as a double-edged sword: it both affirms the character's intelligence and ingenuity but also establishes these qualities as endangering less industrious, enterprising, or attentive white characters.

In a piece published in the *Springfield (MA) Republican* in March 1867, Harte noted that the "quick-witted, patient, obedient and faithful" Chinese

The Tricky Servant in Blackface and Yellowface

were "gradually deposing the Irish from their old, recognized positions in the ranks of labor." He predicted that "John Chinaman" would "eventually supplant Bridget and Patrick in menial occupations."[53] Ah Sin might be understood as a "new type" of theatrical character that also registered new anxieties about Chinese labor. Taking on the multiple occupations of miner, laundryman, and gambler, Ah Sin also becomes the tricky servant, aiding York in his romantic pursuits and entertaining the audience with comic antics. That he does so immediately recalls the servant roles typically given to black comic characters whose presumed racial inferiority—demonstrated through their foolishness and ineptitude—justify their lower social status and servitude; however, the play also departs from simply replicating the terms of blackface.

Eric Lott has characterized the social unconscious of blackface minstrelsy as something that "mediated, and regulated, the formation of white working-class masculinity": a process in which white obsession with and control over black male bodies was enacted through cross-racial impersonations involving eroticism ("love") and the imitation of black slaves in order to appropriate their bodies, labor, and agency ("theft").[54] Yellowface performance in *Ah Sin* appears to head in this direction when Ah Sin agrees to work for York as a seemingly "quick-witted, patient, obedient and faithful" servant. However, what Lott describes for blackface never fully encompasses Ah Sin's unpredictable actions, foreign unintelligibility, and moral ambiguity. Ah Sin's inordinate ability to manipulate and cheat white characters out of money and possessions is coupled with his deep loyalty to his friend Plunkett, suggesting relationships with white characters that are independent of the motivations of servitude and compensation. Thus the performance of Ah Sin unsettles the terms of "love and theft" as defined for the strictly black-and-white, servant-and-master dynamics of blackface minstrel performance. Ultimately it is Ah Sin who engages mainly in the "theft" of white wealth and domestic space, yet these acts of thievery eventually save the white protagonist as well. A happy ending is made possible through a feat of oriental magic when Ah Sin pulls out the crucial evidence of Broderick's incriminating jacket, shows York's innocence, and then reveals that Plunkett is alive just in time to prevent Broderick's lynching. Ah Sin is rewarded with half of Broderick's mining claim and $10,000 as well as *general shouts from the miners* of "*Hurrah for AH SIN!*" (*Ah Sin* 95). More fortunate than his predecessors—other tricky servants who remain in perpetual service and receive no compensation for their work—Ah Sin is literally capable of stealing the show.

5

THE CHINESE LAUNDRY SKETCH

In the song "Uncle Snow," attributed to Thomas Dilward and published in *Christy's New Songster* (1863), the singer identifies himself as "an artist wid de brush by profession" who turns out to be a house painter. His cheeky claim to be "de greatest white washer in all creation," who intends to go to Washington "to try and get a job to whitewash all de black deeds ob dis nation," is undercut by the revelation that his "whitewash bisness" was started "'bout ninety years ago" after he "saved a dime or two" and is located "in a cellar."[1] These humbling details undercut the entrepreneurial boasting of "Uncle Snow" and show the limits of his attempts to improve his social position and political influence. While many minstrel songs and sketches portrayed black characters as slaves or servants, songs such as "Uncle Snow" expressed particular disdain toward self-employed African Americans.

As the previous chapter suggests, the theatrical characterizations of Chinese immigrants were deeply influenced by racial anxieties about their fitness for inclusion in the American workforce and body politic. Chinese men employed as "coolie" labor on railroads, factories, and plantations or as domestic servants were perceived to be threats to white labor and citizenship. Characters such as Ah Sin aroused even more concern by representing Chinese immigrants as free agents. Chinese immigrants sought economic autonomy first as miners and then as the owners of stores, restaurants, and especially laundries. Chinese men began to run hand laundries in San Francisco in the mid-nineteenth century, and by the 1870s these businesses had spread broadly across the nation. These immigrant proprietors faced hard and repetitive work, cultural isolation, and racial animus that did not abate even after exclusion laws barred U.S. immigration and naturalized citizenship for most Chinese after 1882.

Comic representations of these immigrant entrepreneurs, first presented in minstrel and vaudeville sketches and then influential in literature, radio, and film, took on lives of their own. The many incarnations of the Chinese laundry sketch ridiculed the Chinese immigrant for his garbled speech, alien appearance, and strange customs as well as for the unmanly labor of washing clothes. They also expressed concerns about what happens in the absence of white masters and overseers. These sketches no longer emphasized just the comic nature of low-wage servitude or the tricky servant's ineptitude; rather, they highlighted what problems might ensue when cunning Chinese immigrant characters deployed perceptions of their own unintelligibility toward self-serving and devious ends.

This chapter illustrates how the Chinese immigrant was represented in a changing American racial hierarchy as well as the importance of theater in focusing and altering public opinion during the period of Chinese exclusion. It surveys examples of the many versions of the Chinese laundry sketch produced by white performers and describes how, beginning in the 1880s, this ubiquitous theatrical situation was taken up by African American performers in scenes featuring the Chinese laundryman paired with a black customer. At least on the surface, African American renditions of the Chinese laundry sketch maintained the basic patterns of a distinctive racial habit—comic typecasting, ethnic mistrust, and sometimes violent demonstrations of physical abuse and conflict—that was initiated and sustained by white performers. However, some of the African American versions imply different kinds of interracial relationships and even the possibility of common ground between African American and Chinese immigrant characters. A few even suggest how both African Americans and Chinese immigrants experienced similar working conditions and racial restrictions on their ability to work independently and thrive. The chapter ends with a look at how a 1914 short story by the white writer Vachel Lindsay, "The Golden-Faced People," published in the NAACP's magazine *The Crisis*, makes these connections—as well as the continued hold of the Chinese laundry sketch on the American popular imagination—frighteningly clear.

WHITE SKIN, CHINESE LAUNDRIES

As seen in chapter 4, the caricature of Chinese immigrant laundrymen began as the subject of minstrelsy. In the 1870s, a regular part of the San

Francisco Minstrels' repertoire included a popular song sung by one of the troupe's founders, Charles Backus. His version of "The Chinee Laundryman" may have been based on a similar song, "The Chinese Washerman," performed by minstrel Eph Horn in 1856 after Horn returned from a visit to California.[2] "The Chinee Laundryman" depicts a Chinese immigrant man who "workee all day in Chinee laundry," makes rats into potpies, and aspires to becomes an American citizen. This figure was then resurrected in vaudeville acts depicting interactions between the Chinese laundryman and his customers. Many early versions of this sketch emphasized tensions between Chinese and Irish immigrants, the latter of whom were also the objects of comic ridicule. Charles McCarthy, who had been described in an 1884 comment in the *New York Clipper* as "the restless Hiberian-Chinaman,"[3] and George Monroe performed "Grogan's Chinese Laundry." According to the *Musical Courier*, their 1881 appearance at Kelly's Front Street Theatre, with McCarthy as the Chinese character and Monroe as an Irishwoman "with broad accent and robust physique," made "quite a hit" with the audience.[4]

These comic acts demonstrated the wariness with which Chinese men were regarded as competitors in labor and business and threats to white culture and domesticity. One such example is *Allee Samee 'Mellican Man* (1894), a stage monologue published in *Beadle's Dime Dialogues and Speakers*, one of sixty-six volumes designed "for schools, exhibitions, home entertainments, and amateur stages."[5] Center stage is Hop Wong, a Hong Kong immigrant, who appears in "*full 'Chinee' costume, but wearing no pigtail.*" He explains that his lack of a queue is proof that he is "allee samee like 'Mellican man" and "one t'e boys, evely time" and then launches into a story about why he "now go barefoot on top headee" (82). The ensuring tale simultaneously delivers Hop Wong's argument that he has become just like an American man and reveals the legal and cultural differences that render him unassimilable. Hop Wong decides that equality can be earned through American marriage, even though "nobody wantee mally Chinaman," and he proposes to Kate, an Irishwoman who has lost her laundry ticket. After refusing to return her laundry and telling her "no checkee, no washee" (82) he then offers to marry her. Upon seeing his bag of money, Kate agrees.

When later he refuses to give his new wife money, they argue and the police come and lock him up. After he returns from jail, he finds that his alcoholic mother-in-law has moved in, followed by a man Kate claims as her brother, a "big Turk" named Jim. Kate and Hop Wong have a baby, and Hop Wong finds himself "washee all day, walk floor all night" (84) while the others do nothing. Kate asks him for fifty dollars for new clothes, but when he gives her only half the sum, she fights with him. A slapstick scene ensues in which Kate and her mother and brother beat Hop Wong and drag him to the door by his queue, whereupon he cuts it off and they fall down the stairs. A policeman comes and locks him up. When he finally returns home, he declares that he will no longer work and, like Jim and other American men, is content to smoke, eat, and sleep while the women do the laundry. Finally, wary of Jim, he takes the money bag and skips out, justifying his actions by declaring that he is "allee samee 'Mellican man" (86).

Many other versions of the Chinese laundry sketch are much less detailed than *Allee Samee 'Mellican Man*, but their basic plots are similar: a central dispute between the Chinese character and the non-Chinese customer over the latter's failure to produce a claim ticket for the laundry, after which the police are called to intervene. The ensuing conflict not only provides an opportunity for comic dialogue and slapstick violence but also comments on the Chinese character's failure to understand American ways of doing business. As Wolfgang Mieder has noted, the characteristically garbled and repetitive speech given to the Chinese laundryman character, especially variations on "no tickee, no washee," became commonplace expressions.[6]

The Chinese laundry sketch emphasized energetic and sometimes acrobatic movement as well as the linguistic peculiarities of Chinese characters. Due to the popularity of Chinese, Japanese, "Arab," and other acrobatic troupes in circus and minstrel shows throughout the later nineteenth century, oriental bodies were already associated with extraordinary physical dexterity. The laundry sketch, a much more active setting than the opium den, became a popular setting for acrobatics. In 1905, the *Minneapolis Tribune* described the "first-class vaudeville acts" performed at the Roof Garden in Minneapolis and noted, "Of these, the Grotesque Randolphs, in an eccentric aerial act titled 'Fun in a Chinese Laundry,' deserves special mention."[7] When the Chinese laundry sketch was first captured on film, these aspects of physical comedy remained essential, as can be seen in an 1894 Edison kinetoscope film by "Robetta and Doretto," who had performed in vaudeville for Tony Pastor.[8] Showing the "the pursuit of Hop Lee by an irate policeman," the short cinematic sequence features a Chinese character, distinguished by his darkened face and short trousers, smashing a pot over the policeman's head. The two chase one another through a set of stage doors, then the Chinese character pulls himself up on top of the set and drops a board down on the policeman. Edison made this film along with *Chinese Opium Den* (now lost), a title that suggests the additional association of the Chinese immigrant with illicit drugs and gang activity.[9]

Sound recording also captured the Chinese laundry sketch, as shown in a Vitaphone sound skit, "Uncle Josh in a Chinese Laundry," made by Cal Stewart in 1910. In 1903, Stewart became one of the first entertainers to sign a contract with Columbia for his recordings of "Uncle Josh," a humorous "Yankee" character featured for his rural stories. His "Uncle Josh in a Chinese Laundry" provides opportunities to highlight not only the linguistic but also the imagined physical differences between Uncle Josh and a "pig tailed heathen Chineeze" who "looked fer all the world like a picter on Aunt Nancy Smith's tea cups." The allusion to fine china and the queue both feminizes the Chinese character and renders him monstrous: "I've bin around purty considerable. I'd seen all sorts of coorisoties and monstrosities in cirkuses and meenagerys, but that wuz the fust time I'd ever seen a critter with his head and tail on the same end." Though both Uncle Josh and the Chinese character speak with accents, it is clear whose speech is associated with rural "down home" America and whose is extravagantly foreign. On the sound recording Stewart mimics the Chinese character's "outlandish lingo," juxtaposing Uncle Josh's folksy Yankee commentary with what, as Josh describes, "sounded to me like cider runnin' out of a jug, somethin' like—ung tong oowong fang kai moi oo ung we, velly good washee." As in other versions of the Chinese laundry sketch, "Uncle Josh in a Chinese Laundry" emphasizes how the Chinese laundryman uses his unintelligibility to take advantage of customers. Unable to decipher the cryptic laundry ticket, Uncle Josh is met with "no tickee, no shirtee" and loses his clothes.[10]

These dramatic altercations between the Chinese laundryman and his customers showcase not only a cultural divide but also the immigrant character's adherence to rigid, unfathomable, and potentially unscrupulous business practices. Thus the Chinese laundry sketch was far from a harmless piece of fun. One particularly hostile example can be found in the story "The Heathen Chinee," published in a December 1906 issue of the *Elevator Constructor*, a Chicago-based trade periodical published by the International Union of Elevator Constructors. This story concerns a white man, Big Bill, who complains that he has lost his laundry due to a missing ticket. He is told by another man, "Old Twilight," that his loss serves him right for patronizing a "heathen, who wears shoes made in Californy in a planin' mill, an' hez his haid done up behind like yer Aunt Lucy." Old Twilight's diatribe escalates as he imagines "the lep'rous wretches" wearing Big Bill's best shirt-front "at the next fan-tan game and win[ning] enough to tempt a white girl to work for them." Worst of all, Old Twilight rants, there are "lots of decent women in this country only too glad to do your washing—only too glad to make a few cents honestly" but have been laid off in favor of "a pagan who wears his shirt on the wrong side of his pants and burn cornstalks before a pig." Old Twilight then imagines that instead of churchgoing, on Sunday "the sleek yallah people" will indulge in illicit drugs: "pad, pad, pad down the street and foregather in the back room of one uv their points to blow in part of the stuff that white men gave them for daubing their shirt fronts with white."[11] Attributed first to the *Toronto Tribune*, this story reaffirms anti-Asian sentiments published in the *Elevator Constructor* earlier that same year, such as a January 1906 editorial, titled the "Increase of Japs," urging the expansion of the Chinese Exclusion Act to rule out the threat of Japanese immigrants: "Like leeches, they have fastened themselves upon all our unorganized industries—and, like leeches, they will hold on until they are gorged with our gold."[12] A May 1906 issue includes a poem by "a mine worker" lamenting the fate of the white working-class family:

> Mother works in a sweatshop,
> 　Jenny goes out to spin;
> Kit is "cash" in a department store,
> 　Gee whiz, how the money comes in.
> Jimmy picks slate in a breaker,
> 　John is a "blower's dog";
> Everybody works but father,
> 　A "chink's" got his job.[13]

Most versions of the Chinese laundry sketch were much less overtly antagonistic yet derisive nonetheless. As Yuko Matsukawa has noted, potent stereotypes expressing anti-Chinese political sentiment were more broadly circulated through the everyday material culture of advertising and popular fiction for mass consumption.[14] That the Chinese laundry sketch could inject racist sentiments into seemingly innocuous entertainment can be seen in Sheldon Palmer's 1920 farce *Fun in a Chinese Laundry*, written for and originally produced by the Young People's Society of the Presbyterian Church, Springfield, Missouri.[15] In this short play, Ah Sin, the laundry proprietor, is arrested by Hogan, the Irish policeman, after misunderstandings about the laundry ticket. He is also accused of murder and making soup from a pet dog and a little girl, both named Sally, after he mispronounces the word "celery" and says, "Me makee good selly soup" (38). Ah Sin suffers many indignities: he is mistaken for a woman, called a "nassy old China-mans" (9) and an "awful Chinese villain" (36) and mimicked by the young rascal Cholly. Nonetheless, he is staged as a genial rather than menacing comic figure, in accordance with the demands for production by young amateurs; the playscript opens with that declaration that "bright, sparkling fun, a series of side-splitting complications, plenty of brisk action, the absence of anything coarse or vulgar and the total lack of sentimental scenes make this little farce an ideal entertainment for school, club or church societies" (3).

The "fun" of these theatrical sketches inevitably conditioned observations of actual Chinese behavior. Mark Twain, for instance, commented in 1872 that "the chief employment of Chinamen in towns is to wash clothes. They always send a bill, like this below [*illustrations of a laundry ticket with Chinese symbols*], pinned to the clothes. It is mere ceremony, for it does not enlighten the customer much."[16] An 1882 description of the "heathen Chinee" by Alfred Trumble states that "Chinese laundrymen have a method of getting even with customers. When bills are not paid they retain the clothes, and it is sometimes necessary to obtain them by attachment. But the garments are returned in a different condition from that in which they were taken."[17] And in 1885, this short article appeared in African American newspapers such as Alabama's *Huntsville Gazette* and the *New York World*:

> A customer enters and leaves, say, five shirts, eight collars and five
> cuffs. John attaches to each of the lot a linen tag marked in tea-chest
> characters. On each of the shirts is put a tag which reads "Moon"; the
> eight collars are divided into two bundles of four each and likewise
> marked "Moon;" the cuffs are similarly labeled. Other customers
> are given similar tickets with terms such as "horse," "lion," "devil,"
> and "goodness"; these tickets have "a greater significance under
> Chinese law than an ordinary receipt, and may be justly likened to a
> pawn-ticket." Its possession is a badge of ownership. In case of loss
> or destruction that customer should, under Chinese rules, apply
> to a magistrate and enter into an agreement corresponding to the
> American indemnity bond. It takes John a long time to realize that a
> wash-ticket is merely a receipt. Usually three lawsuits and an arrest
> for larceny are required before he recognized the difference between
> Chinese and American law.[18]

BLACK FUN IN THE CHINESE LAUNDRY

The Chinese laundry sketch was taken up by African American actors as early as Japanese Tommy's 1884 performance in "Fun in a Chinese

Laundry"[19] and probably appeared in the 1880s acts of comic impersonators Billy Kersands, Tom Brown, and Harry Fiddler as well. By the first half of the twentieth century, this sketch had become an established part of African American vaudeville and other entertainments. In 1910, J. B. Norton, the stage manager of A. G. Allen's Minstrels, included "a laughable one-act farce" featuring the comedian J. J. Perry along with W. A. Dixon as "Charlie One Lung Lee," a "Chinese laundry man"; this act, the *Freeman* reported, was "a screaming success from beginning to end."[20] In mid-July of the same year, the *Freeman* noted that Dave Lowe played the title role in "Hop Sing, the Chink, or Trouble in the Laundry" at the Swiss Airdome in Dallas and commented that Lowe "is sure good with the 'Chink goods.'"[21] The basic "fun" of the Chinese laundry sketch was easily turned into an altercation between black and Chinese characters. These sketches provided opportunities for wordplay, gymnastics, and comic slapstick violence; an ad for the Harris and Morriss Vaudeville Combination in the Indiana-based *Jasper Weekly Courier* described an act featuring "the trick bill Board" that suggests acrobatics and physical comedy similar to that which appeared in the 1894 Edison kinetoscope film: "It is almost impossible to explain the comedy and fun the Chinaman and Coon get out of this wonderful bill board. Suffice is it to say that they keep the audience in an uproar of laughter from start to finish. When this act was going on in St. Louis, people connected with the house thought there were other actors hidden behind the scenes dressed just like the Chinaman and Coon as it seemed almost impossible for men to fly through doors and windows and back again as they did."[22]

These African American versions of the Chinese laundry sketch continued for decades; in the summer of 1938, Harry Fiddler and Billy Mills performed "Five Minutes in a Chinese Laundry" for Silas Green's company, in which "during the argument in the laundry, Charles Rue steps in as a peacemaker."[23] The Chinese laundry sketch also appeared in films such as *House-Rent Party* (1946), directed by Sam Newfield and produced by Ted Toddy. *House-Rent Party* includes a Chinese character, One Lung Lee (played by Alfred Cortez), who appears in several scenes opposite the comic protagonist Pigmeat (played by the comedian Pigmeat "Alamo" Markham, reputedly the last African American popular entertainer to use blackface).[24] While the film is lost, its catalog summary describes a familiar plotline. When Pigmeat goes to a Chinese laundry to pick up a new shirt for a house-rent party, he fights with One Lung, the laundry proprietor, over the laundry ticket. Later, One Lung and Pigmeat play dice together, and Pigmeat "tries to swindle One Lung, who claims to not know the game." Like other wily

Chinese types, however, One Lung "is merely playing the fool and ends up swindling Pigmeat."[25]

Such descriptions provide little indication that these versions of the Chinese laundry sketch differed appreciably from those performed by white actors. In general, Chinese immigrants were portrayed as both unscrupulous and dangerous to black as well as to white characters. A 1899 song by white writer Paul J. Knox, "I Don't Care If I Never Wake Up," depicted a "yellow coon," a black character who hangs around "at a Chinese laundry" because, he declares, "I likes my hop" (opium).[26] In February 1910, the *Freeman* noted that Dave Merritt's performance as "Wing Lee, the Chinaman," in *Wing Lee's Ragtime Laundry by* "Ed Winn" (perhaps Ed Wynn), "was all that one could wish for" and also credited Winn with "some very good character acting as the 'dope fiend.'"[27]

Yet a few interesting examples also suggested that some African American performers might have put a different valence on the interracial interactions of the Chinese laundry sketch. In 1909, a review republished in the *Freeman* gave high praise to Sam Cook and Jim Stevens's version: "Ordinarily the announcement of a stage Chinaman is a signal to cringe, and when it is coupled with a sketch that suggests a laundry it means to cringe all the harder. But Cook and his partner, Jim Stevens who presents a Negro character that serves as an excellent foil to the Chinaman, make their sketch, No Check-ee, No Wash-ee, the hit of the bill."[28]

That Cook and Stevens delighted the reviewer with "the embodiment of originality" suggests that these African American actors brought new meaning to these all-too-familiar racial performances, ones that by 1909 caused at least some in the audience to "cringe." Cook's innovations are described as adding authenticity and detail to the role: "Cook apparently has discarded the traditional stage Chinaman in to-to; has gone out into Chinatown and studies the Chinaman from life, and then created and embellished a character true to life and, more importantly, to stage art. He gives to John Chinaman some little irresistible touches."[29]

In 1914 and 1916 Gus Stevens would draw similar praise for the convincing nature of his Chinese characters, performed first with Charlie Williams at Gibson's New Standard Theatre in Philadelphia and then at the Bowden Square Theater with Billy Purcell in Boston. Stevens had also played female parts successfully prior to his appearance: "Mr. Stevens appeared here at the Bowden Square Theater several years ago as a female impersonator, with his former partner, Charlie Williams, and their act made a great hit." His

The Chinese Laundry Sketch

Chinese acts, while predictable in title and name, were praised for their verisimilitude:

> These two boys have got the goods and delivered it. Their little sketch is called "Fun in a Chinese Laundry," and I must say it lived up to its title, for there was fun and fun galore. They kept the house in an uproar of laughter, for Billy Purcell, the comedian, is a funny one. He portrayed the character of a shiftless darkey to perfection. He is a natural-born comedian and a great dancer. His partner, Gus Stevens, played the part of One Lung, the Chinaman, so natural, his make-up, dialect and every move was so perfect that few could detect that he wasn't a real Chinaman.[30]

In a 1914 Philadelphia performance, Gus Stevens's Chinese impersonation received even more affirmation. According to the *Freeman*, Stevens was "the talk of the town" as he showcased "his mimetic and dialect ability"; furthermore, "his make-up was perfection, so much so that it really fooled a number of Chinamen who attended regularly every night to see the act. Laughter was almost unceasing."[31] If that same year the white actors Dave Montgomery and Fred Stone in the Broadway hit *Chin-Chin* had been taken aback by a Chinese man's comment that the symbols on their curtain were "just a laundry list," Gus Stevens's yellowface act could fool even some Chinese members of the audience.

Of course, what the reviews lauded as Stevens's and others' attention to authentic detail served mainly to confirm praise for African American actors' mimetic abilities. Theatrical reviews in the African American press consistently highlighted the transformative powers of African American actors in order to emphasize their achievements despite the bias and disregard of white audiences and critics. Thus praise for the realistic makeup and speech of Chinese impersonators did not necessarily translate to a sense of solidarity with the Chinese immigrant characters they played. However, perhaps these sentiments were not entirely lacking. African American versions of the Chinese laundry sketch show little evidence of the vehement anti-Asian hostility demonstrated by works such as the *Elevator Constructor's* "The Heathen Chinee." Instead, certain versions of the laundry sketch could even provide a reminder that African Americans and Chinese immigrants lived, worked, and did business in close proximity to one another.

Other than brief reviews, little can be found to recreate the many "Chinaman and Coon" sketches performed in vaudeville. However, two published dramas—a one-act farce by Henry Llewellyn Williams titled *Waxworks at Play* (1894) and a sketch by Walter Carter, *The Coon and the Chink* (1912)—give some insights into the different ways that interactions between black comic characters and Chinese laundrymen were staged. Williams was a prolific white writer and playwright who composed in multiple genres, including short plays such as *De Black Magician or The Wonderful Beaver, an Ethiopian Comicality in One Scene* (1876) and *Go and Get Tight! An Ethiopian Farce in One Scene* (1880). His *Waxworks at Play* is clearly influenced by the popularity of both blackface minstrelsy and the Chinese laundry sketch. Though the racial identities of the author and performers of Carter's *The Coon and the Chink* are less certain, this sketch itself does hint at the intriguing possibilities of black-Chinese relationships outside the logics of anti-Asian sentiment.

Waxworks at Play does not take place in a Chinese laundry but instead in the interior of a studio owned by a sculptor, Pattern. Pattern's black servant Matthew is discontented with his menial position and wants to use his "liberal eddication" in order to follow his "artistic respirations"; however, according to Pattern, Matthew is too "inquisitive," and Pattern wants to give him a "constructive scare" by posing live people as his waxworks.[32] Much of the play's comic action involves not only the scare that Matthew receives from these pretend waxworks but also his interactions with Pattern's Chinese laundryman, Wing Fat, who repeatedly utters "Me wantee washee" for comic effect. Interestingly enough, *Waxworks at Play* voices its concerns about Chinese immigrant labor from the perspective of black characters. As Matthew argues that his fiancée, Lulu, should be hired instead of Wing Fat, the play makes clear the heated competition between the Chinese laundryman and black female domestics.

> PAT. Matthew, you are always running down that Mongolian, Wing Fat, because you want the job for your steady company—what's her name?
> MAT. Her name gine to be Missis Matthew Spann; but in de meantime—while it is Lulu—yas, she is de card fur washing.
> PAT. But the Chinee comes cheaper.
> MAT. Dat's so; de 'Merican ought to be dearer—see?
> PAT. American? Your Lulu is an African.
> MAT. Well, Africa am nearer dan China, I calc'lates; 'sides she has gone done rejuced her terms on 'count of de hard soap.
> PAT. The hard soap?

MAT. Did I say soap, boss? Hard times—precious little soap about.

PAT. None of your soft soap, Matthew. (Williams 6)

Matthew's fears of Chinese immigrant labor registers the actual conflicts between African American and Chinese laundry workers described by Tera Hunter in her study of nineteenth-century African American women in the South, *To 'Joy My Freedom*. Hunter noted how African American laundresses in Galveston, Texas, led an 1877 strike protesting racism in the laundry business. While these women protested at white-owned steam laundries, they also directed their energies toward ousting the Chinese laundrymen of the city; in one newspaper account, one woman was heard to say, "Chinese got no business coming here taking our work from us."[33]

But ultimately *Waxworks at Play* shows little real interest in either illuminating the working conditions for African American washerwomen or in depicting their real-life competition with Chinese immigrant labor. Instead, it emphasizes slapstick violence and humorous reversals as the black characters are pitted against Wing Fat. Matthew makes Wing Fat sit on the burning stove and then seizes him by his queue, *"slings him out of window,"* and rejoices with Lulu that "we hab got rid ob dat Chinee—'cause he bruck our tings—and you are on de job! An ugger-ly yaller man!" (Williams 10). But in a subsequent scene, a statue of Cupid strikes Wing Fat and Lulu with his arrow, and they fall in love with one another.

WING FAT. (*Appears D.F.*) Me wantee—

LULU. Well, you wont get washee!

WING FAT. No, me wantee you! Me lovee you! We make biz and
    washee-washee.

CUPID in D.F. shows that he made the Chinaman love her. Aims at LULU.

LULU. Why cert! Mat, you are broke! Whar are dem clo'? John, we are
    pardners.

WING FAT. Me tankee you.

MAT. What? (*Snatches club from SANDOW.*) Me spankee you! (*In
    the fight LULU takes away the club and holds WING FAT by the cue
    [queue] so that MAT. cannot shove him out. MAT. gets the hatchet from
    WASHINGTON and strikes a blow. The cue is cut and WING FAT drops
    out with a yell.*) (Williams 12)

This intriguing possibility of an interracial union between Wing Fat and Lulu is ultimately put to rest by Pattern. After Wing Fat is finally ejected from the scene, the white master of the house finally restores the racial order by allowing the black characters to take their more appropriate places as his domestic help.

While *Waxworks at Play* was most likely written for white actors performing in blackface and yellowface, the intended casting of Carter's *The Coon and the Chink* is somewhat more ambiguous, and both of its roles may well have been performed by African Americans. Carter's "Chink" is described in stage directions as a *"short, thin, middle-aged Chinaman. Very stupid and ignorant in disposition"* who wears a *"typical close-shaven wig with queue."* "Coon" is a *"tall, lanky, ignorant and unpolished negro"* in *"comedy black-face"* who, like his white counterparts in other laundry sketches, expresses wonder and derision at the Chinese laundryman and suffers the effects of his unintelligible business practices.[34] Coon points out that Chink has sewn up the wrong hole on his socks, and when Chink subsequently *"scolds COON in Chinese,"* Coon interrupts him to mock his singsong language: "Scuse me suh, scuse me suh, what am de name of dat song?" (Carter 5). Yet even though both *Waxworks at Play* and *The Coon and the Chink* pair stereotypical black and Chinese characters, they show important differences. In *The Chink and the Coon*, the action is not directed by a white character such as Pattern but directed equally by the two nonwhite characters. The focus of the humor shifts from Chinese unintelligibility to black illiteracy as Chink tells Coon, "No tickie—no laundry," and Coon looks at his ledger and then *"turns the book around a few times in confusion then points to one of the characters."*

> COON. Dat one dare look something like my laundry, bring dat one.
> CHINK. Dat one four dollar sixty-two cent.
> COON. I guess dat ain't de one. (Carter 4)

While Chink demonstrates deceitful business practices, Coon is equally untrustworthy. Asked to leave his watch as collateral, Coon gives it to Chink, only to pickpocket him and return it to his own pocket. *The Chink and the Coon* moves from confrontations over the laundry to moments in which the black and Chinese characters share a bowl of "chop suey" that suggests the stereotypically "black" fare of chicken and possum.

> CHINK. You wantie some chop suey?
> COON. Dat depends entirely upon what de ingredients of de concoction am constituted of.
> CHINK. Chicken and—
> COON. Never mind de balance of de explanation—only waltz me to it. (*Chink hands Coon bowl containing chop suey and chop sticks.*) Smells jes like possum-soup. Got a spoon John?

CHINK (*pointing to chop-sticks*). You usie chop-stick.

COON. What! You expect me to eat wif de toothpicks? (Carter 5)

Significantly, *The Coon and the Chink* gives both of its characters an equal measure of the stage action and comic dialogue. Their parallel roles culminate in Coon's final proposal that the two "go on the stage" together. Coon then has an imaginary dialogue with an offstage figure, the manager of the "Metra-prop-olitan Opera House" (Carter 7), requesting a large sum of money. His negotiations include Chink, whom he evidently intends to pay much less. He tells the manager, "Sure we'll work for you, $12,000 for de act? Let's me see—dat's $2000 per night. Couldn't you make it $15,000, Mr. Manager?" and then, "I'll have to give my friend here a dollar or two" (Carter 7). Chink is suitably suspicious, replying in uncharacteristically unaccented English.

> COON (*Turns to* CHINK). Wants to shake hands with you. (*To manager*)
> My friend Mr. Oleo Margarine. (*To* CHINK) Wants to know if you'll
> work for $3 per week?
> CHINK (*to imaginary manager*). What do you take me for?
> COON (*to* CHINK). Says he wouldn't take you for a gift. (*To manager*)
> Oh yes, we'll be there all right. We'll rehearse right away. Good-
> bye Mr. Manager we are paralyzed to meet you. (COON *and* CHINK
> *sing last number.*) CURTAIN. (Carter 7)

This manager figure suggests that white authority over money and employment ultimately reasserts itself in the business dynamics between Coon and Chink. However, unlike Pattern in Williams's *Waxworks at Play*, the white manager of *The Chink and the Coon* never appears. While Coon seemingly emerges as superior to Chink in terms of anticipated financial gain, the meta-theatrical aspects of this ending—with both characters agreeing to enter show business—affirm their mutual benefit in this shared enterprise. Their partnership is also affirmed by musical numbers in which both Coon and Chink in turn sing "*any convenient song*" (Carter 4, 6) and finally perform their last musical number together.

While the more conventional versions of the Chinese laundry sketch pit a white character against the Chinese one, in *The Chink and the Coon* black and Chinese characters, despite their differences, are shown working together rather than competing onstage. Of course these moments might speak more to the camaraderie of two African American vaudevillians than they do to any real relationships between African Americans and Chinese immigrants. Chink's irate question to the imaginary white manager "What do you take me for?" could even allude to the fact that the actor playing the role is angry at being taken for a low-wage "Chink" (Carter 7). However, the details and distinctions in Carter's play do create parallels between the Coon and the Chink figures, even suggesting that they share food and strategies of survival; this is in stark contrast to other Chinese laundry sketches that focus on producing humor out of situations of mistrust, fear, and violence between a Chinese laundryman and his unhappy customers.

A brief description of another vaudeville duo also implies some potential for partnership rather than animosity between black and Chinese characters. According to an account in *Variety*, in 1919 Sam Cook partnered with another performer named Smith to do a laundry sketch at New York's American Roof Garden, adding another instance of a meta-theatrical twist:

> Cook, formerly of Cook and Stevens, is presenting their former
> type of act with a new partner. The characters are the "Coon" and
> "Chink," with Cook portraying the Chinaman. The routine of talk
> is over Smith claiming his laundry from the "Chink" and the latter
> refusing to give it without a check. The dialogue is witty throughout
> and both characterizations are splendidly rendered. However, where
> Cook removes his "queue" and tells Smith it was all a joke, it brings
> forth the fact that Smith does not like the Chinaman, as they are all
> "yellow." This should be eliminated, however, it is not in good taste
> with race conditions are they are in this country. It may be contended
> that this remark is the basis of the cue for Cook to start his song
> of "equality," but it is, nevertheless, in bad taste and really retards
> the value of a perfectly meritorious offering. A good double num-
> ber could take the place of this song and would polish up the turn
> considerably.[35]

This description leaves some ambiguity as to what the reviewer finds in bad taste, given the "race conditions as they are in this country": whether it is the derogatory use of "yellow" (suggesting both a racial slur and cowardice) to level insult at the Chinese, or the meta-theatricality of Cook revealing himself to be African American and then singing a "song of 'equality.'" In addition to referring to Chinese, "yellow" was also a term used for light-skinned African Americans, suggesting another level of ironic self-mockery. It further seems significant that it is Cook, the Chinese impersonator, who sings the "song of 'equality'" (though he sings it after he removes his Chinese disguise). Although the exact nature of "equality" is not specified in the review, the title recalls the well-known song "Human

The Chinese Laundry Sketch

Equality" by abolitionist and suffragist William Lloyd Garrison, which was in turn inspired by the poem "A Man's a Man for A' That" by the Scottish poet Robert Burns (used to illustrate the need for social equality in causes such as labor reform and the abolition of slavery). Arguing that "a common birthright crowns us all / With liberty, for a' that," the song "Human Equality" addressed the need to recognize the equality of women ("Down with all barriers that prevent / Her culture, growth, and a' that!"). In 1902, Garrison's son and namesake would also oppose Chinese exclusion on the grounds that it was contrary to U.S. principles of freedom and "a link in the chain of imperial aggrandizement."[36]

Thus Cook and Smith's rendition of the Chinese laundry sketch seemed to hint, however obliquely, at how racial hostility and inequality were experienced by both African Americans and Chinese immigrants. Where most versions of the laundry sketch emphasized the tensions between the cunning laundryman and his foolish customers, moments such as these suggest parallels between antiblack and anti-Chinese racism, a theme that would be taken up by Vachel Lindsay's short story "The Golden-Faced People."

LINDSAY'S "THE GOLDEN-FACED PEOPLE"

Writing in Chicago's *Broad Ax* in February 1920, NAACP field secretary William Pickens commented that the lesson taught by the 1919 Chicago and Washington riots, in which white violence was met with black retaliation, was one of black heroism: "that the Negro when attacked by white hoodlums is going to fight and not run." He then noted another incident in Chicago in which "two colored youths were passing down the street and a Chinaman came along behind them." Some "white toughs" whom the men passed did not harass the African Americans but instead addressed the Chinese man with "Hello, Chink—Rat-Eater—Slant-Eyes." Pickens was struck by how the Chinese man modeled his response after the African American defiance of racism: "Whereupon, the Chinaman conceived an inspiration and said passionately as he shook his head: 'Me, Nigger, too! Me fight like Nigger at Thirty-ninth street.'"[37]

Pickens's comments suggest how Chinese immigrants may have seen African Americans as models of racial protest. This tentative alliance in itself did not necessarily express a full-fledged political solidarity, but nonetheless, Pickens's account assumed close proximity, common experience, and fellow feeling between African Americans and Chinese immigrants. While such sentiments might be only obliquely registered in theatrical sketches such as Carter's *The Chink and the Coon,* Vachel Lindsay's "The Golden-Faced People" provides a more sustained opportunity to explore these nascent interracial connections. Published in the NAACP's magazine *The Crisis* in 1914, Lindsay opens his story with the typical character of a Chinese laundry-man "who ironed shirts superbly, yet with that irritating air of being a little above his business." The narrator describes a familiar sequence in which "old Yellow-arms clutched my week's washing because I had lost my half of his red ticket."[38] In a hurry to dress for a banquet in honor of Lincoln's birthday, the narrator tries to escape the laundry. This leads to a moment of slapstick violence: "Pushing the money towards him, I jumped for the exit with my goods. He turned out the gas. I heard him scramble over the counter. He was between me and the door. He hit me with the handle of his broom" (36–37).

Based on the Chinese laundry sketch, this opening scene turns into a dream fantasy of racial reversal. After being hit on the head, the white narrator dreams of traveling to a future in which Chinese people are dom-inant and the "pure and pale" are treated with contempt. An alternative racial history unfolds in which the white people enslaved by the Chinese had been liberated by a Chinese leader named "Lin-Kon." As Edlie Wong has illustrated, the white writer Lindsay's story revises a familiar narrative of Chinese as the "yellow peril"; it also speaks to the stigmatizing effects of the "separate but equal" racial structure established by the landmark 1896 Supreme Court case *Plessy v. Ferguson* by projecting black-white relations onto a fantasy of whites enslaved by Chinese.[39] The narrator's dream allows him to feel the fear of racism as well as internalized self-hatred toward his "white and ghastly skin" (40). Now identified with an inferior race of whites, the narrator makes a speech to a "curious audience" (39) of Eurasians, who applaud his plea for equality. He is then asked by the Chinese laundryman (who appears in his dream as his racial superior yet appears to be an ally) to give a similar speech at a banquet celebrating the birthday of "Lin-Kon" attended by pure-blooded Chinese. At that banquet, however, he is faced with disapproval from the Chinese audience, becoming "the cynosure of a thousand reproving and astonished glances." He tries to retrieve the man-uscript of his speech from the laundryman, only to find it changed "to my own bundle of laundry" as the laundryman's face "underwent a complete degradation"; "it shriveled like a leaf in a fire, it became petty and full of hate": "Uttering inarticulate cries he struggled with me for the bundle, and fell on one knee" (41). Enraged by the loss, the laundryman turns the assembly on him.

Threatened by Chinese mob violence, the narrator wakes from his dream to find "the white still supreme," with the realities of U.S. racial violence still operative. While he was unconscious, a white mob had lynched the Chinese laundryman, along with three others: a Japanese, a Greek, and "a nigger" who was hung because the mob "did not want to burn him alive on Lincoln's birthday" and who perhaps was, as the Irish policeman explains, "too free with his lip." The narrator retrieves his laundry bundle, which he opens to find a shirt "not soiled with blood where it would show" and attends the Lincoln's birthday banquet in which Lincoln is commemorated as "the self-made railsplitter and backwoodsman, the perfect pioneer type," without any mention of "the race question or the question of equality" (41–42).

"The Golden-Faced People" was directly influenced by Lindsay's response to the brutal 1911 lynching in Coatsville, Pennsylvania, of black steelworker Zachariah Walker, who was accused of killing a white policemen, as well as by his sympathetic readings of Harriet Beecher Stowe's *Uncle Tom's Cabin* and W. E. B. Du Bois's *The Souls of Black Folk*.[40] With its depiction of the multiracial victims of lynching, the story's finale also acknowledges, as Wong suggests, "the articulation of antiblack violence with nativist attacks on foreign immigrants."[41] Lindsay wrote a number of literary works that repurpose familiar oriental and black stereotypes even while challenging racial oppression and violence. His 1915 poem "The Chinese Nightingale" is rife with oriental fantasies of a mystical China but also presents a sympathetic portrayal of Chang, an immigrant laundryman. Images of Africans as primitive, savage, and superstitious permeate another 1915 poem, "The Congo: A Study of the Negro Race," which implicates colonial exploitation in Africa. In a similar fashion, "The Golden-Faced People" revisits the familiar elements of the Chinese laundry sketch onstage—the unintelligible and incorrigible immigrant entrepreneur, cultural misunderstanding, and the slapstick blows that ensue over the missing laundry ticket—in order to decry violence against African Americans and stigmatized immigrants. Lindsay's short story, directed at both white and African American readers, thus highlights both the numbingly repetitive "fun" of the Chinese laundry sketch and its potential to model and encourage racial hostility in the world outside the theater.

6

"MAYBE NOW AND THEN A CHINAMAN"

AFRICAN AMERICAN IMPERSONATORS
AND CHINESE SPECIALTIES

This chapter and those that follow emphasize how, in the late nineteenth and early twentieth centuries, African Americans who played oriental characters and tropes generated their own distinctive habits of racial performance. At first it appears that these habits differ little from those perpetuated by white actors. African American performers also capitalized on the popular interest in tales of oriental adventure and magic, exotic commodities, and erotic and sensual spectacles. But African American performances were also conditioned by the specific opportunities and constraints that governed black representation in commercial theater. As Robert Toll notes, the theater, and particularly minstrelsy, became "'one of the few opportunities for mobility—geographic, social, and economic' that was open to African Americans in the nineteenth century."[1] James Weldon Johnson observed in *Black Manhattan* that by the 1890s a new generation of experienced African American performers was poised to move away from "the tradition of the Negro as only an irresponsible, happy-go-lucky, wide grinning, loud laughing, shuffling, banjo playing, singing, dancing sort of being" onto "the second phase, or middle period, of the Negro on the theatrical stage in America."[2] This "second phase" included significant numbers of African

Americans in vaudeville, the entertainment form that became popular in the United States during the 1870s and 1880s. Drawing upon the performances of concert saloons, variety shows, the medicine show, and minstrelsy, vaudeville was rendered as "clean" entertainment by Tony Pastor's New York theaters and the chain of "polite vaudeville" houses of Benjamin Franklin Keith and Edward Franklin Albee (adoptive grandfather of the playwright Edward Albee) extending across the United States and Canada. African Americans worked in white-operated vaudeville from its early years on and later established a separate set of theaters and companies. With his theaters in Jacksonville, Florida, and touring troupe, the Rabbit's Foot Company, Pat Chappelle became one of the largest employers of African American vaudeville entertainers. Sherman H. Dudley set up a series of African American owned and operated vaudeville houses in the first decades of the twentieth century, which by the 1920s had developed into the Theatre Owners Booking Association, or TOBA.

Vaudeville's flexible structure, multiple specialty acts, and appeal to all-black as well as integrated audiences allowed African Americans a broader range of theatrical expression, including music and dance numbers, specialty numbers, and characterizations that were not specifically associated with black stereotypes. African American vaudevillians played Jewish, Dutch, German, Irish, Italian, Spanish, American Indian, Hawaiian, Chinese, Japanese, and "Hindoo" characters. This power to represent non-black characters with skill and even some measure of authenticity was seen as particular testimony to African American achievement and artistry. As African Americans affirmed their ability to perform a range of characterizations beyond minstrelsy's caricatures, they also challenged the idea that black bodies were limited to expressing some inherent and natural state of authentic blackness. In her 1934 essay "Characteristics of Negro Expression," Zora Neale Hurston would declare that "the Negro, the world over, is famous as a mimic" and that far from lacking in originality, mimicry "is an art in itself."[3] Cross-racial performance, and the exotic oriental role in particular, could demonstrate the actor's talents in capturing what was seen as the "essence" of another race.

This chapter traces how African American minstrel, vaudeville, and musical performers employed ethnic impersonations, particularly those of Chinese immigrants, not only to showcase their mimetic skills but also to challenge their confinement to stereotypical black roles. More than a half century after the success of Ira Aldridge in Europe and the UK, performing anything outside of minstrel caricature continued to be a hard-won privilege for most African American actors. In the 1890s and after, a new generation of talented performers still faced resistance when trying to prove themselves capable of the same versatility as white actors. The white male actor had long been seen as having a body that could serve as a neutral foundation for enacting characters of all races. In contrast, African American and other non-white performers were thought to be indelibly marked by their skin color and other racial features. In 1907, the African American newspaper the *Philadelphia Tribune* published the comment, "It seems strange that some white people never enjoy seeing the Negro attempt anything classical, but prefer 'coon songs,' etc. They don't care to see a black man imitate the white folk, but they have nothing to say about George Primrose, Billy West, George Thatcher, Lew Dockstader, George Wilson and a number of other white men, who have got rich by blacking their faces and imitating the Negro. I wonder what some white folks will say when they find some of us in heaven?"[4]

W. E. B. Du Bois's description of the "peculiar sensation" of "double-consciousness," a "sense of always looking at one's self through the eyes of others, of measuring one's soul by the tape of a world that looks on in amused contempt and pity," captures this tortured relationship between social actor and black racial role.[5] The ever-present need to hide inner feeling and tailor outward performance to white approval is also expressed in Paul Laurence Dunbar's eloquent lament:

> We wear the mask that grins and lies,
> It hides our cheeks and shades our eyes,—
> This debt we pay to human guile;
> With torn and bleeding hearts we smile,
> And mouth with myriad subtleties.[6]

For African American entertainers, what Dunbar calls "the mask" governed all aspects of their careers and fueled their professional anxieties. Even relatively successful African American stage performers such as Billy McClain, on tour in Australia in 1901, reported to the *Freeman* that "I am still battling along at the same old rate with the view of something better. I have a very good class of singers and specialists, all white. Great things are expected of us as Cordelia and myself are the only colored people on the bill, and I don't know that I am colored until I look in the glass."[7]

For this reason, a number of African American artists and critics expressed their preference for African American audiences. In 1909, the *Freeman* wrote that black venues such as Chicago's Pekin Theater were much more enjoyable, "because the average colored performer can say things in that theater that place him three times funnier than he would be at a white house—he is natural there, and any one is a good deal better, whether singing, dancing, or acting, when natural. Every slang phrase we understand, and of course he opens his heart to us, because he is among his own people."[8] When asked in 1931 by the *Baltimore Afro-American* which kind of house she and her sisters preferred, Mabel Whitman (of the Whitman Sisters, one of the longest-running and best-paid acts on the TOBA circuit) said, "I think beyond question that a colored audience is our favorite, for there we get full appreciation without grudge, for what we do and there is no such thing as a nasty little feeling that we are breaking in where we are not really wanted." Whitman continued, "You never have a real light colored star on the white stage. When we get too light, as we are (humorously), they won't really welcome you, but still it is a pleasure to know that you are able to qualify as a first class entertainer for that kind of audience; but, as for us, give us a colored audience any old day in the week."[9]

However, even when playing in all-black venues or reviewed by other African Americans, African American performers were not necessarily seen as having neutral bodies. Their facial appearance and skin tone were heavily scrutinized, and critics were quick to comment on the amount and kind of makeup they used. African American actresses were subject to particular surveillance, with reviewers leveling pointed criticism at the perceived preference for lighter-skinned female performers or attempts to "act white." In 1904, *Freeman* critic Sylvester Russell emphatically stated, "The problem of women of the colored race depends only upon their ability. Color cuts no figure with a colored actress. The quicker that managers and colored actors find this out the better. The woman with black or brown skin—I say without prejudice—with ability is far more attractive and fascinating to a white audience than light-colored ones."[10] Russell was not alone in his admonitions. Though largely complimenting a 1908 performance of Bert Williams and George Walker in *Bandanna Land*, Burton Beach nonetheless decried aspects of the makeup and movement: "Several members of the company—possibly out of sheer vanity—seek to make up in imitation of this or the other prominent American actress, and most of the women in the chorus affect the manners of white folk—from gait and gesture to rouge pot and powder. Imitation is the sincerest form of flattery, and there is no sociological harm in this instance, of course. But the Negroid illusion is spoiled; the realism, which the originator of the work had in view, is marred by the affectations of Caucasian traits."[11] Elwood Knox (son of *Freeman* owner George Knox) praised the chorus of *The Ruler of the Town*, a 1910 show by the Whitney and

Tutt Comedy Company: "You never saw a more beautiful set of girls in all your days." He added, "I thought they were pretty, because they were natural looking, for they had left off a whole box of rouge and paint, that most chorus girls think they should wear on their face to make them look like what they ain't."[12] Others warned of negative consequences from audiences when light-skinned actresses were paired with African American actors in blackface. Actress Carita Day, described in the *Freeman* as having "a slight tendency to be white" or "very fair with chestnut hair that has an African kink," was criticized for refusing to darken her skin for *Rufus Rastus*, which was perceived to create a "problem for the public to solve when they see Ernest Hogan made up as black as possible, making love to Miss Day, who just dotes on looking as white as she can."[13]

However, other commentary in African American newspapers stressed that racial similitude—whether in terms of skin tone or mannerism—should not be the sole measure of the actor's success. Reviewers emphasized the skills of African American performers in maintaining a degree of separation between actor and character, a skill that was seen as particularly necessary when taking on well-established racial types. A *Freeman* commentary on a 1915 Indianapolis Crown Garden performance of comedian Tim Moore in a one-man version of *Uncle Tom's Cabin* emphasized how each of the characterizations Moore played had become a cliché: "Moore's success depends on that fact solely, that nearly every person has seen the real *Uncle Tom's Cabin* play." The review emphasized Moore's "inimitable" skill and the ease with which he evoked well-known black and white characters through his own performance: "He starts out by making up as Legree and Uncle Tom at once; he daubed one side of his face white with a few touches from his powder box; the other side was already black—there you are. Legree, the cruelest of masters and Uncle Tom, the best of slaves. When the ability of Moore is known as a comedian one can easily imagine how he made this go by his dialogues and actions. He reached the climax of fun making when he meets little Eva in the other world."[14] This review showed that Moore did not disguise his dark skin color but rather turned it into a stage effect. He reduced the familiar characters and actions of *Uncle Tom's Cabin* to mere gestures, emphasizing not only the predictability of the story but also its previous history of cross-racial theatrical production: as a story written by a white woman about African American slaves, and then dramatized both by white performers in blackface and by African Americans.

Moore's version of *Uncle Tom's Cabin* suggests a set of parodic effects similar to that revealed in the history of the cakewalk. Rooted in West

"Maybe Now and Then a Chinaman"

African festive dance traditions brought to the United States by slavery, the popular dance enacted a mockery of white elite society, becoming, as David Krasner writes, "a two-sided parody."[15] Terry Waldo has described the cakewalk as beginning with "slaves who dressed up in 'high fashion' and mimicked the formal dances of their masters"; its movements were subsequently performed by white minstrels and then, in the ragtime era, performed by "blacks imitating whites who were imitating blacks who were imitating whites."[16] Moore's *Uncle Tom's Cabin* thus overtly foregrounded the transformative artistry of the African American actor, suggesting that the endless reincarnations of this story could be rendered obsolete by his "inimitable" versions.

A similar emphasis on the artfulness of the actor—as evidenced by attention to detail, the ability to enliven a role in a new way, and the laughter or admiration of the audience—is evident in reviews of African American performers who played non-black characters. Special praise was given to those who were seen to perform the roles of Jewish, Indian, Italian, Japanese, Hawaiian, Chinese, and other types as convincingly or even more memorably than their white counterparts. A 1911 *Freeman* review of the vaudeville duo H. Quallie Clark and Lena Clark commented that "Mr. Clark's impersonations were refreshingly new and he got away with some very difficult character stuff. I say 'new' advisedly, for it is not only something new to see a performer in black face get away with an impersonation of a Jew, but [it] is a distinct novelty as well." Like many other vaudeville shows, the Clarks' performance included several ethnic characters, including "another song by Mr. Clark, 'Go On, Good-A-Bye,' a Dago ditty," which "was also well received"; however, a Jewish novelty number garnered the most praise for H. Quallie Clark: "His Hebrew song, 'Rebecca,' won him big acknowledgment. At times it was hard for one to believe that he was a colored man, so perfect was his accent and so realistically faithful were his portrayals of a real Jew."[17] In 1913 another *Freeman* reviewer marveled that "Margie Crosby, the girl with a Jewish face," is a "reality" and "a finished performer." Crosby, who had appeared previously as part of a vaudeville duo with Tom Scott, shone in a striking solo number: "She enters singing, 'Ephram Jones' which is done with dash and pleasing movement. She comes back with 'In My Harem' done in Yiddish—a Hebrew impersonation. She shines here as a performer, doing the stunt equal to similar work seen on the best stages."[18]

African Americans also performed American Indian characters in ways that drew similar praise. In his favorable assessment of a 1904 production of Bob Cole's musical comedy *Looney Dreamland* by the Black Patti

Troubadours, Sylvester Russell said that the "most interesting chorus feature of all" was "Big Indian Chief," calling it "the first original development of Indian song music not in rag-time, by Cole and Rosamond Johnson," and concluding that "Negro actors make elegant looking Indians, so everything in that line was perfection."[19] The song "Love Me All of the Time" as sung by Theresa Bluford in a vaudeville act with Barrington Carter also drew acclaim from the *Freeman* in 1906: "Her appearance as an Indian maiden represented the highest grade of art."

> Her make-up is so exact that one seeing her anywhere could not help taking her for one who might be akin to Longfellow's "Hiawatha" or "Minnehaha." She was indeed clever in her gestures. She had the proper amount of that shyness that seems to be the nature of the Indian maiden and represented the highest grade of art when the lover makes his overtures to one. Other teams have failed in this same sort of an act and have failed flatly, and what seemed to be the failure was that they did not possess the talent. Carter and Bluford are extremely great in their portrayal because they have studied every way until they have brought it up to a realistic scene.[20]

In addition to demonstrating the performer's versatility, such ethnic impersonations were seen as evidence of the racial progress of African American theater. In a review of Gus Hill's Smart Set Company in 1905, Milton Lewis reflected upon the movement away from blackface type and toward refinement and universality:

> No disparagement is to be uttered against the black cork regime of the days gone by. They were a necessity from a theatrical standpoint and are, today, but they are not the "whole show." They delighted their tens of thousands, but harped always on a single string. The old order of dark was done and redone and then done again. Not only the uglier and lower phases of Negro life are to be depicted but those of refinement are to be delineated. The public has been artfully educated to give justice to whom justice is due and the ban of oppression gives way to the light of reason that claims the universality of art, the residence place to the contrary notwithstanding.

Lewis saw the Smart Set's show as "a composite study of the stage from a racial viewpoint" that included "every phase of stardom from low Negro comicalities to the most beautiful renditions of bits of opera, operatic in spirit and tone." This range of abilities shown by African American performers,

Lewis stated, would "prove the cramped condition of the colored performer." Not only could African Americans excel at both minstrel "comicalities" and more elite operatic selections, but they could also provide theatrical attractions that were seen as neither black nor white in form. Lewis noted that in this production the "Japanese with rikshaw [sic] excited admiration" and that there is "a superbly costumed chorus of Indian lads and maidens all of which makes a spectacular presentation that helps to make Smart Set's reputation enduring."[21]

For African Americans, moving out of blackface roles into other ethnic and racial types was clearly more than just a novelty act. The opportunity to enact roles that would not be confused with their offstage lives emphasized their skills at transforming into different characters and their ability to perform rather than just inhabit roles. As we have seen both with Ira Aldridge and Thomas Dilward's Japanese Tommy, the playing of oriental types, including Chinese, South Asian, Japanese, and Filipino characters, helped to enlarge the range of roles available to actors and display their versatility during a time in which African American artistic and creative expression was severely limited. The remainder of this chapter examines how the caricatures of Chinese male immigrants helped define a number of careers for African American comic actors, including Harry Fiddler, Tom Brown, Frank Walker, and George Catlin, among others. The praise for the artistry and verisimilitude of their Chinese impersonations would affirm that African Americans, like white actors, could convincingly portray characters who were seen as not only racially different but also particularly foreign in language and culture.

AFRICAN AMERICANS IN CHINESE ACTS

In 1916, Lester A. Walton, the theater critic for the New York–based African American newspaper the *New York Age*, reviewed an adaptation of Irish playwright Dion Boucicault's 1859 melodrama *The Octoroon*, performed by Anita Bush's All-Colored Dramatic Stock Company at Harlem's Lafayette Theatre. Louis Hallet had revised *The Octoroon* with new dialogue, including "a number of broad-minded views on the race question" that won "instant favor with the colored patrons, who evince[d] their approval by hearty applause." Walton found this production revelatory for its cross-racial casting as well; the production featured Charles Gilpin as the villainous white overseer, Jacob McCloskey; Mrs. Charles H. Anderson as the Southern belle, Dora; "Dooley" Wilson as George Peyton; Andrew Bishop as the "lazy

Indian," Wah-no-tee; and Anita Bush as the octoroon, Zoe. He concluded that "the colored performer has taken a long step forward in the realm of dramatic art."[22] In his *Octoroon* review, Walton emphasized, "For years the colored performer has been sadly declaring: 'Our field is limited; our color permits us to appear on the stage as Negroes only, maybe now and then a Chinaman.'"[23] His offhand remark about the occasional "Chinaman" as the exception to the limitations of casting affirms that by the second decade of the twentieth century, Chinese impersonation had become a regular feature of the African American stage.

There are conflicting accounts of when the comic Chinese immigrant character first appeared in African American theater. In 1910, Billy McClain recalled that his many accomplishments as an African American performer included a "first" with Cleveland's Minstrels: "Tom Brown and I were the first to do a sketch of a Chinaman and a 'coon' in Kansas City in 1887 at the Gaiety Theater, where the colored performers' reputation extended from Walnut Street to Independence Avenue, an area of ten blocks."[24] However, a 1921 review of a Darktown Follies production, *A Trip to Chinatown*, named George Catlin as "the first of our race to essay this character, doing it for more than twenty years."[25] Most likely, it was the celebrated comedian Billy Kersands who did the first African American versions of the Chinese immigrant type as part of his multiple comic roles in the 1879 E. S. Getchell operetta, *Urlina, the African Princess. Urlina* featured the well-known Hyers sisters (Anna Madah and Emma Louise) as leads, but according to the *San Francisco Bulletin*, "The comic element rested mainly on the shoulders of Billy Kersands, who personated six characters with marked success," including "'Tin-Ear,' a Christian Chinee." Kersands "was repeatedly recalled" for applause by the audience at the Bush Street Theatre.[26] A 1879 edition of the *New York Dramatic News* also reported on Kersands's "very amusing" Chinese impersonation in Stockton, California,[27] and a 1880 *Oregonian* review of an actual Chinese opera, *The Treaty between the Six Asiatic Nations*, even compared one of the real Chinese performers with Kersands: "The low comedian was funnier than Billy Kersands, of the Hyer[s] sisters' combination, and he was, if possible, uglier."[28]

By the 1890s, Chinese immigrant characters were regularly being performed by African American actors. In subsequent decades, these acts proliferated as a regular part of the professional minstrel, vaudeville, and musical theater stage. In August 1898, Tom Logan performed the sketch "Li Hi's Visit" at the Casino Roof Garden in New York; according to the *Topeka Plaindealer*, he "was 'made up' as Li Hung Chang, and rendered a song in

Chinese, looking so much like the famous statesman, and acting so naturally, that his impersonation was considered a marvel."[29] In 1898, Ernest Hogan's rewritten sketch of "On Jolly Coon-ey Island" for the Black Patti Troubadours also included Logan's "Wong Lung, a good natured Celestial," as well as a "Japanese Song and Dance" by the Meredith Sisters.[30] In the 1899–1900 season, Logan performed this characterization as part of Ernest Hogan's company touring in Honolulu; the *Pacific Commercial Advertiser* noted that in a production of *A Trip to Honolulu*, "Tom Logan gave a clever Chinese impersonation,"[31] while in *A Country Coon*, "Hogan, the basso, plays the heavy, a tough sport, while his namesake has an opportunity to display his skill in interpreting Chinese character and song."[32] The well-known comedian John Rucker (known for his "Alabama Blossom" routine) joined Henry Winfred as part of a successful "Chinaman and Coon" act that booked the Pantages and Loew vaudeville circuits in the United States and Canada in the 1915–16 season.[33] Winfred (also spelled "Winifred" or "Winfield" and a founder of the vocal group the Golden Gate Quartet)[34] had done an earlier version of the sketch in Connecticut in 1914.[35] He might have appeared as well in the April 1928 performance of "The Chinaman and the Coon," described as "a comedy riot with Winfield and Mills," and as part of the stage show accompanying a screening of the Lon Chaney film *The Big City* in Washington, DC.[36]

While many of these performers were much better known for other theatrical roles, Tom Brown, Harry Fiddler, Sam Cook, George Catlin, and Frank Walker became famous for their Chinese impersonations. Tom Brown performed in the late 1880s as an end man with McCabe and Young Minstrels; Henry Sampson speculates that he "could play every part in the show" and was especially notable for "doing a Chinaman under cork."[37] Around the time of the 1893 World's Fair in Chicago, Brown was featured in Richard and Pringle's Minstrels, the largest black minstrel troupe on the road, and his act included impersonations of Italian and Jewish as well as Chinese immigrants; one 1894 program lists him as a "Character Artist, Impersonating Chinese, Hebrew, and Italian."[38] Around 1895, Brown performed his Chinese act in the highly respected B. F. Keith vaudeville circuit.[39] These minstrel company and vaudeville experiences were undoubtedly the basis for the role he performed in the 1897 musical *A Trip to Coontown* and later musicals such as Ernest Hogan's *Rufus Rastus* (1906), which won him praise from the *Freeman* in April 1907: "Brown is one of the notable Negro actors of to-day. His finish makes him a pronounced success as an interlocutor, a monologist, a characterist, and an all-around man of indisputable value. His Chinese and Italian characterizations were especially good."[40]

After *A Trip to Coontown,* Brown partnered with Siren Navarro in a series of Chinese duo acts. A talented dancer, Navarro (also spelled "Nevarro") was hailed by the *New York Age* as "perhaps the only African American woman who has mastered the difficult art of toe dancing" and would later perform as the Filipina dancer and love interest Grizzelle in *The Shoo-Fly Regiment* (1906) as well as choreograph Bob Cole, J. Rosamond Johnson, and James Weldon Johnson's *The Red Moon* (1908). Her partnership with Brown initially ran into difficulties since, according to Sampson, "Brown had trouble convincing vaudeville managers to accept a black woman doing a Chinese part." For several months, "Miss Navarro accompanied Brown as they toured the theatres, Brown paying all the expenses although she was not getting paid. Brown finally won over the managers and Navarro joined the act as a paid performer."[41] This act became part of their two-year tour in Europe as well as developed into a specialty act, "Gimlet and Whirlina," in the star vehicle for Bert Williams, the 1909 musical *Mr. Lode of Koal.* Writing in the *New York Age,* Lester Walton noted that "the Chinese specialty of Tom Brown and Siren Nevarro won several encores."[42] This act was also reviewed favorably by the *Freeman* in 1909:

> Next Mr. Tom Brown, "Gimlet," enters, and when given the cue by Big Smoak he makes a lightning change—clever—and enters once more as the Chinaman that needs no introduction to most of my dear readers, but for the benefit of those who need an explanation regarding Tom Brown, I want to say that Tom Brown is without any reasonable doubt the greatest all-around character actor, "colored," in show business today extant. He sings "Chink, Chink Chinyman [sic]," assisted by eight girls dressed as boys in knickerbockers and blouse waists, playing bean bags. It makes a pretty picture. Tom Brown in the center and all the ponies playing ring around the Chink Chink Chinyman. Miss Navarro enters as a Chinese woman, and when the spotlight is flashed on her, why you go right back to Chinatown. Her makeup was perfect, and the little dialogue that this clever pair of colored artists have arranged is just as big a hit as it was in vaudeville, when presented at Hammerstein's Victoria a short time ago, when I saw them take four bows on second, something unusual for that theatre.[43]

Another famed performer of Chinese types was Harry Jacob Fiddler, recognized since the early 1890s as "the man of a hundred faces" and as a "perfect Chinese impersonator."[44] Fiddler (also occasionally spelled "Fidler")

Harry Fiddler and Reuben Shelton. *Indianapolis Freeman*, July 4, 1908.

did various impersonations for the 1896 Al G. Field musical *Darkest America* (though reviews of that show do not mention a Chinese act) and first played the role of Li Hung Chang in John Isham's 1896 musical revue *Oriental America* before Tom Brown took the role.[45] It is quite possible that he continued this act in other musicals as well: for instance, a review of the second iteration of Isham's musical show *Isham's Octoroons* (first performed in 1895) noted that "Harry Fidler, an eccentric character mimic, is amusing."[46] Fiddler continued to play Chinese characters in vaudeville, most notably in a specialty act with Reuben (Rubie) Byron Shelton that ran from 1908 until at least 1915. A 1908 *Freeman* reported that in their show, Fiddler and Shelton combined their comic impersonations with "straight" work in "wearing correct evening clothes, which they carry exceedingly well."[47] In 1915, the *Freeman* also praised the pair as a "clean, classy and comical act," with Shelton called "a splendid baritone singer and a phenomenal pianist, playing the popular ragtime selections of the classics with equal facility."[48]

Fiddler's mimetic ability was seen as a talent separate from his makeup and costume. A 1915 *Freeman* review stated that "Fiddler does not need the assistance of cork, wig, or whiskers to make him funny or help in his surpassing impersonations. He has complete control of the facial muscles and distorts and contorts them into any desirable position or shape. He has many rivals as a Chinese impersonator, but it is safe to say that Harry stands at the top of the list."[49] In 1938, Fiddler played at the Swingland Café in Omaha, Nebraska, where "his remarkable facial changes alone" were "sufficient to transform him from a Chinaman, Japanese emigrant, woman or chimpanzee to an elegant man about town."[50] Throughout his career, Fiddler was frequently compared with other Chinese impersonators: an 1899 *Topeka Plaindealer* review mentioned the Chinese role of Tom Brown in *A Trip to Coontown*, saying that "about the best compliment that can be paid Brown is to say that he has a clever imitator in the person of Jay Harry Fidler, who is now with Richards and Pringle's minstrels."[51] A 1924 assessment of the singer Jules McGarr in *Billboard* observed that "Jules was introduced thru the medium of the opening song in a Chinese character, which was very good, but Jules is not Harry Fiddler."[52]

But Fiddler too was subject to less favorable comparisons with other Chinese impersonators. In 1908 the *Freeman* noted that he performed "as a Chinaman for a minute or two at the opening" of his act with Shelton and that this "character is well-done," although Fiddler "is suffering this week through following an act in which a Chinaman is also prominent."[53] As suggested by a different *Freeman* review, the act that preceded Fiddler and Shelton was most likely the comic duo of Sam Cook and Jim Stevens, perhaps appearing in their laundry sketch. Comparing the two, this review praised Fiddler for his "extreme versatility" and Cook for his consistency:

> He [Fiddler] is rich in variety, evidencing a reserve fund of material which he can set forth at any moment, assuring a continuity without tiring his audience. For instance, his Chinese character is sufficient in itself for the making of a splendid hit. Stevens and Cook, the team

just preceding Fiddler and Shelton, went big owing to the Chinese impersonation as much as anything else. Cook came on the stage and went off a Chinaman and at no time did he tire. Fiddler's characterization is quite as taking; either would easily be mistaken for the real thing. In fact, Jake's face, his natural face, is in his favor, making him the better Chinaman as to physical appearance. Fiddler holds his Chinese characterization back; he gives just enough to show what he might do if he cared to.[54]

Quoting from *The Star*, *Freeman* reviewer J. D. Howard stressed the originality and uniqueness of Cook and Stevens, probably as a reaction to this comparison with the competing act of Fiddler and Shelton: "There is no place in their work that one can accuse them of theft or copying from others."[55] Howard commented of Cook's Chinese impersonation that "I have seen the 'Chink' of Tom Brown and others, but must say that caricature of the Celestial put forth by the Texas lad was the 'goods,' all wool and a yard wide."[56] Sam Cook was also praised for his Chinese characters in other shows and musicals, first with Billy Kersands's Minstrels in 1903, in the musical *7-11* (1922), and in *Hit and Run* (1924).[57] In 1929, William G. Nunn wrote in the *Pittsburgh Courier* that *7-11* featured a performance by "Chink," who was "the best oriental impersonator of his day."[58]

Like Tom Brown and Harry Fiddler, Frank Walker was known for his multiple impersonations including Chinese characters and also appeared in song-and-dance duos with Chinese themes. Of his 1915 appearance in a skit with Grace Johnson, Salem Tutt Whitney wrote for the *Freeman* that "Chinee Walker is well known as the foremost delineator of Chinese characters."[59] Walker appeared in the musical *Darkydom* (1915) as "Ah Sing, a Chinaman," and was listed as "Chinese Walker" in the cast of *Plantation Days*, which had several productions between 1922 and 1925.[60] Praising Walker's Chinese act in 1911 at the Crown Garden in Indianapolis, J. D. Howard also described his partner, "Little Pinkey," as "a dashing little soubrette, full of life," whose dancing "was a revelation."[61] "As delineators of oriental characters," Howard wrote, "they go to the head of the class," adding that "'Chinee Walker' has already won his spurs as a 'chink' impersonator, and he has about one real rival in all the theatrical field and that is Tom Brown. His 'Dago' is equally as strong and he uses both in the act." Another 1911 *Freeman* review praised Walker's mimicry, saying that "while he is not a real Chinese, he makes it very hard for his audiences to determine the fact, by the perfection of his characterizations," and that "as a Chinese impersonator he stands in a class by himself. He does not resort to the old staid line of stuff adopted by the ordinary performer in the delineations of 'Chink' character, but carves out for himself an individual field in which he stands alone. He makes a good 'Dago' also, and doubtless would be as strong in this character as that of Chinee were he to devote as much of his time to it as he does the Celestial."[62]

If not the first, George Catlin was, as a number of African American newspapers called him, one of the most significant "originators" of the Chinese immigrant act in African American theater, doing it for more than twenty years before retiring to join the business staff of Harlem's Lafayette Theatre.[63] A review of Mahara's Mammoth Minstrels in 1899 said that "George Catlin, the premeir [sic] Chinese impersonator keeps the audience guessing whether he is the genuine article or not."[64] Later in his career, Catlin appeared with Bob "Dad" Kelly in Chinese routines such as "The Chinaman and the Burglar," advertised for the Lafayette Theatre.[65] According to Salem Tutt Whitney, both were well received, with the conclusion that "Bob Kelly and Geo. Catlin, the Chinese and the Coon, are pioneers and originators in their particular line of work, and one of the big time colored acts."[66] Time and again, Catlin received attention for his convincing Chinese portrayals. A 1916 announcement for acts at Philadelphia's Gibson's New Standard Theatre lauded Catlin and Kelly for the skit "The Chinaman and the Coon": "They introduce new songs, new talk, and with the assistance of a new $200 drop they produce much laughter—just what the act is meant to do. Kelley is seen as the 'Cullud Gem'an' without a name, but has a number—that's all and his philosophy is humorous. George Catlin has the reputation of being the best Chinese impersonator in the country and speaks the real language."[67]

There is no evidence that Catlin actually spoke Chinese, but praise for the convincing nature of his impersonation was repeated in a 1900 discussion of African American comedians in the *Topeka Plaindealer*, in which Catlin was said to be someone "who can impersonate a Chinaman without burlesquing it."[68] Another reviewer in the *Plaindealer* observed that in *The Policy Players*, "George Catlin is artistic in his Chinese impersonation, so quiet and life-like, in fact, that the merit of his work is likely to be overlooked."[69] A year later, the *Freeman* favorably noted Catlin's transformation into Chinese roles, "considering the fact that he is of a very dark complextion [sic] with a very heavy mustache," as "something wonderful; while his 'pigeon-English' is remarkable."[70] However, an assessment of *Sons of Ham* in the *New York Telegraph* later that year was much more critical of Catlin's use of makeup to lighten his skin, noting "a small Chinese bit by George Catlin, who makes up too white."[71]

Chinese immigrant characters were regularly included in amateur as well as professional African American theatricals. For instance, a *Negro World* review of a 1922 production of N. R. Harper's "great race drama" *Tallaboo*,[72] presented by the dramatic club of the Marcus Garvey Universal Negro Improvement Association for one night at the Lafayette Theatre, praised the "good acting" of "Mrs. Dasong A. Tobias" playing "Chink, Chinaman."[73] Like the characters played by white actors, these yellowface roles portrayed Chinese immigrant men as not only comically foreign but also deviant and dangerous. Chinese characters were associated with opium addiction, and Chinatown was seen as a lurid place of temptation and dissipation. Sabine Haenni has characterized the gaudy "surface aesthetic" associated with turn-of-the-century New York Chinatown as expressing "the fear that 'Chinese-ness' may be beyond the bounds of an intelligible identity or a coherent self, especially when excessive decorations seem to mark mere profusion and lack of order."[74] For African Americans, visits to Chinatown could well have symbolized the temptations of modern life in the urban North. This seems to drive the storyline of *The Devil*, a 1922 show written and produced by Quintard Miller, in which Eugene Shields plays "One Lung, a Chinaman" alongside other allegorical characters such as "The Devil," "Young Man," "Poverty," and "Purity." The plot summary describes "the attempt of the Devil to lure a young man into the path of ruin and destruction" as directly connected to a Chinatown setting; the play resolves when "a friend of the young man, who was not tempted by the devil, rescues the young man by 'shooting up' the Chinese 'dive' where he (the young man) has been lured."[75]

African American performers continued to enact comic versions of the Chinese immigrant character well into the twentieth century and after (witness Eddie Murphy's portrayal of Mr. Wong in the 2007 film *Norbit*). However, by the early 1900s, African American newspapers were commenting on the distorted and problematic nature of racial and ethnic caricatures as connected to antiblack racism. In April 1904, Sylvester Russell wrote at length protesting the offensive use of racial slurs in songs of the day. Russell argued that similar slurs directed against Jews and Italians were no longer used in the press, stating that "the Negro race has no objections to the word 'coon' and no objections to the word 'darkey.' We care nothing for the words black, colored, or Negro, but we do object to the word 'nigger.'" Russell drew a contrast between two other ethnic groups, first "American

Jews," who "have suffered from American prejudice," and yet "the success-ful Jews, regardless of this fact, are not affected with race prejudice." The Irish, on the other hand, "as it shows by their daily history, are the most prejudiced race of all towards a black man," and "in the North the word . . . comes almost exclusively from this race of children, taught to them in their homes and through the popular songs." Russell noted that this prejudice continued in spite of the fact that the Irish were also the targets of racial stereotype: "Why, the Irish boys told me to my face that they do not like the song 'The Mick Who Threw the Brick.'" He concluded, "Now it is time for us to tell every race under the sun, just for fun, that we do not care for any more ignorant display of the word . . . from chumps of song writers, unfair publishers and crusty stage performers."[76] A similar protest against "coon" was published in the January 1909 *Freeman*, lamenting that "the people, especially the children, are educated that a colored man is a 'coon'" and that "what is meant for a jest is taken seriously." The essay ends by describing how Irish immigrants successfully protested ethnic caricature: "The in-habitants of Butte, Mont. are mostly Irish. Two years ago a burlesque show came there and posted lithographs caricaturing and ridiculing the Irish. The company was arrested, the house closed and the bills torn down and the show had to leave town. Abraham Lincoln once wrote a harsh letter to a man and after considering how the man might feel over it he threw the letter in the stove. Every composer who writes a song with the word 'coon' in it should do the same."[77]

In the decades that followed, terms such as "chink" and "Jap" also came under discussion. In 1919, the *New York Age* reported a campaign under the auspices of the Student Department of the National Board of the YWCA against the use of racial slurs. Posters were sent to white branches of the YWCA throughout the United States with the request to stop these "Things that Sting":

Dago and Sheeney and Chink
Greaser and Nigger and Jap
Lo! We make the stung-man sink
And stab the soul with hateful word
Dago and Nigger and Chink
DO YOU
LYNCH THE SPIRIT
Of those whose heritage
Is different from yours?[78]

"Fiddler and Shelton: Those Two Clever Boys."
Indianapolis Freeman, February 26, 1910.

In the same spirit, a 1934 editorial by Beatrice Murphy in the *Washington Tribune* urged African American readers to think about their own choice of terms:

A well-known comedian on the radio utters a word in speaking of the Negro, and race jumps up in arms. They call it an insult. They threaten to boycott the radio station, the comedian, and the company sponsoring the program.

And that, my dear, is the narrow-minded race to which you and I belong: a race which calls an Italian a wop or a dago; the Chinaman a chink, the members of the Caucasian race ofays, and speaks scornfully of the "dirty Jew." A race which can laugh at and appreciate a joke on any one else in the world but is ready to commit murder when the joke is turned on it. . . . A race which keeps itself in the gutter with its black faced comedians and its smushy jokes and yet expects the world to respect it.[79]

Unfortunately, there is little in the archives that reveals what African American impersonators thought of the Chinese subjects that they mimicked. However, an interesting cartoon in the February 1910 *Freeman* depicts Fiddler and Shelton in their Chinese act. Captioned "Fiddler and Shelton: Those Two Clever Boys," the top frame of the cartoon shows a well-dressed Shelton at the piano with Fiddler in his Chinese impersonation, detailing a comic exchange that draws a direct parallel between acts of racism faced by African American and Chinese immigrant men.[80]

It is not certain whether any actor intended to perform or any audience intended to watch anything more than glitzy tomfoolery. But examples such as these indicate that performers were aware of how racial typecasting was directed at Chinese immigrants as well as at African Americans. This sensibility also seems behind an offhand remark by Harry Fiddler published in the "Stage" section of the *Freeman* in August 1900. Included among the other theatrical news, the comment hinted that at least one African American performer was well aware of the strong anti-Asian sentiments of the time; it read that "Harry Fidler ain't doing his Chinese Turn this season. He is afraid some Irishman will take him for a Chink."[81]

7

· • • •

DIVAS AND DANCERS

ORIENTAL FEMININITY AND
AFRICAN AMERICAN PERFORMANCE

· • • •

Featured as the "Black Venus" in Sam T. Jack's 1890 *Creole Burlesque Show*, Dora Dean later performed with her husband, Charles Johnson, as the "King and Queen of Colored Aristocracy," dancing the cakewalk in impeccable evening dress and receiving top billing in integrated and all-black vaudeville shows. A 1913 review in the *Freeman* gives a glimpse of Dean's flamboyant stage presence, describing how, in addition to being "known the world over as the only lady of color doing the beautiful electrical spectacular production, known as the serpentine fire dance and French plastique poses," she appeared in the latest fashions: "Her wardrobe is par-excellent, she having just received some beautiful Parisian gowns for her next act, which she is now rehearsing." In this particular show, "Queen Dora" also included some "special scenery, which consists of three drops and one large Chinese dragon head."[1]

"Queen Dora" spotlights how the habits of performing race inevitably also entail performances of gender and sexuality. Dean was one of many American female performers who employed oriental touches to add variety, visual pleasure, and in many cases erotic titillation to their acts. While African American men such as Tom Brown, Harry Fiddler, Sam Cook, George Catlin, and Frank Walker became known for playing undesirable Chinese immigrant characters, African American women such as Dean highlighted the allure associated with oriental femininity. But though these were the same roles as those of white female performers—exotic love interests, beautiful princesses, demure and compliant wives, the inhabitants of the seraglio—the cross-racial performances of African American women were subject to the additional pressures of racial typecasting and ideals of appropriate feminine behavior and domesticity.

The blackface minstrel stage had already associated the black female body with licentious display. Caroline Yang has pointed out, for instance, how the figure of the "yellow gal" as desirable mixed-race woman "masks the history of rape and sexual violence against Black female captives and the exploitation of those captives' productive and reproductive labor in slavery."[2] The oriental specialty acts played by African American women likewise utilized but also carefully circumscribed oriental feminine attraction within accepted norms of middle-class respectability. This can be seen in the Chinese duo acts taken up by Sidney Perrin and Goldie Crosby at Chicago's Pekin Theater in 1910, in which Perrin "makes up as a typical Chinaman, uses the language, acts the part and then dances and dances more" and then is joined by Goldie Crosby, described as "a neat little soubrette" who, "much to her credit, 'togs' up in attractive costume." Writing for the *Freeman*, Cary Lewis found that "as a colored act they more than upheld the profession."[3] The well-known Chinese impersonator Frank Walker also took part in a Chinese duo with "Little Pinkey" in a 1913 performance at the Indianapolis Crown Garden Theatre. Walker first sang the song "Chop Suey, Suey" and then was joined by Pinkey for "Tinga Sing" as well as a Chinese dance. A *Freeman* review complimented this "bit of Chinese impersonation" with "rich costumes," finding that "Pinkey as a Chinese lady fits well into her partner's work" and that this team set a standard "that helps largely to show the progress of the race on the stage. Their work is a study as well as entertaining."[4] These reviews of male-female "Chinese duos" suggest a performance far different from the rowdy interracial banter of the two-men "Chinaman and Coon" sketches. Here the Chinese man is no longer seen as a threatening and scheming figure; instead, both he and the attractive "Chinese lady" are quaintly domesticated through song and dance.

While charges of prostitution defined the exclusion of actual nineteenth- and early twentieth-century Chinese immigrant women,[5] musical and theatrical performances channeled their characterizations into respectable monogamy, such as is demonstrated in the lyrics of the popular song "Chinese Blues." Written by the white writers Fred D. Moore and Oscar Gardner in

Divas and Dancers

1915 and incorporated by the "Father of the Blues," W. C. Handy, into his 1926 *Treasury of the Blues*,[6] the song describes a "Chinaman" who "wash 'em laundry all day," is addicted to opium (he "feels his habit coming on again"), and sings the mournful refrain, "I got those Ipsing Hong Kong Ock-a-way Chinese Blues." He has a relationship with a "little China gal," to whom he pleads plaintively,

> Listen to those Chinese Blues,
> Honey gal, I'm crying to you,
> Won't you open that door and let me in.

But while the song imagines a rift between the two (perhaps because he "smoke 'em pipe a long long"), the relationship between him and his "little China gal" ultimately shows her loyalty:

> She love him alright,
> He love little China gal too,
> So he sing to her ev'ry night.[7]

The Chinese female character is pictured as patient, forgiving, and loyal in the face of her beloved's flaws. Her presence ultimately transforms the Chinese immigrant man into a sympathetic figure, seeking refuge from his daily toil and loneliness with his "little China gal." The song was performed by both white and African American singers; for instance, Babe Brown sang the song at the Crown Garden Theatre, Indianapolis, in 1913, prompting the comment that "her last number is the 'Chinese Blues.' Not greatly different to the colored blues, but they are the blues just the same."[8]

The examples in this chapter highlight how oriental characterizations and themes enabled some noteworthy leading roles for African American women. These included displays of passionate intensity and impressive physicality that were carefully managed in keeping with the propriety of middle-class racial respectability. Perceptions of feminized oriental excess were strategically contained through assurances of discipline and management, the refinement of sensuality, the selection of appropriate decorative scenic and costume choices, and virtuosic displays of musical technique and stylized choreography. Though taking on characterizations that were rife with illicit passion and rebellious energy, such as the operatic heroine Selika, the biblical figure of Salome, or the exotic dancer, African American women emphasized the performance of oriental femininity as vigilantly regulated, self-consciously artful, and all in good taste.

AFRICAN AND INDIAN PRINCESSES:
THE HYERS SISTERS' *URLINA*

Beginning in December 1900, an article published in several African American newspapers speculated as to why, despite the popular rage for ragtime and the cakewalk, only two African American companies had "won permanent success," both headed by "women whose voices were of no ordinary metal." The unnamed author credited the success of the companies that included the Black Patti Troubadours (led by Sissieretta Jones) and the Hyers Sisters not only to vocal talent but also to watchful male supervision, whether by Rudolph Voelckel and John J. Nolan, the white managers of the Black Patti Troubadours, or the father of the Hyers sisters, Samuel B. Hyers.

> Twenty years ago the Hyer[s] sisters drew great houses everywhere, their company being made up much after the same model as that of the "Black Patti"—opera, burlesque, and single vaudeville turns, of the best class. The Hyer sisters were popular because they could sing and because they were well managed. It is for the same reason, likely, that the "Black Patti" has had, up to date, five years of unparalleled popularity. She has two managers who understand their business—the operatic, concert and vaudeville. Messrs. Voelckel and Nolan, while manager of the Carnegie Music [H]all of New York, introduced Paderewski to the American public. It is no wonder that in such hands . . . the "Black Patti" company should have been well organized and won a splendid success.[9]

Assurances of cultivation, refinement, and careful male management accompanied the appearances of many successful African American women, particularly those who appeared on integrated stages. The Hyers sisters, Anna Madah Hyers and Emma Louise Hyers, were a prominent example.[10] The *New York Tribune* lauded a 1871 performance at Steinway Hall by saying that they were "by no means mere 'Jubilee' singers" and noting in their program "several airs and duets from 'Martha' and 'Trovatore,' the last being the 'Miserere,' which called forth hearty applause."[11] The *New York Evening Telegram* found that these selections "embraced a high order of music, operatic and otherwise; and were rendered with a taste and grace that elicited frequent applause. One of the young girls possesses a very pure soprano, and the other an equally excellent contralto voice; and singly or together, their execution is marked by a refinement, culture, and attractiveness that deserve first-class audiences and first-class appreciation."[12] While both sisters performed with minstrel companies such as Callender's Colored Minstrels and the racially integrated Ideal Uncle Tom's Cabin Company (in which they played "double" versions of Topsy), they were best known for singing classical opera and concert songs to mixed audiences.[13] Peter Hudson identifies early nineteenth-century African American opera singers and performers such as Anna Madah Hyers and Emma Louise Hyers as some of the earliest "crossover" artists of the nineteenth century: they "transgressed the boundaries between high and low culture by playing the marginal American concert stages . . . as well as minstrel and vaudeville shows" in an attempt to gain success despite frequent restrictions from major (white) American stages and touring circuits.[14]

While their musical talents offered the Hyers sisters some degree of opportunity, the concert stage was far from a level playing field even for these gifted performers. African American singers were often described as naturally suited to spirituals, ragtime, and blues, and their selection of Euro-American operatic selections or art songs was both marveled at and questioned. Most often Anna Madah and Emma Louise offered a blend of opera excerpts, art songs with popular spirituals, "jubilee" songs, and comic minstrelsy. At least one of their productions featured a prominent oriental theme as well.

After a successful set of U.S. tours beginning in 1871, Anna Madah Hyers and Emma Louise Hyers began to perform in musical dramas. The first, written for them by Joseph Bradford, a white playwright and former Union soldier, was *Out of the Wilderness*, later called *Out of Bondage*. Premiering on March 26, 1876, at the Academy of Music in Lynn, Massachusetts, *Out of Bondage* depicted a slave family in the south before and after the Civil War, with musical selections integrated loosely into the plot.[15] In 1878, the Hyers sisters began to juxtapose *Out of Bondage* with another musical play, Ellen S. Getchell's *Urlina, the African Princess*.[16] This "new burlesque" was promoted as being "of African extraction."[17] Its "African" setting has been noted by contemporary scholars as making it "the earliest known African American play set in Africa." Jocelyn L. Buckner has remarked that *Urlina* "marks the beginning of a trend in African American theatrical performances characterized by a stylized longing and desire on behalf of black artists to acknowledge and celebrate their ancestral roots."[18]

Interestingly enough, a review of a 1878 production in Minneapolis characterized the story of *Urlina* as "oriental and gorgeously costumed," and another 1879 review in Victoria, British Columbia, identified *Urlina* as an "original oriental entravaganza [sic]."[19] This conflation of Africa with the Orient was undoubtedly due to *Urlina's* nature as an operatic burlesque that borrowed from a variety of theatrical sources, including Shakespeare's *Tempest*, as summarized in a Victoria review in *The Colonist*.

> The plot embraces the story of a banished princess (Miss Anna Hyers) who is sent to a desert island by a cruel uncle, who is also a usurper of the throne. A witch swears enmity to the usurper because of having sold her children into slavery, and she incites Prince Zurleska (Miss Emma Hyers) the son of the usurper, to rescue the captive princess. The princess is rescued in company with Nubiana, a gushing female who declares that, until the Prince's advent to the island, she "never saw a man." Eventually she is arraigned before the King and sentenced to death by starvation, but the sentence is averted through the instrumentality of the witch and at last the princess ascends to the throne.[20]

Though a burlesque, *Urlina, the African Princess* served as a serious vehicle for the vocal talents of both Hyers sisters. A review in Oregon's *Daily Astorian* noted that Anna Madah's performance was "modest and unassuming," saying that "she sang her numbers with true feeling" and finding the second act solo to be "very sweetly performed."[21] The review contrasted Anna Madah's role as Urlina with the part of Prince Zurleska, a mezzo-soprano "breeches" part played by her sister Emma Louise, who was seen as "vivacious, boyish and dashing." Another review in *The Colonist* praised Anna Madah's soprano voice as being "of rare cultivation and compass," describing how "her upper notes are particularly clear and sweet, and her acting last night was unassuming, but as lifelike as possible," and noting that "she was frequently applauded for the solos allotted to her."[22] Emma Louise was thought to be "a very pleasing actress, full of that dash and vivacity requisite to render the character thoroughly successful, and has a rich contralto voice, over which she possesses perfect control." *Urlina* blended the operatic talents of the Hyers sisters with comic roles enacted by the cross-dressed Willie Lyle as "Nubiana" and by Billy Kersands, who played six different characters: a missionary "African Irishman" and his anxious wife, a pet monkey named "Jumbo," an African "fetish" man, a "wonderful terpsichorean ostrich," and "Tin Ear the musical Chinaman." According to the *Daily Astorian*, Kersands performed "each part with an energy peculiar [to] his own, and provoked frequent ebulitions [*sic*] of pleasure from the audience."[23]

However memorable, Kersands's comic moments as "Tin Ear the musical Chinaman" were clearly not the main reason why several reviews identified the play, set in Africa, as "oriental." While its burlesque elements undercut the seriousness of grand opera, *Urlina* also capitalized on the widespread popularity of another operatic character, a princess designated as both African and oriental. A photograph of Anna Madah Hyers as Urlina shows her wearing an asymmetrically draped skirt with a tight bodice, armbands on her bare arms, elaborate headdress, multiple necklaces, and sandals. This style of dress bears a marked resemblance to the costume worn by soprano Marie Sasse in the role of Selika, a leading role in the highly successful tragic opera *L'Africaine*, the last work of German composer Giacomo Meyerbeer, which premiered at the Opera de Paris in 1865.

Like *Urlina*, Meyerbeer's *L'Africaine* features exotic settings, romantic triangles, and, even more importantly, a degree of ambiguity in the racial identification of its noble heroine. Based on a French libretto by Eugène Scribe, the opera depicts a fictional version of the adventures of Vasco da Gama. The Portuguese explorer is hopelessly loved by Selika, the queen of an undiscovered island.[24] In act 1, Vasco declares adamantly that though called "L'Africaine" because she has been enslaved by Africans, Selika as well as her loyal servant Nelusko are not African slaves; he sings that "their features; strange, too, their garb; and skin / Of bronze—these mark them a tribe yet unknown."[25] Act 4 begins at "the entrance of a Temple of Indian architecture" where "the High Priest of Brahma, Brahmins and Indians of various Castes are assembled," and Nelusko hails them with an oath to the Hindu gods: "Oh Brahma! Vishnu! Siba [Shiva]!" (*L'Africaine* 55). Selika's people are barbaric and superstitious and eager to put strangers to death. Nelusko in particular is full of hatred and treachery, ready to kill all Christians. However, Selika is somewhat redeemed by her tragic love for Vasco and acts altruistically in allowing him to escape with her Portuguese rival in love, Ines.

Selika is clearly a noble figure of sexual attraction and great passion, as shown in act 5, in which the marooned Vasco suddenly feels wild desire for her. But Vasco's all-too-temporary infatuation is interrupted by the voice of Ines, who is being led away to her execution. When Selika realized that Vasco still loves Ines, she moves past her jealous anger and gives them their freedom. After they depart, Selika poisons herself with deadly blossoms and dies in the arms of her loyal Nelusko. This final death-by-flower scene provides another opportunity for an oriental fantasy in which Selika imagines

Emilio Naudin as Vasco da Gama; Marie Battu as Ines; Marie Sasse as Selika; and Jean-Baptiste Faure as Nelusko in the 1865 Paris Opera premiere of Giacomo Meyerbeer's opera *L'Africaine*. Bibliothèque Nationale de France.

that she sees "the bright host / That guard Brahma's abode" and that she is being carried to heaven as

> Fair houris round with smiling glance,
> In mighty circles dance,
> With footsteps light. (*L'Africaine* 81)

Urlina, the African Princess is obviously more comic than tragic; nonetheless, its musical burlesque seems to draw on explicit references to Meyerbeer's opera, especially in its characterization of the title character as hailing from India rather than Africa. This suggestion of oriental origin may have allowed *Urlina* a degree of expressive freedom and to move away from the inevitable stereotypes that would have been associated with "African" representations. By basing the character of Urlina on a noble princess who, despite being labeled as "African," is ambiguously racialized, Anna Madah Hyers at least to some degree could escape the confines of black typecasting. As the *Daily Astorian* noted, "Her action and manner were most graceful, and these qualities, heightened by eminently appropriate costume and ornaments, caused this young lady to make a highly favorable impression as the demi-savage though gentle princess."[26] The echoes of Meyerbeer would have allowed the character of Urlina to express heightened emotions of love

Divas and Dancers

Anna Madah Hyers in the role of Urlina in *Urlina: The African Princess* (1879).
Photograph by Bradley and Rulofson, San Francisco.
Huntington Library, San Marino, CA.

and loyalty that tempered the display of her erotic attractions. Descriptions of Urlina suggest an exotic princess who seems in fact much more sensible and respectable than the jealous and suicidal Selika. Implied comparisons with the well-respected operas of Meyerbeer would have also placed the other "demi-savage" island characters in a more refined light. The *Daily Astorian* review suggested that *Urlina* featured the physical appeal of an African American male chorus, if not dancing houris: "The costumes are beautiful and appropriate, and this greatly enhances the novelty of colored actors appearing as native Africans. The appearance of the colored warriors of the king, all well-built, muscular fellows, in the scanty but becoming costume, is not the least pleasing effect apparent in the piece."[27] Nonetheless, negative perceptions of Africans as savage and barbaric did affect *Urlina's* reception, as suggested by the *San Francisco Bulletin's* comment that "*Urlina, the African Princess*, is a hint of civilization in Zululand, with the incongruous elements of society which would naturally result."[28]

There were probably other incentives for using *L'Africaine* as one of the direct influences for *Urlina, the African Princess*. That the Hyers sisters paired their 1879 performances of *Urlina* not only with *Out of Bondage* but also with Gilbert and Sullivan's 1878 *H.M.S. Pinafore* (in a production featuring Billy Kersands as Dick Deadeye)[29] suggests that they were eager to use audience familiarity with the most popular operas and operettas of their time to demonstrate their musical versatility.[30] A *Daily Astorian* review suggested that the music of *Urlina* was much more serious than that given to the usual "opera-bouffe extravaganza": "The music is meritorious, but does not possess the peculiar pungency and lightness common to extravaganzas, but would be more acceptable in real opera, sans the bouffe."[31] Their production of *Urlina, the African Princess*, moreover, was not the first or last time that talented African American singers looked to Meyerbeer's Selika for a leading role with complexity and power. Carolyne Lamar Jordan has remarked that *L'Africaine* was "a particular favorite of African-American singers."[32] Another renowned African American singer even took "Selika" on as her stage name: Marie Williams (née Smith), a coloratura soprano who sang for Rutherford B. Hayes in 1878 and was the first African American artist to perform in the White House.[33]

Along with Giuseppe Verdi's *Aida* and Giacomo Puccini's *Madama Butterfly*, *L'Africaine* is one of a number of famous operas in which sexual allure and high passion are associated with oriental and African heroines. Sung first by white divas, the female characters of Aida, Cio-Cio-San, and Selika allowed for a degree of racial ambiguity that permitted African American singers to perform leading roles in otherwise all-white companies. Singing in Verdi's *Aida* with Alfredo Salmaggi's company at the New York Hippodrome in 1933, Caterina Jarboro was the first African American woman ever to perform a leading role with a white opera company in the United States; prior to this, Jarboro had performed Selika as well as Aida at the Chicago Grand Opera Company.[34] In 1946, Camilla Williams, the first African American to receive a regular contract with a major American opera company, made her New York City Opera debut as the Japanese Cio-Cio-San in Puccini's

Madama Butterfly.[35] Of course, aspects of these operatic characterizations remain problematic even when sung by African Americans. *L'Africaine* and *Madama Butterfly* center on stories of interracial love, imperial conquest, and exotic women for whom sexual passion leads to tragedy.[36] However, like the operatic selections that would be used in musicals such as *Oriental America* (one of the subjects of the next chapter), these leading roles were significant in making possible at least some opportunities for African American divas to showcase their talents.

ORIENTAL DANCERS AND ABYSSINIAN MAIDENS

Operatic characters such as Selika and Butterfly suggest larger anxieties over the management of female agency and sexual activity; similar concerns were articulated through the figure of the oriental dancing girl. These characterizations became especially popular in the United States with the 1893 World's Columbian Exposition in Chicago. American interest in *danse du ventre*, or belly dance, was galvanized by the displays at the Midway Plaisance such as "A Street in Cairo," where, as Donna Carlton has described, crowds witnessed demonstrations of dance from North Africa and the Middle East such as "Egyptian-style *ghawazi*, Algerian Ouled Nail and handkerchief dancers, and a Turkish-style *cengi*" as well as the imitations of "Parisian dance hall entertainers."[37] Although there were earlier well-attended exhibits of North African and Middle Eastern culture in both Europe and the United States, including the tableaux vivants at the Paris International Exhibition of 1867 and a Tunisian "handkerchief dance" at Philadelphia's 1876 Centennial Exposition,[38] the Chicago Exposition was the defining point in the popular imagination of oriental dance. At the fair and afterward, versions of these oriental dances, some performed by Syrian- or Algerian-born dancers such as Fahreda Mahzar Spyropoulos, Ashea Wabe, and Fatima Djemille and others by "pseudo-Oriental beauties decked out in their exotic best" were regularly featured in amusement parks, carnivals, circuses, vaudeville, burlesque, and film.[39] The spectacular 1892 show *Egypt through the Centuries* at New Jersey's Palisades Amusement Park featured hundreds of "dancers, jugglers, serpent-swallowers, soldiers, camels, and floats,"[40] and Coney Island's popular "Streets of Cairo" exhibit featured Spyropoulos as "Little Egypt" as well as many other similar performances.

European and British fascination with female dancers from the Middle East, North Africa, and South Asia long predated these American appearances. For instance, Carlo Zen, son of the Venetian deputy ambassador to the Ottoman Empire, described a celebration held by Tuscan and Venetian merchants in Istanbul for the carnival of 1524; among the different entertainments were the performances of the *zenghi* (*cengi* in Turkish), "talented, beautiful Turkish girls" who "played instruments and sang," then performed a "very lascivious" dance:

> They were making movements with their heads, twisting their arms, and moving their lips; they were throwing their hair that fell on their shoulders sometimes toward their chin sometimes to their backs. They were raising the cymbals in their hands to their temples gracefully: with these they were making beautiful sounds. At some eastern turns, by stretching themselves, they were making marvelous somersaults: their swift back movements were worth seeing. These were movements that could melt the marble, and believe me, not only at those of youth but also at the Alp Mountains of the elderly I could see that snow was melting down; especially because the women were beautiful and their costumes were small and tight so much so that all their secret parts could be sensed: you can imagine what a beautiful scene it was.[41]

Priya Srinivasan has documented the interest in the oriental dancing girl through ballets such as Taglioni's *La Dieu et la Bayadere* (*The Maid of Cashmere*, 1830), Lucien Petipa's *Sacountala* (1858, based on the Indian poet Kalidasa's play *Sakuntala*), and Marius Petipa's *La Bayadere* (1877).[42] Srinivasan notes that in 1838, temple dancers from South India (*devadasis*) performed in Paris and London as "bayaderes," and a group of Indian "nautch" (an anglicized version of "dance" in Hindi and Urdu) dancers performed in New York as part of interludes for Augustin Daly's *Zanina* in 1881.[43] Dancers from northern India and Sri Lanka were brought from Bombay to perform at Coney Island in 1904, and P. T. Barnum brought another group of dancers from South India and Sri Lanka for his New York shows.[44] Fascination with Japanese female dancers was similarly part of the "Japan craze" in Britain, Europe, and the United States, prompting great interest in tours by the actress and dancer Kawakami Sadayakko from 1899 to 1902.[45]

The figure of the oriental dancer gained particular traction when embedded into the story of Salome, the biblical daughter of Herodias who requests the beheading of John the Baptist. By the late nineteenth century, Salome had become a popular subject in art, literature, and theater, such as in Oscar Wilde's 1892 *Salomé*. Rana Kabbani has suggested how, in European painting, the dance of Salome exemplified oriental feminine allure: "It could portray female nudity, rich and sequestered interiors, jewels, hints of lesbianism, sexual languor and sexual violence; in brief, it encapsulated the painted East."[46] In terms of theatrical performance, it was Canadian-born dancer Maud Allan's "Vision of Salome," inspired by Wilde's play and performed in Vienna in 1906, that gave this dance its most notorious reputation.[47] Allan's scantily clad and impassioned version of Salome immediately inspired a host of other versions of the dance, including a parody in Florenz Ziegfeld Jr.'s *Follies of 1907* and at Mademoiselle Dazie's "school for Salomes," which by 1908 was sending "approximately 150 Salomes every month into the nation's vaudeville circuits."[48]

Lucinda Jarrett has commented on the display of female power inherent in the narrative of Salome: "Sensational without being pornographic, Salome dancers were asked to act out a story and were not asked to address an audience directly or lay claim to the sexuality they enacted. Salome was the symbol of the new woman; she was strong, assertive, and also destructive."[49] This potential power—as well as the explicit expression of female desire—was certainly one of the reasons why the performance of Salome was subject to such censorship. Yet despite her revealing costumes and lurid display of the severed head of John the Baptist, Allan's performances were also noted for their more abstract qualities. A 1908 review in the London *Times Literary Supplement* lauded "the wonderful instrument of expression, the revelation of beauty, the mysterious power, that dance becomes with Miss Maud Allan"[50] and differentiated Allan's Salome from what was considered "lascivious and repulsively ugly" about oriental dancers: "Now it is obvious that this dancer could make no movement or posture that is not beautiful and, in fact, her dancing as Salome, though Eastern in spirit through and through, is absolutely without the slightest suggestion of the vulgarities familiar to the tourists in Cairo or Tangier."[51]

As Amy Koritz has noted, in order to appeal to more elite audiences, Maud Allan "had both to enact the East and to distance herself from that enactment"[52] through playing up the spiritual and aesthetic elements of her Salome role as well as showing herself equally capable of performing dances without oriental coloring. Along with the dance of Salome, Allan also performed more sedate choreography set to Mendelssohn, Schubert, and other classical composers. Judith Walkowitz has illustrated how Allan used oriental fantasies "as a register for female expression" but also incorporated a range of other movement forms, including physical techniques from François Delsarte, theatrical tableaux vivants, and aesthetic modernism, in order to develop a distinctively cosmopolitan bodily idiom: "a solitary, autonomous,

unfettered, mobile, weighted, and scantily clad female body whose movements delineated emotional interiority, shifting states of consciousness, and
autoeroticism."53 Other white dancers such as Isadora Duncan, Loie Fuller,
and Ruth St. Denis also created blended forms of dance emphasizing the
disciplined abstraction of modernist choreography. For example, St. Denis
found success with *East Indian Suite,* which included the dances *Egypta*
(1909) and *Radha* (1906).54 As Rhonda Garelick suggests, Loie Fuller's innovative "veil dance" and lighting backdrops were influenced by her early
experiences in Alfred Thompson's pantomime version of *Aladdin's Wonderful
Lamp* at New York's Standard Theater in 1887, although Fuller never admitted this publicly. This pantomime included "an Indian 'nautch'" dance in
which the female dancers wore filmy, transparent costumes; a "Veil of Vapor
Dance," performed by Fuller behind a translucent "curtain" of steam over
which colored lights were projected; and a "Crypt of the Crimson Crystals"
number in which a "switchboard of electric lights" created a twinkling, jew-
ellike background.55 Stylization and abstraction in choreography, costume,
and background help to mitigate the degree to which these dances could,
like the *danse du ventre,* be charged with unseemly and provocative display.

Oriental dances were identified by a variety of names (such as "belly
dancing," "nautch," "Egyptian," or simply "oriental"), and American performers and spectators purposefully confused not only their geographical
and cultural origins but also their racial associations. Such slippage made
it easier not only to ignore cultural authenticity but also to perpetuate fantasies that made black as well as oriental female dancers into erotic objects
of interest. The oriental dance was even sometimes referred to as "hooch-
ma-cooch," referencing the "cooch" or "hoochy coochy," a black social dance
form popularized at New Orleans Conga Square in the early 1900s. Derived from the French *hochequeue* (*hocher,* "to shake," and *queue,* "tail"), the
"cooch" was suggested to have come from Africa, with its popular name
reflecting Cajun dialect in Louisiana.56 In 1899 the *Musical Courier* would
lament that "society has decreed that ragtime and cake-walking are the thing,
and one reads with amazement and disgust of historical and aristocratic
names joining in this sex dance, for the cakewalk is nothing but an African
danse du ventre, a milder edition of African orgies."57

These interchangeable terms were not the only means by which the
oriental crossed over to black in dance. In the United States, Indian as
well as Middle Eastern and North African dancers were frequently derided
for their dark skin. Srinivasan recounts how in 1880 several performers
from India, contracted by the impresario Augustin Daly as part of his opera

Divas and Dancers

Zanina, played to New York audiences. While reviewers at first showed curiosity about these Indian dancers, they later found these performers "monotonous" and bemoaned their skin color; one commented that "the famous Nautch dancers were four little mulatto girls, who twisted their big ugly hands in the air with the grace of a cow and the animation of a China mandarin."[58] At the 1893 Chicago Midway, spectators responded to oriental dancers with racialized assumptions about physical appearance, movement, and music. The *Illustrated American* wrote that "their kinky hair, dirty-butter complexions, bad features, stained teeth, and tendency to embonpoint [plumpness] are dreadfully disillusioning, and their voices are of a timbre that would drive an American cat in disgrace from any well-regulated neighborhood."[59] The *Savannah Times* criticized the exhibition in racial as well as choreographic terms: "It is not dancing. It is walking about the stage to alleged music with peculiar swaying and jerking of the body, such as tends to excite passion. . . . From association with the negro, American people are apt to conclude that all dark-skinned people are dull, but they will find themselves in error before they get through Midway Plaisance."[60] Both music and choreography were subject to the conflation of black and oriental. Writing for *Etude Music Magazine* in December 1898, one commentator derided ragtime music as "simple syncopation" popularized by the Chicago Exposition: "The negroes of the South employed it in the banjo accompaniments to their songs, but not until the 'midways' of our recent expositions stimulated general appreciation of Oriental rhythms did 'ragtime' find supporters throughout the country."[61]

The racial confusion between oriental and black bodies, movement, and music made it possible for African American women to perform professionally as Egyptian, Turkish, and Indian dancers, as was satirized in a series of songs such as Ed Rogers's song "The Oriental Coon" (1899). The sheet music suggests that "The Oriental Coon" was popularized by a white vaudeville entertainer, the "Petite Vocalist Irene Franklin." The song was also sung by African Americans such as Will H. Dixon in *The Hottest Coon in Dixie* (a "Rousing, Rollicking, Ragtime Revel" that first emerged on tour in 1899).[62]

Rogers's song mocks the "colored child" who sees the oriental dancers at Chicago's Midway Plaisance and declares, "I think, wid a naughty wink, / I could do dat style of dance." She then follows "a fat Turk" who offers to teach her if she will "join my Orient." But upon her return from Europe, her "coon friends" shun her, for "her grand display, for the old midway. / They'd no use for anymore." The chorus emphasizes how the other "color'd folks think she'll go crazy soon," since

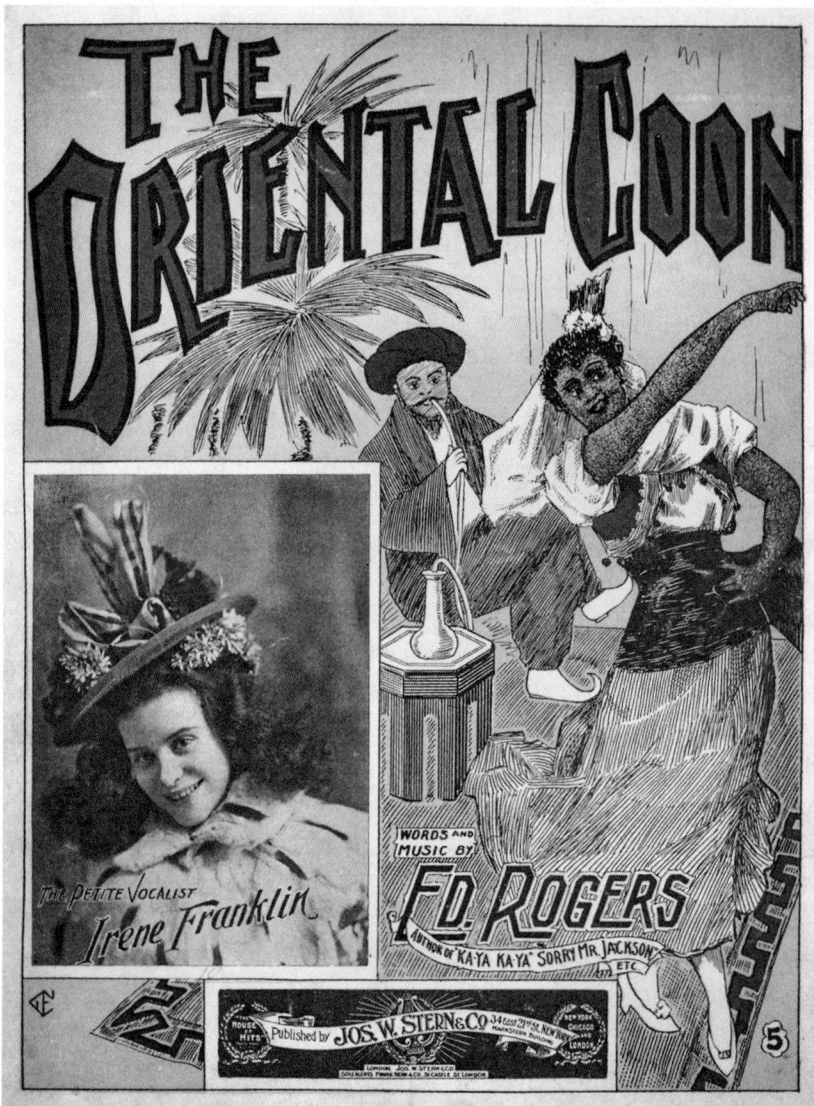

Sheet music for "The Oriental Coon" by Ed. Rogers
(New York: Jos. W. Stern and Co., 1899).
Lester S. Levy Sheet Music Collection,
Johns Hopkins University, Baltimore, MD.

For years she danc'd the bombershay!
Now the Kaya, on the Grand Midway.
For she is an Oriental Coon!

These lyrics emphasize the distinction between the physicality of the black "wench," who is addressed by the "Turk" as "ma burly coon," and the demands of the foreign dance that she has taken on. Even though she might be able to capture "dat style" of dancing (with its "naughty wink") and continues to pose as an oriental dancer on the Midway, she is nevertheless unable to reconcile her new way of moving with her racial identity as a "coon." The song thus satirizes both oriental dances and aspiring African American dancers as novelties of limited interest.

"The Oriental Coon" highlights a degree of anxiety about African American women who moved away from conventionally black forms of movement and took on the eroticized forms of oriental dance. Two songs published in 1908, "The Dusky Salome" (Ben M. Jerome and Edward Madden) and "I'm Going to Get Myself a Black Salome" (Stanley Murphy and Ed Wynn), also address the problem of black females performing in the role of Salome.[63] These songs might have been inspired by both the notorious 1907 Metropolitan Opera production of *Salome* (canceled shortly after its premiere due to concerns about its lascivious nature) and the Salome-themed dance performed by Aida Overton Walker in the musical *Bandanna Land*, which opened at New York's Majestic Theatre on February 3, 1908.

Premiering on December 23, 1908, the musical *Mr. Hamlet of Broadway* featured the white comic singer Maude Raymond singing "The Dusky Salome." Set to a habanera rhythm, its lyrics depict how "the fair Evaline" begins as a "ragtime queen / with a manner sentimental," then is transformed by her desire for "a chance at a classical dance / with a movement oriental."[64] When her suitors, "lovesick coons with ragtime tunes," solicit her favors with "babe, you've got to show me," she answers aggressively:

Bill, you bet I will,
I'm going to dance Salome.
Oh, oh me, that'll show me.

In the second verse, one man decides to watch her: "When she danced 'round the place he just covered his face / But he looked right thro' his fingers." When he offers his "heart and hand," she says, "Give me your head / I'll dance Salome to it." The chorus reaffirms her desire for a man to participate in her fantasy:

I'll make him giggle with a brand new wiggle that'll show me;
In a truly oriental style,
With a necklace and a dreamy smile
I'll dance to the coon who can spoon to the tune of Salome.

Salome's demand "Give me your head" suggests that this uninhibited dance, and the females who dance it for their own pleasure, can end only with tragic consequences. The song varies the conventional take on Salome by staging both her and her male lovers as black characters, whose associations with erotic and violent desires were typical for "coon songs." The aggressive black woman and the seductively slick black man are easily transformed into the sexually demanding Evaline and the "musical coon" who literally might lose his head. Thus the expressed desire for a "coon who can spoon to the tune of Salome" suggests how ragtime romance effortlessly gives way to more openly seductive—and ultimately murderous—oriental desires.

A different kind of contrast is made between black femininity and the figure of Salome in the Ed Wynn and Stanley Murphy song "I'm Going to Get Myself a Black Salome." The song revolves around "Big Bill Jefferson," a "railroad man" who bemoans his lack of money and the fact that his girl-friend spends all his earnings on new clothes. He resolves, "I'm going to get myself a black Salome / A Hootchie-Kootchie dancer from Dahomey." Bill speculates this new woman will be much more economical to maintain, since

All that she'll wear is a yard of lace
And some mosquito netting on her face
A whole new outfit costs about a cent,
And then she can wiggle out of paying rent.[65]

Bill finds his new woman at "Coney Isle" in the form of

A dancer dressed up in a smile,
Oriental ear-rings and a string of pearls,
Surely was the Queen of the Salome girls.

He then takes her "to Ethiopian Hall, / To the dark town fancy ball," where she attracts admiration from other men, who join in the chorus:

She hadn't hardly started in to wiggle about,
When ev'ry colored gentlemen [sic] began to shout.
Oh I'm going to get myself a black Salome.

While it is suggested that both of Big Bill's girlfriends are African American, a definite contrast is set up between his "black Salome" and first girlfriend, who demands "Brinkley hats and Gibson sacks / Long straight fronts and habit backs." If Bill is "tired of my home" and seeks oriental escape, it is because the first girlfriend threatens him with emasculating poverty. The proposed replacement is a Coney Isle version of Salome, the "Queen of the Salome girls," who promises affordable sexual pleasures to the working-class African American man. In these songs, Salome's dance, however enticing to other men, is reduced to an exotic "wiggle" performed for her husband or lover. His "black Salome" no longer demands her beloved's head; any potential for the Salome figure to be powerful and dangerous is now contained through monogamous domesticity.

A strikingly different strategy of containment might have influenced how Aida Overton Walker performed Salome from 1908 to 1912, both in the Bert Williams and George Walker show *Bandanna Land* (for which she also choreographed the sequence "Ethiopia") and in her own featured acts in touring variety shows and at Hammerstein's Roof Garden.[66] Overton's versions of Salome carefully moved away from the titillations of fairground entertainment and the fantasies of conjugal bliss depicted in popular songs and instead balanced the assertive power of the Salome role with what Paula Marie Seniors has called Overton's "Gibson Girl" image of feminine beauty and respectability.[67] David Krasner comments that Overton's version of Salome was notable for its "propriety" and restraint.[68] A undated review of a performance in Chicago commented that her dance included "a few wild figures, and much is made of the sinuous parade which most dancers conceive ·to have been characteristic of the foul-minded daughter of Herodias, but there is nothing of the hoocha-ma-cooch effect which adds a suggestion of sensuality to the exhibitions of other Salomes."[69] Larry Hamberlin points out that "even her treatment of the obligatory severed head was restrained; rather than fondling the head lasciviously, she has it separated from her by a curtain, where a sudden ray of light illuminated it at the climax of the dance."[70]

Such assessments suggest that Overton's performance, like the Salome of Maud Allan, disavowed the popular impression of oriental dance as an indecent Coney Island act and instead gravitated toward modernist stylization. However, like Allan's "beautiful sinuous movements,"[71] Overton's choreography preserved enough of a sensual effect to satisfy audience expectations of oriental character. A reviewer in *Vanity Fair* praised her 1912 Salome: "It's quite possible that Herodia[s]'s daughter had the blood of Sheba in her veins, and there is no gainsaying the fact that Ada is one of the most graceful

Aida Overton Walker, 1912.
New York World-Telegram and the *Sun* Newspaper
Photograph Collection, Library of Congress.

and sinuous dancers on the American stage. Her Pantherine movements have all the languorous grace which is traditionally bound up with Orient dancing."[72] As Jayna Brown has commented, Overton strategically used "the fictions of racial characteristics" in order to present an African American woman as suited for the role of Salome "as a kind of native informer." By operating on assumptions that "all primitive peoples" might "have a proclivity for bodily expression and access to the free spiritual and sexual realms," she could claim to have "a natural right to represent the native woman and . . . translate native movement for a white audience." The oriental role of Salome could be asserted as part of a pan-African modernism: "By associating themselves with the civilized territories of North Africa in their forms of fine art (at a distance from less fully evolved sub-Saharan peoples), African Americans situated themselves as an avant garde, the rightful inheritors of a proud aristocratic African past."[73]

Overton also performed other dance numbers that suggested a similar combination of sinuous and stylized movement. In the first act of *Abyssinia*, Overton led a dance number, "The Lion and the Monk (Die Trying)," with nine chorus members. Her chorus of "Abyssinian Maidens" toured the vaudeville circuit in 1905.[74] She also followed these appearances with her 1909 "Kara Kara" and "Dance L'Afrique," performed with a chorus of "Abyssinian Girls." These dances used her original choreography, described in *Variety* as having "a wild, weird aspect and immense amount of action to it: Eight colored girls are concerned in the act, a splendid octet and active dancers. They have a special act showing a Jungle theme behind them, and Miss Walker leads several numbers."[75]

The emphasis on Overton's offstage respectability and gentility is made evident in a piece written by "Dorothy" in an October 1906 issue of the *Freeman*, which commented on how *Abyssinia* introduced "a bevy of women aspiring for fame and earning a living behind the footlights, singing and dancing themselves into the favor of the audience, and winning their way into the hearts and respect of the general public by their ladylike behavior."[76] While the high visibility of male actors helped in the progress of the race, the article insisted that women also participated in "the upward march by raising the standard of that womanhood that has chosen the stage as a means of service to humanity." The author took care to mention that the "married contingent" of the women in the cast was quite noticeable, and the single women learned "a lesson of self dependence" but also had models for "how a woman can demand and hold the respect of men with whom she is thrown in daily contact without a legal protector." Overton was singled out for particular mention, as someone with "a gentle, refined manner" and "a well-modulated voice that speaks correctly" in addition to being "a born dancer."

Comic songs mocking black Salomes emphasized the imagined differences between African American women (who were seen as more suited to the "bombershay" or to "ragtime") and the "hootchie-kootchie" dancers whom they impersonated. Overton's performances, on the other hand, suggested an inherent connection between the black dancer and more aesthetic modes of oriental role-playing. Yet despite the independence and innovative artistry that she and other female dancers clearly possessed, their performances were conspicuously framed by male-dominated aspects of commercial entertainment. *Bandanna Land* followed Overton's dancing of Salome with a farcical "wench" act performed by Bert Williams that emphasized his huge feet. Williams's parody of Salome was probably offered, as Jayna Brown suggests, "partly to appease a white audience that did not come to see serious black artistry, but expected simple comic relief," thus undermining how Overton's artistic performance "aligned itself with the black bourgeois agenda" by adding "satirical renditions of such black middle-class aspirations."[77] This humor makes clear that Overton's Salome was clearly a radical departure from the kinds of sexualized display for which African American female dancers were best known. Like songs mocking the "Black Salome," the comic versions of Salome attempted to mitigate the effects of a potentially dangerous dance. Daphne Brooks has commented that Overton "dared to dance a metaphor of female sexual *will*."[78] If Overton's performances of Salome served as a hopeful sign that, as Brown states, "black women, too, could be freed of Victorian corsets, free, at least within reason, to express their eternal passionate souls through their bodies,"[79] comic impersonation and parody still tried to keep these desires in check.

AFRICAN AMERICAN SPECIALTIES AND ORIENTAL MAGIC

The final examples of this chapter suggest two other ways in which African American women continued to perform and respond to the erotic and liberatory possibilities of oriental acts, even while negotiating the ever-present demands of black racial respectability. The first is the vaudeville act of Eva Alexander, billed as the "Princess Sotanki," who performed among her other feats of magic a sensational "Hindoo Dance of Death" and whose cosmopolitan glamour suggested versions of black racial uplift removed from the emulation of Eurocentric culture. The second is Alvira Hazzard's one-act play *Mother Liked It* (1928), a gentle comedy that spoofs the oriental impersonations of the "Hindoo" by African American male magicians. Hazzard's play depicts African American women as audience members rather than as performers, yet it also draws attention to the ways that oriental spectacle, and its associations with erotic and magical appeal, became an everyday part of African American leisure and pleasure.

Circus and vaudeville performer Eva Alexander participated in a long tradition of African Americans performing magic, beginning with Richard Potter, the first American-born professional magician of any race, who began performing independently around the Boston area in 1811.[80] Potter and other African American magicians capitalized on the association of the occult with India and other Asian countries, sometimes taking on "Hindoo" identities in order to escape antiblack violence and segregation. As Philip Deslippe notes, by the early part of the twentieth century swamis, yogis, and spirit guides were often conflated with the African spiritual practices of conjuring and hoodoo; by the early part of the twentieth century, the association of African American folk magic and India was common. The *New York Amsterdam News* found that Harlem was "full of turbaned 'wise men'" who were selling herbs and roots, telling fortunes, and offering lucky numbers, and published an illustration of a "Harlem swami" drawing a large crowd, bemoaning the "fakers" (a play on *fakirs*) who appeared "on every avenue."[81]

While most of these acts were performed by men, Eva Alexander, or Princess Sotanki, also built a career out of performing oriental magic. In 1905, the *Freeman* listed her as part of Joseph Terry McCaddon's Company tour of Europe.[82] A 1912 *Freeman* review described her in a show in Louisville, Kentucky, calling her "the Hindoo Wonder, being the only lady of our race doing hypnotic and magic work," and praising her featured act: "Princess Sotanki gets them in a big way with her mammoth snake, when she does the sacred dance of death."[83] In October 1912, Tim Owlsey mused that "after one witnesses the act of Princess Sotanki he is thoroughly convinced that the colored actor or actress offers just as much in the legitimate way of entertaining as his white brother or sister actor or actress." He noted the "new and novel" aspects of her solo act at Indianapolis's Crown Garden Theatre: "The Princess' feat of levitation, suspending the body of a young lady in mid-air, without the aid of a mechanical or human device, held the audience spellbound. Her closing number was a feature within itself, known as the 'Dance of Death,' which she executed with a real live snake twenty feet long and about six inches in diameter. Princess Sotanki's act is exciting, entertaining, and pleasing."[84]

According to a 1914 *Freeman* review, she appeared again at the Crown Garden Theatre performing "a bunch of good tricks which defy solution," including a "Running Turban" that was "especially puzzling" as well as a "wet and dry sand trick" and levitation. This later review was much more critical, noting, "She accomplishes much of her work with a 'species' of incarnation, outlandish prattle and the rattling of a tom-tom or hurdy-gurdy which gives her the appearance of a daughter of Bombay or some other oriental port." Princess Sotanki's magic was characterized as "about the same as that by many of the big magicians," with the skeptical conclusion that "she succeeds in deluding, that's her art."[85] However, another *Freeman* reviewer a year later was clearly enraptured by her performance of the "Hindoo Dance of Death," which was "preceded by the peculiar, weird music known as the snake charming music, noted for its solemnity and monotony—drums much in evidence."[86] Her act also included mesmerism and fortune telling. A 1913 advertisement in the *Savannah Tribune* billed her as the "East India Wonder Worker in the Great Fortune Telling Act," promising, "She tells you what you want to know of your lost property, stolen goods, false friends. Read your life like a book."[87]

As an African American woman performing magic, Alexander was a rarity in her time. Perhaps even more remarkably, she combined this power with a reputation as a capable and trustworthy theatrical manager at a moment in which most African American female performers were supervised by men. The *Freeman* stated in 1913 that Princess Sotanki "never fails to pay the performers on Saturday night, which makes them feel like giving her the best service they can."[88] Furthermore, Alexander maintained this sense of authority even while staging herself as an oriental female, a figure seen as inevitably subjected to the male gaze and endangered by a phallic "mammoth" snake. Descriptions of her act as well as a few undated photographs appearing on souvenir postcards suggest that she imbued her oriental performances both on and off the stage with a distinctive aura of power and control. One such photograph, captioned "Princesse Sotanki, La Charmeuse De Serpents," depicts her reclining seductively and wearing an elaborate headdress and many necklaces.[89] Her costume recalls that of Anna Madah Hyers in the role of Urlina; however, the hookah pipe and half-smiling expression hint at a much less demure character.

Similarly, an extended review in the *Freeman* begins by describing Princess Sotanki in a costume resembling that of other oriental dancers: "She comes on, dazzling, in a bespangled costume. She shines and sparkles all over, enough to charm any kind of 'varmint,' including men." Nonetheless, this review then focuses on her exceptional ability to master both a snake and an audience rather than dwelling solely on the erotic nature of her act:

Slowly she reels about the stage to the music of the orchestra, accompanied by bells in each of her own hands. Some don't see the significance of it all until she stops and drags forth a huge reptile; it is now plain enough. The audience admires the woman's nerve, but no thought or a desire to exchange places with her, not a man, woman, or child. She fondles her great snake, pressing it to her bosom, and other forms of endearment. Finally she pretends to be bitten, gives a piercing scream which has the ring of reality. The audience shudders. Then comes the death scene, which is artistically done that it is good to see. Her death agony has the appearance of the real thing. No laughs at this masterful presentation. The stupefied audience does not know whether to keep silent in contemplation or applaud the artist for her fine work. The curtain rings down.[90]

In 1913, Cleveland's motion picture censor Robert Bartholomew criticized those acts of white female dancers "who endeavored to arouse interest and applause by going through vulgar movements of the body." Bartholomew described a particular theatrical moment in which "a young woman after dancing in such a manner as to set off all the young men and boys in the audience in a state of pandemonium brought onto the stage a large python snake about ten feet long. The snake was first wrapped about the body, then caressed and finally kissed in its mouth."[91] Princess Sotanki was no doubt aware that her "Hindoo Dance of Death" might well arouse similar concerns. The year before Bartholomew's criticisms were published, she issued her own statement directly refuting accusations of cheap sexual display. In 1912, the *Freeman*'s Sylvester Russell wrote that "Princess Sotanki, the East Indian snake charmer who played at the Monogram theater last week, wishes to make it known that she is not an oriental dancer and there was no fear of her dance being immoral at any time during her engagement. She states that the Dance of Death is a snake dance in which her monster live reptile is exhibited. She made a hit and drew big houses and her return will be welcomed."[92]

In disputing charges of indecency that might be attributed to her "Hindoo Dance of Death," Princess Sotanki directly rejected the more negative perceptions of the "oriental dancer." Instead, she used orientalism to cultivate an offstage image blending exotic cosmopolitanism with respectable domesticity. Another postcard, captioned "Princess Sotanki, World's Greatest Lady Hindoo Magician and her troupe of Singalese Dancers; from the Island of Ceylon of the east coast of India," shows an African American woman in Western-style dress and hat festooned with flowers, driving an automobile accompanied by several men wearing turbans and necklaces, as well as by a child in a turban.[93] It is not clear whether these men or the child were part of her act or whether they were actually from Ceylon. However, this photograph does feature Princess Sotanki as the driver of her own car, promoting the image of a modern, capable, and worldly woman on intimate terms with India and the Middle East. This image is maintained in a 1915 *Freeman* review as well.

> A wonderful little lady is Princess Sotanki. It has been her privilege to have the most varied and most wonderful career of any colored performer before the public. She has traveled the world over, giving exhibitions with her husband, who was a Hindustan. She lived among the people of the far East. The Syrians insist she is one of them. She has their features, their language and that different personality that belong to foreigners. The Princess is at home in India, where she learned much of the lore, including magic, snake charming, etc. She has what she calls the reading gift—delving into the future—that occult science about which there is so much dispute. She learned French in France, making four languages which she speaks fluently.[94]

Despite this account, there is no evidence that Princess Sotanki was ever married to an Indian. Jason Dorman has speculated instead that Eva Alexander was at one point married to Walter Brister, an African American man who began his career as "the youngest bandmaster in the world" and later became known as the Indian magician "Armmah Sotanki." Brister later gained broader fame by changing his name to the "Prophet Noble Drew Ali," founding the Moorish Science Temple of America in 1925.

As Dorman has pointed out, Alexander at times cultivated the image of the respectable and happily domesticated African American woman.[95] However, in the theatrical world and public eye, she, like so many other white and African American magicians, created a strategically oriental stage persona and transformed herself into the glamorous and daring Princess Sotanki. In an era in which many other African American stage performers were frustrated by their inability to be seen as equally American, Princess Sotanki suggested an alternative state of being and acting: a cosmopolitan and multilingual persona possessing intimate ties to the "people of the far East" as well an alternative place of belonging "at home in India."

African American vaudevillians, particularly those performing as "Hindoo" magicians, mobilized the figure of the oriental magician not only in order to give themselves additional opportunities but also to access the perceived power, mobility, and glamour of these roles. African American audience members would have been well aware of the desires that inspired these oriental impersonations as well as their potential for deception. A skepticism about racial impersonation is made clear in Alvira Hazzard's one-act play *Mother Liked It*, first published in the June 1928 issue of the *Saturday Evening Quill*.[96] The play pokes fun at the idea of an African American passing as "Hindoo" royalty; however, even as it debunks the oriental magic act, it shows it to be a well-established and ultimately harmless pleasure that is part of African American leisure culture. Unlike the daring career of Princess Sotanki, the play presents the enactment of oriental magic not as a life choice but as a temporary diversion en route to middle-class respectability; thus, this romantic comedy uses a familiar orientalist plot to promote the dictates of racial uplift.

Editors James V. Hatch and Leo Hamalian describe Hazzard's play as "a 'silly' boy/girl comedy in the style of *The Boy Friend* and *Very Good Eddie*." *Mother Liked It* gently mocks the infatuation of Meena Thomas, an eighteen-year-old African American woman, with the performance of "Prince Ali Kahn" after she sees him at a local theater and declares him "adorable" (69). While the normally reserved Meena is riveted, her friends Alta and Tess are more critical of this vaudeville act, with Alta liking everything about the show "except that stupid Indian Prince": "His stunts were all chestnuts, his make-up atrocious, and his manner entirely too artificial" (64). While waiting at a café for a dinner table, Alta schemes to have fun with the shy Meena's infatuation with Ali Kahn's "oriental beauty" (68) by asking her friend Jay to impersonate him. Jay at first refuses. Several days later, the women encounter the Prince at the same restaurant. Thinking that he is Jay in disguise, Alta dares the love-struck Meena, who apparently has been witnessed now "burning incense, and playing 'The Song of India'" (69), to talk to him, and the two finally meet. After the women exit, Jay, "*ridiculously costumed*," enters wearing a "*turban awry, trousers too large*" (70). Jay and the Prince converse, and the Prince reveals that he is not Ali Kahn but Jonas Smithly, a college student who is doing his specialty act to pay his tuition at the University of Chicago. Jonas then confesses the impersonation and his romantic interest in a letter to the delighted Meena.

Mother Liked It blends the gentle comedy of middle-class African American life with the orientalist elements familiar from Molière's *Le Bourgeois Gentilhomme*. The double impersonations by Jay and Jonas of Prince Ali Kahn ridicule the fashionable belief in "Hindoo" mysticism as well as point to cross-racial impersonation of well-known African American magicians, such as the popular "East Indian Psychic" Jovedah de Rajah (the stage name of Arthur Dowling, who performed in the Keith and Orpheum vaudeville circuits and used his stage persona both onstage and off in order to access whites-only hotels, restaurants, and railway cars).[97] But *Mother Liked It* takes a less cynical approach by allowing the oriental disguise, even though a proven hoax, to have a more romantic purpose. The shy Meena's infatuation with the "oriental beauty" of Jonas Smithly leads not to humiliation but to her meeting "a husky college half-back and one-hundred-per cent American" who confesses that his act is only a summer diversion" (71). The conversations among the young black characters also suggest that different oriental pleasures, whether magic acts in vaudeville or the "wonderful food" to be had at Chinese restaurants such as "La Ming," have become integral to the African American bourgeoisie. *Mother Liked It* pokes fun at oriental fakery and magic, but it also implies that the vaudeville act of "Prince Ali Kahn" is entirely consistent with the aims of black racial uplift, providing both a summer job that will help Smithly obtain his college degree and a respectable pathway to marriage for Meena.

A moment in Jessie Fauset's novel *Plum Bun* (1928) finds its African American protagonist inspired by a black speaker whom she compares to "a statue of an East Indian idol" who possesses "some strange quality which made one think of the East": "a completeness, a superb lack of self-consciousness, an odd, arresting beauty wrought by the perfection of his fine, straight nose and his broad scholarly forehead."[98] Vijay Prashad has commented on this passage that "the black man is perfect and complete when he is seen as an Indian, a vision borne partly from U.S. orientalism but also partly from the strong wave of solidarity for the anti-colonial struggles in India that swept parts of black America."[99] Compared with this novelistic moment, Meena's dramatized romantic interest in an oriental prince seems much more opportunistic and mundane in nature. *Mother Liked It* caricatures the fashionable association of India with mysticism and alternative spirituality for African Americans as well as for whites but at the same time gently implies that the ideals of black upward mobility, respectable domesticity, and race progress might easily make use of the racial habits of "oriental magic" to enrich ordinary African American middle-class life and intimate relationships.

8

ORIENTAL FROLICS AND RACIAL UPLIFT IN THE EARLY AFRICAN AMERICAN MUSICAL

The racial habits of theatrical orientalism—spectacular displays of foreign opulence and despotism, fashion and deception, immigrant threats to American labor and business, and nubile female bodies—were distinctively incorporated into the African American musicals that developed during the 1890s. First produced by white managers and then run entirely by African Americans, shows such as *Black America* (1895) and *Darkest America* (1895) relied on blackface stereotypes but also used select oriental characterizations in order to promote images of black racial uplift. Plantation nostalgia and minstrel types served as the imagined points of departure for affirmations of black evolution and respectability, which culminated in Broadway shows such as John W. Isham's *Oriental America* (1896) and Bob Cole and Billy Johnson's *A Trip to Coontown* (1897). Within the sometimes contradictory presentations of racial stasis and progress in these early musicals, oriental impersonations and specialty numbers served not just as diversions but rather as strategic acts that allowed African American performers to show themselves fully capable of more refined forms of entertainment. The adoption of oriental themes also highlighted deeper tensions around narratives of black progress and respectability. Intimations of seductive femininity and the pleasures of the harem affirmed the attractiveness of African American women in works such as Sam T. Jack's *Creole Burlesque Show* (1890). *Oriental America* and *A Trip to Coontown* used oriental themes to satirize as well as celebrate the black bourgeoisie, conveying a degree of skepticism about the ostentatious display and class pretension inherent in middle-class life. Thus, orientalism provided another avenue by which the early African American musical articulated concerns about racial uplift, gender roles, the gap between working-class and more elite forms of culture, and the deceptive nature of American prosperity and belonging.

PROGRESS NARRATIVES IN *BLACK AMERICA* AND *DARKEST AMERICA*

Through the 1890s, African American newspapers reported regularly on the success of several large-scale all-black musical shows as they toured concurrently both in the United States and abroad, playing to white as well as African American audiences. In 1895, a November issue of the *Freeman* proclaimed that "the Afro-American has been decidedly in evidence here this week, in the theatrical world," with *Black America* "at Convention hall, embracing three hundred colored members"; in addition, the article continued, "'On the Mississippi,' at the Academy, carried thirty; and Sam T. Jack's Creoles at Kernan's, numbered not less than fifty."[1] Another bit of "Stage" news in the *Freeman* the following year reported, "The Octoroons are still holding their own in the East," "Oriental America is turning people away in Patterson, N.J. this week," "Sam T. Jack's Creoles are doing their customary good business in Troy, N.Y. this week," and a continuing run of *Darkest America* "is certainly one of the best representations of plantation life on the stage to-day."[2] In December 1897, the *Freeman* announced that Al G. Field's production *Darkest America* "will be seen at the Park Theatre, Indianapolis, soon," while "John W. Isham's 'Octoroons' are touring the United States with success" and Isham's *Oriental America* "is enjoying a most prosperous run through Great Britain and the foreign countries, and it will remain abroad until next May or June before sailing for home."[3] If, as Robert Toll has described, "minstrelsy was one of the few opportunities for mobility—geographic, social, and economic—open to nineteenth-century Negroes,"[4] these shows provided even greater advantages for African Americans working in theatrical entertainment. A 1897 advertisement in the *Trenton Evening Times* billed Field's *Darkest America* not only as "the biggest, best and most expensive colored amusement institution in existence" with "fifty people in the cast" but also as featuring the "highest salaried colored performers in America."[5] Another 1897 article in the *Freeman* quoted the claims of music director Billy McClain that *Black America* was "the largest Negro amusement institution ever organized, carrying 865 people under contract."[6]

The inclusion of a large cast and varied range of entertainments may well have been driven by the same commercial motives that prompted the formation of "mammoth" minstrel companies in the 1870s and 1880s. But the desire to showcase racial progress was also evident in these productions, even those firmly rooted in plantation nostalgia. *Black America*, for instance, was set in a "Negro Village" replete with log cabins, chickens, mules, and bushes decorated with cotton balls, built in Ambrose Park, Brooklyn, New York. The previous summer, Nate Salsbury, the white manager of the show, had staged *Buffalo Bill's Wild West Show* in the same space. He advertised *Black America* as employing "500 genuinely southern negroes" brought "direct from the fields" of Virginia and the Carolinas as "an ethnological exhibit of unique interest."[7] Despite its purported realism, the show featured minstrel numbers such as "Kentucky Home," "Roll, Jordan, Roll," "Carry Me Back to Old Virginia," and "Old Black Joe" and showed its cast happily eating watermelons and dancing a cakewalk. Similarly, the first act of *Darkest America*, produced by the white minstrel performer and manager Al G. Field, was also billed as a "plantation show" that, according to the *Trenton Times*, included "an old-fashioned husking-bee, with all the fun pertaining thereto—the 'possum hunt, the elation of the happy negroes who catch the game, an old Virginia reel, danced as only it can be danced by native negroes." However, these scenes in *Darkest America* were followed by those that showed "a pathetic parting of master and man, slaves made free by the emancipation proclamation of freedom, leaving the old plantation and a happy home to go to out in the world, a new world to the poor, untutored slaves, the battle of life to begin anew under conditions unknown and untried."[8]

The massive scale of these theatrical ventures as well as the central involvement of African American writers, composers, performers, and managers encouraged a much more robust range of racial representation. *Black America* billed itself as "A Gigantic Exhibition of Negro Life and Character," and advertisements made clear an explicit message of race progress, citing the evolution of "the Afro-American in all his phases, from the simplicity of the southern field hand (especially the phenomenal melody of his voice), to his evolution as the northern aspirant of professional musical honors."[9] Though *Black America* was managed by Salsbury, the main source of its musical and narrative structure was likely the notable African American performer and director Billy McClain. Barbara Webb has suggested that some of the material for *Black America* was based on McClain's 1894 play, *Before and after the War*, which was described as showing "The Evolution of the Negro. The Progress of the Afro-American. From a Savage to Congress" and included scenes depicting 1619 Africa, slavery, and emancipation that culminated in showing "the Negro as he is today" in the "reception parlors of Hon. Macon B. Allen," the "first African American lawyer admitted to the bar."[10] Webb also notes *Black America*'s inclusion of a grand chorale display and patriotic pageantry, such as the celebration of the Ninth Calvary, an all-black unit organized in 1866 that was employed in the southwest territories and the Spanish-American War and that participated in the famous 1898 charge up San Juan Hill with Theodore Roosevelt.

In addition to staging minstrel-inspired spectacles of slavery, *Black America* and *Darkest America* also emphasized racial uplift and African American achievement. The *Trenton Evening Times* described the juxtaposition in *Darkest America* of "native negroes" and husking bees with scenes showing technological progress and class mobility. While the first act took place on the plantation, the second was set on the levee at New Orleans at "the greatest steamboat race the world ever knew," between the *Robert E. Lee* and the *Natchez*. The third act highlighted the seedy underworld of black urban life at the "Rabbit Foot gambling saloon, at Jacksonville, Fla.," "the most notorious resort of the kind in the South," but was followed by a fourth act set in "a home of luxury" in Washington, DC. This final act, "sumptuously mounted with magnificent scenic effects" that placed it "on a higher plane,"[11] affirmed how *Darkest America* showed African Americans evolving from the evils of urban life into upper-class respectability. The *Colored American* praised the *Darkest America* cast as being "half a hundred of the best Afro-American talent in the country," depicted as "carrying the race through all its historical phases from the plantation, into reconstruction days and finally painting our people as they are to-day, cultured and accomplished in social graces." This dramatic portrait, the review concludes, "holds the mirror faithfully up to nature."[12]

The vision of racial progress in *Black America* and *Darkest America* followed the lead of the Afro-American Specialty Company, which toured Europe in 1891–92. Its white theatrical manager, William Foote, expressed the need for new material in order to "rescue Negro minstrelsy and bring it again to its former popularity."[13] According to the *New York Age*, Foote's theme of "Negro evolution" was a way to "portray the progress of the Negro from savagery, through slavery to the fullness of his powers as citizen, making the comical side of the Negro's character prominent throughout."[14]

Oriental Frolics and Racial Uplift

The *New York Clipper* reported that Foote "has planned his entertainment, he says, so as to truthfully depict the course of the African, from the jungle to the parlor, and his colored performers will represent the negro's process as a savage, a slave, a soldier, a citizen, and a lawmaker. It ought to be a novel show."[15] The tour was described by W. L. M. Chaise in the *New York Age* as "probably the most refined and elevated Afro-American amusement company ever organized": "All of his stars are new in this line, and instead of making plantation melodies and peculiar dialect their forte, they have a sort of historical bearing in portraying the different evolutions from 1860 to 1891." With leads including "Mme. Marie Selika, leader of the burlesque opera, and her husband Mr. Veloska, baritone [Marie and Sampson Williams]; Mme. Mamie Flowers, a noted soprano as leader of the choruses and Mr. H. E. Jones, as banjoist and guitarist," Chaise noted that "one can see the organizer's intention was to elevate the character of the minstrel show and possibly draw a new interest."[16]

These large-scale shows continued to reanimate familiar black stereotypes, justifying them as points of departure for racial evolution. The desire to please white as well as black audiences, coupled with the added pressures of modeling black respectability, made theater a tricky business for African American performers. As Kevin Gaines has suggested, African American racial uplift envisioned "collective social aspiration, advancement, and struggle" but also generated "a racialized elite identity claiming Negro improvement through class stratification as race progress, which entailed an attenuated conception of bourgeois qualifications for rights and citizenship."[17] There were particular pressures on African American theater artists to conform to rigid ideals of appropriate racial behavior and (as Gaines suggests for photographic portraiture) to maintain a "serious, dignified image," as "anything less than stylized elegance would betray the ideals of race advancement and, indeed, hold the race back."[18]

A June 1897 edition of the *Freeman* reported that the white minstrel impresario Frank Dumont was "busy rewriting" the musical spectacular *Darkest America* and turning the entire third act into "the opera of 'Aladdin.'"[19] Not much else can be found about whether Dumont's operatic *Aladdin* ever took place. Still, the contemplation of this new element for *Darkest America*'s long run, from 1895 to 1904, suggests a move even further away from black stereotypes.[20] As the next examples in this chapter will show, orientalism could be used to highlight the artistic abilities and upward mobility of African Americans; it could also point a finger at the limitations of middle-class respectability and its advocacy of "stylized elegance."

THE HAREM AND THE COLORED GIRL:
SAM T. JACK'S CREOLE SHOW

The white manager Sam T. Jack opened his *Creole Burlesque Show* (often called *The Creole Show*) in Haverhill, Massachusetts, on August 4, 1890, and between 1890 and 1897 the show ran in theaters in Boston, New York, Chicago, and elsewhere. *The Creole Show* preserved the tripartite structure of the minstrel show; however, the first part featured the novelty of a female chorus and female interlocuters along with male end men and numbers. Though the show included dramatic sketches and variety acts, perhaps its greatest appeal lay in its showcasing of attractive African American women, including a chorus of "sixteen light-skinned teenaged girls,"[21] an innovation in burlesque houses.

The Creole Show gave a number of African American women their start in the entertainment business. According to Henry T. Sampson, Dora Dean made her first professional appearance "when Sam T. Jack's Creole show played her home town in Indiana and she applied for a job, having no previous acting or show business experience." Sampson surmises that "she was hired because manager Jack liked her splendid figure and used her as one of the statue girls, and the 'black Venus' was soon heralded all over the country."[22] This casting of African American women challenged racialized assumptions about feminine beauty inherent in the casting of exclusively white chorus girls both in burlesque houses and other theatrical venues. Burlesque had been popularized earlier in the United States by visiting British entertainers such as Lydia Thomson and Pauline Markham and their "British Blondes," who toured the states beginning in 1868.[23] The interest in displays of white feminine beauty later dictated the racial homogeneity of showgirls such as those hired by Florenz Ziegfeld Jr. for his *Ziegfeld Follies,* which was billed as "Glorifying the American Girl" in 1922.[24] In his history *Black Manhattan (1930),* James Weldon Johnson would write that "Sam T. Jack, a prominent burlesque theatre owner and manager, conceived the idea of putting out a Negro show different from anything yet thought of, a show that would glorify the colored girl."[25] For Cedric Robinson, the chorus of African American women in *The Creole Show* subverted "the desperate racist construction of Black women as unattractive," a move that was particularly apparent in "the collision between these beautiful Black bodies and the signifiers of the sexless, de-eroticized Black woman" such as the Mammy figure of Aunt Jemima, who grew to fame at the World's Columbian Exposition in 1893.[26]

Interestingly enough, *The Creole Show* challenged the primacy of white women in burlesque and other musical theater not only through highlighting the black identities of its performers but also through associating them with erotic oriental femininity. A year prior to *The Creole Show*, Jack had staged "Beauty in Dreamland, or The Pearls of the Orient" with his mainly white Lilly Clay Colossal Gaiety Company. The spectacular sketch was set in a harem run by "Islam," a "Shah of Persia," and featured female characters named "Tulip Tint" and "Mossrose" along with male characters such as "Gin Sour, the shah's chief officer"; "Boulanger Jim," the "commanding general of the Persian army"; Flipflop the eunuch; and Legs, "a Persian dude!"[27] "Beauty in Dreamland" was accompanied by song and dance numbers, lady sharpshooters, "Emmerson and Cool, the comedians and acrobats, in a black-face act that brought down the house," and a burlesque of *Robinson Crusoe*; the show culminated in an "Amazonian march" with "a battalion of well-drilled and richly attired beauties."[28] In the spring of 1890, Sam T. Jack announced a new show, billed as an "Oriental Sensation": "a New Revelation to the Amusement World" that was "now being organized in the city of Alexandria, Egypt." He declared his plans to recruit Egyptian performers for this "Oriental Sensation" Company in the *New York Clipper*: "This is the first troupe of its kind ever organized and is composed of fifty people, thirty of whom are Louisiana Creoles, the remainder being young Egyptian women. . . . A purely Egyptian burlesque will be done, the costumes of which will be correct and in Oriental magnificence."[29]

Though by summer the name of the show had been changed from "Oriental Sensation" to "Creole Burlesque,"[30] these announcements highlighted Jack's intention to employ the sexual attractions of the oriental dancer and the harem in order to add novelty to his burlesque shows. According to Irving Zeidman, what began as the more restrained "leg shows" of American burlesque—extravagant musical numbers with dancing chorines in revealing silk tights—later featured increasingly more explicitly sexualized and racialized "cootch" numbers in which "blondes were supplanted by the vogue of 'Oriental' dancers, Little Egypt was followed by Little Africa."[31]

From its inception, *The Creole Show* intentionally created a degree of racial ambiguity in staging its African American female chorus members. Its name suggested that the cast of mixed-race women could be associated both with the French-Spanish colonial aristocracy and the female prostitutes of New Orleans. But, as Lynn Abbott and Doug Seroff note, "the percentage of true 'Louisiana Creoles' in Jack's company was probably about the same as the percentage of 'young Egyptian women,' i.e., not many": the company was in fact "made up of many New York City girls."[32] Yet *The Creole Show* clearly played on the allure of female bodies, both exotically desirable and racially liminal, presented as a spectacular ensemble. The *Haverhill Evening Gazette* of Massachusetts advertised *The Creole Show* as "The Grandest Entertainment under the Canopy of Heaven, Silks, Satins, Glitter and Gold" and hailed "the sultry beauty of the showgirls," described not only as "Enchantresses of the Mississippi" but also as "Charmers of the Nile."[33] Washington, DC, reviews of *The Creole Show* reported it as having "beautiful tableaux," "strange sweet songs," and "graceful and sentimental dances" as well as "many novel specialties," including "the gavotte and grand ensemble, Egyptian pastimes, Creole revelries, vocalists, comedians, acrobats, and fairy like enchantresses in light and gaudy costumes."[34] One opening act, "Tropical Revelries," was presumably "a faithful portrayal of the natural luxuriance of the picturesque land of the Creole."[35] This was followed by a burlesque sketch, "The Beauty of the Nile, or Doomed by Fire." The finale of the show included a "Grand Amazonian March."[36]

Other specialty acts included exotic female performers as well; in August 1893 it was announced that "six women from Honolulu, dancing what manager Jack styles the Hullu-Hullu gavotte, are this week added to the drawing powers of his Creole Burlesquers."[37] *The Creole Show* regularly featured a burlesque number by William Watts, "The Beauty of the Nile, or Doomed by Fire," and the *Freeman* lists the following cast for September 1890: "Nafra, Sadie D. Walfa; Cheop, Florence Hines; Grip, Burnell Hawkins; Zeno, Irving Jones; Isis, his queen, Sarah La Rue; Amasis, King of Theb[e]s, Florence Brisco; Karmack, Mammie Laning; Dinon, Eloise Pousett; Amon, Nina St. Jean; Zoilous, Mary Vorshall; Yeason, Miss Valja; and Mr. and Mrs. Sam Lucas, musical sketch artists."[38] In June 1891, W. L. M. Chaise in the *New York Age* described how "'The Beauties of the Nile,' or 'Doomed by Fire,' an ancient Egyptian burlesque, by twenty young women, nobles, soothsayers, fire worshippers and Nubians, was a gorgeous display of physical development."[39] Later in the show's run at his Chicago Theatre, Jack hired Fahreda Mahzar Spyropoulos, a Syrian-born dancer made famous by her "Little Egypt" performance at the World's Columbian Exposition of 1893, to appear.[40]

While the notable African American entertainer Sam T. Lucas was in charge of *The Creole Show*'s casting and stage production,[41] the show still bore the imprimatur of Sam T. Jack, who promoted his own image as the central force behind the success of his female performers, according to M. J. O'Neill's 1895 biography of Jack, *How He Does It*. Primarily a series of

Oriental Frolics and Racial Uplift

first-person anecdotes, *How He Does It* details Jack's recruitment of performers from New Orleans as well as from the Caribbean, Mexico, Cuba, and Egypt and makes clear Jack's desire to foreground race as part of the erotic attraction of his feminine displays. For instance, Jack gives titillating details about hiring "a very beautiful young Creole lady who was desirous of going on the stage" who appeared to him "clad goddess-like in Nature's raiment only," even while he claims the utmost propriety in his behavior.[42] Jack pointedly avoids any implication of interracial interactions that could result in scandal and describes his "Creole" performers as associated with a privileged class. The young lady and the other African American women described in the book are identified as "Creoles," never as "Negro" or "colored" or "black." Creoles, Jack maintains, are different from the descendants of African slaves: "The Creole is generally a member of the Roman Catholic Church, having received that faith as an inheritance from his French and Spanish ancestors."[43] One performer, Marie Labout, is described as "a beautiful Creole maiden" who was "a maid in waiting to the daughter of a wealthy planter."[44]

In Jack's telling, most of his Creole and other exotic female performers wanted to be in his shows in order to showcase their musical and theatrical talents. In contrast, he depicts the "Egyptian beauty" in his show as someone who "appreciates gold, and is willing to earn it honestly."[45] Jack's account of discovering this most likely fictional Egyptian performer includes a tall tale of travel to Egypt, in which he also acquired "four Eunuchs" whom he presumably tricked a sultan into selling to him. He used the eunuchs to guard his entire company of female performers, presumably from outside harassment but also, it is implied, from their own rebellious tendencies.

"My company of ladies travel on a special car, or on my own special train sometimes, when I run companies over the same territory, and my Eunuchs take up the same position precisely which they formerly occupied in the Harem of the Sultan in the far off Orient. They are big, strapping, good natured fellows, and my ladies are perfectly safe under their care. They are always on guard."

"Do your ladies ever have cause for alarm?"

"Not on my special car, usually, but they are frequently harassed elsewhere by the *genus homo* known as the masher. We have strict discipline, however, both at the theaters and on our traveling coaches. I permit no deviation from my rules. I have never had any rebellion in any of my companies. My ladies comply with all of my requirements, but should any one of them disobey them, I would not hesitate to discharge her and send her home, no matter how good she may be. Every one knows me to be an iron-clad disciplinarian."[46]

Jack's description evokes a fantasy of the harem as ensuring the modesty and privilege of women even while holding them captive. Rather than a sultan, Jack views himself—according to the book—as a benevolent protector whose civilized gallantry removes him from any charges of exploitation or inappropriate racial mixing.

The so-called eunuchs from Egypt were never mentioned in conjunction with Jack's shows. However, Jack's private car for his *Creole Show* performers was a subject of fascination in the *New York Clipper*, which described it as a "Pullman Palace car" "fitted up in regal style" with ladies' "toilet and wardrobe," kitchen, stateroom and private office for Jack, and separate stateroom for the male quartet of African American performers (perhaps the mysterious "four Eunuchs") that was kept "entirely separate from other portions of the car." The *Clipper* commented that "the Creoles are certainly to be congratulated on having such eloquent and commodious quarters in which to travel about the countryside."[47] The *Freeman* also noted how Jack provided a private train for *The Creole Show* performers: "The company has also a private car built by the Pullman Palace Car Company, with a convenient dining room, place to sleep; has also cook and waiters." However, the *Freeman* pointed out the real reason for this means of travel: "When they are refused on account of color, they have their own car in which to eat, sleep, and be merry."[48] What is left unsaid in *How He Does It* is how Jack's "special car" is needed not just to safeguard the virtue of the "daughters of the Nile" but also to adhere to U.S. segregation laws barring the show's "Creole belles" from riding freely on public railway cars.

While it is hard to know whether any of Jack's bombastic stories (which also include curing a woman of insanity, flying a hot-air balloon, and fighting a bull in Havana) were actually true, what is clear is that he embellished his biography, and the productions of *The Creole Show*, with visions of exotic female performers who were imagined as at once sexually available and safely contained. *How He Does It* makes careful and selective use of oriental stories of adventure, conquest, and prostitution; these notes seem to have been sounded in the staging of *The Creole Show* as well. The erotic desires and salacious fantasies related to oriental femininity had already made yellowface and brownface popular for white female performers. African American women, however, had to negotiate their participation in representations

Oriental Frolics and Racial Uplift

of female captivity or the harem with much more care, since a long history of slavery and disenfranchisement already associated them with sexual availability. African American women displayed onstage as objects of erotic desire recalled the dynamics of the auction block or brothel. As Jayna Brown describes, the "light-skinned, limber-legged, and boisterous black women on the burlesque stage carried with them the history of the fancy girl trade and practice of plaçage centered in New Orleans and extending across the Caribbean."[49] Thus the use of an explicitly oriental setting or characterization could help project enslavement and domination onto a foreign space or character; it allowed the figurative harem, even when inhabited by African American women, to maintain a respectable distance from the history of slavery in the United States.

The overtly sexualized appeal of the many non-white women in Jack's show still had the potential to create both sensation and consternation, especially for those trying to ensure the respectability of African American female performers. As Paula Marie Seniors has suggested, African American newspapers stressed the need to manage *The Creole Show*'s eroticism and ensure the respectability of its female acts.[50] The *Freeman* noted with relief that some changes had been made to *The Creole Show* by 1896: "Sam T. Jack's Creoles are playing to excellent business. Mr. Jack is presenting a much cleaner show this season than heretofore, which is commendable to himself and members of his company."[51] Leigh Whipper, the first African American member of Actors Equity (founded in 1913) and founding member of the Negro Actors Guild of America (1937), asserted that the African American women of *The Creole Show* "were not like the white women who were featured in the 'strip-tease act' in burlesque" but rather were "sensational in spangled costumes with skirts split at the side."[52] Composer and musical director Will Marion Cook also found Sam T. Jack's show to be "the most classy and best singing Negro show on [the] road."[53] Such statements suggest how these shows were expected to both arouse and keep in check those desires projected onto the bodies of African American women. Thus Jack's "Creole belles" would come to be praised by James Weldon Johnson as entertainment that would serve to "glorify the colored girl" rather than degrade her.[54]

ISHAM'S *ORIENTAL AMERICA*

The Creole Show's success inspired John W. Isham, the advance agent for Jack's *Creole Show*, to produce his own burlesque-inspired show in 1895.

According to Henry Sampson, Isham was a light-skinned African American man who "frequently passed for white and thereby was able to secure responsible positions with various show companies, which allowed him to acquire valuable experience in the management and advertising end of the business."[55] Coproduced with Ernest Graff, Isham's show also featured an African American female chorus. First called *Isham's Creole Opera Company* and later changed to *Isham's Octoroons*, the show was noted less for its display of female bodies and more for its specialty acts and sketches. An 1896 *Freeman* review of *Isham's Octoroons*, for instance, noted the participation of "Fred Piper, Madame Flowers, Tom Brown, [Anna] Madah Hyer[s], and the Mallory Bros.," who are "fine artists" with "already brilliant reputations"; moreover, "the entertainment they give is clean, bright, humorous and full of new and attractive features."[56] Moving even further away from the minstrel show format that undergirded *The Creole Show*, *Isham's Octoroons* opened with what would have been the afterpiece, with humorous sketches such as "The Blackville Derby," "Darktown Outing at Blackville Park," "A Tenderloin Coon," and "7-11-77."[57] The show also dispensed with the semicircle of the Interlocuter, Tambo, and Bones and instead followed the specialty acts of the olio with a musical extravaganza, "30 Minutes around the Operas," featuring well-known operatic excerpts such as the "Anvil Chorus."[58] One performance was lauded by the *Brooklyn Daily Eagle* for the "high quality of its singing," commenting that "these colored singers have given selections from many of the grand operas, which have surprised and pleased the audiences by the remarkable quality of the voices." The show engaged popular entertainers such as Belle Davis, who drew high praise from the reviewer at the *Eagle*, who stated that Davis "made a reputation last summer by the naturalness with which she sang many of the coon songs introduced by white singers." The *Eagle* also mentioned the appearance of "Harry Fidler, the mimic," although it is unclear whether or not Fiddler included his Chinese act among his other impersonations in the show.[59]

In 1896, Isham developed a larger and more ambitious show that he called *Oriental America*. *Oriental America* had a similar format to *Isham's Octoroons*, opening with a comic sketch, an olio with star specialties, and a finale with the cast performing from popular operas and operettas. It also recycled "The Blackville Derby" from *Isham's Octoroons*. That *Oriental America* still relied on a measure of minstrel-style entertainment is clear from the London *Era*'s description of a performance in Liverpool during a tour in the 1897–98 season, which said that the show presented "in a vivid way the picturesque features of the more pleasant side of the old slave life" and included

Oriental Frolics and Racial Uplift

"John W. Isham's Oriental America: 40 Minutes of Grand Opera" lithograph
(Cincinnati and New York: Strobridge Lithograph Company, ca. 1896).
Theatrical Poster Collection, Library of Congress.

"quaint and characteristic melodies, sand and buck dancing, [and] graphic illustrations of what is known as the 'cake walk' (one of the merriest and liveliest festivals of the American coloured native)." However, the *Era* also noted that *Oriental America* culminated in "a grand operatic performance in which great musical talent is displayed by the principals" and concluded that "no more striking evidence of the progress of the colored race can be found in America than that which is to be met with in the Oriental America performance under the direction of John W. Isham who has displayed the very wisest discretion in the selection of his coloured company."[60]

Like *Black America* and *Darkest America*, *Oriental America* emphasized an imagined progression from the less refined elements of minstrelsy and burlesque toward celebrations of African American artistry and elite culture. A series of lithographs highlights its selections from ballet and opera, showing tenor Sidney Woodward as one of the "Great Singers of the Century" and several female dancers in tasteful poses in "Le Ballet des Fleurs." Another lithograph is captioned "40 Minutes of Grand Opera" and depicts librettos from *Rigoletto, Faust, Lucia de Lammermoor,* and *The Queen's Lace Handker-chief* as well as male and female figures in operatic costume.

Stylishly dressed and elegantly posed, nearly all the figures in these litho-graphs are depicted with light skin. Next to the clock labeled "40 Minutes of Grand Opera" stands a somewhat darker-skinned woman in a pink dress, holding sheet music; however, in another lithograph labeled "Operatic Ce-lebrities," the same woman appears to have the same pale complexion as the other singers. That the performers of *Oriental America* actually demon-strated a range of skin tones is confirmed by the British reviewer in the *Era,* who noted that "the whole of the members of the combination with scarcely a single exception are genuine Negroes, mulattos, or quadroons."[61] The whitening of skin in these lithographs thus suggests the distancing of these performers from more stereotypical black roles, a sentiment implied in the praise of the *Morning Times* of Washington, DC, for *Oriental America*'s cast as "the cream of the colored race."[62]

This theatrical version of racial uplift was accomplished through an emphasis on elite cultural forms. The *Clipper* wrote of *Oriental America* that "the first part was more like a high class ballad or operatic concert than a minstrel show."[63] In this, *Oriental America* may well have been influenced by the success of those white minstrel troupes with much more patrician offerings as well as by African American companies such as Foote's Afro-American Specialty Company. The 1881 U.S. tour of Sam Hague's tour-ing British minstrels did not use blackface characters, employed a much larger orchestra, and highlighted the vocal ability of its performers, who wore evening dress. In the 1880s the lavish spectacles of Primrose and West, the "Millionaires of Minstrelsy," also eschewed blackface for scenes of "lawn tennis, baseball, bicycle riding, yacht racing, polo on skates, and fox hunting."[64] These influences may well have inspired *Oriental America*'s costumes and scenic choices as well as its music. Its inclusion of a "hunting scene and opening chorus from the *Bells of Cornville*"[65] is referenced in the "40 Minutes of Grand Opera" lithograph by an image of men and women dressed for a fox hunt, complete with red coats, white wigs, riding crops, and dogs. Another *Oriental America* lithograph also includes a fox-hunting scene captioned with "Grand Hunting Chorus," an image that flanks a por-trait of a pale-skinned Isham posed in a writerly fashion, leaning on a set of books and papers. This lithograph also shows a set of identical men sporting monocles next to a chorus of women in bloomers with bicycles, identified as the "The Manhattan Club," along with a caption reading "It's English as You See It on Broadway."

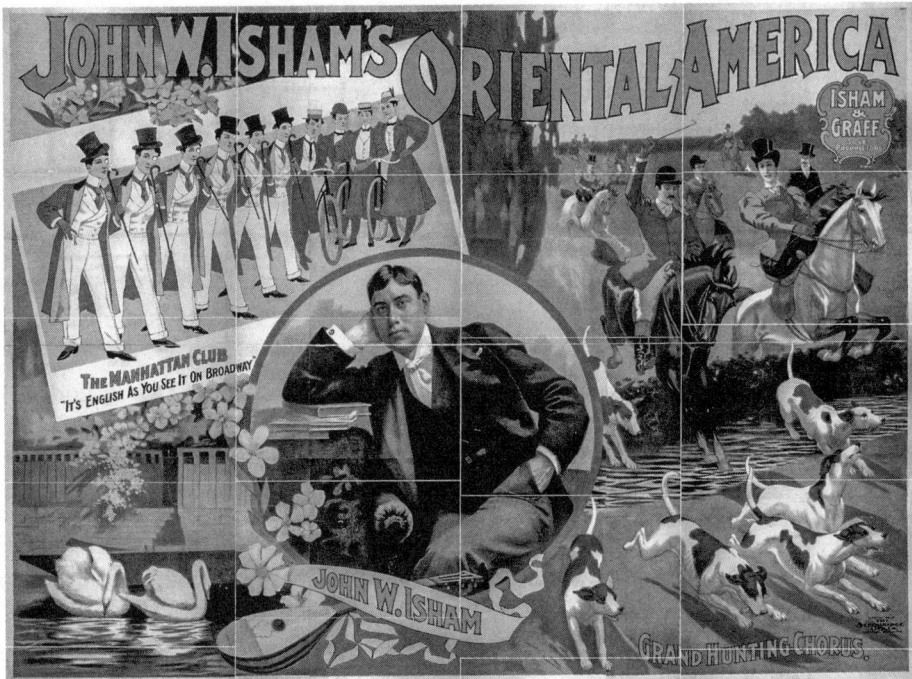

"John W. Isham's Oriental America: The Manhattan Club,
Grand Hunting Chorus" lithograph (Cincinnati and New York:
Strobridge Lithograph Company, ca. 1896).
Theatrical Poster Collection, Library of Congress.

Despite its celebration of genteel refinement, some versions of *Oriental America* also gently lampooned the upward mobility of African Americans with a sketch titled "Mrs. Waldorf's Fifth Anniversary," preserved in typescript at the Library of Congress.[66] The sketch opens in "the exterior of a handsome hotel on the Florida coast" owned by Mr. and Mrs. Waldorf, who are celebrating their anniversary with a "Lawn Fete." The plot of the sketch emphasizes the prosperity of the Waldorfs, who not only stage lavish musical numbers for their elite guests but also have labor disputes with disgruntled employees. Johnson, a waiter, is fired after confronting one of the guests about his table manners, and he, along with the cook, interrupts the party and threatens to take over the hotel. However, this altercation between Johnson and the Waldorfs is not explored in any depth. Johnson is quick to anger but just as quick to change his mind about his rebellion; later in the play he reenters, dressed in style, and tells Mr. Waldorf that he has decided not to buy the hotel. He returns to working for Waldorf, but not until he sings "Hot Tamale Alley" at Waldorf's request.

Yet it seems significant that the class differences in "Mrs. Waldorf's Fifth Anniversary" are highlighted by a diverse offering of specialty acts, including the waiter Jerome singing "Things No One Seems to Understand" and two tramps who are expelled quickly after their song and dance, only to return and blend in unnoticed with the other guests. The magical resolution of the dispute between Johnson and the Waldorfs, as well as between the more elite and the more impoverished characters, adds a satirical touch to the depiction of the Waldorfs' "Lawn Fete" and identifies divides in class and generation. The leisure and pleasure afforded the wealthy is signaled by ensemble numbers enacted by male members of the "Magnolia Golf Club," female lawn tennis players, well-dressed "Manhattan sports," and the "Twentieth Century Bicycle Maids," who perform a specialty act on bicycles. In "Mrs. Waldorf's Fifth Anniversary," the disgruntled Johnson is particularly aghast at the prospect of catering to this young crowd, stating his objection to "checking bikes for New Women" and grumbling that "dudes that call themselves Manhattan sports and women that wear men's clothes can't get any of my time." His consternation pokes fun at the stuffiness of an older generation of African Americans who adhere to strict notions of respectability and gender conformity.

The oriental elements of Isham's *Oriental America* included an ensemble of women dressed as "Oriental Hussars" in brocaded jackets and tights, led by Belle Davis. This female chorus, reminiscent of both *The Creole Show* and *Isham's Octoroons*, drew special praise from the *Washington Bee*, which hailed Davis as having "one of the most perfect figures of any lady on the stage."[67] Oriental costumes were also used in another musical number. A November 1896 *Morning Times* remarked that a "Japanese dance" was "cleverly rendered by Fanny Rutledge, Pearl Meredith, Alice Mackey and Carrie Meredith, who sang and danced equally well" and also "were prominent in all the ensemble scenes of the performance."[68] This specialty is introduced in "Mrs. Waldorf's Fifth Anniversary" as "four little Japs from the flowery kingdom," of whom Mr. Waldorf quips, "I know they will please you and you must treat them nicely or they will cut off your supply of tea." Although it is not certain which song they performed with this "Japanese" number, the influence of the famous trio "Three Little Maids" from Gilbert and Sullivan's *The Mikado* is made clear in another *Oriental America* lithograph. Captioned "Fantaisies D'Orient," the lithograph places the quartet of "Japanese women" front and center, with a number of performers in operatic costume on one end and other women playing instruments on the other. These exotic

"John W. Isham's Oriental America: Fantaisies d'Orient" lithograph
(Cincinnati and New York: Strobridge Lithograph Company, ca. 1896).
Theatrical Poster Collection, Library of Congress.

aspects added to the refined nature of *Oriental America*, associating the show
with fashionable British culture as well as with quaint oriental display.

One 1896 account of *Oriental America* in the *Freeman* noted yet another oriental attraction in the show: Harry Fiddler in the part of "Li Hung
Chang" in the olio, who met "with much success."[69] A similar Chinese impersonation also appeared in the show two weeks later, this time with Tom
Brown, who received effusive praise from the *Washington Bee*: "There is no
comedian on the stage more popular than Tom Brown. His imitation of Li
Hung Chang was one of the greatest hits on the program. Billie Eldridge, the
secretary and interpreter of Li Hung Chang, is enough to make a dying man
come to life. Li wants to know whether the proprietor of Waldorf is married.
After he has been told yes, he requests his interpreter to ask the proprietor
if his wife is married. The questions that Li ask[s] are too funny to repeat."[70]

Like the hapless Chinese immigrant laundryman, the distinguished Chinese statesman and diplomat Li Hongzhang often was treated, at least in name, as a subject of parody in works such as W. C. Robey's 1897 burlesque comedy *Li Hung Chang's Reception*, Joseph Herbert's 1893 parody *The Geezer*, and Mark Twain's unproduced 1898 farce *Is He Dead?* No lines are indicated for Tom Brown as Li Hung Chang in the sketch "Mrs. Waldorf's Fifth Anniversary." However, the *Bee's* description suggests that Brown's Li Hung Chang might have been portrayed as an eminent visitor to the Waldorf hotel rather than an abject immigrant laundryman, cook, or domestic servant. While the *Washington Bee* account makes clear that the role still pokes fun at the cultural and linguistic estrangement of the Chinese man, it also suggests a more elite and distinguished status that would have complemented the overall picture of black gentility at the Waldorfs' party.

By showcasing the artistic refinement of its offerings, *Oriental America* clearly adhered to the overall goals of demonstrating racial uplift and progress toward African American middle-class respectability. Isham refused to play *Oriental America* in less reputable burlesque houses,[71] and an 1896 production was described by the *Washington Bee* as "crowded this week with Washington's most classic and cultured people." This review expressed hope that *Oriental America* heralded a time when African American performers would not only excel but in fact dominate commercial theater: "The presentation of this show has no doubt convinced the most skeptical that Afro-Americans will in a few years monopolize the stage."[72] Another *Washington Bee* commentary in 1898 was similarly optimistic about how Isham's work, praised as "A Tower of Merit to Stand Forever," epitomized the future of black musical theater.

> Truly may it be said: "Times change and we change with them."—
> Few there are who cannot easily remember when the stage was almost entirely the realm of white actors and with few, very few exceptions there were no colored professional artists. Then, it was said that colored singers had a peculiar melody of their own, and were patronized for that, (jubilee singers) but actors and companies composed of colored artists, producing clever skits, original comedy sketches and even daring the most difficult operatic productions—never! Such a fete, however has been accomplished by Mr. John W. Isham of Octoroon and Oriental America fame. Starting at the bottom of a mountain that it had never been thought possible to surmount on account of the numberless difficulties and great opposition to be overcome

Oriental Frolics and Racial Uplift

both from the stage, and worst of all, a prejudice blinded public, Mr. Isham bravely set out to the task, and with a superabundance of tact, business ability and an indomitable will, has succeeded beyond his most sanguine expectations, and today he has an aggregation second to none on the stage of comedy.[73]

After its initial tour, *Oriental America* opened August 3, 1896, at New York's Palmer Theatre, becoming the first show with an entirely African American cast to play in a Broadway house.[74] The Broadway production was not a commercial success, according to Perry Bradford, because it was too "classy" for its largely white audiences.[75] Even though the show was not commercially successful, it nonetheless provided opportunities for individual artists as well as legitimated efforts to move further away from the representational rigidity of minstrel types and plantation scenes. In doing so, it also reiterated orientalism's association with patrician culture. Yet even as this musical celebrated middle-class respectability and refinement, at least one of its comic sketches, "Mrs. Waldorf's Fifth Anniversary," suggested a certain skepticism about these aims. *A Trip to Coontown* would continue to develop the tension between promoting and parodying African American racial progress.

A TRIP TO COONTOWN

Robert Allen "Bob" Cole received his start working with white producers and managers. Performing in Sam T. Jack's *The Creole Show* in 1891, he developed the character of a tramp, Willie Wayside, who would later reappear in multiple shows, including *A Trip to Coontown*. In 1894, Cole would form his own company, the All-Star Stock Company, which included composer Will Marion Cook as well as performers such as the Farrell Brothers, Gussie Davis, Cole's wife Stella Wiley, and William "Billy" Johnson. In 1896, the members of Cole's company began working with the Black Patti Troubadours, and Cole and Johnson wrote the music, lyrics, and book for a "merry musical farce" titled "On Jolly Coon-ey Island" for this company. This sketch was a parody of the 1896 James Sheridan Mathews and Harry Bulger farce *At Gay Coney Island*. According to the *Freeman*, "On Jolly Coon-ey Island" included a range of familiar black types such as a "Coon Singer," a "buck dancer," a "Bunco Steerer," and a "Con Man" with a "glad hand" as well as oriental characters such as a "'Couchee Couchee' girl from the midway." The *Freeman* described it as "full of 'hot stuff,'" a stage fantasy set at a "resort by the sea" where "song, story, and dance in which the entire company invest all the enthusiasm characteristic of their race, reigns supreme for forty minutes."[76] Among the characters that would be reused in Cole and Johnson's later *Trip to Coontown* were Cole's Willie Wayside and Johnson's Jim Flimflammer, a comic duo described as "looking for the best of it,"[77] as well as the hypocritical preacher Reverend Sly.

Disillusioned by their experiences with Rudolph Voelckel and John J. Nolan, the white managers of the Black Patti Troubadours, Cole and Johnson left a year later, taking their materials and some of the performers with them.[78] The creation of *A Trip to Coontown* was part of the larger struggle for the self-determination of African American performers, as Cole insisted: "We are going to have our own shows. We are going to write them ourselves, we are going to have our own stage managers, our own orchestra leader and our own manager out front to count up. No divided houses—our race must be seated from the boxes back."[79] Despite positive reviews in the fall of 1897, initial obstacles for *A Trip to Coontown* included a boycott organized by Voelckel and Nolan that made it impossible for the show to be produced except in third-rate American and Canadian theaters. In the spring of 1898, Klaw and Erlanger, one of the major theatrical booking agencies in New York City, finally broke the boycott, and *A Trip to Coontown* opened at the Third Avenue Theater on April 4, 1898, the first full-length Broadway musical comedy to be written, directed, performed, and managed by African Americans. It would go on to tour until 1900, appearing in New York City two more times before it closed.

In February 1900, an unidentified Boston reviewer suggested the strong connections of *A Trip to Coontown* to some of the oriental variety acts used both in *Oriental America* and "On Jolly Coon-ey Island."

> The first act ended with the most astonishing demonstration of the facility with which the African face can be made to represent other dark-skinned races. It was an elaborate ballet. Four misses looked and acted more like Japanese girls than most white chorus girls in comic opera. A group of men made perfect Arabs. Three more girls were vivid Egyptians, with sinuous suggestion. Two men represented Chinamen. One group was of Spanish girls. All of these were remarkable in their way, and interesting food for reflection. The costuming was rich and tasteful, and the dancing pretty and vivacious in a manner not specially recalling the usual ragtime steps.[80]

An advertisement in the *Philadelphia Times* for an October 1899 production of *A Trip to Coontown* highlighted the show's "oriental frolics" alongside its

Oriental Frolics and Racial Uplift

"coon comedy" and "coon songs."[81] These "oriental frolics" included not only the addition of a now-standard comic "Chinaman" character but also more thematic references to oriental fantasy and deception. An illusory "Chinatown" is behind the play's imagining of "Coontown," a fictive space in which black characters escape their mundane lives through adventure, leisure, and excess, and oriental fantasies figure prominently in the play's entertaining succession of tall tales, lies, and scams.

A Trip to Coontown openly borrows both its title and its central premise—the unfulfilled promise of travel to an exotic destination—from Charles H. Hoyt's 1891 Broadway hit, *A Trip to Chinatown*. Despite its title, Hoyt's musical play does not actually take place in Chinatown; rather, its well-to-do young white characters pretend to leave for a slumming trip to Chinatown as a ruse in order to escape the rigid control of their guardian. Like many musical shows of the time, Hoyt's *A Trip to Chinatown* includes a few casual moments of stage orientalism as well as a "coon" song: a fun-loving widow appears in "white Chinese dress and does Chinese specialty" and later sings "Push Dem Clouds Away" to demonstrate her winsome sense of adventure.

> If de train am a-speedin' an' you can't catch on,
> When you push dem clouds away!
> You're a coon dat's gone, and wuss dan none,
> When you push dem clouds away![82]

As in Hoyt's musical, the plot of *A Trip to Coontown* also revolves around a succession of schemes to fool a wealthy older man.[83] Silas Green Sr. has received a $5,000 pension, which makes him not only the sudden object of attention from the Widow Brown but also a target for two con men, Flimflammer and Wayside.

Flimflammer schemes to sell Green a deserted and waterless property that he builds up as a pleasure resort, "Coontown." Like Hoyt's version of "Chinatown," this place exists only in imagination. Flimflammer's "Coontown" riffs on Cole and Johnson's earlier version of "Jolly Coon-ey Island," an oriental space of black pleasure combining the appeal of the "Couchee Couchee" girl on the midway with black figures such as the "Coon Singer" or "buck dancer." Coontown becomes a similar kind of pleasure dome, promising luxury and excess tailored to the appetites of its imagined "coon" occupants:

> FLIM. On the summit of lowland mountain overlooking the most
>   beautiful stretch of scenery man's eyes ever beheld. In addition

to this, sir, you will find in the southeastern corner of my strip an area of two miles yielding valuable minerals. You'll find fruits of all descriptions, including the red and rosy watermelon.

SILAS, SR. Watermelons?

FLIM. Yes, sir, the air is as fresh as the milk that comes from a Jersey cow, there are fourteen mineral springs within 100 yards of a most magnificent hotel erected in the midst of a beautiful garden of flowers, able to accommodate one thousand persons.

The merging of oriental and black fantasy in "Coontown" is followed in the second act by another kind of oriental deception. After their attempts to bilk Green out of his money go awry, Flimflammer and Wayside visit Green at his new house, and Wayside pretends to be "Prince Daffy from Dahomey" (a plot device familiar from *Le Bourgeois Gentilhomme* and its many oriental-themed imitations). Accounts indicate that Bob Cole played the character of Wayside in whiteface, meaning that his turn as "Prince Daffy" necessitated another racial impersonation from whiteface to black-face. But even though "Prince Daffy" presumably hails from Dahomey, his comic confusion with a kind of oriental royalty is made clear later in the scene, after the detective Billy Binkerton announces a reward for the arrest and return of "Prince Daffy" to Dahomey.

WAY. Ah what is the charge?

BINK. Kidnapping.

WAY. Why I never napped a kid in my life.

FLIM. No sir, I can vouch for that myself.

WAY. Oh, kidnapped who pray?

BINK. Count Buckaciac from the royal courts of Soudan.

WAY. Why I never was in Shangh[a]i in my life.

Flimflammer and Wayside blithely use oriental-style deception to scam Green, portrayed as a newly rich member of the black bourgeoisie who is gullible enough to buy the fantasy of "Coontown" and to be fooled by the playing of "Prince Daffy." Like the sketch "Mrs. Waldorf's Fifth Anniversary" in *Oriental America*, the second act of *A Trip to Coontown* features a grand reception at Green's newly acquired and luxurious home that includes operatic entertainment. But while this part of *A Trip to Coontown* seems to celebrate African American social mobility and racial uplift, the musical also offers the idea that class status might well be a form of deception or, at best, a temporary delight.

While *A Trip to Coontown* is often hailed as a theatrical instance of racial progress, it actually mocks the tropes of heroism and economic success associated with black uplift. The musical's orientalist satire exposes some of the many spectacular illusions of status, leisure, and power that enrapture black characters. "Prince Daffy from Dahomey" is but the final ruse in a succession of tall tales told by characters. In addition to its musical numbers, *A Trip to Coontown*'s entertainment value also relies on a series of creative fictions told or played out by different characters. These begin when Captain Fleetfoot delivers his well-worn war stories of medals won for "the great flank movement at Manases," "bravery at the battle of Bull Run," and the "famous Black Moguls." His accounts are undercut by Mrs. Brown, who says that "he did nothing in the army but drive the Commisary wagon," and by Silas Green Jr., who says that "chances are that the only war he knows anything about is the South before the war." Another pleasurable dream is described by the younger Silas Green while he courts the young Fannie; he lapses into reverie even as he tells Fannie that he intends to reform his gambling ways:

SILAS, JR. No more race horsing. No more staying out at night at
     the Young Mens' Investment Club trying to make a bob tail flush
     stand up for the real thing. Say, Fannie, have you ever taken one
     card to a four heart flush and caught a club?
FANNIE. Why, what in the world are you talking about?
SILAS, JR. Oh, I was talking about a friend of mine—Jack Pots.

Each character's overblown fantasies—promised and sometimes delivered through gambling, drugs, speculation, love, or even spirituality (in the figure of the hard-drinking Reverend Sly)—are skewered in turn. Even African American participation in politics receives its due, as Green declares that "every colored man in Washington plays the colored peoples' national game," which he identifies as "policy."

A Chinese role played by Tom Brown introduced another kind of oriental characterization in keeping with these broader themes of deception, fantasy, and disguise. This character was one of several cross-racial impersonations by Brown and others in the play. Cole played the tramp Willie Wayside in "white make-up which makes it almost impossible to guess his particular tint," a performance that has been noted by David Krasner as "revolutionary" for shifting "the emphasis from a specific ethnic group to a general appearance of an itinerant hobo."[84] Writing for the *Freeman*, J. Harry Jackson commended Cole for showing "that he is capable of playing any white part far better than most Negro comedians play black ones." Jackson's review likewise praised Tom Brown's Chinese impersonation as being "as fine an imitation as was ever given by either Charles Parsloe or James T. Powers."[85] Other reviewers also praised Brown's Chinese impersonation, at times giving it more notice than Bob Cole's whiteface performance. Springfield's *Illinois Record* commented that "Tom Brown is not only the most versatile Negro on the American stage, but he is also one of the best character actor[s], playing the characters of a 'Rube,' an Italian, a Chinaman and an up-to-date parlor monolougest [sic]."[86] The *Topeka Plaindealer* found that "Tom Brown, character comedian, still retains his impersonations of the Chinaman and the Dago, and he also retains his hold upon the popular pulse of the people, judging from the applause with which he was frequently interrupted."[87]

Brown's Chinese role clearly allowed for some improvisation; Jackson's review highlighted the addition of an unpublished parody of Ernest Hogan's 1895 song "All Coons Look Alike to Me," commenting that "it was worth the price of admission merely to hear the blackest Negro in the company sing, 'All Chinks Look Alike to Me.'"[88] Hogan's popular song had inspired multiple variations, including in *Darkest America*, in which Billy McClain performed the song in German, and a version by Billy Miller, "All Spaniards Look Alike to Me."[89] Jackson's comment suggests that Hogan's satire of "coons" as indistinguishable from one another was redirected at the Chinese. Yet Jackson also mentioned that the number was sung by "the blackest Negro in the company," a choice that reinforced the song's irony. If sung in yellowface, the song would not only redirect racial hostility away from African Americans toward Chinese subjects but also imply that both groups were capable of internalized racism.

Another song for *A Trip to Coontown* brings together black and Chinese characters. Performed by Flimflammer and Wayside at the end of the first act, only the song's title is mentioned in the script of the play. However, both the lyrics for "The Wedding of the Chinee and the Coon" and the cover illustration of the sheet music depict an elaborate and fanciful wedding scene between an African American man and a Chinese woman.[90]

As Julia H. Lee has noted, the song's offering of a black-Chinese marriage wavers "between attraction and anxiety," which speaks directly to turn-of-the-century fears of miscegenation and multiracial children, as registered by the song's "slightly apocalyptic flourish."[91] The lyrics predict an "awful jumble" produced by "this strange amalgamation / Twixt these two funny nations" that culminates in "a great sensation / Over the whole creation" as a

Oriental Frolics and Racial Uplift

Sheet music for "The Wedding of the Chinee and the Coon" by Billy Johnson (lyrics), Bob Cole (music), and Theodore F. Morse (arranger) (New York: Howley, Haviland and Co., 1897). New York Public Library.

set of black and Chinese types witness an imagined interracial wedding. The song describes how the wedding feast includes "chop suey that will puff you like a balloon" and relates a dispute over the officiant that produces "razors in the air" and causes the "Chinese preacher" to lose his "cue." However, the song also envisions an occasion for interracial community:

> All Diplomats from coonville must be ready
> To join in with the band
> Of the heathen chinamen.

As Julia Lee has suggested, this presents the possibility that an "intimate Afro-Asian relationship could develop without the inclusion of a white participant."[92] Admittedly, this vision of a marriage between black and Chinese characters figures as only one of many fantasies in the play. Unlike the other fictions of this musical, however, the song's whimsy does less to mock African American escapism and self-delusion and more to conjure up the prospect of intimacy between "heathen chinamen" and the inhabitants of "coonville." As we shall see in the next chapter, this connection will be explored further in the African American musicals that followed *A Trip to Coontown*.

9

. . . .

PLEASURE DOMES AND
JOURNEYS HOME

IN DAHOMEY, ABYSSINIA, THE CHILDREN
OF THE SUN, AND SHUFFLE ALONG

. . . .

The previous chapter has suggested how all-black musical shows in the 1890s offered not only employment but also new opportunities for African American performers to expand their range of stage roles. However, this theatrical path to racial progress proved difficult and uneven. Long-standing practices of blackface performance and racial typecasting continued even as the early African American musical paved the way for the relative success of entertainers such as Bert Williams and George Walker, whose success on the vaudeville stage led to their being featured in musicals such as *In Dahomey* (1902), *Abyssinia* (1906), and *Bandanna Land* (1907).

In December 1907, *Variety* published a letter from Albert Ross, a professor at Western University, to Williams and Walker. Ross begins by noting the great effect that Williams and Walker had in providing black models to African American audiences: "You have a wonderful opportunity in this country. Your name is magic to our people, the characters you bring out in your plays, the vim and dash of Negro young manhood and womanhood have the effect of ideals which almost every Negro boy and girl, however far distant in the backwoods, seems to pounce upon, imitate, emulate and follow as the standard." However, Ross asks why they continue to depict "the old plantation

Negro and the ludicrous darky and the scheming 'grafter'" rather than more heroic characterizations such as the prominent African Americans "[Alain] Locke, the Negro student at Oxford, England . . . [William] Pickens, who won the prize at Yale; Roscoe Conkling Bruce, who led the oratorical contest at Harvard, or the great colored football or baseball stars at Harvard." He urges them to forgo the "'good time' Negro" that is "the curse of the day" and instead turn their influence toward representations of black accomplishment and progress.[1]

Variety also published, in the same edition, the reply of Williams and Walker, in which they defended their continuing to perform racial stereotypes. For them, the heroes suggested by Ross, though "worthy examples," were "in a public sense . . . obscure and surely away from the type," which rendered them theatrically "uninteresting." They pointed to the race progress inherent in their own success, which registered a difference from "a few years back" when "most all the 'so-called' Negro performers were engaged in 'cake-walking,' buck dancing, and 'slap-stick' comicalities, together with all manner of absurd antics which might please the non-sympathetic, biased and prejudiced white man." They asserted proudly that "all of our shows were written, staged and produced by Negroes" and that these "required some thought and very careful deliberation before attempting to present them before the public." "Our task was no easy one, but rather difficult, because the colored theatre 'goer,' taken collectively, only wants to see when he attends a negro show such characters as remind him of 'white folks,' while on the other hand the white patrons only want to see him portray the antebellum 'darkey'; but our aim is to average and simply use characters most familiar to-day; and in doing so, we do it with every regard for art['s] sake—for in true art there is no color line."

Variety's exchange of letters foregrounds both the significance of theatrical representation to the project of racial uplift and the difficulty faced by African American performers in adhering strictly to this charge. Like many other African Americans involved in the theater, Williams and Walker were keenly aware of the real damage that racial typecasting could do. However, their emphasis was on the practical attainment of the same goals and privileges that white entertainers possessed: to be recognized as performers who could bring a variety of characters to life. Their response to Ross recalled a strategy that they used earlier in their careers when billing themselves as "the Two Real Coons."[2] With Williams in blackface and Walker as the impeccably dressed straight man, the two reappropriated the figures of the comic fool and the urban dandy with the claim that they could outdo white actors at the game of black representation. As Camille Forbes suggests in her biography of Williams, even as "black audiences read against the grain of such performances, undercutting prevailing stereotypes that rendered blacks a despised and alien population, white audiences accepted those representations." Thus, though this "conditional acceptance" helped African Americans gain a foothold in theater and popular entertainment, it also "ossified stereotypical images, despite performers' attempts to resist them."[3] Karen Sotiropoulous has eloquently described the predicament of many African American artists who, like Williams and Walker, carefully negotiated their self-presentation:

> African Americans were hyperconscious of how much their self-presentation on stage would be read through stereotype and how a modern sensibility required distancing oneself from pervasive black imagery. Black entertainers consciously used racist stereotypes in their performances in part to distance themselves from these images, since it was abundantly clear (at least to themselves and their black audiences) that they were *performing* these roles, not embracing them as representative behavior. They sought to show their audiences how much they were skilled actors—professionals—playing stereotypes in an effort to expose the fictions within the imagery.[4]

However different their visions, these letters also highlight the importance of all-black theater for African American audience members. Ross stresses the value of Williams and Walker in creating "ideals" for a younger generation of African American viewers who "pounce upon, imitate, emulate and follow [them] as the standard." Williams and Walker also emphasize that their performances no longer have to please just "the non-sympathetic, biased and prejudiced white man," even while they chafe against restricting themselves to roles based on respectable behavior, heroism, and achievement geared toward "the colored theatre 'goer'" who "only wants to see when he attends a negro show such characters as remind him of 'white folks.'" In 1926, W. E. B. Du Bois would famously state the directive of the newly formed Krigwa Players Little Negro Theatre in Harlem: to produce plays devoted to African American artists and spectators as defined in the following terms:

> The plays of a real Negro theatre must be: 1. "about us." That is, they must have plays which reveal Negro life as it is. 2. "By us." That is, they must be written by Negro authors who understand from birth and continued association just what it means to be a Negro today.

3. "For us." That is, the theatre must cater primarily to Negro audiences and be supported and sustained by their entertainment and approval. 4. "Near us." The theatre must be in a Negro neighborhood near the mass of ordinary Negro peoples.[5]

Decades prior to Krigwa's "real Negro theatre," Ross, Williams, and Walker had already asserted the importance of not only producing shows "written, staged and produced by Negroes" but also acknowledging the "entertainment and approval" of African American audiences by developing plots, characterizations, and spectacles that spoke directly to black spectators.

In the early decades of the twentieth century, a new generation of producers and artists carefully integrated this awareness into musical and theatrical entertainment. While still needing to appeal to integrated audiences, these plays also insisted on the value of imagining spaces—however patently make-believe—in which black characters might be free from white control and judgment. These plays also critiqued white behavior and accomplishment as the only standards for African Americans and challenged ideals of black racial uplift that relied on white imitation.

As evidenced by 1890s musicals such as *Oriental America* and *A Trip to Coontown*, oriental elements could be used in constructing alternative worlds of black pleasure and escape as well as in criticizing black bourgeois aspiration. In the early decades of the twentieth century, a new generation of African American performing artists would turn to oriental characterizations and themes in order not only to showcase their artistic skills and escape minstrel caricature but also to imagine different modes of black expression and action. While on the surface these oriental elements still resembled the familiar comic turns and lavish show numbers that proliferated in white American theatrical entertainments, their incorporation into African American musicals made them appreciably different in function. As seen in previous chapters, African American theater artists put their own spin on tropes of oriental luxury and deception and on types such as the comic Chinese immigrant and reworked the racial habits of theatrical orientalism just as they reappropriated the blackface stereotype. Through their use of oriental tropes, they reinforced how their productions were designed not just to please white audiences but also—and sometimes more significantly—to speak to the "colored theatre 'goer'" whose desires, needs, and tastes were changing.

This chapter highlights this strategic repurposing in four musicals—the Bert Williams and George Walker vehicles *In Dahomey* and *Abyssinia*, Salem

Tutt Whitney and J. Homer Tutt's *The Children of the Sun* (1919), and Noble Sissle and Eubie Blake's *Shuffle Along* (1921). In the first three, fantastical settings in foreign lands and exotic adventures allowed black characters respite from the drudgery of everyday life, the demands of racial uplift, and the oppression of American racism. *In Dahomey* and *Abyssinia* used orientalist motifs to help imagine spectacular African kingdoms, despotic rulers, and beautiful maidens. These two musicals included comic characterizations of Chinese immigrants but showed them in close proximity to African Americans and as the targets of racial hostility. *The Children of the Sun* envisioned African American and Asian peoples as linked through mythic histories, and *Shuffle Along* showed how oriental themes might be easily assimilated into a modern and cosmopolitan amalgamation of styles. Thus, each of these different theatrical productions used orientalism to articulate concerns about racial mobility and aspiration, national belonging, and the possibility of intimate connections between black and Chinese characters.

IN DAHOMEY

Since the venue for *A Trip to Coontown* was a less prestigious New York theater, Will Marion Cook and Paul Laurence Dunbar's *Clorindy; or, The Origin of the Cake Walk*, opening July 4, 1898, at the Roof Garden of the Casino Theatre, is sometimes hailed as the first all-black Broadway musical. However, because *Clorindy* was only a one-act show (adapted for the Roof Garden and serving as an afterpiece to Casino manager Edward E. Rice's *Summer Nights*), it is *In Dahomey* that has the distinction of being the first full-length musical written and played by African Americans at a major Broadway house. Written by Cook (music) and Dunbar (lyrics), with a book by Jesse A. Shipp, *In Dahomey* starred Bert Williams and George Walker and began its first New York production on February 18, 1903, at the New York Theatre.[6] Both prior to and after this New York run, *In Dahomey* toured successfully in both the United States and Great Britain (including a performance at Buckingham Palace for the royal family) and was revived on Broadway at the Grand Opera House from August 27 to September 19, 1904. The creative team of Cook, Dunbar, and Shipp would later also produce other musicals featuring Williams and Walker such as *Abyssinia* (opening February 20, 1906, at the Majestic Theatre) and *Bandanna Land* (opening at the Majestic on February 3, 1908).

The first act of *In Dahomey* opens with a minstrel duo of Tambo, a banjo player, and the comedian Bones, followed by an attempt by the fakir

"Dr. Straight" to sell hair- and skin-bleaching products. Shylock Homestead (Williams) and Rareback Pinkerton (Walker), two down-and-out characters, agree to serve as detectives to find a missing silver casket belonging to Mr. Cicero Lightfoot, the president of a group of African Americans, the Colonization Society, intent on relocating to Dahomey. On a tip from Hustling Charlie, they follow the wealthy Lightfoot down to his home in Gatorville, Florida, in order to try to swindle some money. Much of the action in the second act takes place in Florida as the two attempt to take advantage of Lightfoot, and Lightfoot finds a chest of gold in his backyard. The third act takes place in a fanciful kingdom of Dahomey as Shylock and Rareback are hailed as caboceers (governors) by the Dahomian natives, the missing box is found, and Lightfoot decides to return to Florida.

As Daphne Brooks has described, this convoluted plot registers the "heterogeneity of black cultural identity formation,"[7] combining familiar blackface representations with an elaborate fantasy of Dahomey that, like the fictional Orient, is linked to opulence and self-deception. In an opening dialogue, Moses Lightfoot, the agent of the Dahomian Colonization Society, imagines Dahomey to be a land of plenty, echoing the fantasies expressed in *A Trip to Coontown*: "They tell me that gold and silver in Dahomey is plentiful as the whiskey is on election day in Boston. The climate's fine—just the right thing for raisin' chickens and watermelons. It never snows so you don't need no clothes—(*pause*) such as the people wear here, and who know but what you can get a few franchises from the king [to] start street lights, 'lectric lights, and saloons to running" (*In Dahomey* l). The con man Hustling Charlie presents the Colonization Society's aims as speculation and profit in a new territory: "Well, there's a society down in Florida that's been piling up coin for years. Now that they're flush, they're goin' to go blow. They ain't satisfied, see. Their noodles ain't swelled on account of their dough, but they figure this country's a dead one. Some bloke tipped off Dahome as the original Klondyke and they're goin' against the brace hook, line, and sinker" (*In Dahomey* lvi).

But what makes this musical's setting of Dahomey different from the pleasures of Cole and Johnson's fictional "Coontown" is that this space is already seen as inhabited. When Lightfoot declares that "I'se just naturally disgusted with the frivolities of the colored population of dis country," Henry Stampfield, a postal worker, retorts, "I'll dare say you'll find the population of Dahomey quite as much a source of annoyance as the colored population of this country. Your exalted opinion of the ideal life to be found in a barbarous country is beyond my comprehension" (*In Dahomey* l). Stampfield brings up the possibility that the Dahomians will resist colonization: "You've fine, big ideas, but suppose the natives don't take kindly to the new order of things and refuse to be electric lighted, salooned and otherwise fixed up with blessings of civilization. Suppose—they look upon you as intruders and instead of receiving you with open arms (*pause*) make war on you?" Lightfoot then replies, "If it comes to that, we'll arrange with dem gentlemen like Uncle Sam did with the Indians," meaning, "Kick the stuffin' out of dem and put them on a reservation" (*In Dahomey* l). The musical's representations of what it means to be "in Dahomey" is indeed referred to as "colonization" rather than cultural exchange, just as the fictional setting is imagined as a place of profit rather than repatriation.

In 1906, Walker recalled in *Theatre Magazine* how he and Williams were employed to impersonate Dahomian natives in San Francisco's Midwinter Fair in 1893. After the actual performers from Dahomey arrived, Williams and Walker visited their exhibition. "It was there, for the first time, that we were brought into close touch with the native Africans, and the study of those natives interested us very much. We were not long in deciding that if we ever reached the point of having a show of our own, we would delineate and feature native African characters as far as we could, and still remain American, and make our acting interesting and entertaining to American audiences."[8]

Despite this desire to "delineate and feature native African characters," the musical sustains a marked degree of distance between its black American and its Dahomian characters. The succession of "Dahomian" spectacles in the third act makes explicit the fantastical aspects of the play's staging of Africa and its people. Here the play's earlier moments of escapism, such as the fabulations of Rareback Pinkerton or the hunt for buried treasure, give way to an even more spectacular expression of wealth, power, and exotic adventure. Beginning with a "Ballet or chorus, costumed as frogs," the extravagant show numbers then move to the "Gardens of Dahomey" and the song "My Dahomian Queen," in which the King sings of a "Moorish maid," a "dusky turtle dove" who is "so sweet and serene / Fresh from the jungle green," who reminds him of the Hawaiian queen Liliuokalani; "she is my Kai-o ka-lo-nian, / Royal Dahomian queen" (*In Dahomey* lxvii, 98–102). This reference to the U.S. overthrow of the Kingdom of Hawai'i reinforces, as Monica White Ndounou notes, the musical's "subversive undertones" even as it celebrates black female beauty.[9] The royal wedding of the king and queen of Dahomey is pictured as a spectacle much like those in *Aladdin*.

When I become a king,
All the jingle bells will ring,
While through the streets on palanquins we're borne.
'Twill be the grandest thing,
Just to hear the natives sing,
As loyally they fall before my throne.
Cabosieurs [caboceers] will be our sentry,
'Rabian knights will be our gentry,
The wonder of the twentieth century. (*In Dahomey* 99–100)

Other highlights of act 3 include a display of dancing girls as "Amazons" in a pageant reminiscent of *The Creole Show*, followed by a royal procession and a display of mass adulation as a chorus of "*African chiefs, soldiers, natives, dancing girls*" impressively fall "*prostrate on floor on faces to greet* SHYLOCK HOMESTEAD *and* RAREBACK PUNKERTON *dressed as Caboceers*" and sing "Evah Dahkey [Every Darky] Is a King" (*In Dahomey* lxvii). The London Shaftesbury Theatre program, according to the Kansas City *Rising Son*, suggested that an "Execution Tower" was part of the backdrop, highlighting the resemblance of the Dahomian king to the familiar figure of the oriental despot.[10]

Scenes such as these recall the lavish presentations of royalty, wealth, and women so familiar to the theatrical Orient; they also suggest new possibilities for formerly unrecognized black characters to find fulfillment in uncivilized lands. For Brooks, the song "imagines a world where the sun has finally set over colonial empires, 'fading' into a new era of black self-rule," and a sybaritic version of "Africa" as "an extravagant fantastical landscape of promise and renewal."[11] Nonetheless, the scene also maintains a sense of distance between the black American characters and the exotic natives as well as misgivings about colonial rule. In a *Freeman* review of a September 1902 production in Stamford, Connecticut, Sylvester Russell suggested that Jesse Shipp should "scratch his head and write the third act over again," since "there is no literary merit to be found in a band of American Negroes taking a trip to Dahomey merely to bluff the people around after they get there."[12] By October of that same year, he commented that in the New York production the third act had been greatly improved, though it was still mystifying: "Only one bluff is now made at the natives of Dahomey but the natives in some mysterious way take things into their own hands—then they don't—nobody understands just what[']s what, but the music plays and the king's chair is discovered in the beautiful garden." Furthermore, Russell noted that Rareback and Shylock willingly abdicate their Dahomian thrones: "The journey has made them tired. They want to go home and question the natives regarding the journey."[13]

Despite its many enticements, the fictional kingdom of Dahomey is portrayed as a foreign and alien culture rather than an ancient homeland. Even if America disenfranchises its black subjects, they nonetheless wish to return. *In Dahomey* included songs such as "The Czar of Dixie" and "That's How the Cake Walk's Done" that further emphasized American homelands through southern nostalgia. The lyrics of "That's How the Cake Walk's Done" state that while those from other nations such as France might attempt "ze cake walk," they are clearly inadequate to the task of perform- ing a dance that is "native" to the United States; the song states that "the folks from Paree / In this cake walk would have no chance." Furthermore, cake-walking is identified as originating in the U.S. South, with no mention of any African influence.

> The Cake-walking craze, it's a fad nowadays
> With black folks and white folks too
> And I really declare it's done ev'rywhere,
> Though it may be something new to you.
> 'Twas introduced years ago down in Dixie you know,
> By black folks from Tennessee,
> So just to show you, I'm going to do
> A cake walk of a high degree. (*In Dahomey* 163–65)

Like so many other exotic oriental settings, the fictional Dahomey is pre- sented as a temporary space of adventure rather than as a viable home. Early in the play, Shylock expresses initial reservations at Rareback's plan to go to Dahomey: "Say, man, have you got any idea how fast you're carrying me through life? Ten minutes ago, I was a soldier in the Salvation Army. Five minutes after that I'm a detective, and now you want me to be an emigrant" (*In Dahomey* lvii). This comment expresses not just a refusal to identify with Dahomian natives but also a rejection of "emigrant" status. It brings into focus how *In Dahomey* harbors another even more incongruous "emigrant" figure: the Chinese immigrant cook Me Sing.

Originally played by George Catlin, Me Sing appears in two scenes and is paired with another comic character, Mrs. Stringer (played by Lottie Williams, wife of Bert). In the first, Mrs. Stringer calls for a passerby to knock on the door of Me Sing's restaurant. When the passerby does so, Me Sing appears singing and tells the passerby to leave or he'll call the police.

The passerby responds with "Get out, you pigtail. You've got rats in your kitchen." Me Sing continues onstage, "*quarreling in dialect*." Mrs. Stringer then orders "Chinese ham and eggs," bird's nest soup, and an order of "shark fins" for herself and her friends. Me Sing "*repeats the orders in dialect*" and exits (*In Dahomey* lv). The suggestion that Me Sing has rats in his kitchen underscores the racism with which he is seen. At the same time, it is not clear whether the racism of the passerby—who also calls him "pigtail"—is designed to warn the audience about the dangers of Chinese food or to criticize those who harass Chinese immigrants. Certainly the main characters of *In Dahomey*, while they consider Me Sing strange, are far from hostile to him.

While Catlin's impersonation is clearly based on the familiar caricature of the barely intelligible Chinese immigrant man, the comedy of these exchanges is also directed at the assertive African American woman, Mrs. Stringer, who relies on his cooking. Both *In Dahomey* and the later Williams and Walker musical *Abyssinia* juxtapose stereotypes of emasculated Chinese men with those of assertive and voracious black women. Chapter 3 discussed how Mammy figures, such as Aunt Paradise in Walter Ben Hare's 1916 play *Abbu San of Old Japan*, caricature black femininity as both aggressively outspoken and obsessed with food. Importantly, Mrs. Stringer is not pictured as a Mammy but as an independent woman, a widow who writes "the fashion notes in the *Beanville Agitator*, the leading colored paper of Boston" (*In Dahomey* lviii). Still, her character satirizes both African American female independence and obsession with status and leisure. Like the African American girlfriend comically portrayed in the Stanley Murphy and Ed Wynn song "I'm Going to Get Myself a Black Salome," Mrs. Stringer's interest in clothes goes hand-in-hand with her laziness (telling a passerby to knock on Me Sing's door rather than do this herself) and her class privilege in hiring a Chinese cook. Her penchant for Chinese food is as much the subject of humor as is Me Sing's cooking: if exotic foods such as "Chinese ham and eggs," bird's nest soup, and "shark fins" are mentioned as being on Me Sing's menu, it is Mrs. Stringer and her friends who order them.

Mrs. Stringer's interactions with Me Sing in the second act also satirize the imagined self-indulgence of the black female character along with the alien qualities of Chinese immigrant labor. When she visits Mrs. Lightfoot (the wife of the president of the Colonization Society), Mrs. Stringer complains of having to walk from the station to the house and is "*accompanied by Me Sing with boxes, bundles, etc.*" When a startled Mrs. Lightfoot exclaims, "For heaven's sake. He's a Chinaman," Mrs. Stringer retorts, "Don't get excited. He won't bite you." She then explains that "my doctor's put me on a chop suey diet and I'm compelled to have him" (*In Dahomey* lix–lx). This scene not only affirms Me Sing as Mrs. Stringer's constant companion but even offers some sexual innuendo in her line "I'm compelled to have him," after which Mrs. Lightfoot tells her daughter Rosetta to "Show Mr. Chop Suey to Mrs. Stringer's room."

Apart from Mrs. Stringer, it is not fully clear what the characters of *In Dahomey* make of Me Sing. He seems to remain an alienated figure of ridicule, yet his presence also reinforces the sense of familiarity between Chinese immigrants and African Americans, indicating an ongoing relationship as well as close proximity. This sense of intimacy seems consistent with the frequent impersonations of Chinese immigrants by Catlin and others actors already noted. As illustrated in chapter 6, comic banter between a "Chinaman" and a "Coon" had already become an established part of African American musical entertainments. The familiar nature of this interracial exchange seems evident in a brief interaction recorded in the British version of the script of *In Dahomey*.[14] Immediately before scene 3's finale in the "Garden of Caboceers," the con men Hustling Charlie and Dr. Straight express disdain for the Dahomians, with Hustling Charlie telling Dr. Straight, "Doc, if these chocolate drops get gay around here, prescribe rough on rats. We've got to keep discipline" (*In Dahomey* lxx). Me Sing then appears briefly, first in an exchange with Rareback and Shylock: "ME SING *talks Chinese to* RAREBACK. *Bus. for* RAREBACK *and* SHYLOCK. RAREBACK *and* SHYLOCK *exit*." This is followed by unspecified stage business with Dr. Straight and Hustling Charlie: "DR. STRAIGHT *and* HUSTLING CHARLIE *enter and bus. with the Chinaman and exit. Chinaman sings*" (*In Dahomey* lxxi). While the script does not specify either the comic business or song, this order of these exchanges and the suggestion that Me Sing "*talks Chinese*" to Rareback could imply more affinity with the duo of Rareback and Shylock than with the less sympathetic characters of Hustling Charlie and Dr. Straight. In either case, Me Sing clearly has familiar stage business with both.

After *In Dahomey* was performed at London's Shaftesbury Theatre in 1903, one critic remarked that the show produced a novel effect.

From a casual glance at the notices we had vaguely supposed *In Dahomey* to be like any other "musical comedy" save in the complexion of its performers; and it was in an idle kill-time mood we visited the Shaftesbury Theatre. We found something quite unexpected; a new aesthetic "thrill," the fascination of the beautiful-uncanny, and a widening in the world of the horizon of the humorous. Here, indeed, was *aliquid novi ex Africa* [something important and new from Africa]. Since the Japanese performances of *Sada Yacco* we had seen nothing so curiously disquieting as *In Dahomey*. The resultant impression left on our mind was one of strangeness, the strangeness of the colored race blended with the strangeness of certain American things.[15]

These remarks highlight the "strangeness" created in the gap between what was expected of black performers and the expectations of "musical comedy" and the confusion that might have ensued as white London theatergoers tried to distinguish between African American performers and African representations. Even more interesting is how the reviewer compared this "curiously disquieting" response to *In Dahomey* to "the Japanese performances of *Sada Yacco.*" The emotional and physical intensity of the kabuki-inspired performances of Japanese actress and dancer Kawakami Sadayakko, who toured in 1899–1902, galvanized audiences who were used to the patently inauthentic versions of Japanese culture performed in *The Mikado* or Sidney Jones's *The Geisha*. This comparison suggests how *In Dahomey* may well have also been important as a showcase of the show's virtuosity: how its exaggeration and spectacle defamiliarized racial types and produced "disquieting" effects that thrilled with the "fascination of the beautiful-uncanny."

While George Catlin's Me Sing isn't mentioned in this review, such comments nonetheless draw attention back to *In Dahomey*'s comic juxtaposition of the Chinese male immigrant and African American "emigrants" to Dahomey. Just as Me Sing makes clear the unassimilable nature of the "Chinaman," so does the black characters' visit to Dahomey emphasize that imitating white colonial power leads to a dead end. *In Dahomey*'s hyperbolic and extravagant performances link African American disenfranchisement to the Chinese immigrant's "perpetual foreignness." These parallels invite larger questions about who is and who is not included in the body politic of both African and American countries, questions that would be continued much more explicitly in *Abyssinia*.

ABYSSINIA

Only the third act of *In Dahomey* is set in Africa, and its vision of Dahomey is populated with fantastical beings: dancing and singing frogs and Amazons as well as natives. *Abyssinia* is likewise full of fanciful elements; however, it

Pleasure Domes and Journeys Home

provides a somewhat more realistic staging based on Abyssinia, an African nation that had successfully resisted nineteenth-century European colonization, including Italy's attempts to take control in 1896. Located in an elaborate version of Addis Ababa, with settings that include a waterfall and live camels, it presents a number of more developed Abyssinian characters, including one based on the actual King Menelik II. It also incorporates Abyssinian words such as "Janhol" ("King"), "Ras" (a "prince") and "Esshi" ("All right").[16]

Like *In Dahomey*, *Abyssinia*'s plot involves the African travels of African American characters. A caravan of American visitors including a Baptist pastor, his choir, several of his congregants, and a Chinese cook have gone to Addis Ababa. With them are two comic figures, Rastus "Ras" Johnson (George Walker) and Jasamine "Jas" Jenkins (Bert Williams), who are mistaken for a prince and a general. Ras falls in love with Miriam, a local woman (Aida Overton Walker), but their courting is interrupted when he is mistaken for an enemy chief. Jas is also arrested for stealing a vase. Subsequently both are threatened with severe punishment by King Menelik II. Miriam and the Americans intercede on behalf of Ras, and the two ultimately are released.

Aside from the scenes with Me Sing, oriental allusions in *In Dahomey* seem rather cursory, with only oblique references to the tales of the *Arabian Nights*, oriental despots, and harem girls. In contrast, *Abyssinia* more thoroughly explores the possibility of foreign worlds in which African American characters can find love, power, and respect in addition to its more typical displays of exotic pageantry, colorful marketplaces, beautiful maidens, and royal despotism. King Menelik evokes a familiar oriental cruelty as he punishes cheating merchants and thieves.[17] Scene 6 is set in the Throne Room of Menelik's palace and includes a march of Abyssinian priests, royalty, and soldiers, followed by a *"dance (Minuet) of Priests followed by Turkish women, Hawaiian and Native Abyssinian women."*[18] An October 1906 review of *Abyssinia* in the *Freeman* declared that "the Oriental hue gave excellent opportunity for the scores of beautiful colored girls who needed but little making up to appear as the native born."[19]

Dream sequences also provided additional opportunities for oriental spectacle. In scene 4, Miriam, mistaking Ras for royalty, asks about the village in which he is presumably king. He then sings "It's Hard to Find a King Like Me," whose chorus imagines "competent and loyal subjects" paying tribute to their king as well as the "magnificent eminent Queen of the Orient" on "the Isle of Content." Stage directions indicate the spectacle of *"Jas in Oriental make up and six women, three on a side chained to bracelets* on his arms," and "*the market scene is transformed to grotto or foliage surrounding with chorus grouped as follows: All women reclining [with] servants (Men) fanning them and serving them in different ways to remain the same throughout.*" This stage direction is highlighted by the prompt "See page 9406 Laura Jean Libby's 'Dream of The Orient,'" presumably a sensationalized scene from one of writer Laura Jean Libbey's popular dime novels. The evocation of the enslaved harem through this display of women chained to Jas seems especially ironic given that King Menelik II of Ethiopia was known for his opposition to slavery. Nonetheless, this oriental spectacle accompanies Ras's hyperbolic fantasy of power as he sings of his superiority over a host of other rulers such as "Mister Roosevelt," the "Sultan of Turkey," "the High Mogue of China Lan," and "the wise gazabe that rules Japan" and brags about his many wives: "Of Brigham Young you all have heard old Utah's famous son, / He looks like three small dimes to me, I've got six-teen to his one."

This fantasy of despotic and sexual power contrasts Walker's exuberant Ras with the more woebegone Jas played by Williams. In scene 5, after King Menelik II has declared Jas to be a thief and sentenced him to amputation, Jas sings "Here It Comes Again," a song that emphasizes how he is the bearer of continual misfortunes (a familiar characterization for Williams). He details his many woes, including lack of money, alcoholism, violence, gambling, and addiction. Verse 7 describes a trip to Chinatown, where a "'Chink' presented me a pipe that gave me funny dreams": "I dreamt a lovely fairy came and sat upon my knee, / She said that I was handsome and she loved no one but me." At this point Williams lights a pipe onstage and presents his opium-induced dream.

> Here she comes again. Oh! joy and rapture here she comes again,
> I'm bound to marry that sweet fairy, Oh! lady tell me when,
> She answered with a pretty pout, that she is mine without a doubt,
> But shucks! My pipe is going out, Dod burn it, there she comes again.

Jas's depression is magically alleviated by a fairy who inspires his love; however, this fantasy is just as quickly snuffed out. As with Ras's scene of romance with Miriam in "It's Hard to Find a King Like Me," a vision of exotic femininity highlights the dream of black masculine power and fulfillment. Yet oriental rapture is seen as only a temporary and illusory alternative to a bleak reality.

George Catlin's pipe-smoking Chinese immigrant also returns in *Abyssinia* in the character of Wong Foo. As with *In Dahomey*, this character is paired with a demanding black female character. The third scene of *Abyssinia* highlights not only Wong Foo's mangled English in expressions like "Washa malla?" but also the open suspicion with which the cantankerous Aunt Cally Parker treats him. She find his very appearance to be a bad omen: "Yes, I always did b'lieve in signs. When I was home and a cat crossed my path something always happened. Well, that Chinaman is just like a cat. He's always slippin' and slidin' and you never kin hear him and every time he's passed in front of me yet, something happened." However, Aunt Cally's anxiety over Wong Foo's stealthy movements is not shared by the other characters. Wong Foo not only appears to be useful as the cook but also has endeared himself to others. After Aunt Cally's accusation, Lucinda defends him as "real clever" and tells Aunt Cally, "I've been teaching him how to sing native American songs." She and Wong Foo then stage a performance for Aunt Cally.

> LUCINDA. Mrs. Audience, allow me to introduce the singing marvel
> of the 20th Century, Mr. Wong Foo. (*Addressing Wong Foo*) Didn't
> I tell you, you must always bow to your audience? (*Wong Foo
> bows to Aunt Cally, who nearly falls from seat.*) Now sing after me.
> (*Sing chorus of any popular song, line at a time, each line repeated in
> turn by Wong Foo. When Wong Foo is through, Aunt Cally applauds
> violently. Seat is turned over and Aunt Cally is caught in arms of
> Elder Fowler who enters back of Aunt Cally just as Wong Foo finishes.
> Chinaman busy at tripod with tea-pot—while water is heating, smokes
> Chinee pipe.*)

Wong Foo's attempts to imitate a popular American song suggests Lucinda's dedicated tutelage as well as the limitations of his assimilation, and even Aunt Cally applauds her appreciation of his efforts. Wong Foo's song recalls the song of Mark Twain and Bret Harte's Ah Sin, perhaps singing the minstrel song "The Chinee Laundryman." In this scene, however, the humor is found not only in Wong Foo's peculiarities but also in the comic character of Aunt Cally, whose flirtation with Elder Fowler continues as Wong Foo returns to the background with his "*Chinee pipe.*"

The initial appearance of Wong Foo, like Me Sing in *In Dahomey*, suggests that a Chinese cook can have a familiar and even welcome presence in this black community. However, later he reappears under circumstances that comment more seriously on the divergent aspects of citizenship and belonging for Chinese immigrants. In scene 3, Wong Foo is left to wait for Ras and Jas while the remainder of the American caravan party seek shelter from an approaching storm. He is accosted by Abyssinian soldiers, including Tegulet, King Menelik's chief justice, and Captain Bolasso, Tegulet's nephew, a captain in Menelik's army. They are surprised to learn that this "Chinaman" is part of the caravan from America. Tegulet asks, "What part of America does this strange tribe inhabit?" and Bolasso replies, "They are not natives of America, but many thousands have migrated there."

If the earlier scene suggested a benign acceptance of Wong Foo as "real clever" and capable of learning American songs, this scene emphasizes the perceived lack of affinity that Wong Foo, the only character without African roots, has with both the African American and African characters. It makes clear that though Wong Foo travels with those he calls "Melican man Ras," and "Melican man Jas," he still is a member of a "strange" tribe. As they exit, Tegulet and Bolasso reinforce this distinction. Tegulet wonders about Chinese migration to the West, "Has that strange type of Humanity invaded the European Countries?" and Bolasso laughingly replies, "You'll find a few anywhere and everywhere." In *Abyssinia*, African as well as American characters picture the Chinese as "invaders" of Euro-American countries. Yet Tegulet and Bolasso release Wong Foo without violence and resolve the scene with the conclusion that just "a few" Chinese are "anywhere and everywhere." Both reassuringly familiar and perpetually alienated, the Chinese character provides a way of contemplating the hard limits of national and racial belonging.

The larger plot of *Abyssinia* relies on the confusion generated when Ras and Jas are easily mistaken for Abyssinian princes and generals, despite their comically exaggerated makeup and wigs (what Daphne Brooks memorably calls Dahomian "drag").[20] Within this logic of black belonging, African Americans are accepted within Abyssinia even though they are distinctively named as "Americans." The "Chinaman" Wong Foo, however, remains an outsider anywhere and everywhere. If the oriental dancing girl and the cruel despot provided models for Abyssinian maidens and African kings, Chinese immigrant figures, in contrast, continued to serve as comic reminders of another kind of racial abjection.

THE CHILDREN OF THE SUN

African American musicals regularly used oriental elements, whether displays of wealth and power or choruses of beautiful women, to emphasize how black protagonists might inhabit alternative lands and spaces. These new worlds were sometimes imagined within the boundaries of the United States (such as the fantasies of "Coontown") and sometimes outside (in the fantastical lands of Dahomey or Abyssinia). While most of these oriental characterizations stayed on the level of whimsy, some lent themselves to contemplation of more serious and sustained connections between Africans and Asians, whether through Afrocentric histories that envisioned common roots or through a present-day black internationalism.

Published in 1917 in the *Journal of Negro History*, George Wells Parker's lecture "The African Origin of the Grecian Civilization" argued that the classical civilizations of Mesopotamia and Greece originated in Africa. In 1918 Parker would publish *The Children of the Sun*, which postulated ancient connections between Egypt and Ethiopia as extending farther and including areas of Asia and Europe. Parker's writings suggest not only the construction of pan-African roots that boasted of advanced societies with high social and technological achievements but also ties between several ancient cultures that would prove "the African race as the real founder of human civilization" and counter the impression of African cultures as primitive and backwards.[21] Parker argued that archeological evidence as well as cultural and physiological similarity proved that the classical Greek and Roman worlds had their origins in African, not Aryan, civilization, thus challenging the "ethnic fetish of the Caucasian race" in Europe.[22] He also argued that African peoples once ruled ancient Assyria, Babylonia, Persia, India, and other parts of Asia and the Middle East, commenting that "it appears that the entire continent of Asia was originally the home of many black races and that these races were the pioneers in establishing the wonderful civilizations that have flourished throughout this vast continent."[23] In particular, Ethiopia was seen as "the mother of nations," one that "nourished and reared not only Egypt, but many of the nations of Asia and even gave to Greece her gods, laws, and civilizations."[24]

Like other African American intellectuals, Parker used the Old Testament's Psalm 68:31 ("Princes shall come out of Egypt; Ethiopia shall soon stretch out her hands unto God") in order to construct an inspirational past, showing "great potentialities in that race which gave Egypt to the sum of human things."[25] In this he drew on the biblical interpretation that each continent was populated by the descendants of the sons of Noah: Africa (Ham), Asia (Shem), and Europe (Japheth). Though the Old Testament makes no mention of race, by the nineteenth century white southern Christians had used the story that Noah cursed Ham's descendants and relegated them to servitude as justification for U.S. slavery. Parker, however, used the tripartite division to mark the "sons of Ham" as "the first race to spread itself over the world and to nourish the beginnings of culture which eventually showed their highest manifestations in the civilizations around the Mediterranean" and in which "the African was the master and not the slave, the conqueror and not the conquered, the civilized and not the savage."[26]

Imagined racial connections between cultures were not only projected onto the past. As Marc Gallicchio has described, in the decades before World War II, African American writers sensed the connections between a burgeoning U.S. empire and the European partitioning of Africa and "developed a view of world affairs that drew a connection between the discrimination they faced at home and the expansion of the empire abroad."[27] Black internationalism articulated "the extent to which many African Americans believed that color (or race) determined world politics" and envisioned a commonality among the world's "darker races" of Africa and Asia, who "shared a common interest in overthrowing white supremacy and creating an international order based on racial equality."[28] A number of prominent African American leaders drew parallels between American slavery and segregation and British colonial influence in India, connecting Euro-American imperialism to racism in the United States. For instance, a 1915 essay published in the *Atlantic* by W. E. B. Du Bois argued that the ruling classes in the industrial world had placated white workers by sharing small amounts of wealth stolen from Africa and Asia and beguiled them into fearing competition with "colored labor."[29] Reginald Kearney has also noted how African Americans stated their admiration for Japan's defeat of Russia in the Japanese-Russo War (1904–5) and shared a sense of racial pride as Japan became the only non-white imperial nation.[30]

Aspects of *In Dahomey* and *Abyssinia* also posited imagined connections between African and Asian peoples, albeit circuitously. For instance, Thomas Riis notes that one of the 1903 productions of *In Dahomey* at the Shaftesbury Theatre added a musical number, "Minuet, à l'Africaine,'" performed by Aida Overton Walker with a male chorus,[31] to replace the song "A Rich Coon's Babe," which had been performed earlier in the same London run. Riis speculates that this unnamed minuet was probably the lullaby in triple meter "Sur mes genoux, fils du soleil" from Giacomo Meyerbeer's *L'Africaine*, which was particularly popular with African American concert singers. The opportunity to replace a "coon song" with a rendition of a well-known operatic aria was no doubt another move to demonstrate the talent and respectability of the African American cast. It also allowed the appropriation of Meyerbeer's phrase "child of the sun," sung by Selika about the sleeping Vasco.[32] Act 2 of U.S. performances of *In Dahomey* included the song "For Florida," identifying African Americans as the divinely ordained "children of the sun."

> We are the children of the sun.
> Upon our brows His work is done.
> Tho' rude and black our faces be,
> Our hearts are brave, our hands are free.
> And as we sing, so shall we strive,
> As long as loyalty's alive. (*In Dahomey* lviii)

However, with the possible exception of works that addressed U.S. imperialism in the Philippines (such as *The Shoo-Fly Regiment*, the subject of the next chapter), there were few attempts by African American musicals at depictions of Asia and the Pacific that did not fall immediately into caricature. Thus two works by Salem Tutt Whitney and J. Homer Tutt, *Darkest Americans* (1918) and *The Children of the Sun*, seem especially noteworthy in this regard. While no scripts are available for either, reviews suggest that both of these works make use of George Wells Parker's ideas on Afro-Asian connections in a more sustained, if not profound, way.

Following their work with musical troupes such as the Tennessee Warblers, the Oriental Troubadours, and Baynard and Whitney's Famous Troubadours, Salem Tutt Whitney and his brother J. Homer Tutt joined the Smart Set Company, now run by Sherman H. Dudley, for which they wrote and produced over forty shows.[33] These included *Darkest Americans* and *The Children of the Sun*. *Darkest Americans*, with music by Charles "Lucky" Roberts, drew praise less for any serious message than for spectacular scenery ("scenes in mid-ocean, at the base of the pyramids, in the Arctic regions and in the land of the midnight sun, all depicted with the most gorgeous scenic and lighting effects"), impressive costumes (one particular set was described as running "the gamut from pale violet to orange and then from royal blue to scarlet" and making "their wearers look like lovely tropic birds of variant plumage"), chorus numbers ("large and lively"), and "the catchiest kind of music."[34] Its songs included familiar subjects such as "Stepping Po' Chile," "My Dark Brown Jewel of the River Nile," and "For the Samboes and the Sammies Are Together Over There."[35] Whitney and Tutt played an equally predictable duo of tricksters, Abraham Dubois Washington and Gabriel Douglass (or "Abe" and "Gabe"), who "have insinuated themselves through false representations" and whose efforts "to fit into their highbrow environment make for laughter a plenty."[36]

Darkest Americans billed itself in New York as pure entertainment, a "Riotous Hit" that was "Just Brimming Over with New Songs, Dances, and Novelties," and in Washington, DC, as a "Sensational Two Act Comedy" with an appealingly large cast ("35—people—35") that consisted of "mostly girls on account of the draft."[37] Yet *Darkest Americans* may also have struck a more serious note with one of its characters, "Dean Kelly Miller," based on the influential professor and dean at Howard University. Academics had been included in African American musicals before, such as in the Williams and Walker musical *Sons of Ham* (1900), which depicted humorous goings-on at Riske Industrial College, where the fraudulent Professor Skinnerbunch and Professor Switchem teach the reluctant students Willie Wataboy, Gabby Slangtry, Tobias Wormwood, and Harty Lafter.[38] In Bob Cole, J. Rosamond Johnson, and James Weldon Johnson's *The Shoo-Fly Regiment* (1906), Irving Allen and Sam Lucas as "Bro. DoLittle" and "Bro. DoLess" mocked book learning in their song "De Bo'd of Education."[39] However, the inclusion of a character based on Dean Miller lent an interesting gravitas to *Darkest Americans*. Miller was the first African American to attend Johns Hopkins University, a recipient of a law degree as well as a master's in mathematics, a professor of sociology and dean of arts and sciences at Howard, and coeditor with W. E. B. Du Bois of *The Crisis*. *Darkest Americans* was also set at the distinguished institution of Howard University, where education no longer served as industrial training but emphasized intellectual as well as economic uplift. Herbert Aptheker has detailed how African American enrollment in colleges grew from 355,215 in 1910 to 597,682 in 1920 and then to 1,188,532 in 1930.[40] In 1915 the *New York Age* called Howard University "one of the landmarks of Negro-American civilization."[41] Whitney commented in the *Washington Bee* that *Darkest Americans*, while dealing with "the humorous side of college life," can bring out "a lot of fun, without any sacrifice of dignity or violation of any of the properties."[42]

In *Darkest Americans*, the dean's disappearance leads to a second act in which Abe and Gabe travel around the world searching for him. Miller himself was active internationally; in the same July 1918 column as the first mention of *Darkest Americans*, the *Washington Bee* included the news that "Prof. Kelly Miller of Howard University has been on an extended lecture tour of the Far West and South. He has been well received everywhere."[43] Thus the second act gave the play a plausibly cosmopolitan aspect. The

Washington Bee anticipated, "The first act should interest the people of Washington, as it is laid at the Howard University, and from there to all parts of the globe in quick action," and the *St. Paul Appeal* wrote, "When the two adventurers are named to seek the lost president and trot clear around the globe in his pursuit the thrills come along in bunches."[44]

The exotic travels of Abe and Gabe would be repurposed in *The Children of the Sun*, Whitney and Tutt's sequel to *Darkest Americans*. A plot summary in the *New York Age* indicated that *The Children of the Sun* begins when the character of Dean Miller returns from a "successful voyage of archeological research, where he discovers valuable records which he claims establishes the antiquity of the Negro race"; these records "speak of Ethiopia as the mother of nations" and her offspring as "Children of the Sun." Miller's findings not only echo the arguments of George Wells Parker but also provide an excuse for the comic pair of Abe and Gabe, now experienced world travelers, to depart upon another expedition, since "the legend concludes with the prophecy that whoever locates the original site of the 'Children of the Sun' will discover a mountain of gold." Interestingly enough, it is suggested that "a Japanese student attending Howard tells of his people being sun worshippers, which causes an expedition to immediate[ly] proceed to Japan." With this lead, Abe and Gabe adventure "through Japan, Persia, India, and Egypt in a fruitless search, at last arrive at the site of ancient Ethiopia, and learn the true story of the 'Children of the Sun.'" [45]

While the presentation undoubtedly filled the need for the standard pleasures of musical comedy, it seemed to also operate as a vehicle by which to spread Parker's ideas on the Afrocentric origins of Western civilization. Lester Walton wrote that "as in all their other productions, Salem Tutt Whitney and J. Homer Tutt have sought to develop something which is woefully lacking among colored Americas—*race consciousness*—and in 'The Children of the Sun' the black man is strikingly set forth as the pioneer of civilization. In order to do this the theatregoer is taken to Japan, India, Persia, Egypt and finally to Abyssinia." He commented that this kind of theater ought to serve as a model for others seeking to educate a popular audience:

> Just as the Whitney boys are doing on the stage to offset the propaganda which the Caucasian has for years carried on in America to misrepresent historical facts concerning the black man, it would be fitting, especially at this time for other race educators and leaders in the various avenues of endeavor to adopt a similar policy and teach

the masses of our people that the Negro rocked the cradle of civilization and that he should be proud of his racial identity: that all white is not a virtue and all black is not a vice.[46]

In another review of the show a year later, Walton called *The Children of the Sun* "one of the best musical shows seen at the Lafayette in months," with "more of a plot than the average colored musical production." He said that "Salem Tutt Whitney and J. Homer Tutt adroitly carry out the underlying motive—to make the Negro proud of himself and his history—a history which did not begin in America. This is timely propaganda and should help combat plots conducted by those who would have the Negro and others believe that one's status should be chiefly determined by the color of their skin."[47]

Advertising and descriptions of *The Children of the Sun* regularly mentioned Parker's hand in the play.[48] A review written in the Ohio *Sun-Dial* and reprinted in the *Kansas City Advocate* in January 1920 opens with the first paragraph of Parker's introduction to *The Children of the Sun*: "In the morning of the world, when the fingers of Love swept aside the curtains of Time, our dusky mother, Ethiopia, held the stage. It was she who wooed civilization and gave birth to nations. Egypt was her first born and to Ur of the Chaldees she sent her sons and daughters, who scattered empires in Asia as the wanton winds of autumn scatter the seeds of flowers."[49] At the same time, the musical balanced out its history lessons with comedy, song, and dance. The *Kansas City Advocate* advertised the musical as "Clean—Classy—Clever—Historical" while praising Whitney as "the funniest colored man on the stage today" and drawing attention to "a stunningly gowned chorus of brown-skinned beauties well worth hearing."[50] The *Baltimore Evening Sun* noted that the first scene "brings out plantation songs along the banks of the old Swanee River, with Dixie wit and suggestions of the rich, old Virginia background," and the "unusually good songs" include "Travelin', We'se Travelin'" and "Dear Old Dixie Home," which, sung "without trace of the dialect," are "purely racial inspirations."[51]

The musical's staging of the search for Afrocentric roots thus seemed designed to work less as a convincing illustration of George Wells Parker's "scientific" approach and more as a theatrical romp through mythical time and space. The Ohio *Sun-Dial* described how "the company under Salem Tutt Whitney and J. Homer Tutt, opened the play full of pep with Mr. Jass on the wing as Lee Boots Marshall and ended in the hands of the Gods of the Sun, with Abraham Washington as king, played by Whitney"; the reviewer

Pleasure Domes and Journeys Home

rejoiced that "everybody in the Xenia play hou[s]es on Thursday, November 18, 1919 was ruled by a black king once if never again. Tell me the Smarter Set is not smarter."[52]

There also seemed to be strategic choices made as to which parts of Parker's history deserved staging. In the middle of his book, Parker argues that "Asia was the home of the black races as well as Africa"[53] and emphasizes the indebtedness of European to African culture in order to debunk "the great claims made by the white race as the developers of civilization."[54] Whitney and Tutt took on Parker's challenge to Eurocentric notions of black cultural inferiority much more implicitly, taking their audiences not to Greece or Rome but rather to Japan, Persia, India, Egypt, and Ethiopia. The *Baltimore Evening Sun* noted that *The Children of the Sun* was a form of "racial propaganda," since it was "based upon a book written by a well-known Negro archaeologist, who traveled and studied extensively to further this theory of tracing black, yellow and Oriental races back to the ancient Ethiopian race, classifying them all as 'Children of the Sun.'" However, the incendiary radicalism of Parker's thesis was strategically tempered not only by comedy and music but also by its focus on "black, yellow and Oriental" rather than on white and European. The *Sun* commented that "therefore, while such a plot, even though it is hung together lightly with song, dance and travesty, is not offensive to the white race, it may not please the proud East Indian rajah, a Japanese diplomat or statesman, a Persin [sic] philosopher, an Egyptian prince or an Abyssinian king. It, nevertheless, would have a tendency to boost racial pride among the Negroes, and allay any desire on their part to change their color."[55]

The lack of access to scripts or additional production records makes it difficult to ascertain more precisely how Whitney and Tutt imagined the "yellow and Oriental" aspects of their show or how audiences would have responded to those elements. Yet *The Children of the Sun* does seem to mark a definitive shift in the early African American musical away from earlier character types such as the oriental despot or the abject Chinese immigrant. Within its story line, the pleasure domes of stage orientalism present not only wistful fantasies about alternative spaces of adventure and profit but also tantalizing glimpses into Afro-Asian solidarity and black internationalism. The comic team of Abe and Gabe resemble the pairings of earlier musicals, such as Williams and Walker's Rareback and Shylock, or Ras and Jas, who journey to foreign lands in search of easy profits and discover racial pride. But these oriental spaces, while still spectacularly different and exotic, have become fully reconfigured as African American homelands extending throughout Asia and the Middle East. Perhaps most interesting of the details on *The Children of the Sun* is the comment in the *New York Age* that it is a "Japanese student attending Howard" who initiates the expedition to Japan and beyond by mention of "his people being sun worshippers."[56] This puts into play the possibility that Japanese as well as black characters take an active interest in both black educational institutions and the shared roots of Asian and African cultures.

The Children of the Sun was certainly neither the first nor the last theatrical work to imagine familial connections between the peoples of Africa, Asia, and Europe as the "sons of Ham." Zora Neale Huston's *The First One* (1927) stages how, three years after the flood, a drunken Noah is tricked into cursing Ham into servitude and turning his skin black. At the end of Hurston's play, Ham rejects his family and decides to follow his wife, Eve, "to where the sun shines forever."[57] Hurston's depiction of this solo departure suggests that Ham and his descendants will remain isolated and separate from their Asian as well as European brethren. In contrast, in the joyous and clever musicals of Whitney and Tutt, Ham's children discover their connection with other "children of the sun," thus offering the possibility that African Americans and Asians might act as fellow travelers in search of education, adventure, and cultural roots.

SHUFFLE ALONG

Unlike *The Children of the Sun*, the majority of African American musicals used oriental characters and tropes without any attempt at profundity, as suggested by a steady stream of show numbers such as "Chop Suey Sue" in *Darkydom* (1915), "Chink, Chink Babe" in *Darktown Follies* (1916), "Japanese Sandman" and "China Town" in Billy King's *China Town* (1920), and "Down Again in China Town" in *Wift Waff Warblers* (1921).[58] By the early 1920s, these elements were regular features that seemed to have little real connection to other aspects of the show. Yet as *Shuffle Along* reveals, even the occasional and casual nature of oriental effects can say something interesting about the early African American musical.

The first African American musical on Broadway since *Bandanna Land*'s New York production in 1908, *Shuffle Along* had an extensive Broadway run after opening at the rather dilapidated Sixty-Third Street Music Hall (a theater remote from the rest of what was considered Broadway) and was revived in several New York–based and touring versions. In 1923, the New York *Amsterdam News* reported that the "third company" of *Shuffle Along* (the first

Pleasure Domes and Journeys Home

being the 1921 original, the second the 1922 touring company) had opened at Harlem's Lafayette Theatre "to one of the biggest starts made around here." This company, featuring veteran performers Salem Tutt Whitney and J. Homer Tutt in the leading roles, enjoyed standing-room-only crowds that were "almost six deep."[59] The show launched the careers of a number of performers such as Florence Mills, Fredi Washington, Adelaide Hall, and Josephine Baker and inspired many other artists, most famously Langston Hughes, who hailed the show as a catalyst for the Harlem Renaissance.

The plot of *Shuffle Along* satirized the small-town politics of a mayoral election in "Jimtown in Dixieland." The comedians Flournoy E. Miller and Aubrey Lyles, whose vaudeville sketch "The Mayor of Dixie" served as the basis for the libretto, played the political rivals Steve Jenkins and Sam Peck. The plot revolved around them and a third mayoral candidate, the virtuous Harry Walton (Roger Matthews), who can marry his beloved Jessie (a role first played by Gertrude Saunders and then by Florence Mills) only if he wins the election.[60] Its most famous song was "I'm Just Wild about Harry," later chosen by Harry S. Truman for his 1948 presidential campaign.

Within these many notable features, it is easy to overlook *Shuffle Along*'s one big oriental number, whose origins seem quite accidental. According to Eubie Blake's biographer Al Rose, the previously written "Oriental Blues" was included in the show because Sissle and Blake found some "vaguely Orientalish costumes" left over from Frank Fay's revue *Fables*.[61] "Oriental Blues" is sung in act 2 after Tom, a political boss played by Noble Sissle, tells Sam about Aladdin's "marvelous lamp": "Well that was the old lamp they found and when they rubbed it, a Genii came up and any question you would ask him, he would answer it, and any wish you would make, he would grant it" (*Shuffle Along* 328). Tom and the female chorus then sing "Oriental Blues." As Lyn Schenbeck and Lawrence Schenbeck have noted, the music of the song included multiple oriental motifs: "All but the first 8 and last 4 bars of the refrain consist of 4-bar vignettes that reference China, India, Persia, Arabia, and Egypt with familiar musical depictions—drone basses, repetitive rhythms, parallel fifths, and chromaticism or modalism."[62] The corresponding lyrics also run through a list of oriental characterizations.

> If I only had an oil lamp like Aladdin,
> With its mystic power from his mystic bower,
> I'd call old Genii to my side.
> Precious stones nor riches
> Would not be my wishes,

But on bended knee,
I would implore old Genii
To let my conscience be his guide.
I'm so lonely and there's only
One place that will ease my mind,
It's that land where gentle oriental maidens you will find.

Chorus:
I've got those Oriental Blues,
I've got those Oriental Blues.
I'd like to take a trip across the China Sea to old Shanghai,
And sip a cup of China tea with poor Butterfly.
Then spend a day at old Bombay,
Watching those Hindoo maidens sway,
With a night's repose where grows the Persian rose.
At dawn on an Arabian steed,
At an Arabian speed,
Let me whirl with a Bedouin girl.
Then in Cairo town, I'd like to settle down.
Oh, I've got those mysterious, doggone delirious Oriental Blues.
I've got those Blues. (*Shuffle Along* 328–48)

The inclusion of "Oriental Blues" provided yet another way to stage a chorus line of attractive dancers, admired by Lester Walton in the *New York Age*: "Mr. Sissle is assisted by Oriental gals who look the part in every way. Most attractive are these maidens to gaze upon."[63] The array of women recalls the carefully managed displays of *The Creole Show*, with each chorus member dressed as a different type: a multi-ethnic dancing harem carefully positioned around Sissle's singing sultan. At the same time, these oriental women also seemed interchangeable, with the song's lyrics hinting that each promised, like Shakespeare's Cleopatra, an "infinite variety" of erotic pleasures.

These oriental roles were added to an already full slate of appearances for three female choruses: the Jazz Jasmines, the Happy Honeysuckles, and the Majestic Magnolias. In contrast, there was only one male chorus, the Syncopating Sunflowers. Like many African American musicals after *The Creole Show*, *Shuffle Along* made the most of its chorines both in terms of costumed spectacle and in varied dance numbers. Photographs show the female choruses in various costumes: "cotton picker" overalls with straw

Noble Sissle and chorus from *Shuffle Along*, ca. 1921.
Photograph by White Studio. © Billy Rose Theatre Division,
New York Public Library for the Performing Arts.

hats, dapper top hats and shiny one-piece outfits, elaborately draped satin gowns.[64] Like the costuming and arrangement of "Oriental Blues," each of these appearances defines an easily recognizable type, yet their quick succession conveys a sense of the black female body as much more protean. The lyrics of the song "If You've Never Been Vamped by a Brownskin, You've Never Been Vamped at All" imply that dark skin itself works as a kind of superficial costume or a surface that immediately signifies sexual appeal.

A high brown gal will make you break out of jail,
A choc'late brown will make a tadpole smack a whale,
But a pretty seal skin brown, I mean one long and tall,
Would make the silent sphinx out in the desert bawl.
(*Shuffle Along* 322–25)

This effect suggested yet again by the song "I'm Just Simply Full of Jazz," sung by the character of Ruth Little, a woman who declares herself not interested in marriage because she is "simply too full of jazz" (106). Her performance along with the Jazz Jasmines insists that while each of their movements suggests a different cultural character, these stock modes of racial performance no longer strictly define their dancing. The quick changes and far-ranging repertoire move quickly from oriental to Hawaiian to black, thus showing the Jazz Jasmines to be versatile performers liberated by their improvisatory choreography.

Just because I like to do a wiggle,
In a regular Salome style,
Just because I like to do a little wriggle,
Like on a Hawaiian Isle,
'Cause I kick like a donkey and jump way back,
'Cause I act like a monkey, and "Ball the Jack,"
And like Miss Minnie, I do the Shimmie,
Keep my shoulders shaking 'til you hear them crack,
Just 'cause you see my feet a-shufflin',
Just because I act like a Razz,
Though I seem a little hazy,
I ain't crazy;
I'm just simply full of Jazz. (*Shuffle Along* 113–19)

In "I'm Just Simply Full of Jazz," the distinctions between non-white cultures—oriental, Hawaiian, black—are lost in the rapid tempo of choreographic gestures performed by virtuosic African American bodies. This dynamic movement across so many racial styles demonstrated the chorus line's artistry and ability to transform into a variety of roles. At the same time, it highlighted the excitement and creative potential in a specifically black-identified but also racially amalgamated form of jazz.

In her 1934 essay "Characteristics of Negro Expression," Zora Neale Hurston would comment on "the lack of symmetry which makes Negro dancing so difficult for white dancers to learn." Hurston emphasized that in African American dance forms, "there is always rhythm, but it is the rhythm of segments. Each unit has a rhythm of its own, but when the whole is assembled it is lacking in symmetry. But easily workable to a Negro who is accustomed to the break in going from one part to another, so that he adjusts himself to the new tempo."[65] Hurston differentiates between how "the white dancer attempts to express fully" but "the Negro is restrained," even while "gripping the beholder by forcing him to finish the action the performer suggests." She concludes, "Since no art can ever express all the variations conceivable, the Negro must be considered the greater artist, his dancing is realistic suggestion, and that is about all a great artist can do." Hurston calls this the "dynamic suggestion" of the black dancer: "No matter how violent it may appear to the beholder, every posture gives the impression that the dancer will do much more." These characteristic "abrupt and unexpected changes" of "Negro dancing" appear in *Shuffle Along* as a rapid succession of racial styles, reducing a set of easily recognizable racial characterizations to a kind of theatrical shorthand.[66] The multiple chorus numbers of *Shuffle Along* treat different racial characterizations like Hurston's "dynamic suggestion," throwing out a constantly changing set of riffs in the show's many improvisatory moments.

Of course, this emphasis on variety and racial mélange could be found in a number of white-produced Broadway shows. Just a few years prior to *Shuffle Along*, Dave Montgomery and Fred Stone's adaptation of *Aladdin*, *Chin-Chin* (1914), had presented a different mash-up of blackface and oriental numbers. Gerald Bordman recalls that in the *Ziegfeld Follies of 1917*, "Fanny Brice vamped as an Egyptian odalisque" while an Eddie Cantor in blackface "played the college-educated son of a porter," as played by Bert Williams. Ziegfeld also had "a set simulating Chinese lacquer" with "fifty Ziegfeld beauties scampering up and down red and gold ladders against a black blackground."[67] *Sinbad*, with book and lyrics by Harold Atteridge and music by Sigmund Romberg, became the most successful Broadway musical of 1918–19, marking one of the early successes of Al Jolson, who played "a porter in old Bagdad" who "meets a series of characters from the Arabian Nights (including Sinbad) and goes to exotic settings Cabin of the Good Ship Whale, Grotto of the Valley of Diamonds, Island of Eternal Youth." Its songs included "Rock-a-Bye Your Baby with a Dixie Melody," "My Mammy," and "Swanee" (George Gershwin's first hit recording, written with Irving Caesar), sung on a ramp from the stage in blackface and white gloves.[68]

However, *Shuffle Along*'s use of racial pastiche must be understood in terms of the considerable difficulties that African American performers continued to face in trying to appeal to white audience members. David Krasner has suggested that *Shuffle Along* had two aims: "first, to create progressively minded musical characters with integrity and capable of romance; and second, to appeal successfully to white nostalgia for minstrel humor and Dixie."[69] The former is highlighted by a tender love scene between Ruth and Harry singing "Love Will Find a Way," which Krasner notes as a "breakthrough" since it presented "a decent, mature relationship against the backdrop of comic mayhem."[70] The latter shows itself in *Shuffle Along*'s continued reliance on minstrel types and plantation nostalgia. Both Miller and Lyles wore blackface for their roles, and the show featured songs such as "Uncle Tom and Old Black Joe," "And They Called It Dixieland," and "Sing Me to Sleep, Dear Mammy." Lester Walton noted that there were "more than the usual number of comedians under cork in one show."[71]

Thus, a third aim might be added to this list, as prompted by *Shuffle Along*'s celebration of the versatile and virtuosic African American performer. The show undeniably showcased the rapid-fire delivery of song and dance numbers by the leads as well as by chorines who could change their choreographic character—and thus the racial connotations of their own bodies—as quickly as they did their costumes. Expertly played and quickly discarded, these varied gestures highlighted the superficial nature of the racial types, including those of blackface nostalgia, used in the show. "Oriental Blues" was not the only *Shuffle Along* number inspired by recycled costumes: Lyn and Lawrence Schenbeck write that "after finding some plantation costumes and scenery, Sissle and Blake wrote 'Bandana Days' and pulled other Southern numbers from their song trunk so those items could be used."[72] The repetition of familiar spectacles of plantation nostalgia, like the oriental scenes, offered a practical response to an initially limited budget, but they also became only a few of the multiple options for performers.

Shuffle Along's varied shifts in choreographic and musical gesture and visual spectacle emphasized the artful repetition of old racial habits rather than their representational truth. Still, white reviewers seemed to appreciate the dance numbers only insofar as they confirmed a sense of black movement as inherently excessive, chaotic, and animalistic. "How they enjoyed themselves," the *New York American* marveled of what it called the "darky musical" of *Shuffle Along*: "How they jiggled and pranced and cavorted, and wriggled, and laughed."[73] The *New York Herald* wrote, "It is when the chorus and principals of a company that is said to contain the best negro troupers in these parts gets going in the dances that the world seems a brighter place to live in. They wriggle and shimmy in a fashion to outdo a congress of eels, and they fling their limbs about without stopping to make sure that they are securely fastened on."[74] Such impressions were an integral part of how blackface minstrelsy had framed black physicality as "peculiar" and "eccentric." Sianne Ngai suggests how figures such as Topsy in *Uncle Tom's Cabin* demonstrate how "the affective qualities of liveliness, effusiveness, spontaneity, and zeal" are harnessed to race, and such animation "function(s) as bodily (hence self-evident) signs of the race subject's naturalness or authenticity."[75] However, African American reviews of *Shuffle Along*, such as one appearing in the *Kansas City Advocate*, highlighted the precision and dexterity entailed in its energetic succession of styles: "There are more delightful song numbers, and alluring music in 'Shuffle Along' than in any other production of its kind in existence, and they are given so fast and furious that you don't even get time to think and audiences simply rise to their feet clamoring for more."[76]

It is important to keep in mind that breaking ground on the Great White Way was not *Shuffle Along*'s only aim. The musical operated as the latest work in what was by now a firmly established touring tradition of all-black shows that bore a special meaning for African American audience members. Demonstrations of masterful control over the variety and tempo of movement challenged the implied slowness and backward qualities of nostalgic plantation minstrel types. Jayna Brown emphasizes the importance of seeing these dance numbers in terms of black modern mobility: "For a black constituency during the 1920s, black chorus women were important figures of hopeful migratory movement, urban ebullience, and promise. Moving in sinuous unstoppable unison, black chorus girls' agile mobility became the triumphant and pleasure-filled affirmation of opportunities gained."[77] Numbers such as "Oriental Blues," or Sissle and Blake's "Vision Girl," added later to the run, might have enhanced this impression as well by alluding to foreign travel and adventure ("Vision Girl" lauds the "sweet and gentle charms" of a woman, a "mysterious pearl" residing "way down in Pyramid Land" [*Shuffle Along* 447–71]) and suggesting the exotic oriental maiden as one of many possible roles realized by the black female body.

Aided by its mastery of oriental form, *Shuffle Along* evidenced both new forms of black social mobility and cosmopolitan sophistication geared for African American audiences. This was demonstrated not only in the show itself but in related entertainments, such as an example described by Lucien White in the *New York Age* in November 1921. A post-show entertainment at the New Star Casino included the orchestra from *Shuffle Along* under the direction of Eubie Blake, popular song and dance numbers by Florence Parham and "Little Cleo, the Baby Vamp," circus acts, and a midnight cakewalk, all hosted by the magician Black Carl (Edward Johnson). Performed while the Broadway run of *Shuffle Along* was still in full swing, this post-show event suggests a much looser format without the constraints of plot and character, thus relaxing the terms by which *Shuffle Along* was tasked with representing black characters to white audience members.[78] The show's terms of judgment, whether for acrobatic moves or dance, highlighted refinement, artistry, and control: "At twelve o'clock, the cake walk was begun, and for a half-hour some dozen or more couples girated [*sic*] and pranced about the floor in such bewildering grace and accuracy of step as to make the selecting of the winners a task of no mean proportions." Moments of pleasurable excess were reserved for afterward, with *Shuffle Along* musicians and the New Amsterdam Musical Association dance orchestra "dispensing dance music for the lovers of Terpsichore," as "the light fantastic toe was swung in joyous abandon until after four o'clock in the morning of Monday." [79]

Notably, this post-show performance also included players who did oriental acts. White described how the appearance of two groups in particular, the "Ishii Japs" and "a troupe of Arabs—the Lightning Six (a misnomer, as there were eight in the group)," gave a "program of rare excellence" that was "received with enthusiastic approval." These specialty acts confirmed how the infectious music and dance of *Shuffle Along* complemented fantasies of oriental physicality and extraordinary skill. The "Ishii Japs" and the "Lightning Six" apparently exhibited riveting physical control and athletic skill. White declared, "From the entrance of the Japs until the last whirl of the Arabs there was not a dull moment." The "Lightning Six" in particular gave a memorable demonstration of acrobatics and balancing: "The Arabs gave a breath-taking act of tumbling and whirling backward, forward, sideways, concluding with the building of a pyramid in which one man supported the bodies of his seven companions, who stood on his head, his shoulders, and swung onto his body at various points." While it is not certain whether the "Ishii Japs" or the "Lightning Six" were actually touring Japanese, Middle Eastern, or North African acrobats, or their African American imitators, these "breath-taking" performances served as a reminder that both oriental and black acrobats had been popular since the 1860s and 1870s in the spectacles of the "Wild West" show, the circus, "mammoth" minstrel troupes, and vaudeville and burlesque specialties.[80] For instance, Moroccan,

Algerian, and Lebanese men under the management of Hassan Ben Ali toured nationally with the Sells Brothers Circus in the late 1890s and were famous for acts such as "the pyramid in which up to ten men and boys stood in decorative formation upon the shoulders of a single man."[81]

Shuffle Along is most often remembered for the successes of its African American performers as they aspired to and to some extent achieved mainstream white commercial success. But it is important to assert how the show, and the success of its creators, was also measured by other standards that were understood as black or, at times, even oriental. A May 1922 article in the *Savannah Tribune* noted how the "Messrs. Miller and Lyle[s] and Sissle and Blake seems [*sic*] to have no end to their activities since the remarkable success scored by Shuffle Along" and reported that producers were now backing Miller and Lyles's comedy-drama *The Flat Below* as well as other all-black shows such as *The Bandanna Land Revue*, "a midnight show savoring of the levee."[82] The *Savannah Tribune* then described how the producers of *Shuffle Along* had been made rich by the show: "We would not be surprised to learn that the 'boys' have purchased a theatre on Broadway as 'Variety[,]' the theatrical weekly, tells us they are rolling in wealth, sporting high priced buzz wagons and diamonds that would make an Indian Rajah envious." As superficial and temporary as they might have been, *Shuffle Along*'s oriental markings—whether in costumed bodies, choreographic gestures, or box office gains—added another dimension to its highly symbolic success.

10

. . . .

FANTASY ISLANDS

STAGING THE PHILIPPINES, 1900–1914

. . . .

Prior to the Spanish-American War, the Philippines was depicted as but one of many exotic oriental locales on the American stage. Owen Hall's London and New York hit *Florodora* (1899) staged romance and adventure on a mythical island in the Philippines. The Chicago-based musical *The Isle of Bong Bong* (1905) was also presumably set in the Philippines, but this time imagined as a floating island.[1] In 1893, J. Cheever Goodwin and Woolson Morse premiered *Panjandrum*, a sequel to their previous 1891 New York hit, *Wang*, a comic opera set in a fantastical version of Thailand. Staged by the DeWolf Hopper Opera Company, *Panjandrum* imagined the Philippines as yet another whimsical oriental land and featured a bullfighting scene as well as the savage antics of a native tribe ruled by King Panjandrum. Both the king and the title were publicity stunts; as producer DeWolf Hopper related, "We purposely called the play by the meaningless syllables, 'Panjandrum.' Rather than stumble over 'Panjandrum,' the public asked for seats for Hopper, as we intended they should."[2]

As the United States became involved in the conflicts of the Spanish-American War (1898), the Filipino-American War (1899–1902), and the Moro Rebellion (1899–1902), these theatrical fantasies gave way to plays that showcased more dramatic scenes of U.S. imperialism and military fervor. Not all of these had serious intentions. Frank Dumont's 1899 *Witmark Amateur Minstrel Guide and Burnt Cork Encyclopedia* includes "The War

Correspondent," a minstrel sketch in which a brief romantic dialogue between the "Filipina girl" Inez and her fiancé, Juan, a Filipino soldier, leads to a comic scene with two American tramps, Jake and Pete, who visit the Philippines as war correspondents. Wearing "misfit military costumes" and pretending to be Filipino soldiers, they sneak into the home of Emilio Aguinaldo, the Filipino independence leader. When he confronts them as imposters, they hide in the nursery, and Jake pretends to be a baby. Finally they are discovered by Filipino soldiers; as the soldiers aim their guns at them, Jake and Pete "pull small American flags out of bosoms and wave them at soldiers," declaring, "Fire on this if you dare!" The scene concludes with a fantasy of U.S. imperial power: "*Music Yankee Doodle. Jake and Pete dancing. Soldiers and rest are cowering . . . Filipinos baffled.*"[3] African American productions such as the Black Patti Troubadours sketch "A Filipino Misfit" (1902) provided a similarly humorous take on the conflicts in the Philippines. This one-act farce cast the well-known comic actor John Rucker and Leslie Triplet as "Bo-Ho and Ho-Ho," the "Filipino Misfits," and Ida Larkins as "Miss O So Ot," described as "a warm member," and provided a female chorus with names such as "Miss Co Co," "Miss Lo Lo," and "Miss Do Do."[4]

However, a number of full-length works set in the Philippines injected more serious notes into their productions, reflecting not only the gravity of war but also anxieties linking American imperialism with issues of race. Patriotic tableaux, thrilling conflicts with Filipino insurgents, and choruses of alluring Filipina maidens would be staged repeatedly by both white and African American actors in ways that blended melodrama, comedy, and romance. This chapter compares several full-length plays authored by white playwrights—Charles E. Blaney's melodrama *Across the Pacific* (1900), Clyde Fitch's society melodrama *Her Own Way* (1903), and George Ade's comic operetta *Sultan of Sulu* (1902)—with a distinctive trio of musical shows by and about African Americans. Bob Cole, James Weldon Johnson, and J. Rosamond Johnson's *The Shoo-Fly Regiment* (1906), the Pekin Stock Company's *Captain Rufus* (1907), and the Black Patti Troubadours' *Captain Jasper* (1913) provide a very different perspective on the racial tensions inherent in U.S. expansionism. Each of these works emphasizes the virtues of patriotic military service and "Rough Rider" masculinity. However, for African American male characters, the wars in the Philippines served both as a path toward racial uplift and as a reminder of racism in America. While the Philippines was staged for both white and African American men as a place of interracial desire as well as imperial adventure, *The Shoo-Fly Regiment, Captain Rufus*, and *Captain Jasper* balanced out the more conventional depictions of Filipinas as exotic temptresses by also picturing them as legitimate love interests.

ROUGH RIDERS AND RACIAL LOGICS: *ACROSS THE PACIFIC* AND *HER OWN WAY*

The script of Charles E. Blaney's *Across the Pacific* has been lost, but Blaney's novel of the same title, written in 1904, is based closely on this melodrama.[5] Its story begins with a patriotic group of Montana miners who volunteer to fight in the Philippines. Led by the courageous Captain Joe Lanier, the men head for Luzon, stopping along the way in San Francisco to visit a Chinese opium den. These various settings provide opportunity for scenic effects as well as an array of racial types that contrast white American virtue with danger and treachery in the form of Chinese immigrants and Filipino insurgents. The inhabitants of the Montana mining camp include a knife-wielding servant, Sing Lee (called a "rat-catcher" and "the equal of any dog in the community"[6]); another Chinese immigrant appears as the dubiously genial proprietor of an opium den. These Chinese characters foreshadow the conflicts with Filipino insurgents by showing oriental dangers already present within U.S. borders.

Described in the novel as "yellow devils," Blaney's Filipinos are suggested to be similar to both the Chinese and the white but "dark-complexioned" villains who become spies for Emilio Aguinaldo (Blaney 103). Their portrayal reflects the shift from the imagined American "liberation" of the Philippines from the Spanish into U.S. military action maintaining colonial control against the efforts of Emilio Aguinaldo and other Filipinos fighting for independence. Caroline Levander has suggested that "just as the perception and media portrayal of Cubans as noble freedom fighters underwent a radical change when U.S. forces journeyed abroad and engaged an opposing army in the Caribbean in 1898," so did Filipinos "undergo a radical metamorphosis from ally to enemy" and become "'othered' to the point of being unrecognizable." Levander notes that Filipinos were described as "part-Spanish" but also as "niggers," "Malays," and "Mongols" and that Theodore Roosevelt referred to them as "Apaches and Oceala." One report even "declared that Filipinos were 'spotted' and 'striped.'"[7] John Cullen Gruesser relates that letters from African American military men stationed in the Philippines commented with disgust on how white soldiers used the word "nigger" to describe Filipinos as well as "lamented the actrocities perpetrated on native soldiers and civilians."[8]

Like other dramatizations of these wars in the Philippines, *Across the Pacific* featured a thrilling and realistic battle scene pitting white Americans against dark-skinned Filipino insurgents. Reviews praised how "one sees the soldiers in action and with fidelity enough to cause one frequently to rise in his seat with a desire to shout out his approval of the boys from the States" and pointed out the use of "a real Gatling gun . . . spitting out 260 shots to the minute"[9] and the "roar and crash of the fire arms, and the blind struggle of the little bond of Americans defending themselves against overwhelming odds [which] afford a stage representation seldom excelled."[10] The inclusion of musical numbers by "Blaney's Rough Rider band"[11] helped support the transformation of Blaney's Montana miners into a unified band of brothers fulfilling the dictates of Manifest Destiny. The heroic image of the Rough Riders (the first U.S. volunteer cavalry) drew from frontier mythology (slouched hats and horses) and military history, most famously the decisive battle fought at San Juan Hill in Cuba on July 1, 1898. Though rife with casualties for both the Spanish and the U.S. sides, this battle became emblematic of U.S. military prowess in the Spanish-American War, in part due to popular dramatic reenactments given in Wild West and minstrel shows as well as to its active use in the political promotion of Theodore Roosevelt. Tales of heroism in the Spanish-American War, as Amy Kaplan has noted, spoke to the recuperation of white American masculinity after the divisiveness of the Civil War, uniting the North and the South "against a common external enemy";[12] they also echoed the frontier rhetoric lauding the conquest of Indigenous lands and celebrated American technological progress in the development of the rapid-fire Gatling gun.

While emphasizing all of these elements of white American patriotic fervor, Blaney's battle scenes included an additional scene of racial transformation involving the character of a journalist, Willie Live. Live, played by Blaney's brother, Harry Clay Blaney, was central to the story's entertainment value; reviewers praised how Live "furnishes a large assortment of laughs and provides several good songs"[13] and how "his brilliant wit, his ever-ready kodak, and his sure-shot revolvers . . . [are] sufficient guarantee that there will be 'something doing' every minute."[14] But in the frenzied final battle scene, Willie transforms himself into a very different figure—a Rough Rider hero—in a dramatic moment that is also described by Blaney's novel as an act of blacking-up.

In the battle that followed, Willie Live fought like a demon. He seemed to bear a charmed life. The bullets whizzed about him, yet he remained unscratched.

Hatless and coatless he fought, and every time his rifle cracked a Filipino fell.

In a few minutes his face, arms and hands became so black with powder from his own weapons that he might easily have been mistaken for a negro. (Blaney 122)

This symbolic moment works on two levels, allowing Willie to appropriate the imagined strength and virility of the black body (and, however obliquely, the presence of the African American soldier in the Philippines) while insisting on the racial superiority of whiteness that is presumed to undergird U.S. imperial might. Willie's transformation from educated white journalist into battlefield "demon" reflects what Paula Marie Seniors has described as the popular image of Roosevelt as "the civilized white man who in fighting the Spanish American War sacrificed his life of luxury and privilege by taking on the white man's burden by fighting for the black, mulatto, and white Cubans."[15] This and other scenes of melodramatic conquest in *Across the Pacific* thus promoted, according to a review in the *Washington Post*, the play's "educational value," insofar that "thousands of people are afforded a glimpse of war, and the terrible realities of such a conflict as the government has been engaged in on the other side of the world. The stage pictures, the Filipinos, the Chinese, the sailors, the soldiers, all teach valuable lessons."[16]

Clyde Fitch's *Her Own Way* revolves around a similar idea in which military service in the Philippines helps to distinguish a white American hero from both his romantic rivals and his racial enemies. A vehicle for the popular actress Maxine Elliott, the play lacks any scenes in the Philippines but is nonetheless preoccupied with imperial mastery as defined not only by victory in battle but also by the successful regulation of primal energy and sexual desire.[17] *Her Own Way* depicts the romantic troubles of the beautiful yet somehow unspoiled socialite Georgiana Carley. Georgiana rejects the advances of the wealthy but conniving Sam Coast in favor of the heroic Dick Coleman, a lieutenant who has just been ordered to the Philippines. Coleman's voluntary military service caps off his other virtues, among them his anti-union work to help "stop a strike of street cars in Brooklyn" (Fitch 8). His firm management of discontented labor in New York is consistent with his attitude toward Filipinos. As Georgiana worries about his being subject to "unfair, cruel, unlawful warfare," Coleman responds, "I suppose that's what it's likely to be with the natives until we teach them a thorough lesson on every one of the infernal islands" (Fitch 65).

In addition to rebellious natives, the perils of the Philippines also include sexual temptations that might lead upstanding American military men astray. Georgiana's mother blithely tells Coleman that "we'll watch the papers to see what brave things you do, and don't fall in love with any of the décolleté young nigger ladies we read about" (Fitch 123–24). The fear of sexual defilement through interracial desire is also voiced by Georgina's hairdresser, Bella Shindle, who worries about her beloved, a Mr. Gootch, who has enlisted in Coleman's regiment. Bella is not only worried about Gootch's safety in battle but also nervous "that he's right there among all those black creatures, whose manners is very free, I'm told, and whose style of dressing is peculiar." She frets that "Mr. Gootch always did favor dark-complexioned people" (Fitch 193).

Bella's jealousy is not shared by Georgiana, who never once questions Coleman's sexual loyalty even when she is not always sure of his love. Yet this separation between civilized American values and Filipino savagery is sustained through her romantic choices as well. When Coleman's rival, the unscrupulous Sam Coast, tries to force Georgina to marry him, she tells him, "You don't know what love is!" and delivers an impassioned speech: "Love doesn't make beasts of men, it makes men of beasts. It doesn't take all for itself—it sacrifices all for another. Love isn't an enemy that lays traps and makes ambushes,—love is a friend whose heart is a divine magnet!" (Fitch 181). If Coast's impulsive desires mark him as a "beast," the hero Coleman demonstrates his civilized masculinity in both his restrained and respectful courtship and his military service in the Philippines. Georgiana's words directly admonish Coast for his attempts to blackmail her but also subtly echo the larger terms of American imperial interests in the Philippines. In 1898, President McKinley famously stated his aims for the military administration "to win the confidence, respect, and affection of the inhabitants of the Philippines by . . . proving to them that the mission of the United States is one of benevolent assimilation."[18] Though quite different in tone from Blaney's *Across the Pacific*, *Her Own Way* also equates skin color and virtue, as both the hero, Coleman, and the heroine, Georgiana, successfully manage their encounters with danger and Filipinos are portrayed as the unseen "dark-complexioned" people who must be wooed into "confidence, respect, and affection."

BROWNFACE AND BLACKFACE IN *THE SULTAN OF SULU*

Her Own Way references taboos against interracial romance, marriage, and sex between American military men and Filipinas, themes which receive a more satirical treatment in George Ade's operetta *The Sultan of Sulu*. Ade references real-life events in the Muslim Sulu region of the southern part of the Philippines. As President McKinley declared sovereignty over the region, the Bates Treaty offered a salary to the historical sultan of Sulu, Hadji Mohammad Jamalul Kiram, in exchange for his help with American commerce and settlement.[19] As Victor Mendoza points out, the play's portrayal of Ki-Ram and his eight wives also registers the early twentieth-century American public's fascination with the "twin relics of barbarism," slavery and polygamy, associated with the Philippines.[20] But rather than realistic reportage, *The Sultan of Sulu* took the form of a comic opera influenced by works such as Gilbert and Sullivan's *The Mikado* (which Ade performed during his undergraduate days at Purdue University) and *Florodora*. Ki-Ram resembles a cross between Gilbert and Sullivan's characters Koko and the Mikado, and Ade's Galula, "an elderly female, all of whose native charms have long since disappeared" (Ade 30), resembles Katisha. The female chorus of Filipina wives who sing "a bolero refrain" while demonstrating "gay castanetting" (Ade 2) suggest the popular chorus of "Spanish (Filipina) girls" in *Florodora*. *The Sultan of Sulu* makes light of imperial enterprise, soothing any anxieties over the forced imposition of American rule. One St. Louis reviewer called Ade's "excruciatingly funny" play "the best thing we've gotten out [of the] Philippines yet. . . . It almost reconciles one to the $20,000,000 we blew in for the archipelago."[21] As in many other depictions of the Spanish-American War, there are spectacular battle effects, as when in act 1 "*a body of United States Volunteers in khaki and marines in white pours on the stage in pell-mell confusion.*" Yet the play still supports a picture of imperial power as comically benign, as these troops sing,

> Though we come in warlike guise
> All battle-front arrayed,
> It's all a business enterprise;
> We're seeking foreign trade. (Ade 11)

According to one of his contemporaries, James McKee, Ade was a writer who "just thought the idea of Americans trying to transform the Filipinos into Asiatic carbon copies of American democrats was almost too absurd for words."[22] But *The Sultan of Sulu* does address the question of Filipino transformation through staging two distinctively racialized characters: Ki-Ram's beautiful wives, who are pictured as easily assimilable, and his two "*Nubian slaves,*" who are not. The casting of white actresses as the chorus of wives supported the impression that Ki-Ram's Filipina wives are ideal

Fantasy Islands

subjects for American colonization. Aside from elaborate headpieces, the white actresses wore no makeup or dress in the original production to suggest that they were racially distinct from white American women. One wife, Pepita, is described as "the Gibson girl of the Philippine Islands" (Ade 4). By the end of the play, the wives reappear in fashionable American dress, eagerly anticipating their divorce from Ki-Ram and matched up with various American soldiers. This transformation becomes a source of humor, as one of the male characters marvels, "Only to think—yesterday morning an untamed creature of the jungle, and now, thanks to our new policy, a genuine American girl" (Ade 119). His phrase "untamed creature of the jungle" recalls the "dark-complexioned" and "free" women imagined by Bella Shindle in *Her Own Way*. But the easy assimilation of Ki-Ram's wives is aided not just by the transparency of their cross-racial casting but also by the perception that Filipina wives were already "Spanish," as prior colonization presumably erased the native identities of Filipinas. This onstage depiction was supported by popular ethnographies of the time. In *The Philippine Islands and Their People*, Dean C. Worcester, secretary of the Interior of the Philippine Islands, declared mixed-race Filipinas to be distinct from Native women, though as exotically beautiful: "Many of the *mestiza* women and girls are very attractive, and like the native women they have beautiful hair, which not infrequently reaches to their heels, and of which they are inordinately proud."[23]

The Sultan of Sulu adds another element to shore up the color line between the "Spanish" and the "native" chorus girl. To highlight their entry into American identity, Ki-Ram's wives, already played by white actresses, embrace dimensions of blackface minstrelsy. In the second act, the performance of a "Sulu battle-hymn" (described as *"Oriental music"* sung by the *"chorus of Natives"*) is quickly dismissed in favor of what the white American businessman, Jones, calls the *"popular* songs of a truly progressive and refined people" (Ade 95–96). The American characters begin by performing "Rosabella, Rosabella Clancy" complete with a *"walk around,"* and they are followed by one of Ki-Ram's wives, Chiquita, who announces a performance of "the song they like the best of all," which entails a

> syncopated serenade,
> Beneath the lime-light's glow,
> About a dusky darky maid. (Ade 97)

Stage directions emphasize how "the music swings into a coon melody" as the leading characters form *"a minstrel semicircle"* (Ade 97). The principal characters, both white and Filipino, then sing a song about "Miss Delia," a "saddle-cullud Venus" who is being urged by her lover to "come to de cabin window" (Ade 98). These musical moments layer cross-racial imitations: white performers play Filipino characters who are demonstrating their successful assimilation into American culture through a blackface number.

The easy assimilation of the female chorus is offset by male characters who are much less harmoniously integrated into American imperialism. Ki-Ram's "*Nubian slaves*" are overtly based on blackface types, as suggested by their names "Didymos" and "Rastos." They dance, appear in the song "My Sulu Lulu Loo," and have a key moment in which they are told, "You are slaves no longer, but free citizens of Sulu. Serve the Governor, if you choose, but compel him to pay union wages and tip you liberally" (Ade 54). Upon gaining this American freedom, they later appear "*smartly attired as waiters*" who perform "*an impertinent break-down*" directed at Ki-Ram, who is told to restrain his irritation at them: "Governor, be careful. You are now an office-holder. This is the president and vice-president of the waiters' union. You can't afford to antagonise the colored vote" (Ade 64–65). In the final act, after Ki-Ram is imprisoned for scheming to dispense with his wives, they reappear "*in frock-coat costumes and tall hats*" during a political parade displaying different versions of the Democratic and Republican Marching Clubs in Sulu and perform "*a lively dance*" (Ade 124). Didymos and Rastos are then announced as the Democratic and Republican candidates for governor. However, the American official, told that he must "preserve order in Sulu" but not "interfere with any of the local laws or customs," finally restores Ki-Ram as sultan of Sulu. The two blackface characters are pictured "kneel[ing] in trepidation" after which Ki-Ram tells them, "You two statesmen hurry and get me a throne" (Ade 127).

While Ki-Ram's wives are imagined as easily assimilated into liberated American wives, his slaves Didymos and Rastos are relegated back to servitude. Through picturing Didymos and Rastos as nearly gaining their freedom through the imposition of American democracy, *The Sultan of Sulu* wrestles black enslavement away from its more sobering American contexts; slavery is instead presented as an obsolete Filipino custom that American imperialism might hold in check. *The Sultan of Sulu* suggests how the "benevolent assimilation" of Filipinos into American ways goes only so far and satirizes not only the servile conditions of Didymos and Rastos but also their uppity demeanor as part of the consequences of American democracy.

MILITARY HEROISM IN *THE SHOO-FLY*
REGIMENT AND *CAPTAIN RUFUS*

No complete scripts of *The Shoo-Fly Regiment, Captain Rufus*, or *Captain Jasper* are available. However, reviews and other accounts suggest how these musicals present African Americans as central to U.S. military involvement in the Philippines. Christine Bold has described how in the late nineteenth and early twentieth centuries "African-American image makers forged a distinctively black popular culture around these soldiers, celebrating them as a source of race pride and solidarity among peoples of colour—national and international."[24] While African Americans served with distinction in battles against Native Americans and in the Civil War and Spanish-American War, their military accomplishments were inevitably undervalued or erased. In 1898 Roosevelt acknowledged white and African American participation in the pivotal Battle of San Juan, recalling that "we went up absolutely intermingled, so that no one could tell whether it was the Rough Riders or the men of the Ninth who came forward with the greater courage to offer their lives in the service of their country."[25] However, by the following April 1899, Roosevelt published a very different account in his serialized memoirs in *Scribner's Magazine*, suggesting that black soldiers were, "of course, peculiarly dependent upon their white officers" and changing his version of the Battle of San Juan: "None of the white regulars or Rough Riders showed the slightest sign of weakening; but under the strain the colored infantrymen (who had none of their officers) began to get a little uneasy and to drift to the rear."[26]

All three musicals refuted these insinuations of weakness and cowardice. Sylvester Russell wrote that *The Shoo-Fly Regiment* "presented a better side to the stage picture of a black soldier, who is braver and more loyal to his country than any playwright who ever lived."[27] *Freeman* critic Juli Jones (William Foster) recalled a specific scene in *The Shoo-Fly Regiment*: "When the lieutenant asked for volunteers to take a dangerous fort, every man stepped forward and volunteered to sacrifice his life for his country; it was a question at every performance whether the audience would applaud or laugh."[28] *The Shoo-Fly Regiment* featured the song "The Old Flag Never Touched the Ground," which, according to Bob Cole's sister, Carribel Cole-Plummer, was inspired by the story of Sergeant William H. Carney of the Fifty-Fourth Massachusetts Regiment, an all-black combat unit that fought in the Civil War battle of Fort Wagner, South Carolina. During the battle, the bearer of the national flag was killed, but the standard was taken up by Sergeant Carney. Despite severe wounds to his chest, he held the flag aloft and returned to his comrades, saying, "The old flag never touched the ground."[29] The published sheet music for "The Old Flag Never Touched the Ground" was "respectfully dedicated to Sergeant Carney of the 54th. Mass.," connecting African American heroism during the Civil War with military service in the Philippines.[30] J. Rosamond Johnson as Jackson garnered special praise for his performance of the song: "On more than one occasion the situations were intensely dramatic; he was equal to them especially when he stood waving the American flag, insisting that it never touched the ground."[31]

The Pekin Theater's *Captain Rufus* similarly highlighted the remembered bravery of African American soldiers fighting in the Philippines. The *Broad Ax* noted that "the great battle scene which closes the second act is a veritable triumph . . . and presents the thrilling and realistic picture of a real skirmish between American troops and Philippine insurgents."[32] Sylvester Russell also found effective the musical's final climax, "when soldiers came to the footlights to sing over bodies, dead men's graves."[33] A *Chicago Defender* review of the revival pointed out "the military feature, which affects every human heart, thrills you, and all the more so when real soldiers appear and an actual battle takes place."[34]

As Seniors has noted, the refusal of the U.S. military to appoint African Americans as commanding officers was directly challenged in *The Shoo-Fly Regiment* by the "decision to make J. Rosamond Johnson's character, Edward Jackson, an officer in the production, and to costume him in an officers' uniform."[35] *Captain Rufus* and *Captain Jasper* both followed suit, designating a number of characters as corporals, captains, majors, and lieutenants. These three musicals also highlighted the military veterans in the audience. The 1906 Chicago production of *The Shoo-Fly Regiment* gave a special performance for the Eighth Illinois Regiment that had served in Cuba during the Spanish-American War; the *Broad Ax* announced that "the entire regiment will attend the performance in uniform" and that "the gold lace and brass buttons of the regiment in the audience will prove a most interesting sight as well as a most distinctively social feature ever given in a first class theatre at a play of this kind." During that performance, the *Broad Ax* said, "the theatre will be appropriately decorated with the colors of the regiment and the national colors, which will bring out the strong patriotic sentiment that pervades the performance of *The Shoo-Fly Regiment*."[36] Similarly, in the 1914 revival of *Captain Rufus*, L. W. Washington commented in the *Broad Ax* that "when *Captain Rufus* and the chorus . . . sang 'The Sword and the Flag' and guards raised the American flag, I saw private Hightower, a member of the Eighth Ill. National Guards who was present, stand with head uncovered in the midst of that vast audience, so impressive was this scene."[37]

Accounts of these plays invariably address the conflicts in the Philippines as the "Spanish-American War," in which Americans allied with Filipinos against colonial Spain. Yet these three dramatizations portrayed African Americans as pitted against insurgent Filipinos fighting for independence in the Filipino-American War. This elision suggests a calculated avoidance of some of the more troubling tensions around U.S. imperialism and race. The celebration of African Americans as military patriots obscured the wariness with which many African Americans approached American imperialism abroad. While some African Americans openly opposed annexation, their political choices were limited. As John Gruesser relates, "The election of 1900 became a referendum on U.S. imperialism generally and the effort to subjugate the Filipinos specifically."[38] African Americans were limited to voting either for "the proexpansionist Republican incumbent McKinley, who had done little to protect the rights of blacks, or the anti-imperialist Democrat William Jennings Bryan, who unabashedly advocated white supremacy." "Faced with this difficult choice," Gruesser remarks, "most blacks regarded McKinley as the lesser of two evils." As Scot Ngozi-Brown has noted, "The fates of African-Americans and Filipinos were bound by their common disenfranchisement," with neither "regarded to be capable of full political participation and self-determination." Ngozi-Brown comments, "The turn-of-the-century American quest for empire abroad occurred at a time when the specter of disenfranchisement, economic dislocation, mob violence, and terrorism plagued the black population at home in the United States." The African American soldier serving in the Philippines was both made the target of racial animosity from white American soldiers and placed in the position of firsthand witness to the racism against Filipinos: "He endured open hostility from his white colleagues and officers, and he watched how they imposed 'home treatment for colored peoples' on Filipinos."[39]

In the *Freeman*, critic Sylvester Russell accused the writers of *Captain Rufus* of copying "military material" from *The Shoo-Fly Regiment*.[40] While this may well have been true—and Black Patti's *Captain Jasper* in turn imitated other aspects of *Captain Rufus*—what is perhaps more salient is how each of these plays uniquely configured its theatrical elements in order to challenge some of prevailing typecasting of both African Americans and Filipino characters. Given that the most moving scenes of these musicals celebrate U.S. military heroism, it is more difficult to discern in them more guarded views on annexation. Yet though these three plays glorify the loyal African American soldier, they also provide some awareness of the complex racial dynamics inherent in U.S. imperial expansion.

THE OLD MINSTREL AND THE NEW
SOLDIER: *THE SHOO-FLY REGIMENT*

Produced by Bob Cole and J. Rosamond Johnson, *The Shoo-Fly Regiment* is described by James Weldon Johnson (who wrote the lyrics) in his autobiography as being "in three scenes; time, the outbreak of the Spanish-American War; the first and third scene in a Negro industrial school in the South, the second scene in the Philippines."[41] The first act at the Lincolnville Institute, an industrial college in Alabama, depicts a love story between Edward Jackson (J. Rosamond Johnson), a graduate of Tuskegee who is being offered a position at the school, and Rose (Inez Clough, later Fanny Wise), the daughter of the principal. Act 2 takes place as Jackson and other leading characters fight insurgents in the Philippines, featuring what the *New York Age* called "a touch of military melodrama, with a battle scene and gun play"; in the third act, the regiment returns to Alabama, where the lovers are reunited.[42]

The love story between Jackson and Rose spoke directly to the concerns expressed by Aida Overton Walker that the "popular prejudice against love scenes enacted by Negroes" on the part of white audiences discouraged African American musicals from presenting onstage romance.[43] In February 1908, the *Freeman* commented that the play "gives an opportunity to show to the incredulous white that the Negro has ability and talent to produce a play, teeming with music, humor and an interesting love story."[44] Despite its dramatic displays of military heroism and touching romance, *The Shoo-Fly Regiment* was billed as a comedy and praised for familiar humorous characterizations such as R. A. Kelly's "old-time plantation negro" or "Ophelia, the Village Pride," a cross-dressed role played by Andrew Tribble, and for specialty songs in dialect such as "Ghost of Deacon Brown."[45]

That the first and final act of *The Shoo-Fly Regiment* are set in the United States suggests how the concerns of imperialism are intricately interwoven with the presentation of both minstrel comedy and black racial uplift. The play opens at the fictional Lincolnville Institute, a "colored industrial school in the South, with a cotton field in the background,"[46] suggesting the Hampton-Tuskegee models for black education in service and skilled trades. For Booker T. Washington, industrial education allowed valuable lessons in self-employment, thrift, and industry as well as preparation for work already associated with African American slaves.[47] W. E. B. Du Bois was much more skeptical, accusing this model of perpetuating the caste system of plantation and domestic black labor in the service of white masters. *The Shoo-Fly Regiment* plays both sides of the question, suggesting racial uplift through hard work and meticulous service but also affirming education as producing opportunities for new kinds of employment. Choruses of students celebrate cooking, blacksmithing, and dressmaking as crafts that require management and design as well as manual production.

> We know just how to fit both fat and thin,
> And make them appear just as neat as a pin.
> Gingham and calico, muslin and lawn,
> Under our fingers so skillful take on
> Shapes that are very trim, stylish and neat;
> Our work, so people say, is dainty and sweet.[48]

The industrial school is pictured as fulfilling a need not only for service labor and basic literacy but also for artisanal craft and scientific knowledge. New methods of farming are contrasted with the old agricultural economy, as a male chorus declares, "We are the boys who've learned the worth / Of a plow, and a hoe, and an acre of earth." Their words emphasize the sustenance and advancement of the African American farmer, rather than a white master; agriculture is now informed by modern techniques rather than manual labor: "We've learned that the way to deal with land / Is to work it with the head as well as with the hand." Without forgetting that "our forefathers also raised some cotton; / With the help of a mule and the use of a hoe," they hail "the brand new farmer man" who does "farming on a chemical plan": "Not only do we know how to plow and hoe, / But we know what makes the cotton grow." By the end of this number, the entire ensemble reaffirms this transformation from a familiar minstrel scene of plantation nostalgia to a paean to the educated African American worker.

> You now can see,
> As plain as we,
> Just how this whole plantation
> Has, far and nigh,
> Been transformed by
> Industrial education.

Young and vigorous characters, who demonstrate their vigor both in school and in battle, are contrasted with black plantation types, such as "Bro.

DoLittle" and "Bro. DoLess" (played by veteran actors Irving Allen and Sam Lucas),[49] who satirize how

> A man kin study hard in books,
> And graduate f'om school,
> And yet dat man kin be wid ease
> De bigges' kind o' fool

in the song "De Bo'd of Education."

Both education and military service are seen as integral to African American racial uplift, as the different acts move from the Lincolnville Institute to military action in the Philippines and back again. The heroic Edward Jackson, "a graduate of Tuskegee," is celebrated for his military valor in the Philippines. His return to the South in the final act of the play links colonial endeavors abroad to American claims on domestic territory. This is emphasized in the inclusion of the second act song "O, Southland" by the male chorus.

> Long years our fathers 'neath thy sun,
> Bent under weary toil,
> They felled thy forest, and brought forth
> The treasures of thy soil;
> And so thy sun, thy soil, thy rocks,
> Thy forests, streams, and flowers,
> By right of toil, by right of birth,
> By right of love are ours.

In the song, labor by enslaved Africans becomes the basis for claiming U.S. territory as well as citizenship, suggesting the blended logics of U.S. imperialism and colonial expansion. Notably, while Filipino natives appear in *The Shoo-Fly Regiment* as rebellious insurgents, Native Americans do not. Indigenous presence is erased as African Americans are uplifted into the role of colonial settlers.

A similarly troubled claiming of American identity at the expense of Native American presence would be reinforced in a 1908 musical by Cole and Johnson, *The Red Moon*. *The Red Moon*, a love story between the black character Plunk Green and his half-black, half-Indian beloved, Minnehaha, depicts Green at odds with a rival, Red Feather, who is favored by Minnehaha's father, Chief Lowdog. As Seniors suggests, the story incorporated hopes for interracial cooperation and black racial progress as well as drew on the interactions between Native American and African American students and teachers, including Booker T. Washington, who served as a "house father" to Native American male students at Hampton Institute in 1880 before founding Tuskegee in 1881.[50] The romance between Green (played by J. Rosamond Johnson) and Minnehaha (played by Abbie Mitchell) was considered groundbreaking. However, like the Filipino characters in *The Shoo-Fly Regiment*, the Indian characters of *The Red Moon* seemed based less on actual people and more on conventional romantic or villainous stereotypes. In his *Freeman* review of *The Red Moon*, J. D. Howard commented that "there is a bit of evolution interwoven throughout the story that is sure to have a beneficial effect upon American whites as regards their opinion of the Negro" but added that Cole and Johnson "have succeeded in bringing out to a nicety the natural degenerate tendency of the Indian and show correspondingly well the ambition and progressive tendency of the Negro."[51]

CAPTAIN RUFUS

Written by J. Ed. Green and Alfred Anderson, the Pekin Stock Company's *Captain Rufus* opened July 20, 1907, at the Pekin Theater in Chicago; it later appeared at the Harlem Music Hall in New York in August 1907 and was revived again at the Pekin in 1914. The plot concerns what *Variety* described as "two roustabouts," Rufus Jones and U. R. Swift, who leave New Orleans to escape the police and are shipwrecked off the coast of the Philippine Islands. A U.S. regiment mistakes Rufus Jones for "Captain Rufus," and in a similar fashion, Filipino insurgents hail Swift "as their heaven sent leader," even though "both men are utterly ignorant of military tactics and customs."[52] Despite the comic focus on these dissolute "roustabouts," the Pekin's *Captain Rufus* was hailed as a positive sign of African American racial progress. The *Chicago Defender* began its review of the 1914 revival with "If you want to see a show that will make you feel proud of your race; if you desire to be moved to tears or laughter, your heart to respond to real, genuine sentiment; if you like artistic acting, superb singing, enjoy a military musical comedy of the highest class, just go to the Pekin Theater and see 'Captain Rufus,' which is there for a 'run.'"[53]

As with *The Shoo-Fly Regiment*, *Captain Rufus* also blended different genres and stock characterizations with heroics, with the *Chicago Daily Tribune* calling it "a curious mixture of musical comedy, burlesque, extravaganza, and melodrama."[54] In describing the racially mixed audience of the 1907 New York performances, Lester Walton emphasized the importance of balancing the more serious aspects of the play with comedy and music: "While not playing to crowded houses, the attendance is good, and it seems that the size of the audience increases with each performance. Both whites and colored were amazed last week at the manner in which 'Captain Rufus' was put on, and the Pekin Stock Company is demonstrating that the whites will take us seriously from a dramatic standpoint, when applied in the proper doses."[55] The humor of Harrison Stewart and Mat Marshall as the two "roustabouts" helped to offset the melodramatic dimensions of the more serious war scenes, sometimes, as noted by Sylvester Russell, to detrimental effect: "His [Stewart's] waving of the American flag was novel, but the waving of the American flag and white flag together was unapprovable."[56] This juxtaposition of comic and heroic roles also more subtly affirmed that the roles of both the ne'er-do-well and the romantic lead were now available to African American men. According to the New York Age, as Rufus Jones, "Mr. Stewart went through his comical paces with a mock gravity that brought him into immediate good standing with the audience."[57] The real "Captain Rufus" could also be played by Sidney Kuppatuck, as the Chicago Defender commented, in ways that were "stately and commanding": he "acted and spoke without a fault, and rendered a baritone solo that was sweet in tone and rich with resonance."[58]

Captain Rufus had another racial twist in its plotline; not only is Jones mistaken for "'Captain Rufus,'" but his partner-in-crime, Swift, becomes chieftain of a band of insurgent Filipinos."[59] Furthermore, Swift's incompetent leadership is contrasted with the appearance of an actual Filipino leader (played by Lawrence Chenault in 1907 and Charles Liverpool in 1914). It is unclear whether this performance went beyond villainous caricature; however, reviews did note that the role of "Leon Carlos" did have some importance. The Broad Ax commended Chenault "in the role of an insurgent chief" who has "striking make-up and portrays his part with fidelity."[60] Both the Freeman and the Defender praised the opportunity for an exciting stage fight as performed by two African American actors. Sylvester Russell lauded this "duel scene with swords" between Chenault and Jerry Mills (as the African American Major Drummond) as "the best I have ever seen by colored actors," commenting at length that "it was something finer than a grand opera duel; it was not by West Point cadets, but with such an exhibition of military art by two colored actors, representing a colored major and a Filipino desperado, that it was just as good."[61] The Defender mentioned the "fine qualities" of Mills as Drummond in the revival: "especially was this evident in the duel between him and Charles Liverpool, who took the part of Leon Carlos, leader of the Phillippines [sic]," and noted for both men, "Their acting received generous applause."[62] That an African American character could be easily mistaken for a Filipino one and that an African American actor could earn praise for playing a Filipino insurgent suggest that *Captain Rufus* employed—perhaps inadvertently—significant degrees of representational flexibility. This also points to the possibilities of racial slippage between African American and Filipinos, or pro-annexation Americans and Filipino nationalists. This slippage moved to an even deeper level in the musical's Filipina characterizations and treatments of interracial romance.

FILIPINA DANCING GIRLS AND DIVAS

Both *The Shoo-Fly Regiment* and *Captain Rufus* featured Filipino antagonists appearing in battle scenes, such as the dueling Leon Carlos or the "Philippine Spy" (played by Herbert Amos) listed in the cast for the 1906 version of *The Shoo-Fly Regiment*.[63] They also showcased memorable characterizations of Filipinas through songs such as "On the Gay Luneta" (with music by James Reese Europe) and "La Philipena" in *The Shoo-Fly Regiment* and "Amazon Land" in *Captain Rufus*.[64] At least one of these numbers celebrates interracial romance. Sung by Lieutenant Dixon (Theodore Pankey) and chorus, "On the Gay Luneta" speaks of a past encounter in a bucolic setting:

> When the moon was shining over Manila Bay
> I went strolling away,
> To the Luneta gay.[65]

The song recalls a "Manila Bella," characteristically figured as a "Spanish maiden" whose eyes "out-twinkle the stars."[66] Although the outcome of their love affair is not related, the chorus indicates that this romantic encounter is set in the past: "I never will forget her, / This gay Grizzelle." The exotic attractions of this Filipina figure are affirmed in the related dance number choreographed and performed in the 1906 production by Siren Navarro.[67] In a later production in 1907, Navarro's role was taken by Nettie Glenn (originally playing the role of Jackson's sister Virginia in the 1906 production); different accounts in the *Freeman* in March 1907 praised "Nettie Glenn, the pretty little dancer," whom audiences had "admired so much as the Philippine dancer."[68]

Both Paula Marie Seniors and Lucy Mae San Pablo Burns suggest that *The Shoo-Fly Regiment* included a love scene between Lieutenant Dixon and Grizzelle featuring the song "On the Gay Luneta." However, they provide very different interpretations of what such a scene might mean. Seniors argues that the romance in *The Shoo-Fly Regiment* "simultaneously broke the love scene taboo" that Aida Overton Walker describes and "the taboo against interracial romance" as enacted by African American actors.[69] However, Burns finds the song "On the Gay Luneta" to have more disturbing implications, whereby "the national body of the Philippines is conflated with the body of the Filipina woman, both feminized into softness and serenity under the desiring gaze of the American military officer."[70] Interracial romance and marriage in fact did reveal conflicting attitudes toward imperialism in the Philippines as well as U.S. racial divides. Ngozi-Brown has commented that "a large number of African-American soldiers married Filipino women, and a significant number of them remained in the Philippines and stayed with their Filipino families," with some African American soldiers believing in "African-American mass migration to the Philippines . . . [as] a solution to the oppression they faced in the U.S."[71] He notes that T. Thomas Fortune, a prominent black journalist and advocate of African American civil rights who traveled extensively throughout the Philippines during the early 1900s, said that white and African American men approached interracial romance quite differently: "A white American never marries a Filipino woman, but a great many of them live with Filipino women in Manila, and in the provinces. When they are ready to leave for the United States, they do so without regard to their obligations to Filipino women and children."[72]

In "On the Gay Luneta," interracial romance is indeed offered as a possibility for African American men just as it might be for white military men. However, other moments of *The Shoo-Fly Regiment* express reservations about such relationships. The manuscript version includes in the first act finale an assurance from Edward Jackson that even in the heat of "the bloody field of battle," his regiment will maintain their sexual self-control.

> But though the shot come fast and hot,
> And the bullets rain like sixty,
> You still can bet we won't forget
> The girls we leave in Dixie.
> Then a kiss and a sigh, and a fond good-bye,
> And remember our vote is,
> No Filipino girl, not the fairest in the world,
> Will ever claim our notice.

Denying these imperial sexual temptations affirms the respectability of the African American soldier, who is imagined to be as loyal to his American sweetheart as he is to his flag. At the same time, *The Shoo-Fly Regiment* used its female chorus to showcase the temptations of Filipina exoticism in the form of the "Spanish" chorus. The *New York Age* described how in the second act, "the scene shifts to the Philippines, where the colored girls appear as senoritas with characteristic music and dances."[73]

These cross-racial performances affirmed the ability of the African American actress to enact both racial difference and similarity. Just as Ade's *The Sultan of Sulu* insinuated that white women could instantly become Filipinas through simple changes of costume and a few castanets, so could African American actresses likewise convincingly inhabit both of these roles. In both cases, Filipina characters were pictured as benefiting from American military presence, thus exemplifying the white or black "affection" of benevolent assimilation. But what complicated this cross-racial casting further in the case of African American actresses was that they were seen as resembling two different perceptions of Filipina character: the already colonized mestiza and the native "untamed creature of the jungle" feared by Bella in Clyde Fitch's *Her Own Way*. This confusion was intensified even more by the racial ambiguity seen within African American female roles and chorus numbers, whose casting favored light-skinned women. Seniors points out how African American touring shows offered "extremely light-skinned performers who fueled the white obsession with black skin color," with white reviewers referring to these women as "white octoroons" or quadroons and "describing them as light as Spanish or French women, and lighter than Italians."[74] Henry T. Sampson explains how "in order to secure booking in vaudeville, many light-skinned blacks who chose not to 'darken up' frequently passed for white or concealed their racial identity by billing themselves as 'Two Creole Maids' or the 'Filipino Beauties.'"[75] The attractiveness of these women was tied to the perception of their mixed-blood heritage and the sexual availability it implied.

Both *The Shoo-Fly Regiment* and *Captain Rufus* may have capitalized on these associations, preferring lighter-skinned African American women for their version of the "Filipino Beauties." At least one reviewer of *The Shoo-Fly Regiment* described the chorus "most evenly matched, all the young ladies being of the same shade of complexion, color of hair and same average size."[76] However, both Sylvester Russell and Lester Walton criticized the performers in the company for making up as if they were white actresses. Russell commented that "Anna Cook-Pankey, as lady principal of Lincolnville Institute was painted too red (so was the chorus)" and complained that her later song "La Philipena," though "richly interpreted both by the singer and chorus," should have been presented as a solo number: "If Mrs.

Pankey wants to advance in important positions, it is best that she omit red paint altogether and take a few lessons from Black Patti."[77] Walton urged the performers to resist "white powder in wholesale" applied with "the principal aim of making yourself look white or very near white": "Let the dark people make up dark, the brown people brown, the yellow people yellow and the light people light. Please 'amputate' that idea of trying to make a colored show look like a guessing contest to decide just what your original color is."[78]

Of course, Russell's and Walton's reservations about the use of makeup were not just confined to their reviews of *The Shoo-Fly Regiment* and *Captain Rufus*. However, in these musicals the cross-racial performance of Filipino/a characters, imagined as both colonial subjects who are racially mobile and as natives who are racially inferior, marked a particular area of both opportunity and limitation for African American performers. Casting African American women as Filipinas highlighted their transformational abilities, giving them the same artistic privilege as white actresses. However, these cross-racial performances also foregrounded their perceived likeness to the colonial subjects they played.

Seniors has discussed how oriental performance helped create more respectable and dignified roles for African American women: "The playing of refined and delicate femininity as Chinese, Japanese, or Filipino maidens, for instance, countered the ways that African American women were associated with unbridled sexuality and uncivilized behaviors in characters such as Topsy."[79] These aims are apparent in a 1907 feature by "Dorothy" in the *Freeman* recognizing the "even dozen women" who made up *The Shoo-Fly Regiment*'s female cast. Of these "maids and matrons," Dorothy noted, "One-fourth of the number are making their first experience in limelight and are interestingly enthusiastic, anxious and determined to 'tread successfully where others have trodden.'" Dorothy described their aims as similar to that of other involvements in racial uplift: "With proper encouragement and the desire to present to theatre goers the Negro in a new class of Negro show, these women are making their part good, and the effort is excellent."[80]

But not all the actresses in *The Shoo-Fly Regiment* faithfully toed the line of black respectability. After Fanny Wise (who initially played "Truscolina," a student) replaced Inez Clough as Rose, she apparently added some stage business to the song "Won't You Be My Little Brown Bear" by throwing teddy bears and dolls into the audience and calling male spectators to join her onstage. (The teddy bear was associated with Theodore Roosevelt, whose refusal to shoot a captured bear inspired a 1902 *Washington Post* cartoon and then the popular stuffed animal.)[81] That her actions did add sex appeal to the flirtatious song is confirmed by an offhand comment in the *Freeman* during the show's 1907 run: "There are plenty of grizzly, black and cinnamon brown 'bears' who are dead willing to go with Miss Fannie Wise, the leading lady of the 'Shoo Fly Regiment,' most anywhere."[82] But both Sylvester Russell and Lester Walton criticized this aspect of her performance, especially in light of the show's racially mixed audience. Russell found that "Fanny Wise as the Professor's daughter, is a soubrette, quite fair to look upon with a very good singing voice for her line of business," but said that in "Won't You Be My Little Brown Bear," "I dare not think of her legitimately even if she does do as white actresses," since "the method of throwing Teddy Bears and doll babies into an audience is simply a trick of the variety stage and a good excuse for actresses who have a limit of talent and unlimited nerve." He concluded, "But let us be mild and ask Miss Wise to be wiser and do something better next season."[83] Walton is similarly prescriptive:

> Miss Fannie Wise should thank her stars that she is of that little and cute [word intelligible] with a manner modest and retiring, for I hear there are times she would be made [to] feel very cheap. The bidding of some one in the audience to come on the stage is, I think, a little suggestive—and that would not be so bad, but the male members of the white race who are invariably with women folks, are called on the stage. One pale face brother, sitting in a box with his lady friends, was made the object of Miss Wise's attention the night I saw the show and when she threw him the Teddy bear he quickly returned it with no little force, thereby showing his displeasure.[84]

In light of the strict restrictions placed on the openly sexualized expression of African American actresses, playing the Filipina was clearly preferable to the openly flirtatious vamp. However, both kinds of female roles were seen as in need of the firm management to prevent charges of lewdness and scandal. In contrast, not a whiff of impropriety would be suggested in the presentation of black or Filipina characters in the Black Patti Troubadours' *Captain Jasper*.

CAPTAIN JASPER GLORIFIES THE FILIPINO GIRL

The sizable cast of *Captain Rufus* evidently included "a large chorus of Filipino men and girls" as well as "soldiers and American tourists."[85] The musical also gave memorable dramatic moments to "Cheteka, a Filipino girl," played in the first productions by Lottie Grady, according to the *Freeman*:

"Lottie Grady, as the Filipino girl, was given a chance to display considerable emotion in a tragic scene which soared beyond the heights of either comedy or melodrama. In a struggle scene, she rose to her feet too quickly and her emotional breathing ceased too abruptly, but Miss Grady can claim a bright future for, to her credit it can be said that, she posses[ses] the good qualities of a real actress."[86] A 1914 *Freeman* article confirming the importance of the role of Cheteka in the revival highlighted "the costume to be worn by Miss Elizabeth Wallace, who takes the leading part in '*Captain Rufus*,'" detailing that her dress "was made in New York and especially designed by a Parisian modiste." It continued, "Miss Wallace is a Filipino girl and all of her costumes are of the richest material from that country. Her song, 'Amazon Land,' is expected to be the song hit of the show."[87] Subsequently, Wallace received acclaim in this role from the *Chicago Defender*: "Miss Lizzie Wallace as Cheteka Castro, pride of the Filipinos, was extremely clever with her lines and acting, and was the big hit of the evening singing 'Amazon Land.' She received six encores and a huge bunch of American beauties."[88] Her performance was also described with enthusiasm in the *Broad Ax*: she "took the house by storm, her enchores [*sic*] were so great that she had to quit, and the audience realizing how hard it was upon her, covered her with flowers."[89]

Although no music or lyrics for "Amazon Land" are available, the title as well as these descriptions of stage costume and reception suggest a powerful and memorable stage presence for those playing Cheteka. This highlights the divide between the representational and the presentational aspects of musical theater; while the character of Cheteka could be powerless and subservient, her enactment could demonstrate the dramatic skills and vocal command of the actress. In this, *Captain Rufus* offers a tantalizing glimpse of a more developed characterization for the "Filipino girl." Unfortunately not much more can be gleaned from available archival materials; however, some clues might be found in a later production by the Black Patti Musical Comedy Company (the successor to the Black Patti Troubadours), *Captain Jasper*, which ran touring productions beginning August 1912 through the spring of 1913.[90] That *Captain Jasper* took the Pekin's *Captain Rufus* as its inspiration is clear not only by the confusion of dates and authors[91] but also by the obvious similarities of plotlines concerning military events in the Philippines and mistaken identities and of characters, including a "Filipino girl" named Cheteka (Lottie Grady in the initial production), a Colonel Warsaw, a Major Drummond, and even a comic character named "U. R. Swift."

Prior to *Captain Jasper*, the Black Patti Troubadours had incorporated scenes set in the Philippines into several of the company's shows. "A

Filipino Misfit" was followed by versions of *Darktown Circus Day* (1903) that included an act "Around the Camp Fires in the Philippines" performed by James Crosby and the "Bon Mots of 1903." The second iteration of *Darktown Circus Day* included "a new sketch," titled "Life in the Philippines," along with "a realistic tenting scene embellished by a ladies' quartet of Red Cross nuns" alongside "Netti Goff, lady trombonist, and Bob Kelley, the hen roost inspector."[92] A number of other shows featuring Sissieretta Jones also had choruses of "Philippine girls" and Filipino characters in song and dance numbers. A 1912 *Freeman* review of a Black Patti show in Little Rock, Arkansas, reported, "Everybody in the company doing well. Jeannette Murphy and her dancing girls, namely, Marie Hendricks, Johnny Livingston, Ada Donegan, Blanch Howell, Edith and Mamie Rowe, are getting along fine in their portrayal of the Philippine girls. They intend to have a dance that will startle everybody when they get back East. Eddie Borden will be the Phillippine [*sic*] king, with John Grant and John Phillips as voodoo kings."[93]

As described in a number of newspapers, *Captain Jasper* had a much more involved plot than was suggested for these earlier Black Patti shows, and it featured both characterizations of African American men serving in the Philippines and leading roles for Filipina characters and chorus members. Credited to Will A. Cooke, the plot of *Captain Jasper* moves from a first act set in U.S. military barracks at the Presidio in San Francisco. There the American Colonel Warsaw and his daughter Lucy discover the theft of valuable government papers, including secret plans for "attack on the Philippine stronghold," as well as documents of landholdings that had been entrusted to the colonel by his friend Sergeant Jackson, which were intended for Jackson's daughter Cheteka when she became of age. Major Drummond, who has been commissioned to the Philippines, is identified as the thief. The second act takes place in a mountain pass in the Philippines, where the heroic Captain Jasper has been sent to look for Drummond. Jackson's estranged wife (formerly Cheteka Castro, described as a native of the Philippines) decides to return with her daughter Cheteka. The daughter meets up with the unscrupulous Drummond, who convinces her to sign over her property rights to him. But just as he is about to cheat her of her valuable legacy, he is detected by U. R. Swift and his friend Captain Jasper Charcoal. Charcoal is mistaken for the actual Captain Jasper. In the third act, set at a "Lawn Fete, Golden Gate Park near Fort Mason, Cal.," the characters have returned to the United States, and "Major Drummond dies in an effort to escape, and the stolen papers are returned."[94]

Despite this complicated plot (which Sylvester Russell called "theoretical and stagy"),[95] the musical received praise for its musical numbers and comic turns. In particular, the renowned Sissieretta Jones had star billing as the displaced Filipina Cheteka Jackson. She sang "Sun-Blest Are You, O Golden Land" (with lyrics by Lillian B. Rice and music by Joseph Melville),[96] "The Nightingale" in the second act, and "Belle of New York" in the third. Her role as Cheteka Jackson was her seventeenth consecutive season (and sadly, her last) as a star of the Black Patti Musical Comedy Company. A review of one of the closing performances at the Grand Opera House in New York City, May 1913, concluded with its tribute to "a voice so far famed and one that we deem a rare treat to hear." This *Freeman* review continued, "Mme. Patti has an exceptional gift as a vocalist, and added to this her appearance in carefully selected and costly costumes charmed the audience. As she smilingly stepped forth and began to sing, the reception she received halted her for a moment, but she acknowledged it with the grace of a real duchess and began to sing. I need say no more of her singing, as we all know she stands in a class by herself."[97] Clearly this role was created to give Jones an opportunity to demonstrate her vocal prowess. It also cast her as a proud Filipina character who is married to an African American military officer and is the mother of a biracial daughter, a leading part that is substantively different from the humorous Filipino/a characters of "On Jolly Coon-ey Island" or "A Filipino Misfit."

Not much indicates that Jones enacted the character in ways that would mark her as Filipino in "native" or even "Spanish" terms. Rather, her choice of well-known hymns, spirituals, and art songs and characteristically American costumes affirmed her celebrity image rather than the character she played. A performance at the Majestic Theatre in Fort Worth in October detailed an "overflowing" audience, who enthusiastically received Jones when she appeared "majestically" dressed in a large white picture hat, white serge suit, white gloves, and white shoes. The *Fort Worth Star-Telegram* commented, "She is booked in the play as 'Cheteka,' queen of a Philippine tribe, this was rather more clothes than might have been expected, especially as the scene was laid in the summertime."[98] Watching a 1913 performance, Sylvester Russell noted that her singing "again brought forth the same message of truth that her wonderful preservation and perfect schooling still ranks her as supreme in vocal distinction" and that songs were met with "a rousing reception." He also suggested that her costume changes were an effective part of the spectacle: "In 'The Belle of New York,' in the last act, her pale silk costume embroidered with beaded lace, diamonds and a white plume were rich to behold."[99] The *Washington Bee* emphasized a telling detail of her stage costume in *Captain Jasper*: "Her vast array of diamonds seem to have taken on a more brilliant sparkle."[100]

The success of Sissieretta Jones as Cheteka Jackson recalls how other African American singers also took on yellowface and brownface roles as Cio-Cio-San or Selika. However, that she was Cheteka Jackson, imagined as "queen of a Philippine tribe," makes clear *Captain Jasper*'s specific involvement in questions of U.S. imperialism in the Philippines. At the very least, the musical indicates a non-tragic outcome for a Filipina and the success of an interracial marriage. *Captain Jasper*'s plot suggests that while Cheteka Jackson has lost aristocratic privileges in her now-colonized native land, her daughter will be rightfully restored to her legacy by her African American father. African American, Filipino, and biracial characters are now acknowledged as the legitimate owners of property in the Philippines, and refinement, respectability, and elite status await a new generation of black characters in what are now presented as Filipino-American homelands.

WALTER LOVING AND PRINCE MUNGO

The trio of African American musicals that we have just examined not only incorporated the celebratory rhetoric of American patriotism but also staged more complex and even ambivalent representations of U.S. imperial power in the Philippines. Clearly, opinions about military involvement, policies of benevolent assimilation, and Filipino independence differed within the many theatrical performances devoted to this subject. These complicated cultural, national, and territorial negotiations and affinities required a fine-tuning of how we might understand more conventional habits of black and oriental representation in response to situations of imperial contact and conflict. One final set of comparisons affirms this need as well.

In a February 1907 article appearing in the *Freeman*, Frederic J. Haskin described a number of praiseworthy African Americans whose success might counter the impressions of racial discontent, such as the "trouble with the Negro soldiers at Brownsville, and race disturbances elsewhere." Among those listed was the musician and military officer Lieutenant Walter H. Loving, "the Negro bandmaster who captivated the crowd at the St. Louis exposition with his Filipino band of eighty pieces." Loving was a former U.S. Army regimental band leader who directed the principal military band of the Philippine Constabulary, the U.S. colonial government's police force in the Philippines created in 1901 to replace the Spanish colonial civil guard.

Haskin detailed Loving's accomplishments at the 1904 Louisiana Purchase Exposition (also known as the St. Louis World's Fair) contest, in which he led the Philippine Constabulary Band to a second-place finish, and emphasized Loving's impressive disciplining of his military musicians: "He studied in Boston and organized two army bands before going to the Philippines, where he had to master the Spanish, Tagalog and Ilocane languages in order to make himself understood by his men. He rehearsed eight hours a day on the ship which brought his band to America and continued the daily drill until the opening of the exposition, at which time his men were thoroughly familiar with over one thousand selections."[101]

Overall, the World's Fair exhibit on the Philippines emphasized the need for U.S. control over the uncivilized islands of the Philippines. It drew immense crowds to a "Philippine Village" inhabited by approximately 1,200 Filipinos, including Igorots (from Bontoc, Suyoc, and other regions), Manobos, Moros, Visayans, and Negritos, where popular demonstrations of Igorot dog-eating and revealing native dress suggested savage Filipinos greatly in need of American guidance and tutelage.[102] Thus the demonstrations of the musicianship of the Constabulary Band, headed by an African American, seemed to confirm the potential for Filipino progress under American imperial control.

Yet not all interactions between African Americans and Filipinos could be encompassed within the related logics of benevolent assimilation and racial uplift. Among the many late-nineteenth and early twentieth-century circus performers was a "Prince Mungo," who claimed to be from the Philippines.[103] Prince Mungo made his living traveling with various circus and exhibition venues such as the different partnerships of the Sells-Floto Circus, the Hagenbeck-Wallace Shows, and the Cole Brothers Circus. He was known as a "ballyhoo" man, whose banter, songs, and jokes would attract audiences at the beginning of the show; a September 1911 account in the *Freeman* commented, "His weird native songs and dances are both amusing and instructive, and he is capable of giving ten minutes of strange and fascinating amusement." The review continued, "Prince Mungo has traveled with all of the larger circuses and is considered one of the best attractions ever imported from the Philippine Islands. As a bally-hoo proposition he stands without a peer, as this is one of his strongest assets, both in front of a kid show top or in the lobby of any theatre."[104] In 1914, the *Freeman* mentioned Prince Mungo, "labeled from the Luzon of the Archaepelago [*sic*] of the Philippines," as "a cracker jack attraction" in the Sells-Floto performances in Indianapolis.[105]

The September 1911 *Freeman* article included a photograph of a dark-skinned man with an elaborate headdress, necklaces, and cape and the caption "Prince Mungo, Descendent of the Bhogirattes." There is not much to indicate that Prince Mungo was actually from the Philippines. The term "Bhogirattes" does not identify an ethnic or tribal affiliation. Though some indigenous Filipino tribal members did wear feathered headpieces, the arrangement of feathers on Prince Mungo's headdress more resembles that of a Native American headpiece than those of native Filipinos.[106] And of course the name "Mungo," though reminiscent of the Tagalog word *munggo* (for mung bean, or balatong), harkens back to the popular slave character from *The Padlock*. Moreover, he is consistently suggested to be part of a community of African American performers. For instance, the *Freeman* review of the Hagenbeck-Wallace Shows in Indianapolis commented that the side show "is still the home of the Colored folk" in terms of audience and indicated that "Prince Mungo is among the notable attractions of the side show owing to his dark skin."[107]

While it might be intriguing to think of Prince Mungo not only as someone who was "known to all performers as the greatest single ballahoo man in the business"[108] but also as a Filipino who found solidarity with African American performers, it is much more likely that he was an African American who appropriated an exotic Filipino identity that seemed consistent with the popular exhibits at the 1904 St. Louis World's Fair. But ultimately, what remains interesting is that Prince Mungo, at least early in his career, did not avoid issues of Filipino national independence. The *Topeka Plaindealer* commented in 1903 that "Prince Mungo, of the Philippine Islands, with his Caraboo Ox, has been secured by the Sells & Downs show at an enormous price. Prince Mungo is a follower of Aguinaldo, and it is very interesting to hear him talk about it."[109] Such a linking of Prince Mungo with the Filipino insurgency might well have played up his enactment of the savage warrior or the romantic former royal. Yet the idea of spectators brought into conversation with Prince Mungo over the politics of Filipino independence provides a reminder of those African Americans who supported the resistance to American occupation and contemplated the intertwined concerns of American racism and imperialism.

Conclusion

RACIAL PUZZLES, CHOP SUEY, AND JUANITA LONG HALL IN *Flower Drum Song*

From the nineteenth century onward, different actors, playwrights, and producers brought oriental fantasies to life on the American stage. Their lavish displays, comic stereotypes, exotic dancing girls, and magical remakes of *Aladdin* expressed desires for adventure and luxury, anxieties about economic competition, and fascination with imperial power. Whether performed by white or African American performers, theatrical orientalism not only shared space with blackface but also became deeply entangled with black representation. However, African American performances of orientalism did more than simply mimic the prevailing racial habits of the American commercial stage. Rather, they operated in ways that sometimes paralleled, complicated, or purposefully obfuscated blackface impersonation and caricature; they also remarked upon the afterlife of American slavery, the violence of segregation, and the aspirations of racial uplift.

Oriental characters were still mostly pictured as abject figures who existed at a far remove from black life. Yet there were various impersonators, singers, and dancers who took on more dignified roles such as Selika, Salome, or Grizzelle. These performances, along with Salem Tutt Whitney and J. Homer Tutt's staging of ancient Afro-Asian roots in *The Children of the Sun*, suggest more complex ways of connecting black and oriental representation.

Some African American performers—Thomas Dilward as Japanese Tommy, Eva Alexander as Princess Sotanki, and the ballyhoo great Prince Mungo— sustained cross-racial impersonations for years, blending their onstage oriental personae and offstage black identity. Unfortunately, little can be found to indicate whether they, or any of the many African American vaudevillians such as Harry Fiddler, Tom Brown, Sam Cook, or George Catlin, ever had any meaningful interactions with the people they mimicked on stage.

In general, the theatrical record falls far short in demonstrating the kinds of Afro-Asian political solidarity imagined in the writings of W. E. B. Du Bois and other intellectuals. While Du Bois famously described the twentieth-century problems of the "color line" as extending to "the relation of the darker to the lighter races of men in Asia and Africa, in America and the islands of the sea,"[1] we can only speculate on any affinities that may have been felt between Asian peoples and those African American performers who played them on the musical stage. In 1914, the *Freeman* praised Gus Stevens's Chinese vaudeville act at Gibson's New Standard Theatre in Philadelphia, saying that "his make-up was perfection, so much so that it really fooled a number of Chinamen who attended regularly every night to see the act. Laughter was almost unceasing."[2] Were Chinese men in the audience also the objects of this "unceasing" laughter? Or did they laugh along with white and African American spectators in recognition of Stevens's artful foolery? These questions are impossible to answer with certainty.

Yet this book concludes with the hope that something other than mimicry or mockery conditioned these African American performances of orientalism. This concluding section contemplates how relationships between African American performers and Chinese immigrants might have included moments of close proximity and even familial intimacy through three key examples: the career of Lily Yuen, a theatrical performer of both African American and Chinese descent; the African American consumption of a quintessentially Chinese American food, chop suey; and the appearance of Juanita Long Hall as Madam Liang in Richard Rodgers and Oscar Hammerstein's 1958 musical, *Flower Drum Song*, a later production that bears reframing in terms of the long-standing connections between black and oriental theatrical representation.

THE RACIAL PUZZLE OF LILY YUEN

Previous chapters have considered how characterizations of the "Chinaman" as paired with the "Coon" might have indicated not only pervasive xenophobia but also common experiences of menial domestic labor, racism, and physical violence. Musicals such as *In Dahomey* and *Abyssinia* similarly reminded audiences of the close proximity of African Americans and Chinese immigrants in the late nineteenth and early twentieth centuries. These theatrical representations suggested how, despite their differing cultural backgrounds and legal status, African Americans and Chinese immigrants shared some common ground. Valued as a source of cheap labor to replace emancipated African Americans and reviled as emblems of "wage slavery," Chinese immigrants were already viewed through a lens of antiblack racism. Anti-Asian sentiment and exclusion laws successively restricted aspects of Chinese migrant labor, mobility, marriage, and property rights, just as Jim Crow laws and continued racial violence restricted the ability of newly emancipated slaves to live, travel, work, and thrive. African Americans occupied many of the same jobs as well as lived in the same urban areas as Chinese immigrants. Both faced the disadvantages of poverty, poor working conditions, and urban blight; both shared experiences of racist violence as well as strategies of sustenance and survival. And in the early decades of the twentieth century, both groups would appear on the American stage, struggling to be seen as credible performing artists rather than as the limited black and oriental stereotypes they offered for public consumption.

As theatrical entertainers, Chinese and other Asian immigrants rarely achieved even the modest levels of fame reached by African Americans. Krystyn Moon's foundational study *Yellowface* has carefully documented the few professional Chinese and Chinese American vaudevillians performing in the early twentieth century. These included solo performers such as the "first Chinese baritone" Lee Tung Foo (Frank Lee), ensembles such as the Chung Hwa Comedy Four or "the Chinese Quartet," and male-female duos such as Rose Moy (Rose Yuen Ow) and her husband and partner, Joe Chong (Chong Yow Haw), or Dong Fong Gue ("Minnie") and Harry Gee Haw (later known as "Honorable Wu"). Like their African American counterparts, these performers were clearly aware of the limitations that race placed upon their modes of expression. Many avoided what Moon calls the period's "grosser 'Heathen Chinee' laundryman, or servant stereotypes," but instead sang and danced in a variety of styles and were costumed in tuxedos, ball gowns, elaborate Chinese costumes, or even (for "Scottish" numbers) kilts.[3]

Unsurprisingly, these vaudevillians included many performing acts based on blackface minstrel or "coon songs." According to Moon, Chee Toy (Chee Tai), who toured with her father, the internationally renowned magician Ching Ling Foo (Chee Ling Qua), sang "Waiting for the Robert E. Lee" at her debut in 1912, and one critic commented that "the little Chinese Miss sang it with a purity of diction many American soubrettes might emulate."⁴ Yen Wah and Chan Tock (Tak Wha Chan) included blackface impersonations in their acts from 1922 to 1927, including "a Negro specialty, singing 'blues' numbers," and a cakewalk. One review was unsure whether they were Chinese who were "sufficiently authentic to make them as colored men" or "African Americans performing in yellowface."⁵ These relatively few Chinese and Chinese American vaudeville performers joined with their African American counterparts in performing what was in broad commercial demand, whether it came in the form of blackface plantation nostalgia or stereotypes of the exotically or abjectly foreign Chinese. Yet the dissonance expressed in seeing these performers take on roles usually reserved for whites was also part of these acts; both their mimetic and artistic skills unsettled the primacy of the white actor as cross-racial impersonator.

Their many different vaudeville specialties affirmed that Chinese American as well as white and African American performers were equally capable of performing white, black, and oriental roles. We can only speculate as to whether new kinds of interracial connections might have been generated by African American and Chinese Americans performers waiting together in the wings and socializing backstage. But in the case of Lily Yuen, a theatrical performer of both African American and Chinese descent, the gap between African American and Chinese American experience was bridged in a different way.

Yuen was featured in the vaudeville revues *Broadway Rastus* (1919), *Jones Syncopated Syncopaters* (1923), *Brownskin Models* (1925), and *Miss Georgia Brown* (1925), among other shows.⁶ Henry Sampson lists her as dancing with the comedian Gallie (Melton) DeGaston on the TOBA vaudeville circuit.⁷ While she appeared as a hula dancer in a 1921 show with Jules McGarr and His Ragtime Steppers at the Pekin Theater,⁸ Yuen was not professionally identified as anything other than a black performer. Numerous reviews hailed her performances in African American shows. The *Kansas City Advocate* said that she was "now a full recognized star in her line and exceptionally in the Charleston realm"; the New Orleans *Times-Picayune* called her "the wonder dancer"; the *Inter-State Tattler* of New York referred to her as a "slim bronze beauty" with "winsome smile and flying feet";⁹ and the *New York Age* described her as a "statuesque" or "long-limbed beauty."¹⁰ In 1929, the *New York Age* wrote that in the musical comedy *Lucky Stars* "the tall and gorgeous Lily Yuen contrasts with adorable little Baby Banks"¹¹ and noted in 1930 a "new revue absurdity" called *S'prise Me!* in which Yuen had "a raggedy dancing and singing turn that wins several encores."[12]

The professional use of her surname signaled that Lily Yuen never hid her Chinese descent. However, even while she appeared in entertainments that included oriental acts (for instance, the 1932 revue *Yeah Man* that also featured Harry Fiddler as "a splendid 'Chinaman'"),[13] this part of her heritage was rarely mentioned in the press. One exception was a profile titled "Artist Here from Savannah Had Chinese Father," published in Baltimore's *Afro-American* in June 1925. The article detailed how Yuen, featured with the Miller Company at the Regent Theatre, "in appearance is typically Negro, and yet she is the daughter of a Chinese subject and of a colored woman." The article maintained that her professional talents as well as appearance bore "little resemblance to her father"; instead, the dancing skills of this "tall, agile, brown girl" came from her maternal side: "Three years has the actress followed her chosen profession, and in her dancing which seems to be her forte there is all of the skill of her Negro ancestors, and none of the usually deliberate movement associated with natives of China." The article noted that she had "the slightly slanting eyes common to Orientals," which indicated a stereotypical inscrutability: "Replies to the interviewer's questions were obligingly answered after evident deliberation, but the questioner seemed to catch, now and then, the stolid shrewd glance of the inhabitants of the Celestial Kingdom."[14]

The *Afro-American* thus presented Yuen as what it called "A Racial Puzzle," emphasizing the story of her parents' courtship in ways that combined the familiar image of the Chinese immigrant laundryman with a whiff of fairy-tale romance: "Tom Yuen came to this country many years ago, after satisfying the immigration authorities and settled in Savannah, Ga. Like so many of his thrifty countrymen he embarked in the laundry business. Having acquired honest American dollars which far exceeded the neus [*sic*], fans, and candareens of his home city via the cleansing and ironing of sundry shirts, collars and cuffs, Pappa Yuen looked about for a helpmate. His celestial gaze fell upon the present Mrs. Yuen, he proposed, was accepted and they have been living happily ever afterward." While this account predictably categorized Yuen's father as one of many "celestials" who started hand laundries, it also included certain details about the legal exclusion and economic uncertainties facing Chinese immigrants during the era of Asian exclusion. If vaudeville sketches turned the Chinese laundryman into a figure of comic mockery, this account suggested a much more sympathetic picture. Not only was Tom Yuen given a measure of romantic credibility, but he was also affirmed as having legitimacy in entering the United States only "after satisfying the immigration authorities." He was described as "thrifty" (an unsurprising description for an immigrant entrepreneur) but also "honest," in contrast to the unscrupulous stereotype of the "Chinaman." The story ended with a hopeful projection of interracial harmony despite cultural and geographical distance: "It's a far cry from the city of Hong Kong, China to Savannah, Ga., and yet when we disclose our little tale perhaps you'll agree that it's only a little world after all." The article noted, "Six children have been born of the union," most of whom "closely resemble the mother," with the "slightly slanting eyes" of Tom Yuen "marked strongly in the actress daughter."[15]

Of course, there were few if any performers of interracial Afro-Asian descent other than Lily Yuen whose stories could confirm this idealized vision that "it's only a little world after all." Nonetheless, the *Afro-American* portrayed Lily Yuen's patrilineage in ways that moved beyond the usual typecasting of Chinese as exotic and abject foreigner; it not only affirmed the close and personal ties of an African American performer to her Chinese immigrant father but also pictured an interracial family in intimate and celebratory ways.

CHOP SUEY AND THE AFRICAN AMERICAN MUSICAL

With book by Jesse A. Shipp, lyrics by Alex Rogers, and music by J. Rosamond Johnson, the 1909 musical *Mr. Lode of Koal* served as a vehicle for Bert Williams, after his theatrical partner George Walker became too ill to perform. Williams's title character was Chester A. Lode, who escapes his humble origins and makes his way to the fantastical land of Koal, a world infused with familiar oriental elements. After taking on the identity of King Smoak and consuming the "sleep-compelling" fruit of the island, Chester enjoys "one of the most satisfying and delightful dreams that he could have wished for, had he the magic of Aladdin's lamp at his command."[16] The dream sequences included numbers such as Al Johns's "In Far Off Mandalay," evoking fair exotic maidens and the "sacred lotus,"[17] and "Chink Chink Chinaman" as sung by Tom Brown, joined by Siren Navarro and "eight girls dressed as boys in knickerbockers and blouse waists, playing bean bags." This song and dance number, according to the *Freeman*, made a "pretty picture," with "Tom Brown in the center and all the ponies [chorines] playing ring around the Chink Chink Chinyman."[18] The lyrics of "Chink Chink Chinaman" belie this quaint and pleasing spectacle with a more sober situation, in which a Chinese immigrant man who keeps a "chop suey house" bemoans how he is tormented by racist taunts.[19] The song was written by Alexander "Alex" Claude Rogers, a prolific lyricist who during the course of his career wrote the words to almost 2,000 songs as well as most of the lyrics for Williams and Walker's musicals.[20]

As Caroline Yang has pointed out, "Chink Chink Chinaman" pointedly differentiates the Chinese immigrant's racial status from that of African Americans.[21] That the Chinese man can open his chop suey house in a white neighborhood is a sign of his privilege and mobility in a time of segregation. Yet the Chinese character by no means escapes racism. After facing the derision of "heap white boys," he moves his restaurant to a black neighborhood, only to face the same ridicule from "heap black boys." The song makes the point that both sets of tormentors sing the same "clazy song" with the refrain "Chink, chink, chink, chink chineeman run away wi' loyster can." The Chinese man points out that these words are nonsensical: "Wat dis chink chink loystercan got to do wi' chineeman?" Even as the song foregrounds his despair and creates a measure of sympathy for him, it also repeats these words incessantly, echoing as well as underscoring the hostility that he faces from both whites and blacks: "White boy, black boy loud as can sing / chink, chink, chink, chink, chineeman."

It is unclear whether Tom Brown's delivery of "Chink Chink Chinaman" was designed to prompt mockery or sympathy, or perhaps both. Yet in all of these cases, the song's words affirm that African Americans and Chinese lived in close proximity to one another and that they both experienced intense though different kinds of racial hostility. What also seems significant is that the "Chinaman" is portrayed less as an exotic foreigner than as a familiar figure who keeps a chop suey house in a black neighborhood. Thus the number's inclusion in *Mr. Lode of Koal* reaffirms a pattern established in the earlier musicals *In Dahomey* and *Abyssinia*, by which Chinese immigrant characters are seen entering into African American inner circles and even homes. George Catlin's Me Sing follows Mrs. Stringer to Florida because she can't give up her chop suey. Similarly, the cook Wong Foo becomes an integral part of the American caravan to Abyssinia. These portrayals suggest the possibility of close, reciprocal, and even nurturing relationships between Chinese immigrants and African Americans.

There are many other instances of African American theatrical and musical performance that make reference to "chop suey" as a favorite dish of African American customers. Allusions to chop suey abounded in song titles such as "Chop Suey Sue"[22] and in vaudeville sketches such as Williams and Stevens as "two Chinese cooks" in "Chop Suey Restaurant" or Fiddler and Stevens performing in "Troubles in a Chop Suey Café."[23] One casual yet striking reference made in the 1901 song by Sherman Boone, "The Coon with the Raglan Craze," makes fun of African American fashions. The playful lyrics depict a man's overwhelming passion for his "mighty fine Raglan overcoat" that he wears "most everywhere," even to the point of excess: "I eats in it, an' I sleeps in it; even keeps it on when I takes my bath." This ode to the "Raglan Craze" opens with a specific reference to other trends: "Most all the coons are raving destracted 'bout 'poke' chops and good things to eat. / An' brags 'bout the chicken chop sueys they buy, an' says it's the only treat."[24] That "chicken chop suey" is mentioned in a song satirizing African American fashion highlights Chinese food as an integral part of early twentieth-century African American social life and commodity culture.

In the later nineteenth century, Chinese restaurants became increasingly popular in the United States, first within the Chinese immigrant community and then for non-Chinese patrons, including African Americans. In his history, *Chop Suey USA*, Yong Chen mentions a 1901 article in the *New York Tribune* reporting that African Americans frequented the city's Chinese dining establishments "in disproportionately large numbers," commenting, "They seemed to like the Chinese, and, indeed, the noise in the kitchen reminds one of the similar condition of southern kitchens under negro management."[25] Chen points out, "The ambiance was not the only reason that attracted them to the Chinese restaurant; it was one of the few public places that welcomed them." By 1928, the *New York Age* would write, "In the past ten years the Chinese restaurants have become quite a vogue in New York but they have attained their greatest popularity in Harlem."[26]

The Chinese restaurant, like the Chinese laundry, was at times the site of economic competition and interracial tension. In 1928, the *New York Age* articulated fears that Chinese restaurants, like Chinese laundries, were posing serious threats to African American businesses: "It is interesting to note that the most prosperous Harlem restaurants are owned and controlled by Chinese and they started as 'Chop Suey' joints. On Eighth, Seventh, and Lenox avenues, between 125th and 145th streets, there are no less than twenty of these restaurants and all of them are under selling the Negro places, both as to price and the quality of food."[27]

The segregation of dining establishments also worried another commentator in the *New York Age* in April 1917: "The drawing of the color line has reached the fine point in this city, and winds its slimy way from the churches to the Chinese chop suey joints."[28] In January 1927, the *Negro*

World published a call "To the Negroes of Harlem" to boycott the Bamboo Inn on Seventh Avenue, fearing that the restaurant was "drawing the color line, closing its doors to Negroes, so that white patrons and Chinese, East and West, may meet indeed in frolic unconfined."[29] Despite these concerns, a year later the Bamboo Inn was still open to Harlemites, advertising in African American newspapers such as the *Inter-State Tattler* that its pleasures included "sheered silken ceilings and walls, revolving lights, Hendi Saparo's Band, Marjorie Sipp and Katy Crippen to entertain you" as well as "Chinese-American cuisine."[30]

Though criticized for competing for business with black-owned establishments or segregating customers, Chinese restaurants were also seen as employing African American performers as well as encouraging intercultural exploration. According to Jimmy Durante, the nightclub cabaret originated in New York's Chinatown, at a concert saloon called the Melodeon that opened in 1859.[31] Many late-night establishments in major cities hosted African American musicians and catered to African American patrons. James Weldon Johnson's novel *The Autobiography of an Ex-Colored Man*, first published in 1912, describes in detail a club, "the most famous place of its kind in New York," that is frequented by African American as well as whites. This "center of colored bohemians and sports" had in its basement a Chinese restaurant, and Johnson mentions that "the Chinaman who kept it did an exceptionally good business; for chop-suey was a favourite dish among the frequenters of the place."[32]

The opening scene of *A Night in New York's Chinatown*, produced at Chicago's Pekin Theater in 1910, depicted "a mysterious phase of oriental life, including a tragedy in pantomime." While this production delivered dire warnings about the evils of opium, gambling, prostitution, and dissolution associated with Chinatown, its musical comedy format also offered specialty numbers and chorus girls. According to Sylvester Russell, Tom Brown played the character of "Ah Sing," a "highbinder" in earlier productions, and then was replaced by Frank Walker in Walker's first Pekin appearance. Russell noted that "Charles Gilpin as a buffet boss, W. H. Elkins as a soldier and Jerry Mills as a sleeper and a policemen were all merry spectacles of delight" and that Lloyd Gibbs and Carroll Amos played "the waiters in the cafe roughly handled." He found the pantomime scene "true to life and not overdone" and praised the playwright, Jesse A. Shipp, who appeared as "Ling Lee" in this "grave and dramatically interesting" scene.[33] His description affirmed how Chinese food establishments—however staged as dens of iniquity—were heavily frequented by African Americans.

New York was not the only place where African Americans patronized Chinese restaurants. In an August 1902 article in the *Freeman*, J. D. Howard described being part of a "slumming party" in St. Louis, Missouri, that visited "John Hop's restaurant." He portrayed Hop as an entrepreneur, "a Chinaman strictly progressive and keenly alive to the fact that the American public is nothing if not curiosity seeker" who "has shrewdly figured that the Chinaman has ever proven a subject of interest to the American." Both Hop's restaurant and its immediate neighborhood were, according to Howard, "thickly infested with the almond eyed Celestials," and his offerings were seen as catering mainly to Chinese patrons: "No American ideas are pandered to here from the fact that fully one-half of Hop's patronage is composed of his countrymen, who demand and must have the 'real thing.'" Thus for Howard, John Hop's restaurant was not a "toy supported by the wealthy classes for the amusement afforded, but a real Chinese restaurant, such as one might expect to find in Pekin, Canton or any Chinese metropolis," serving tea, duck, noodles, and "raw sliced fish with a hot sauce, which was called 'e joke.'" However, despite this reassurance of cultural authenticity, Howard noted that in the front part of the restaurant, "the customers were equally divided between whites, blacks and Chinese," and "all were served without discrimination." "Too often," Howard remarked, "the casual tourist is liable to leave the large cities of this great country utterly ignorant of many of their cosmopolitan customs and institutions that proper investigation would prove intensely interesting and plentifully supplied with a wealth of educational value." Howard described John Hop's Chinese restaurant not only as an adventuresome place for dining but as a place that welcomed African American customers in particular. His closing observation emphasized that: "It seemed to be understood by all that a Bohemianizing spirit actuated the presence of each, and the mongrel makeup of the crowd only seemed to add to its good nature."[34]

If Chinese restaurants provided accessible experiences of foreign culture conveniently located in American cities, one menu item in particular stood out for its blend of exoticism and familiarity. First associated with Chinese restaurants in the late nineteenth century, chop suey has multiple origin stories,[35] and its popularity grew quickly with non-Chinese patrons. African American newspapers in the early twentieth century made repeated references to chop suey parties and published home recipes for the dish using ingredients such as banana or rabbit.[36] While frequently featured in ads for Chinese restaurants, the dish was also outed as not being authentically Chinese. In 1912, the *Washington Bee* repeated comments from the *New*

York Telegraph that "Chop Suey is not a Chinese dish in China. It is not known anywhere in the entire empire."[37] Like the Chinese restaurant, chop suey became symbolic of the cultural and racial blending seen as possible in American culture. Its patently inauthentic mélange of ingredients could signify both American assimilation and misguided amalgamation. A short opinion essay in the September 1926 *Broad Ax* contemplating the question "What is jazz?" cynically concluded that "jazz is a razz of aborted syncopation and instrumentation. . . . Its origin cannot be definitely described. It has no limitations. It is the 'chop suey' of the musical world—but the world seems to want more of it, sad though that fact be."[38]

JUANITA LONG HALL IN *FLOWER DRUM SONG*

In the 1958 Broadway premiere and 1961 film versions of *Flower Drum Song* by Richard Rodgers, Oscar Hammerstein II, and Joseph Fields, Juanita Long Hall played Madam Liang, an immigrant Chinese woman. This was not her first oriental role; Hall had already won success playing the Tonkinese (Vietnamese) Bloody Mary in *South Pacific*, for which she won a Tony Award for Best Supporting Actress, the first Tony ever given to an African American. In many ways, however, her cross-racial performance in *Flower Drum Song* was even more distinctive. With the exception of a few characters, including Hall's Madam Liang, *Flower Drum Song* cast Asian or Asian American actors in nearly all of its roles, the first Broadway musical to do so in a casting feat that would not be repeated until Stephen Sondheim's 1976 *Pacific Overtures*.

Like Rodgers and Hammerstein's previous oriental musicals *South Pacific* (1949) and *The King and I* (1951), *Flower Drum Song* demonstrated a fascination with particular locales and cultures in the Asia and Pacific as conditioned by what Christina Klein calls "Cold War orientalism": efforts at intercultural exchange driven by American military and economic interests, fears of communism, and the promotion of U.S. global superiority as a model of multiracial democracy.[39] *Flower Drum Song* in particular fixated on the possibility of assimilating Chinese immigrants, who in the past had been shunned as undesirable aliens but now could be featured as model minority exemplars of American racial harmony. As Robert Lee and Heidi Kim have suggested, the musical presented Chinese Americans as hardworking, college-educated, entrepreneurial, and eager to adapt themselves to white culture.[40] Its story contrasts an old-fashioned Chinese father, Master Wang, with his English-speaking sons. Cultural differences affect the romantic choices of Wang's eldest son, Ta, who at first prefers the Americanized and enticingly assertive Linda Low, a nightclub dancer, but then falls for the demure new immigrant, Mei Li. While the plot does involve Mei Li's lack of legal immigration documents, the musical forgoes directly debating the history of Chinese exclusion laws, in marked contrast with the novel that inspired it, C. Y. Lee's 1957 best seller, *The Flower Drum Song*.

In its rush to celebrate the assimilation of its Chinese American characters, the musical version of *Flower Drum Song* downplays significant aspects of American racism. One striking example occurs in the memorable song "Chop Suey." When Juanita Hall begins the song, her lighthearted delivery seems well in keeping with the musical's genial celebration of American multiculturalism through Asian American success. "Chop Suey" is sung to celebrate Madam Liang's new citizenship and Wang Ta's graduation, and the lyrics suggest the diversity of American life by describing a mix of notable events, places, artists, politicians, celebrities, and commodities:

> Hula hoops and nuclear war
> Dr. Salk and Zsa Zsa Gabor
> Harry Truman, Truman Capote, and Dewey
> Chop Suey![41]

While Hall as Madam Liang leads other characters in the musical reflection that "living here is very much like chop suey" with experiences "good and bad, intelligent, mad, and screwy . . . Sad and funny, sour and honey dewy," overall "Chop Suey" presents American life for its Chinese characters in optimistic ways: "Mixed with all the hokum and bally hooey" is something "real and glowing grand" that "sheds a light all over the land."

Using chop suey as metaphor for cultural amalgamation, the song erases a violent history of racial, colonial, and imperial division in favor of viewing late-1950s America as a liberal nation that finds space for even the formerly reviled Chinese immigrant. Processes of assimilation and erasure are crucial to this vision. While the verses mention a diverse array of cultural objects and practices, they also imply that these can be rendered palatable only through commodifying them for white audiences and consumers:

> Hear that lovely La Paloma,
> Lullaby by Perry Como.
> Dreaming in my Maid'nform bra,
> Dreamed I danced the Cha-Cha-Cha.

The ideal Chinese American subject is also seen as adhering to this principle. Hall's character, Madam Liang, declares without self-consciousness

Juanita Long Hall as Madam Liang and ensemble in *Flower Drum Song* (1958).
Photograph by Fred Fehl. © Billy Rose Theatre Division,
New York Public Library for the Performing Arts.

that she is happy to be "both Chinese and American" before launching into "Chop Suey." Like the other Chinese American characters, Madam Liang does not register bitterness at past racisms or reservations about her social status or quality of life in the United States. With the exception of Mei Li's illegal entry (conveniently resolved by Mei Li's own ingenuity and perhaps one of the "hundred million miracles" foreshadowed by her opening song), no real racial worries come into play here or elsewhere in the musical. Ultimately, the conflicts are seen as coming from the characters' misunderstandings or resistance to cultural change rather than from larger structures of segregation, exploitation, or violence.

In order to celebrate the ease with which Chinese immigrants become integrated into the American mix, *Flower Drum Song* carefully segregates its own setting and musical numbers. No black characters are included in the musical; instead, this version of San Francisco's Chinatown is inhabited exclusively by Chinese characters. Explicit references to African American culture are also conspicuously absent from the story. In the "Chop Suey" dance number, the ensemble incorporates not only quaint "Chinese" bowing but also square dancing, waltzes, and popular social dances such as the Charleston and the Watusi. While some of these dance forms are clearly indebted to black culture, they receive no such explicit attribution. *Flower Drum Song* erases any mention of black musicians, dancers, or performers, even in the jazzy numbers sung by the nightclub entertainer Linda Low.

In much the same way, Juanita Long Hall's cross-racial casting was barely acknowledged by the mainstream white press, despite earlier acclaim for her playing of Bloody Mary.[42] A *Time* magazine article on the Broadway *Flower Drum Song*, featuring the female leads Miyoshi Umeki and Pat Suzuki on the magazine's cover, touted the novelty of a mainly Asian and Asian American cast as well as the musical's attractive female leads and chorus.[43] The article emphasized the difficulty of casting the ensemble numbers, stating that "assembling this chorus line took on a scope that recalled nothing less than the recruitment of Kublai Khan's harem," with casting agents ultimately selecting on the basis of racial appearance rather than ethnic background: "The scouts could not possibly hope to find a full bag of authentic Chinese, settling for any vaguely Oriental features."[44] This article gave considerable space to the Japanese and Japanese American backgrounds of the show's female leads. It also noted that one of the leading characters, the wisecracking nightclub owner Sammy Fong, was played by the white actor Larry Storch, later replaced by Larry Blyden. However, it did not identify Hall even in mentioning her trademark song from *South Pacific*, "Bali Ha'i," as the fastest composition that Rodgers ever wrote.[45] The article's omission of Hall's cross-racial performance seems consistent with larger efforts in the musical to celebrate the "model minority" acceptance of Chinese Americans and to erase reminders of more systemic and troubling racial struggles.

However, the African American press insisted on highlighting Hall's racial identity as crucial rather than incidental to *Flower Drum Song*. Kathryn Edney has commented that while the white mainstream media of the late 1950s "essentially ignored Juanita Hall as the sole African-American actor within a musical about Asian-Americans penned by white men," in contrast, African American newspapers "wholeheartedly embraced both Hall and her role in *Flower Drum Song* while generally ignoring the five other Broadway Asian-themed plays that opened in that year."[46] According to Edney, "Many African-American newspapers billed Hall as the star of *Flower Drum Song* rather than as a supporting player." A magazine feature in *Ebony* was devoted to Hall as "the lone Negro in the cast of 59," detailing her approach to playing Madam Liang. It included many photographs of Hall in the show as well as offstage with Broadway star Mary Martin and director Gene Kelly and opened with a picture of Hall with the ensemble of "Chop Suey." The opening caption implied how Hall saw a clear difference between her *South*

Pacific role as Bloody Mary, a "raucous Tonkinese woman," and Madam Liang's "mature Chinese lady," the "dignified and most emphatic sister-in-law of a widower" who "delivers a series of sage observations on men, women, and teen-agers."[47] While Hall's "method in achieving authentic Oriental quality for the part of Bloody Mary in *South Pacific* was to play the part as nearly Chinese as she could," in contrast, "as Madam Liang, she says, 'I *am* Chinese.'"[48]

As suggested in a previous chapter, impersonations of Chinese immigrants by African American vaudeville and musical theater performers a half century prior to *Flower Drum Song* were noted for their distinctive uses of authenticating detail. Sam Cook was praised for having "discarded the traditional stage Chinaman in to-to" and for having "gone out into Chinatown and studie[d] the Chinaman from life, and then created and embellished a character true to life and, more importantly, to stage art."[49] Gus Stevens was commended for playing "the part of One Lung, the Chinaman, so natural, his make-up, dialect and every move was so perfect that few could detect that he wasn't a real Chinaman."[50] That these performers succeeded in pleasing not only African American and white audience members but also Chinese spectators is implied by the *Freeman*'s praise of Stevens's 1914 vaudeville act, which "really fooled a number of Chinamen who attended regularly every night to see the act."[51] *Ebony* validated Hall's performance as Madam Liang in similar ways. Its backstage pictures illustrated how "Juanita applies make-up which emphasizes her naturally Oriental features" and revealed her "specially-made hairpiece which accentuates [the] Oriental cast of her face." It also commented that an ad for the show in New York Chinese language newspapers "caused the child of Chinese friends of Miss Hall's to exclaim triumphantly to her parents: 'You see, Juanita Hall is Chinese after all. She's been passing for colored all the time!"[52]

If *Time* portrayed the *Flower Drum Song* chorus as selected mainly on the basis of "vaguely Oriental features," *Ebony*, in contrast, insisted that Hall's performance of Madam Liang was successful not just because she fit a racial phenotype but because of her close and respectful relations with Chinese Americans. *Ebony* declared that "Juanita's profound respect for Chinese people and their culture will not allow her to caricature Chinese types on the stage" and emphasized her many Chinese and Chinese American fans: "Since *Flower Drum Song* opened, a steady stream of Chinese visitors has appeared at her dressing room to congratulate her warmly on a believable and dignified performance."[53] *Ebony*'s feature on Hall ended with a section titled "Chinese Like Performance," which made clear that "Juanita Hall, whose portrayal of the flighty, impulsive, strong-willed Madam Liang earned admiring approval from drama critics, has never been to the Orient." The article described her understanding of Chinese culture as beginning instead with her encounter with a Chinese American laundryman.

> The first Chinese person she met was Charlie Lee, who ran a laundry in Keyport, N.J., where she was born. When she told her grandmother stories she heard at school about Mr. Lee cutting off girls' hair and eating rats, she was taken to meet the town laundryman whom she found to be a warm, kind, gentle man.
>
> "You see, Juanita," her grandmother told her, "there's no real difference between you and Mr. Lee. He merely happened to be born on the other side of the world, while you were born right here."[54]

In Hall's account, her initial fear and revulsion were corrected by her grandmother's admonition and an actual encounter with a Chinese laundryman who proved her racial assumptions wrong. Through imagining these personal experiences, Hall's performance as Madam Liang took on a different cast: she was described as bringing to the role not just her mimetic abilities but her own childhood experiences of familial reassurance that there was "no real difference" between her own identity and that of a Chinese immigrant man.

According to *Ebony*, author C. Y. Lee, whose novel served as the basis for the musical, was "so impressed with Juanita's convincing performance as a Chinese lady that he told her: 'You have a good deal of Chinese blood in you, don't you? I ask because I think you are more Chinese than any one else in the cast.'"[55] The article continued, "There was a time when she [Hall] quickly corrected such mistaken impressions by explaining proudly, 'I'm a Negro.' Now, a little older, wiser, more tolerant, she smiles, says, 'I'm an American.'" Hall's response to C. Y. Lee might seem to be not only a declaration that she lacked Chinese heritage but also a disclaimer of black identity in favor of a race-neutral vision of being "American." In context, however, this exchange between Lee and Hall implies that both were aware that they shared common challenges in claiming "American" status. Hall's performance as Madam Liang is less an active erasure of Hall's blackness in order to celebrate Chinese American inclusion in the "melting pot" and more of an affirmation that African Americans and Chinese Americans have their own distinctive experiences of interracial encounter.

Thus Juanita Long Hall's indisputably black presence in *Flower Drum Song* added another dimension to the show's affirmation of the American "melting pot," and her singing of "Chop Suey" calls for a reassessment of the song's central metaphor. As sung by Hall, "Chop Suey" no longer just illustrates the processes of American assimilation, envisioned as amalgamated and undifferentiated ingredients of a thoroughly Americanized dish. The song also provides a subtle reminder that Chinese American food as well as oriental performances were already integral parts of African American culture. While *Flower Drum Song* has been hailed mainly as a breakthrough for Asian American actors on a white-dominated stage, Hall's performance gestures toward moments in which African Americans and Asian Americans lived, worked, and ate alongside one another in restaurants that were, as J. D. Howard once put it, "equally divided between whites, blacks and Chinese."

After considering the well-established tradition of oriental impersonation in African American theater, Hall's roles as Bloody Mary and Madam Liang take on a new light. Her yellowface performances were neither singular nor exceptional but two instances among many that challenged the exclusive privilege of white actors to define cross-racial performance in both blackface and oriental roles. A century before *Flower Drum Song*, white minstrels had partitioned off American racial identities, picturing blackface characters as comical fixtures of the plantation home and Chinese immigrant characters as inherently alien. "What can all de Chinese do Along side ob de Nigger?" asked an 1870 number, "Nigger versus Chinese." This minstrel song by Harry F. Lorraine emphasized the inability of Chinese immigrants to assimilate into American culture, as demonstrated by their inability to perform black music:

> Dey cannot learn to play the fiddle,
> Or pick the ole Banjo,
> Or stave de head ob de [t]amborine,
> Dey are so mighty slow.[56]

Flower Drum Song still retained some very old elements of oriental caricature. It also erased appropriations of black music, dance, and performance in favor of celebrating "model minority" characters. However, with Juanita Long Hall as Madam Liang joining its cast, *Flower Drum Song* allowed a host of new players to attempt to prove themselves as competent cross-racial actors, thus making significant changes to some of the persistent habits that had been ingrained into American theater.

Notes

INTRODUCTION

1. The Mudcat Café (online forum), accessed August 20, 2021, https://mudcat.org /thread.cfm?threadid=27210/.

2. J. Rosamond Johnson (music), Bob Cole, and James Weldon Johnson, "My Castle on the Nile," Frances G. Spencer Collection of American Popular Sheet Music, Baylor University. The sheet music advertises the song as being one of Bert Williams's numbers. Thomas Riis notes that J. Rosamond Johnson includes a brief chord progression from "Su! Del Nil al sacro lido," a chorus from Verdi's *Aida* about the Nile River. Thomas L. Riis, *Just before Jazz: Black Musical Theater in New York, 1890–1915* (Washington, DC: Smithsonian Institution Press, 1989), 88.

3. Edison's trade paper comments that "possibly because of his great success in singing coon and ragtime songs for the Edison Phonograph some people seem to have gained the impression that Arthur Collins is a colored man. Such an impression is naturally amusing to Mr. Collins. It is complimentary, however, to imitate the colored race so closely as to be mistaken for the real article." *Edison Phonograph Monthly*, July 1905, 10.

4. Famously performed by Judy Garland and Margaret O'Brien in *Meet Me in St. Louis* (1944).

5. It is listed as one of the "camp songs" on the web page of Camp Lake Hubert in Minnesota, accessed August 20, 2021, www.lincoln-lakehubert.com/girls-camp/girls-songs/.

6. Edward W. Said, *Orientalism* (New York: Random House, 1978), 3.

7. Samuel Taylor Coleridge, "Kubla Khan; or, A Vision in a Dream. A Fragment," in *Poems* (New York: Knopf, 2014), 11.

8. For instance, see Bridget Orr, *Empire on the English Stage: 1660–1714* (Cambridge: Cambridge University Press, 2001); and Susan Nance, *How the Arabian Nights Inspired the American Dream, 1790–1935* (Chapel Hill: University of North Carolina Press, 2009).

9. Esther Kim Lee, *Made-Up Asians: Yellowface during the Exclusion Era* (Ann Arbor: University of Michigan Press, 2022).

10. Lawrence Senelick, *Jacques Offenbach and the Making of Modern Culture* (Cambridge: Cambridge University Press, 2017), 129.

11. Willard Spenser, *The Little Tycoon: A Comic Opera in Two Acts* (New York: William S. Gottsberger, 1882), 127.

12. The title referred to Anson Burlingame, the American diplomatic minister to China from 1861 to 1867, who had returned to the United States in 1868 as the imperial envoy

for the first Chinese embassy. The Chinese, with Burlingame's assistance, negotiated a new treaty within the United States that was supposed to improve trade relations for both nations and protect the rights of Chinese immigrants, much to the anger of many supporters of anti-Chinese legislation.

13. Gerald Bordman, *American Musical Theatre: A Chronicle*, 3rd ed. (New York: Oxford University Press, 2000), 28; Krystyn R. Moon, *Yellowface: Creating the Chinese in American Popular Music and Performance, 1850s–1920s* (New Brunswick, NJ: Rutgers University Press, 2005), 25.

14. Bordman, *American Musical Theatre*, 97.

15. Said, *Orientalism*, 63.

16. The 1921 song "The Sheik of Araby" was written by Harry B. Smith and Francis Wheeler (lyrics) and Ted Snyder (music) and was subsequently performed and recorded by both white and African American singers, including Eddie Cantor, who sang it in the 1922 Shubert musical *Make It Snappy*, and Fats Waller, who recorded it in 1938. The *Tin Pan Alley* version adds additional lyrics and close-harmony vocalizing. Waller's "Honeysuckle Rose" is also used in *Tin Pan Alley*.

17. A survey can be found at Josephine Lee, "Yellowface: Historical and Contemporary Contexts," in *The Oxford Encyclopedia of Asian American Literature and Culture*, ed. Josephine Lee, Floyd Cheung, Jennifer Ann Ho, Anita Mannur, and Cathy Schlund-Vials (New York: Oxford University Press, 2020), 1205–23; online at http://oxfordre.com/literature/view/10.1093/acrefore/9780190201098.001.0001/acrefore-9780190201098-e-834/. Also see John Kuo Wei Tchen, *New York before Chinatown* (Baltimore: Johns Hopkins University Press, 1999); Moon, *Yellowface*; and E. Lee, *Made-Up Asians*.

18. Konstantin Stanislavski, quoted in David Magarshack, "Stanislavsky," in *The Theory of the Modern Stage*, ed. Eric Bentley (New York: Penguin, 1968), 221–22.

19. Eddie S. Glaude Jr., *Democracy in Black: How Race Still Enslaves the American Soul* (New York: Crown, 2016), 55.

20. Pierre Bourdieu, "Habitus," in *Habitus: A Sense of Place*, ed. Jean Hillier and Emma Rooksby (Aldershot, UK: Ashgate, 2002), 27–28.

21. Pierre Bourdieu, *Outline of a Theory of Practice*, trans. Richard Nice (Cambridge: Cambridge University Press, 1977), 22.

22. Harvey Young, *Embodying Black Experience: Stillness, Critical Memory, and the Black Body* (Ann Arbor: University of Michigan Press, 2010), 4, 7.

23. Young, 22.

24. Helen Ngo, *The Habits of Racism: A Phenomenology of Racism and Racialized Embodiment* (Lanham, MD: Lexington Books, 2017), x.

25. Annemarie Bean, James V. Hatch, and Brooks McNamara, eds., *Inside the Minstrel Mask: Readings in Nineteenth-Century Blackface Minstrelsy* (Hanover, NH: Wesleyan University Press, 1996), xi.

26. Robert Toll, *Blacking Up: The Minstrel Show in Nineteenth-Century America* (New York: Oxford University Press, 1974), 34.

27. St. Claire Drake, *Black Folk Here and There: An Essay in History and Anthropology* (Los Angeles: University of California Center for Afro-American Studies, 1991), 302.

28. Toll, *Blacking Up*, 34–35.

29. See Toll, chap. 7.

30. Marvin McAllister, *Whiting Up: Whiteface Minstrels and Stage Europeans in African American Performance* (Chapel Hill: University of North Carolina Press, 2011), 1.

31. *Kim-Ka!* is included in Dave Williams, *The Chinese Other, 1850–1925* (Lanham, MD: University Press of America 1997), 7, 2. Krystyn Moon gives an earlier date than Williams; see *Yellowface*, 25–26.

32. Tchen, *New York before Chinatown*, 8.

33. Nancy Davis, *The Chinese Lady: Afong Moy in Early America* (New York: Oxford University Press, 2019), 208; Tchen, *New York before Chinatown*, 118.

34. Philip B. Kunhardt, *P.T. Barnum: America's Greatest Showman* (New York: Knopf, 1995), 147.

35. Tchen, *New York before Chinatown*, 118, 113.

36. Tchen, 325.

37. Thomas Richard Whitney, *The Republic: A Monthly Magazine of American Literature, Politics, and Art* 1–4 (1851): 285.

38. According to Edward Le Roy Price, the Buckleys leased the space for a minstrel hall in June 1853 and remained three years. See Price, *Monarchs of Minstrelsy, from "Daddy" Rice to Date* (New York: Kenny Publishing, 1911), 16.

39. Tom Miller, *Daytonian in Manhattan* (blog), June 3, 2013, accessed August 20, 2021, http://daytoninmanhattan.blogspot.com/2013/06/the-lost-1882-casino-theatre-39th.html/.

40. Doug Reside, "Musical of the Month: Florodora," New York Public Library blog, July 8, 2011, www.nypl.org/blog/2011/07/08/musical-month-florodora/.

41. Maurice Peress, *Dvorak to Duke Ellington: A Conductor Explores America's Music and Its African American Roots* (New York: Oxford University Press, 2004), 55.

42. *The Alaskan*'s book was by Joseph Blethen and Max Figman, with music by Harry Girard, and the show was reviewed in the *New York Sun* on August 11, 1907.

43. An 1899 American Mutoscope and Biograph Company film of this "famous Parisian chanteuse in the rag-time cake-walk, 'Hello, Ma Baby,' with which she made such a sensation at the New York Theatre" (Biograph picture catalog) has been archived at the Library of Congress, www.loc.gov/item/96520410/ (accessed August 20, 2021).

44. Hammerstein would later recount that he "had him dressed up as a Persian, provided him with a retinue of native servants," and billed him as the "Court Magician to the Shah of Persia." "When I landed with him in New York," Hammerstein said, "the ship news reporters printed so much matter that he was a sensation for a summer." Morris Gest, "The Famous Freaks of Hammerstein's," *Green Book Magazine* 12 (September 1914): 555.

45. Lee Tung Foo appeared along with the "slang sketch 'Hogan's Visit' and 'Lord Islington,' a 'new short comedy,' an act by Ben Welch 'in Hebrew and Italian,' Henry French 'actor, juggler, mimic, and impersonator,' and 'Cremation,' which shows 'a living woman transformed to ashes on the stage.'" *New York Times*, August 4, 1907. For more on Foo, See Krystyn Moon, "Lee Tung Foo and the Making of a Chinese American Vaudevillian, 1900s–1920s," *Journal of Asian American Studies* 8, no. 1 (February 2005): 23–48.

46. "Mid-Summer Offerings," *New York Times*, August 4, 1907; "More New Musical Plays," *New York Sun*, August 11, 1907.

47. Edward W. Said, "Orientalism Reconsidered," in *Reflections on Exile and Other Literary and Cultural Essays* (London: Granta Books, 2000), 199.

48. Julia H. Lee, *Interracial Encounters: Reciprocal Representations in African and Asian American Literatures, 1896–1937* (New York: New York University Press, 2011), 5.

49. Alain Locke, "Steps toward the Negro Theatre," in *The Works of Alain Locke*, ed. Charles Molesworth (New York: Oxford University Press, 2012), 93.

50. See Bill V. Mullen, *Afro-Orientalism* (Minneapolis: University of Minnesota Press, 2004); and Vijay Prashad, *Everybody Was Kung Fu Fighting: Afro-Asian Connections and the Myth of Cultural Purity* (Boston: Beacon Press, 2002). Helen H. Jun also includes an illuminating reading of how Anna Julia Cooper's writings evidence "an ideologically complex paradigm of modern black womanhood" in pointed contrast to depictions of the "subjugated Oriental woman" in *Race for Citizenship: Black Orientalism and Asian Uplift from Pre-emancipation to Neoliberal America* (New York: New York University Press, 2011), 34.

51. W. E. B. Du Bois, *The Souls of Black Folk* (Chicago: A. C. McClerg and Co., 1903; repr., New Haven: Yale University Press, 2015), 12. For discussion of writings on the subject of interracial alliance by Du Bois and other African Americans, see Marc Gallicchio, *The African American Encounter with Japan and China: Black Internationalism in Asia, 1895–1945* (Chapel Hill: University of North Carolina Press, 2000); and Yuichiro Onishi, *Transpacific Antiracism: Afro-Asian Solidarity in 20th-Century Black America, Japan, and Okinawa* (New York: New York University Press, 2013).

52. W. E. B. Du Bois, "Egypt and India," *The Crisis* 18, no. 2 (June 1919): 62.

53. Mullen, *Afro-Orientalism*, xx.

54. Julia Lee, *Interracial Encounters*, 6.

CHAPTER ONE

1. Kayleigh Donaldson, "Aladdin: How Guy Ritchie Beat Low Expectations and Made a Disney Hit," *Screenrant*, May 30, 2019, https://screenrant.com/aladdin-movie-2019-good-success-disney/.

2. The exception was Fipilina actress Lea Salonga, who provided the singing voice of Jasmine.

3. According to *Variety*, changes to the opening song were made the following year following protests from the American-Arab Anti-Discrimination committee (removing lines such as "Where they cut off your ear / If they don't like your face" but preserving "It's barbaric, but hey, it's home"). John Evan Frook, "'Aladdin' Lyrics Altered," *Variety*, July 12, 1993.

4. Jack G. Shaheen, "Arab Caricatures Deface Disney's 'Aladdin,'" *Los Angeles Times*, December 21, 1992. See also "It's Racist, but Hey, It's Disney," *New York Times*, July 14, 1993; and Evelyn Alsultany, "How the New 'Aladdin' Stacks Up against a Century of Hollywood Stereotyping," *The Conversation*, May 26, 2019, https://theconversation.com/how-the-new-aladdin-stacks-up-against-a-century-of-hollywood-stereotyping-115608/.

5. Joseph Berger, "His Tunes Make Disney's World Go Round," *New York Times*, July 13, 1997.

6. Thomas Allston Brown, *A History of the New York Stage from the First Performance in 1732 to 1901, Volume One* (New York: Dodd and Mead, 1903), 19.

7. Peter J. Kitson, *Forging Romantic China: Sino-British Cultural Exchange, 1760–1840* (Cambridge: Cambridge University Press, 2013) 229; Anne Veronica Witchard, *Thomas*

Burke's Dark Chinoiserie: Limehouse Nights and the Queer Spell of Chinatown (London: Routledge, 2009), 31–32.

8. Marina Warner, *Stranger Magic: Charmed States and the Arabian Nights* (Cambridge, MA: Harvard University Press, 2012), 24.

9. Arafat A. Razzaque, "Who Was the Real Aladdin? From Chinese to Arab in 300 Years," Ajam Media Collective, August 10, 2017, https://ajammc.com/2017/08/10/who -was-the-real-aladdin/, and "Who 'Wrote' Aladdin? The Forgotten Syrian Storyteller," Ajam Media Collective, September 14, 2017, https://ajammc.com/2017/09/14/who-wrote -aladdin/. Yasmine Seale, who retranslated the Aladdin story from French into English in 2018, also has said that Galland based his "Aladdin" on "the story he was told by a young Syrian traveler named Hanna Diyab" and that the story is "both a product of France and also of the Arab world." Wendy Smith, "Yasmine Seale Has Retranslated 'Aladdin,'" *Publishers Weekly*, October 19, 2018.

10. The setting is described as being in "the Capital of one of the large and richest Provinces of the Kingdom of *China*, the Name of which has at present escap'd [the narrator's] Memory." "The Story of Aladdin: Or, the Wonderful Lamp," Antoine Galland, trans., *Arabian Nights Entertainments. Consisting of One Thousand and One Stories*, vol. 9 (London: W. Taylor, W. Chetwood, and S. Chapmar, 1722), 89.

11. Witchard, *Thomas Burke's Dark Chinoiserie*, 32.

12. Ross Forman, *China and the Victorian Imagination: Empires Entwined* (Cambridge: Cambridge University Press, 2013), 163. Though Disney no longer set its 1992 animated *Aladdin* in China, the movie gives a nod to this well-established tradition with the song "A Whole New World," in which the magic carpet ride of Aladdin and Princess Jasmine concludes with a grand view of a lion dance and fireworks at the Imperial Palace in Beijing.

13. *Songs, Choruses, &c, in the Grand Melo Dramatic Romance Called Aladdin; or, The Wonderful Lamp: as performed at the Philadelphia Theatre* (Philadelphia: T. Desilver, 1816), 8.

14. John O'Keeffe, *The Recitatives, Airs, Choruses, &c. in Aladin; or, The Wonderful Lamp. A Pantomime Entertainment Performed at the Theatre-Royal, Covent-Garden* (London: T. Cadell, 1788), 8, 11, 13.

15. O'Keeffe, 12.

16. Edward Litt Leman Blanchard, *Aladdin; or Harlequin and the Wonderful Lamp, a Grand Comic Christmas Pantomime* (1874), in *English Plays of the Nineteenth Century, Volume 5*, ed. Michael Booth (Oxford: Clarendon Press/Oxford University Press, 1976), 337–77, 343.

17. "Amusements," *New York Daily Times*, March 17, 1856.

18. Susan Nance, *How the Arabian Nights Inspired the American Dream, 1790–1935* (Chapel Hill: University of North Carolina Press, 2009), 11–12.

19. Galland, "Story of Aladdin," 9:105–6.

20. No script for the 1826 Drury Lane *Aladdin* by George Soane (libretto) and Henry Rowley Bishop (music) is available, but a playbill is included in Kristan Tetens, "Scheherazade on the English Stage: The Arabian Nights' Entertainments and the Georgian Repertoire," in the blog *The Victorian Peeper: Nineteenth-Century British through the Looking Glass*, October 1, 2016, http://victorianpeeper.blogspot.com/2015/03/scheherazade-on -english-stage-arabian.html/.

21. Blanchard, *Aladdin* (1874), 343.

22. "Drury Lane Theatre: Aladdin," *Illustrated Sporting and Dramatic News*, January 2, 1875.

23. Dere was an old Nigga, dey call'd him Uncle Ned. / He's dead long ago, long ago! / He had no wool on de top ob his head / De place whar de wool ought to grow (Stephen Foster, "Old Uncle Ned," 1848. Lyrics at Song of America, accessed August 20, 2021, https://songofamerica.net/song/old-uncle-ned/).

24. J. Wilton Jones, *The Entirely New and Strictly Original Comic Grand Christmas Pantomime, Aladdin and the Wonderful Lamp; or, Harlequin and the Fairies of the Jewel Cavern*, overture, incidental, and ballet music specially composed and arranged by D. Gribbin (Leeds: F. R. Spark, 1880), 25.

25. Henry J. Byron, *Aladdin: or, The Wonderful Scamp! An Original Burlesque Extravaganza, in One Act* (London: Samuel French, 1861), 24.

26. Byron, 37–38.

27. J. W. Jones, *Entirely New and Strictly Original*, 12, 27.

28. See Michael Booth's introduction to Blanchard, *Aladdin* (1874), 339, 341.

29. Blanchard, *Aladdin* (1874), 371, 375–77.

30. Krystyn R. Moon, *Yellowface: Creating the Chinese in American Popular Music and Performance, 1850s–1920s* (New Brunswick, NJ: Rutgers University Press, 2005), 23–24.

31. Moon, 24.

32. Hattie Starr, "Little Alabama Coon" (New York: Willis Woodward and Co., 1893).

33. "The Stage," *Freeman* (Indianapolis, IN), June 19, 1897.

34. *New York Age*, April 27, 1929. *Aladdin* is announced as one of a series of upcoming pantomimes for children in the *Inter-state Tattler* (*New York Age*, May 24, 1929) and as the last of the seven plays in 1934–35 season by the Children's Theatre Group of the Community Committee of the Phyllis Wheatley YWCA, as dramatized by Clare Tree Major ("'Aladdin,' Magic Drama Is Slated for Children's Group," *Washington [DC] Tribune*, April 13, 1935). Later versions included a marionette show at Camp Pleasant in Virginia (*Washington Tribune*, July 31, 1937) and a dance version by the Mary Bruce dance revue, "Bobo, the Aladdin of Harlem," starring child star Valentino Whitaker (Herbert L. Nichols, "The Jazz Life," *New York Age*, July 12, 1941). A version by Daniel A. Reed was also staged at the Harlem Boy's Club (*New York Age*, June 2, 1945).

35. "The Aladdin Cruise to West Indies and South American Attracts Many," *New York Age*, September 27, 1924.

36. Nance, *Arabian Nights*, 20.

37. "A Little Learning," *New York Age*, September 5, 1931.

38. Galland, "Story of Aladdin," 9:23–24.

39. Galland, 10:42.

40. *Aladdin, or The Wonderful Lamp: A Drama in Three Acts as Performed at the Chestnut St. Theatre, Philadelphia*, in *Alexander's Modern Acting Drama: Consisting of the Most Popular Plays Produced at the Philadelphia Theatres and Elsewhere, Volume VI* (Philadelphia: Carey and Hart, C. Alexander, and W. Marshall and Co., 1835), 127. This version is very similar to *Aladdin: or, the Wonderful Lamp, a Drama, in Three Acts, with Original Casts, Costumes, and the Whole of the Stage Business Correctly Marked and Arranged by J. B. Wright, Assistant Manager of the Boston Theatre*, number 90 in the series "Spencer's Boston Theatre" published in Boston by William V. Spencer between 1857–58.

41. Blanchard, *Aladdin* (1874), 347.

42. John Robert O'Neill, *Aladdin, or The Wonderful Lamp: A Piece of Oriental Extravaganze in One Act* (London: G. H. Davidson, 1855), 16. The original opera is by Michael William Balfe, with lyrics by Alfred Bunn.

43. Galland, "Story of Aladdin," 9:122, 10:31.

44. "Vanderheyden Fyles' Letter of New York Theatrical News," *Times-Picayune* (New Orleans), November 1, 1914.

45. "Vanderheyden Fyles' Letter of New York Theatrical News."

46. Playbill for *Chin-Chin* at the Illinois Theatre (Chicago), March 5, 1916, Library of Congress Rare Books and Special Collections Division, Washington, DC.

47. "At the Playhouses," *New Orleans Herald*, December 6, 1917.

48. Fred Stone, *Rolling Stone* (New York: McGraw-Hill, 1945), 188–89.

49. Anne Caldwell (music) and Ivan Caryll (lyrics), "Ragtime Temple Bells" (New York: Chappell, 1914), Lester S. Levy Sheet Music Collection, John Hopkins University.

50. Stone, *Rolling Stone*, 62.

51. David R. Roediger, *The Wages of Whiteness: Race and the Making of the American Working Class* (London: Verso, 1999), 116.

52. Gerald Bordman, *American Musical Theatre: A Chronicle*, 3rd ed. (New York: Oxford University Press, 2000), 346.

53. Bordman, 218.

54. African American actors playing the Genie have included Broadway actors Michael James Scott, Trevor Dion Nicholas, and Anthony Murphy. Major Attaway, Juwan Crawley, and Deonte L. Warren have also played the character in Broadway and touring productions.

55. *Illustrated London News*, August 17, 1844.

56. See Frederick Burwick, *Romantic Drama: Acting and Reacting* (Cambridge: Cambridge University Press, 2009), 165.

57. *Alexander's Modern Acting Drama* (1835), act one, 109; act two, 120, 124; ending 136.

58. Blanchard, *Aladdin* (1874), 347.

59. Grimaldi's *Memoirs* notes that "on Easter Monday, 1813, the melodrama of 'Aladdin, or the Wonderful Lamp,' written by Mr. Farley, was acted for the first time, Grimaldi playing the character of Kasrac, a dumb slave, which became one of his most popular characters." Joseph Grimaldi, *Memoirs of Joseph Grimaldi* (London: George Routledge and Sons, 1853), 185. For a detailed account of Grimaldi's clowning, see Esther Kim Lee, *Made-Up Asians: Yellowface during the Exclusion Era* (Ann Arbor: University of Michigan Press, 2022), chap. 1.

60. *Alexander's Modern Acting Drama* (1835), 122.

61. Blanchard, *Aladdin* (1874), 360.

62. Jeffrey Richards, *The Golden Age of Pantomime: Slapstick, Spectacle, and Subversion in Victorian England* (London: I. B. Tauris, 2015), 327.

63. *Times* (London), December 27, 1865, quoted in Richards, 261.

64. *Punch* (January 9, 1886), 9.

65. "The Garrick of Animal Mimes," *The Playgoer: An Illustrated Magazine of the Stage and All Entertainments*, ed. Fred Dangerfield, May 1902, 97–104.

66. Richards, *Golden Age of Pantomime*, 346.

67. "Character Sketches from 'Aladdin' at Drury-Lane, and 'Cinderella' at the Crystal Palace," *Illustrated London News*, January 16, 1886.

68. *Songs, Choruses* (1816), 5.

69. *Aladdin . . . Marked and Arranged by J. B. Wright . . .*, 2.

70. J. W. Jones, *Entirely New and Strictly Original*, 2.

71. Jacqueline L. Romeo, "Comic Coolie: Charles T. Parsloe and Nineteenth-Century American Frontier Melodrama" (PhD diss., Tufts University, 2008), 79.

72. Lawrence Hutton, *Curiosities of the American Stage* (New York: Harper and Bros., 1890), 200.

73. This production was performed at the Broadway Theatre on April 8, 1895, with a book by J. Cheever Goodwin and music by W. H. Batchelor, W. F. Gloves, and Jesse Williams. Crambo was played by comedian John J. Burke, whom the *San Francisco Call* praised as an "artistic fun-maker" with a "singing voice that is extremely agreeable." "At the Theaters," *San Francisco Call*, December 18, 1894.

74. *Alexander's Modern Acting Drama* (1835), 130.

CHAPTER TWO

1. Along with biographers Herbert Marshall and Mildred Stock, Bernth Lindfors argues that Aldridge made his London debut at the Royal Coburg Theatre on October 10, 1825, playing the role of Oroonoko in *The Revolt of Surinam; or, a Slave's Revenge* (an adaption of Thomas Southerne's *Oroonoko*) rather than Othello, as sometimes is suggested. Bernth Lindfors, "Ira Aldridge's London Debut," *Theatre Notebook* 60, no. 1 (2006): 30–44, 30. See also Herbert Marshall and Mildred Stock, *Ira Aldridge: The Negro Tragedian* (New York: Macmillan, 1958; repr., Washington, DC: Howard University Press, 1993).

2. "Aussi son entrée en scène fut-elle magnifique: c'était Othello lui-même comme l'a créé Shakespeare, avec ses yeux à demi fermés et comme éblouis du soleil d'Afrique, sa nonchalante attitude orientale et cette désinvolture de nègre qu'aucun Européen ne peut imiter." Théophile Gautier, *Voyage en Russie* (Paris: Charpentier, 1867), 254–55.

3. See Christy Desmet, "Confessions; or, the Blind Heart: An Antebellum Othello," *Borrowers and Lenders: The Journal of Shakespeare and Appropriation* 1, no. 1 (2005): 1–24; and Atesede Makonnen, "'Our Blackamoor or Negro Othello': Rejecting the Affective Power of Blackness," *European Romantic Review* 29, no. 3 (2018): 347–55.

4. Myra Lynn Stephenson, "Ira Aldridge: A Black Othello on the Nineteenth-Century English Stage" (MA thesis, Shakespeare Institute, University of Birmingham, 1977), 11–12, quoted in Bernth Lindfors, *Ira Aldridge: The Vagabond Years, 1833–1852* (Rochester, NY: University of Rochester Press, 2011), 170.

5. Lindfors, *Vagabond Years*, 31, 36.

6. *Cork Evening Herald*, March 24, 1834, quoted in Lindfors, *Vagabond Years*, 31.

7. *Cork Weekly Times and Commercial Economist*, March 21, 1834, quoted in Lindfors, *Vagabond Years*, 31.

8. Bernth Lindfors, *Ira Aldridge: Performing Shakespeare in Europe, 1852–1855* (Rochester, NY: University of Rochester Press, 2013), 4.

9. Lindfors, *Vagabond Years*, 92.

10. *Ayr Observer* (Scotland), December 3, 1839, and *Stanraer Advertiser* (Scotland), November 28, 1839, quoted in Lindfors, *Vagabond Years*, 81.

11. Quoted in Jenna M. Gibbs, *Performing the Temple of Liberty: Slavery, Theater, and Popular Culture in London and Philadelphia, 1760–1850* (Baltimore: Johns Hopkins University Press, 2014), 44.

12. The son was later known as Charles Dibdin the Younger, who became a noted dramatist and proprietor of Sadlers Wells Theatre in London.

13. William Dunlap, *A History of the American Theatre* (New York: J. and J. Harper, 1832), 31.

14. Gibbs, *Performing the Temple of Liberty*, 59.

15. Marshall and Stock, *Ira Aldridge*, 76.

16. *Kilkenny Moderator* (Ireland), February 4, 1835, quoted in Lindfors, *Vagabond Years*, 38–39.

17. *Carmarthen Journal* (Wales), December 15, 1843, quoted in Lindfors, *Vagabond Years*, 96.

18. Isaac John Bickerstaff, *The Padlock* (1768), reprinted in *Slavery, Abolition and Emancipation: Writings in the British Romantic Period, Volume 5*, ed. Jeffrey N. Cox (London: Pickering and Chatto, 1999), 88.

19. Rana Kabbani, *Europe's Myths of Orient* (Houndsmill, UK: Macmillan, 1986), 19.

20. Bickerstaff, *Padlock*, 89.

21. David Brion Davis, *The Problem of Slavery in Western Culture* (Ithaca: Cornell University Press, 1966), 43.

22. Edward Said, *Orientalism* (New York: Random House, 1978), 59–60.

23. See Kabbani, *Europe's Myths of Orient*, chap. 3.

24. Bickerstaff, *Padlock*, 96.

25. Marshall and Stock, *Ira Aldridge*, 54.

26. "As sung by Mr. Mathews, in his Entertainment called A TRIP TO AMERICA And Arranged Expressly for him," by T. Philipps (I. Willis and Co.), quoted in Marshall and Stock, *Ira Aldridge*, 42–43. An advertisement for Aldridge as the "African Roscius" on August 14, 1855, in a performance of "Gambia, the Slave in Morton's 'The Slave; or, the Blessings of Liberty!' paired with *The Padlock* lists several featured songs including 'Dear Heart, what a terrible Life I'm led,' 'Opossum up a Gum Tree,' and 'Negro Boy,'" in Langston Hughes and Milton Meltzer, *Black Magic: A Pictorial History of the Negro in American Entertainment* (Englewood Cliffs, NJ: Prentice-Hall, 1967), 45.

27. *The Virginia Mummy*, arranged by C. White was published as vol. 14, no. 25, of *Dick's Standard Plays* (London: John Dicks). *The Virginia Mummy* appears alongside John Poole's *Intrigue*, a play performed at the Theatre Royal in 1814. The date is uncertain; the University of Minnesota Libraries estimates that it was published between 1840 and 1849. *The Virginia Mummy* was reprinted later in London and New York by Samuel French.

28. The C. White version is presumably the version of the play that Aldridge performed as the Surrey Theatre in March to April 1848 and is the source of several quotations in the text. W. T. Lhamon republished another version of the script in his collection *Jump Jim Crow: Lost Plays, Lyrics, and Street Prose of the First Atlantic Popular Culture* (Cambridge, MA: Harvard University Press, 2003). This work is the source of several in-text citations later in the chapter. According to Lindfors, Lhamon republished the imperfect manuscript of this farce held at the British Library among the plays submitted to the Lord Chamberlain's office (Add. Mss. 42940, ff. 822–67), supplementing it with materials from printed sources; a fuller manuscript based on Rice's adaptation is held in the Pettingell Collection at the Templeton Library, University of Kent at Canterbury (Lindfors, *Vagabond Years*, 205n111). Mobile's *Commercial Register* confirms a performance of *The Virginia Mummy* at a benefit held by Noah Ludlow in Mobile, Alabama, on April 22, 1835, and says that the

play was "written especially for the occasion, by Mr. Rice," with Rice playing Ginger Blue (Lhamon, *Jump Jim Crow*, 425n1).

29. William Bayle Bernard, *The Mummy: A Farce in One Act* (Boston: W. V. Spencer, 1856). In-text citations are to this work.

30. William Wycherley, *The Country Wife*, ed. Thomas Hikaru Fujimura (Lincoln: University of Nebraska Press, 1965), 99.

31. Lhamon, *Jump Jim Crow*, 48.

32. David R. Roediger, *The Wages of Whiteness: Race and the Making of the American Working Class* (London: Verso, 1999), 117.

33. Lhamon, *Jump Jim Crow*, 175, 165.

34. Lindfors, *Vagabond Years*, 88. Brackets are Lindfors's.

35. Sheffield Theatre playbill, November 22, 1841, quoted in Lindfors, *Vagabond Years*, 80.

36. *Derby Mercury* (England), December 29, 1841, quoted in Lindfors, *Vagabond Years*, 80.

37. *Westmeath Guardian and Longford News-letter* (Ireland), September 5, 1839, quoted in Lindfors, *Vagabond Years*, 80.

38. *Doncaster Chronicle and Farmer's Journal* (England), March 6, 1841, quoted in Lindfors, *Vagabond Years*, 80.

39. John Coleman, *Fifty Years of an Actor's Life* (London: Hutchinson, 1904), 91–92, quoted in Lindfors, *Vagabond Years*, 112.

40. *Drogheda Journal* (Ireland), September 21, 1839, quoted in Lindfors, *Vagabond Years*, 80.

41. *Era* (London), October 25, 1846, quoted in Lindfors, *Vagabond Years*, 134.

42. "Mr. Aldridge, the African Tragedian," *Illustrated London News*, July 3, 1858.

43. *British Press*, October 11, 1825, quoted in Lindfors, *Vagabond Years*, 2.

44. Felicity A. Nussbaum, "The Theatre of Empire: Racial Counterfeit; Racial Realism," in *A New Imperial History: Culture, Identity and Modernity in Britain and the Empire, 1660–1840*, ed. Kathleen Wilson (Cambridge: Cambridge University Press, 2004), 89.

CHAPTER THREE

1. Sarah Meers, *Uncle Tom Mania: Slavery, Minstrelsy and Transatlantic Culture in the 1850s* (Athens: University of Georgia Press, 2005), 15.

2. W. T. Lhamon, *Jump Jim Crow: Lost Plays, Lyrics, and Street Prose of the First Atlantic Popular Culture* (Cambridge, MA: Harvard University Press, 2003), 65.

3. David Mayer, *Harlequin in His Element: The English Pantomime, 1806–1836* (Cambridge, MA: Harvard University Press, 1969), 94.

4. Michael Pickering, *Blackface Minstrelsy in Britain* (Aldershot, UK: Ashgate, 2008).

5. David Worrall, *Harlequin Empire: Race, Ethnicity, and the Drama of the Popular Enlightenment* (New York: Routledge, 2015), 25.

6. Robert Toll, *Blacking Up: The Minstrel Show in Nineteenth-Century America* (New York: Oxford University Press, 1974), 171.

7. Toll, 171.

8. Program for Christy's Minstrels and the Mohawk Minstrels reproduced in Harry Reynolds, *Minstrel Memories: The Story of Burnt Cork Minstrelsy in Great Britain from 1836–1927* (London: Alston Rivers, 1928), 138–39.

9. Josephine Lee, *The Japan of Pure Invention: Gilbert and Sullivan's "The Mikado"* (Minneapolis: University of Minnesota Press, 2010), 89.

10. Mari Yoshihara, *Embracing the East: White Women and American Orientalism* (New York: Oxford University Press, 2002), 17.

11. J. Ed. Green, "Big Minstrel Festival of the Richards and Pringle-Rusco and Holland Troupes," *Freeman*, January 8, 1900.

12. Henry T. Sampson, *The Ghost Walks: A Chronological History of Blacks in Show Business, 1865–1910* (Metuchen, NJ: Scarecrow Press, 1988), 218.

13. Toll, *Blacking Up*, 34.

14. Stephanie Dunson, "The Minstrel in the Parlor: Nineteenth-Century Sheet Music and the Domestication of Blackface Minstrelsy," *American Transcendental Quarterly* 16, no. 4 (2002): 244.

15. See Yoshihara, *Embracing the East*; and Josephine Lee, "Decorative Orientalism," in *Asian American Literature in Transition: 1850–1930*, ed. Josephine Lee and Julia H. Lee (Cambridge: Cambridge University Press, 2021).

16. Toll, *Blacking Up*, 197–98.

17. Eileen Southern, "The Georgia Minstrels: The Early Years," in *Inside the Minstrel Mask: Readings in Nineteenth-Century Blackface Minstrelsy*, ed. Annemarie Bean, James V. Hatch, and Brooks McNamara (Hanover, NH: University Press of New England, 1996), 166.

18. "City and Suburban News: Brooklyn," *New York Times*, March 4, 1882.

19. "'Japanese Tommy's' Funeral," *New York Times*, July 13, 1887.

20. "Variety," *New York Clipper*, January 5, 1884; Toll, *Blacking Up*, 197–98.

21. Edward Le Roy Price, *Monarchs of Minstrelsy, from "Daddy" Rice to Date* (New York: Kenny Publishing, 1911), 116.

22. Reynolds, *Minstrel Memories*, 210, 164.

23. W. Anthony Sheppard, *Extreme Exoticism: Japan in the American Musical Imagination* (New York: Oxford University Press, 2019), 465–66n16.

24. "Variety," *New York Clipper*, January 5, 1884.

25. John Russell Bartlett, *Dictionary of Americanisms*, 4th ed. (Boston, Little, Brown, 1877), 304.

26. Harry Reynolds, *Minstrel Memories*, 169. For information on the broom, see Dale Cockrell, *Demons of Disorder: Early Blackface Minstrels and Their World* (Cambridge: Cambridge University Press, 1997), 47, 49, 50.

27. E. Byron Christy and William E. Christy, *Christy's New Songster and Black Joker Containing All the Most Popular and Original Songs, Choruses, Stump Speeches, Witticisms, Jokes, Conundrums, etc., etc., as Sung and Delivered by the World-Renowned Christy's Minstrels at Their Opera Houses* (New York: Dick and Fitzgerald, 1863), 59–60.

28. This 1866 studio photograph of Dilward dressed for a female role in an elaborate dress and bonnet, taken by Fisher's of Boston, was auctioned in 2020: https://web.archive .org/web/20200212131104/https://www.cowanauctions.com/lot/remarkable-cdv-of -japanese-tommy-in-drag-ca-1866-3997721/ (accessed August 20, 2021).

29. Dunson, "Minstrel in the Parlor," 246.

30. Masao Miyoshi, *As We Saw Them: The First Japanese Embassy to the United States (1860)* (Berkeley: University of California Press, 1979), 43–45, 65, 67, 69, 79, 146–47, 160–61, 184.

31. *Philadelphia Inquirer,* June 15, 1860, and *New York Herald,* June 17, 1860, quoted in Miyoshi, *As We Saw Them,* 43.

32. "A Day at Willards," *New York Tribune,* May 26, 1860, quoted in Joel D. Treese, "The Japanese Mission of 1860," White House Historical Association, April 23, 2015, accessed August 20, 2021, www.whitehousehistory.org/the-japanese-mission-of-1860/.

33. "News of the Niagara: What the Japs Think of Their Visit to America," *New York Times,* August 20, 1860.

34. Japan–NYC 1860–2010, Consulate General of Japan in New York website, accessed August 20, 2021, www.ny.us.emb-japan.go.jp/150JapanNY/en/tommy.html/.

35. *Harper's Weekly,* June 30, 1860. For more on this, see Josephine Lee, *Japan of Pure Invention,* 96–97.

36. *Bristol Times and Mirror* (UK), March 15, 1869.

37. Frank Dumont, "The Golden Days of Minstrelsy," *New York Clipper,* December 19, 1914.

38. Bluford Adams, *E Pluribus Barnum: The Great Showman and the Making of U.S. Popular Culture* (Minneapolis: University of Minnesota Press, 1997), 158.

39. "Amusements," *New York Times,* July 8, 1860.

40. "Things Theatrical," *Spirit of the Times,* March 16, 1861.

41. William J. Mahar, *Behind the Burnt Cork Mask: Early Blackface Minstrelsy and Antebellum American Popular Culture* (Urbana: University of Illinois Press, 1999), 312.

42. Eric Lott, *Love and Theft: Blackface Minstrelsy and the American Working Class* (New York: Oxford University Press, 1993), 19.

43. Lott, 25.

44. Thomas Allston Brown, *A History of the New York Stage from the First Performance in 1732 to 1901, Volume One* (New York: Dodd, Mead, 1903), 237.

45. According to John Jeremiah Sullivan, Juba gave his year of birth as 1830 to the *Manchester Guardian,* contradicting the year 1825 often given in modern encyclopedias. "*Shuffle Along* and the Lost History of Black Performance in America," *New York Times Magazine,* March 24, 2016.

46. *Manchester Guardian,* October 18, 1848.

47. Toll, *Blacking Up,* 43.

48. Mark Knowles, *Tap Roots: The Early History of Tap Dancing* (New York: McFarland, 2002), 87–90.

49. Charles Dickens, *Pictures from Italy, and American Notes for General Circulation* (Boston: Houghton, Osgood, 1880), 274–75.

50. See Marian Hannah Winter, "Juba and American Minstrelsy," *Dance Index* 6, no. 2 (February 1947): 28–47; and Constance Valis Hill, *Tap Dancing America: A Cultural History* (New York: Oxford University Press, 2009), 12.

51. *Manchester Guardian,* October 18, 1848.

52. Lott, *Love and Theft,* 160–61.

53. *Manchester Guardian,* October 18, 1848.

54. Stephen Johnson, "Gender Trumps Race? Cross-Dressing Juba in Early Blackface Minstrelsy," in *When Men Dance: Choreographing Masculinities across Borders,* ed. Jennifer Fisher and Anthony Shay (New York: Oxford University Press, 2009), 237.

55. Lott, *Love and Theft,* 52.

56. Sianne Ngai, *Our Aesthetic Categories: Zany, Cute, Interesting* (Cambridge, MA: Harvard University Press, 2012), 15, 3.

57. Clipping, American minstrel show collection, 1823–1947, MS Thr 556 (98), Harvard Theatre Collection, Houghton Library, Harvard University.

58. "Amusements," *New York Times*, July 4, 1860.

59. "The Theatres on the Fourth," *New York Times*, July 4, 1860.

60. "Theatres on the Fourth."

61. Frank Dumont, *The Witmark Amateur Minstrel Guide and Burnt Cork Encyclopedia* (Chicago: M. Witmark and Sons, 1899), 1.

62. Dumont, 39.

63. *New York Clipper*, August 10, 1895, quoted in Lynn Abbott and Doug Seroff, *Out of Sight: The Rise of African American Popular Music, 1889–1895* (Jackson: University Press of Mississippi, 2002), 330.

64. The song is listed as "Yung-Go-Wap" by Hubbard T. Smith (music) and Jim Anderson (lyrics) in the 1899 Witmark's catalog (Library of Congress). A 1914 copyright is listed for a new four-part arrangement of "Yung Go Wap" by W. C. O'Hare on October 21, 1914 (Library of Congress Copyright Entries, 1914, Musical Compositions, part 3, 1356).

65. Dumont, *Amateur Minstrel*, 34–35. "Two Little Japanese Dolls: An Oriental Romance" by Hattie Star was published by M. Witmark and Sons in 1894. The song was also mentioned as "one of the latest efforts from the pen of Hattie Starr, composer of 'Somebody Loves Me' and 'Little Alabama Coon' in the sheet music of Starr's song, 'You're So Good, Daddy' published by M. Witmark and Sons in 1896."

66. Barbara Schulman, "Blackface Minstrelsy: Instructional Handbooks for the Amateur, 1899–1921" (PhD diss., University of Minnesota, 2018).

67. Toll, *Blacking Up*, 138; Annemarie Bean, "Double Inversion and Black Minstrelsy, circa 1890," in *African American Performance and Theater History: A Critical Reader*, ed. Harry J. Elam Jr. and David Krasner (New York: Oxford University Press, 2001), 174. Seymour Stark has also suggested that "the first female performers, the 'Sable Sisters' (Annette, Angeline and Pauline) played at the Apollo Rooms in November 1844 and that the same year, the 'Lady Minstrels' performed at Peale's New York Museum with 'Prof. Pesch's Celebrated Band of Female Minstrels.'" *Men in Blackface: True Stories of the Minstrel Show* (Xlibris, 2001), not paginated.

68. Dumont, *Amateur Minstrel*, 2.

69. Sheppard describes this song as depicting a "male Japanese doll [who] commits suicide after his beloved is purchased." *Extreme Exoticism*, 57.

70. Dumont, *Amateur Minstrel*, 112–15.

71. Yoshihara, *Embracing the East*, 18.

72. Walter Ben Hare, *Abbu San of Old Japan: Comedy-Drama in Two Acts for Fifteen Girls* (Chicago: T. S. Denison, 1916). This is the source of the following in-text citations.

73. A 1919 production at St. Mary's College in Notre Dame, Indiana, for instance: "Through the courtesy of the Expression Class, the Exhibition Hall was transformed into a little bit of Japan. 'Abbu San of Old Japan,' a refreshing three act play, was presented amidst incense and chrysanthemums. Lucile Miller as Abbu San, the princess, did full justice to the leading role. While Esther Carrico the Black Mammy from 'Old Virginy,'

proved an interesting character in picturesque Japan." *St. Mary's Chimes* (Notre Dame), March 1919, 124.

74. Yoshihara, *Embracing the East*, 95–100.

75. See Josephine Lee, *Japan of Pure Invention*, chap. 4.

76. Lott, *Love and Theft*, 26–27.

77. For more on the Aunt Jemima advertising campaign, see Maurice M. Manring, "Aunt Jemima Explained: The Old South, the Absent Mistress, and the Slave in a Box," *Southern Cultures* 2, no. 1 (Fall 1995): 19–44.

78. Isabel Wilkerson, *Caste: The Origins of Our Discontents* (New York: Random House, 2020), 138.

CHAPTER FOUR

1. Robert Toll, *Blacking Up: The Minstrel Show in Nineteenth-Century America* (New York: Oxford University Press, 1974), 170.

2. Bret Harte, *Two Men of Sandy Bar. A Drama* (Boston: Houghton, Mifflin, 1888), 58.

3. Robert G. Lee, *Orientals: Asian Americans in Popular Culture* (Philadelphia: Temple University Press, 1999), 3.

4. "John Chinaman," reprinted in Richard A. Dwyer and Richard E. Lingenfelter, *The Songs of the Gold Rush* (Berkeley: University of California Press, 1963), 15–16, quoted in R. Lee, *Orientals*, 43.

5. R. Lee, *Orientals*, 34, 76–77.

6. Moon-Ho Jung, "Outlawing 'Coolies': Race, Nation, and Empire in the Age of Emancipation," *American Quarterly* 57, no. 3 (2005): 690.

7. Lisa Lowe, *The Intimacies of Four Continents* (Durham, NC: Duke University Press, 2015), 24.

8. Moon-Ho Jung, "Coolie," in *Keywords for American Cultural Studies*, ed. Bruce Burgett and Glenn Hendler (New York: New York University Press, 2007), 64.

9. Caroline H. Yang, *The Peculiar Afterlife of Slavery: The Chinese Worker and the Minstrel Form* (Stanford: Stanford University Press, 2020), 19.

10. Ronald Takaki, *Iron Cages: Race and Culture in 19th-Century America* (Oxford: Oxford University Press, 1978), ix.

11. Francesca Schironi, "The Trickster Onstage: The Cunning Slave from Plautus to *Commedia dell'Arte*," in *Ancient Comedy and Reception: Essays in Honor of Jeffrey Henderson*, ed. S. Douglas Olson (New York: De Gruyter, 2013), 447–78.

12. Sianne Ngai, *Our Aesthetic Categories: Zany, Cute, Interesting* (Cambridge, MA: Harvard University Press, 2012), 193.

13. Isaac John Bickerstaff, *The Padlock* (1768), reprinted in *Slavery, Abolition and Emancipation: Writings in the British Romantic Period, Volume 5*, ed. Jeffrey N. Cox (London: Pickering and Chatto, 1999), 86–87.

14. Robert Hornback, *Racism and Early Blackface Comic Traditions* (Cham, Switz.: Palgrave Macmillan, 2018), 56, 54.

15. William Courtright, *The Complete Minstrel Guide* (Chicago: Dramatic Publishing Co., 1901), 107–13. In-text citations are to this work.

16. Heidi Kim, *Invisible Subjects: Asian America in Postwar Culture* (New York: Oxford University Press, 2016), 62.

17. R. Lee, *Orientals*, 99.

18. James J. McCloskey, *Across the Continent; or, Scenes from New York Life and the Pacific Railroad*, in *Davy Crockett and Other Plays*, ed. Isaac Goldberg and Hubert Heffner (Princeton: Princeton University Press, 1940), 23–56. In-text citations are to this work.

19. Kenneth J. Cerniglia, "Negotiating American Identity through Ethnic Stereotypes in J. J. McCloskey's *Across the Continent* (1870) and Edward Harrigan's *The Mulligan Guard Ball* (1879)," *Theatre Annual* 61 (2008): 23–56, 29.

20. Classical names were given to slave characters in works such as *The Politicians; or, A State of Things* (1798) by Philadelphian John Murdock, which depicts the freed slave Sambo debating the "pros and cons of French versus American republicanism with two slave friends, Pompey and Caesar" (Jenna M. Gibbs, *Performing the Temple of Liberty: Slavery, Theater, and Popular Culture in London and Philadelphia, 1760–1850* [Baltimore: Johns Hopkins University Press, 2014], 45). "Caesar Augustus" recalls the earlier incarnations of happy black servant characters in American plays such as the "affectionate, garrulous, irresponsible, and highly loyal" Caesar in Washington Irving's *Salmagundi* (1807) or the similar character of "Agamemnon" in James Fenimore Cooper's *The Spy* (1821); see Joseph Boskin, *Sambo: The Rise and Demise of an American Jester* (New York: Oxford University Press, 1986), 96.

21. Hornback, *Racism and Early Blackface*, 238.

22. The Fifteenth Amendment was ratified February 3, 1870, and prohibited the federal government and states from denying the right to vote based on race, color, or previous condition of servitude.

23. Goldberg and Heffner, introduction to McCloskey, *Across the Continent*, xvii.

24. Rosemary K. Bank, "Frontier Melodrama," *Dutch Quarterly Review of Anglo-American Letters* 19, no. 2 (1989): 136–45, 137.

25. Roger Allan Hall, *Performing the American Frontier, 1870–1906* (Cambridge: Cambridge University Press, 2001), 12.

26. *New York Evening Post* (February 15, 1881), quoted in Jacqueline L. Romeo, "Comic Coolie: Charles T. Parsloe and Nineteenth-Century American Frontier Melodrama" (PhD diss., Tufts University, 2008), 23.

27. Bret Harte, "Plain Language from Truthful James," *Overland Monthly* 5, no. 3 (1870): 287–88.

28. Gary Scharnhorst, *Bret Harte: Opening the American Literary West* (Norman: University of Oklahoma Press, 2000), 52.

29. Bret Harte and Mark Twain, *Ah Sin*, in *The Chinese Other, 1850–1925: An Anthology of Plays*, ed. Dave Williams (Lanham, MD: University Press of America, 1997), 40. In-text citations are to this work.

30. "Ah Sin. Mary Clemmer's Description of Mark Twain and Bret Harte's New Play," *San Francisco Daily Evening Bulletin*, May 21, 1877.

31. Quoted in Sean Metzger, *Chinese Looks: Fashion, Performance, Race* (Bloomington: Indiana University Press, 2014), 43.

32. Gerald Bordman describes an appearance by Charles Parsloe in Edgar Wilson (Bill) Nye's *The Cadi* on September 21, 1891: "Nye at least attempted something different in 'Orientalia,' allowing his exotica to take place in New York. A mischievous boy (Minnie Dupree) leads a Wyoming postmaster to believe he has been made Turkish consul in Manhattan. Enlivened by the cavortings of Thomas Q. Seabrooke as the postmaster and

Charles Parsloe as a pigtailed, pidgin-English-speaking Chinese, the piece played until 19 December." Gerald Bordman, *American Musical Theatre: A Chronicle*, 3rd ed. (New York: Oxford University Press, 2000), 125–26.

33. Quoted in Metzger, *Chinese Looks*, 56.

34. "Mark Twain and Bret Harte's New Play at the Fifth Avenue Theatre, New York—Mark Twain's Funny Speech," *San Francisco Daily Evening Bulletin*, August 9, 1877.

35. Washington correspondence, *St. Louis Globe-Democrat*, "Ah Sin on the Stage. An Interesting Sketch of an Interesting New Play," reprinted in the *Denver Daily Rocky Mountain News*, May 19, 1877.

36. "Amusements. Fifth Avenue Theatre," *New York Times*, August 1, 1877.

37. "'Ah Sin' at the Fifth Avenue Theatre," *New York Herald*, August 1, 1877.

38. "Amusements: Ah Sin," *New York Sun*, August 5, 1877.

39. *Spirit of the Times*, August 4, 1877.

40. Romeo, "Comic Coolie," 6–7, 66, 67.

41. Romeo, 76–79.

42. *New York Clipper*, January 29, 1898, quoted in Romeo, "Comic Coolie," 73.

43. *New York Herald*, May 8, 1871, and *New York Times*, May 9, 1871, quoted in Romeo, "Comic Coolie," 91.

44. Sharon McCoy notes Twain's particular affinity for the San Francisco Minstrels, a popular troupe that began in San Francisco and moved to New York in 1865 who performed a particular blend of political satire and "manic improvisation." Sharon D. McCoy, "'The Trouble Begins at Eight': Mark Twain, the San Francisco Minstrels, and the Unsettling Legacy of Blackface Minstrelsy," *American Literary Realism* 41, no. 3 (Spring 2009): 232–48, 235.

45. Stuart W. Hyde, "The Chinese Stereotype in American Melodrama," *California Historical Society Quarterly* 34 (December 1955): 357–65, quoted in Alexander Saxton, "Blackface Minstrelsy and Jacksonian Ideology," *American Quarterly* 27, no. 1 (March 1975): 3–28, 25–26.

46. A later version, "All-A-Same; or, The Chinee Laundryman," was published in 1880 by Frank Dumont. The cover notes that it was written for Charles Backus of the San Francisco Minstrels but credits Dumont with the words and music. Frank Dumont, "All-A-Same; or, The Chinee Laundryman" (Philadelphia: Chas. F. Escher Jr., 1880), Lester S. Levy Sheet Music Collection, Johns Hopkins University.

47. "Mark Twain and Bret Harte's New Play at the Fifth Avenue Theatre."

48. *New York Sun*, August 5, 1877.

49. Harte himself did not intend the violent anti-Chinese sentiment that the poem was used by others to support; in later years he disavowed it as "trash," calling it "the worst poem I ever wrote, possibly the worst poem anyone ever wrote." Gary Scharnhorst, "'Ways That Are Dark': Appropriations of Bret Harte's 'Plain Language from Truthful James,'" *Nineteenth-Century Literature* 51, no. 3 (December 1996): 377–99, 380.

50. Hsin-yun Ou, "Mark Twain's Racial Ideologies and His Portrayal of the Chinese," *Concentric* 36, no. 2 (September 2010): 33–59.

51. Yusha Pan, "Intention versus Reception: The Representation of the Chinese in *Ah Sin*," in *Constructing Identities: The Interaction of National, Gender and Racial Borders*, ed. Antonio Medina-Rivera and Lee Wilberschied (Newcastle upon Tyne: Cambridge Scholars Publishing, 2013), 54.

52. Pan, 59.

53. Bret Harte, *Bret Harte's California: Letters to the "Springfield Republican" and "Christian Register," 1866–67*, ed. Gary Scharnhorst (Albuquerque: University of New Mexico Press, 1990), 114.

54. Eric Lott, *Love and Theft: Blackface Minstrelsy and the American Working Class* (New York: Oxford University Press, 1993), 86.

CHAPTER FIVE

1. E. Byron Christy and William E. Christy, *Christy's New Songster and Black Joker Containing All the Most Popular and Original Songs, Choruses, Stump Speeches, Witticisms, Jokes, Conundrums, etc., etc., as Sung and Delivered by the World-Renowned Christy's Minstrels at Their Opera Houses* (New York: Dick and Fitzgerald, 1863), 59.

2. Stuart W. Hyde, "The Chinese Stereotype in American Melodrama," *California Historical Society Quarterly* 34 (December 1955): 357–65, quoted in Alexander Saxton, "Blackface Minstrelsy and Jacksonian Ideology," *American Quarterly* 27, no. 1 (March 1975): 25–26.

3. "Circus, Minstrel, and Variety Gossip," *New York Clipper*, January 5, 1884.

4. "Correspondents' Notes" for *Musical Courier*, September 10, 1881, quoted in Jennifer Mooney, *Irish Stereotypes in Vaudeville, 1865–1905* (New York: Palgrave Macmillan, 2015), 137.

5. J. C. C., *Allee Samee 'Mellican Man*, in *Beadle's Dime Dialogues*, no. 41 (New York: Beadle and Adams, 1894), 82–86. In-text citations are to this work.

6. Wolfgang Mieder, "'No Tickee, No Washee': Subtleties of a Proverbial Slur," *Western Folklore* 55 (Winter 1996): 8–9.

7. "Attractions at the Theater, Vaudeville: At the Roof Garden," *Minneapolis Tribune*, November 26, 1905.

8. "Robetta and Doretta, [no. 2] Chinese laundry," filmed around November 26, 1894, in Edison's Black Maria studio in West Orange, New Jersey, Library of Congress Motion Picture, Broadcasting and Recorded Sound Division, accessed August 20, 2021, http:// hdl.loc.gov/loc.mbrsmi/edmp.4032/.

9. See Michael Starks, *Cocaine Fiends and Reefer Madness: An Illustrated History of Drugs in the Movies, 1894–1978* (Berkeley: Ronin, 2015), 13–14; and Jason Grant McKahan, "Substance Abuse Film and the Gothic: Typology, Narrative, and Hallucination," in *Monsters in and among Us: Towards a Gothic Criminology*, ed. Caroline Joan (Kay) Picart and Cecil E. Greek (Madison, NJ: Fairleigh Dickinson University Press, 2007), 122–23.

10. Vitaphone sound skit of Cal Stewart in "Uncle Josh in a Chinese Laundry" (1910) is linked to Jeff Cohen, "Fun in a Chinese Laundry," in *Vitaphone Varieties* blog post, January 7, 2007, http://vitaphone.blogspot.com/2007/01/fun-in-chinese-laundry.html/. The electronic edition of Cal Stewart, *Uncle Josh's Punkin Centre Stories*, can be found at Project Gutenberg: www.gutenberg.org/files/970/970-h/970-h.htm#link2H_4_0005/ (accessed August 20, 2021).

11. "The Heathen Chinee," *Elevator Constructor* 3, no. 12 (December 1906): 20.

12. Anonymous, "Increase of Japs," *Elevator Constructor* 3, no. 1 (January 1906): 34.

13. "Father's Side of It," *Elevator Constructor* 3, no. 5 (May 1906): 15.

14. Yuko Matsukawa, "Representing the Oriental in Nineteenth-Century Trade Cards,"

in *Re/collecting Early Asian America*, ed. Josephine Lee, Imogene Lim, and Yuko Matsukawa (Philadelphia: Temple University Press, 2002), 200–217.

15. Sheldon Palmer, *Fun in a Chinese Laundry* (Chicago: T. S. Denison, 1920). In-text citations are to this work.

16. Mark Twain, *Roughing It* (Hartford, CT: American Publishing Co., 1872), 392.

17. Alfred Trumble, *The Heathen Chinee at Home and Abroad* (New York: Fox, 1882), 50.

18. "Washee-Checkee. The Complicated Process by Which Chinese Laundrymen Check Their Goods," reprinted from *New York World* in the *Huntsville (AL) Gazette*, April 25, 1885.

19. "Variety," *New York Clipper*, January 5, 1884.

20. "A. G. Allen's Minstrels," *Freeman*, January 1, 1910.

21. The same review also noted that "the Indian and the Coon sketch by Burns and Sam Mobley was a scream, and called for more encores than their wind would allow," *Freeman*, July 23, 1910.

22. *Jasper (IN) Weekly Courier*, October 26, 1906.

23. "Fiddler Is Playing in Omaha, Neb.," *Chicago Defender*, December 17, 1938.

24. Kliph Nesteroff, "Last Man in Blackface: The World of Pigmeat Markham," *WFMU's Beware of the Blog*, November 2010, https://web.archive.org/web/20200910140714/https://blog.wfmu.org/freeform/2010/11/the-forgotten-pigmeat-markham.html/.

25. Alan Gevingson, ed., *Within Our Gates: Ethnicity in American Feature Films, 1911–1960*, American Film Institute Catalog (Berkeley: University of California Press, 1997), 471.

26. Paul J. Knox, "I Don't Care If I Never Wake Up" (Chicago: Will Rossiter, 1899).

27. *Freeman*, February 29, 1910.

28. J. D. Howard, "Cook and Stevens," *Freeman*, October 23, 1909.

29. *The Star*, quoted by Howard in "Cook and Stevens."

30. "Boston, Mass., Theatrical Notes," *Freeman*, January 22, 1916.

31. "Gibson's New Standard Theater," *Freeman*, June 27, 1914.

32. Henry Llewellyn Williams, *Waxworks at Play* (Chicago: T. S. Denison, 1894), 3. In-text citations are to this work.

33. Tera Hunter, *To 'Joy My Freedom: Southern Black Women's Lives and Labors after the Civil War* (Cambridge, MA: Harvard University Press, 1997), 78.

34. Walter Carter, *The Coon and the Chink: A Vaudeville Sketch in One Act* (New York: Dick and Fitzgerald, 1912), 2. In-text citations are to this work.

35. "New Acts This Week," *Variety*, October 24, 1919.

36. "Chinese Exclusion—Is It in Harmony with the Moral Principles of the Single Tax?," *New York Times*, January 13, 1902.

37. [Williams] Pickens, "Me Nigger, Too!," *Broad Ax* (Chicago), February 28, 1920.

38. Nicholas Vachel Lindsay, "The Golden-Faced People: A Story of the Chinese Conquest of America," *The Crisis* 9, no. 1 (November 1914): 36. Additional in-text citations are also to this work.

39. See Edlie L. Wong, *Racial Reconstruction: Black Inclusion, Chinese Exclusion, and the Fictions of Citizenship* (New York: New York University Press, 2015), chap. 3.

40. Wong, *Racial Reconstruction*, 168.

41. Wong, 173.

CHAPTER SIX

1. Robert Toll, *Blacking Up: The Minstrel Show in Nineteenth-Century America* (New York: Oxford University Press, 1974), 223.

2. James Weldon Johnson, *Black Manhattan* (1930; repr., New York: Arno, 1967), 87.

3. Zora Neale Hurston, "Characteristics of Negro Expression," in *Negro: An Anthology*, ed. Nancy Cunard (London: Wishart, 1934), 59.

4. *Philadelphia Tribune*, May 10, 1907.

5. W. E. B. Du Bois, *The Souls of Black Folk* (Chicago: A. C. McClerg and Co., 1903; repr., New Haven: Yale University Press, 2015), 215.

6. Paul Laurence Dunbar, "We Wear the Mask," in *Lyrics of Lowly Life* (New York: Dodd, Mead, 1896), reprinted in *The Collected Poetry of Paul Laurence Dunbar*, ed. Joanne M. Braxton (Charlottesville: University Press of Virginia, 1993), 71.

7. "The Stage," *Freeman*, September 17, 1901.

8. "The Pekin and Ollie Demsey Always Make Good," *Freeman*, August 21, 1909.

9. *Baltimore Afro-American*, December 1931, quoted in Henry T. Sampson, *Blacks in Blackface: A Sourcebook on Early Black Musical Shows*, 2nd ed. (Lanham, MD: Scarecrow Press 2014), 68.

10. Sylvester Russell, "Should Respectable Girls Adopt the Stage?," *Freeman*, April 15, 1904.

11. "*Bandanna Land* by Burton Beach, Majestic Theatre, New York City," *Freeman*, February 15, 1908.

12. Elwood Knox, "Whitney and Tutt Comedy Company, 'The Ruler of the Town,'" *Freeman*, February 5, 1910.

13. "Carita Day's 'I Wont,'" *Freeman*, January 19, 1907.

14. "Tim Moore—One Man Uncle Tom's Cabin Act," *Freeman*, October 16, 1915.

15. David Krasner, *Resistance, Parody, and Double Consciousness in African American Theatre, 1895–1910* (New York: St. Martin's Press, 1997).

16. Terry Waldo, *This Is Ragtime* (New York: Hawthorn Books, 1976; repr., New York: Da Capo Press, 1991), 25.

17. "Clarks, Reviewed at the Crown Garden Theatre," *Freeman*, May 6, 1911.

18. "At the New Crown Garden: Margie Crosby—the Girl with a Jew Face," *Freeman*, August 16, 1913. The song "Uncle Ephram" might have been a variation on "Old Uncle Eph" (published with music by Bob Allen by White, Smith and Co., Boston, 1878) or the song later recorded as "Uncle Eph's Got the Coon" (see the listing at the Traditional Ballad Index, California State University–Fresno, accessed August 20, 2021, www.csufresno.edu/folklore/ballads/RcUncEph.html/).

19. Sylvester Russell, "The Black Patti Show," *Freeman*, August 16, 1904.

20. "Free Lance," "Carter & Bluford," *Freeman*, November 24, 1906.

21. Milton Lewis, "The Smart Set Company," *Freeman*, December 23, 1905.

22. Lester A. Walton, "The Octoroon," *New York Age*, January 13, 1916.

23. Walton, "The Octoroon."

24. "Billy McClain—Originator of the Cake Walk," *Freeman*, April 16, 1910.

25. "*Trip to Chinatown*—Darktown Follies Company, Reviewed at the Avenue Theatre, Chicago," *Billboard*, January 1, 1921.

26. "Amusements," *San Francisco Bulletin*, April 1, 1879.

27. Krystyn Moon, *Yellowface: Creating the Chinese in American Popular Music and Performance, 1850s–1920s* (New Brunswick: Rutgers University Press, 2005), 134.

28. On August 19, 1880, a Chinese opera, *The Treaty between the Six Asiatic Nations*, was performed in a new venue in Portland, Oregon ("Coung Ye Lung & Co's new theater, corner of Second and Alder streets"), witnessed by a full house: "five-sixths of the audience being Celestials and one-sixth Caucasians" with "about 30 Chinese women" in the gallery. Much of the description is devoted to describing how "a Chinese theatrical performance, like a Chinaman, is peculiar" ("The Chinese Theatre," *Oregonian* [Portland], August 20, 1880).

29. "From Table Talk, Sydney, Australia," reprinted in *Topeka Plaindealer*, March 9, 1900, 1.

30. Henry T. Sampson, *The Ghost Walks: A Chronological History of Blacks in Show Business, 1850–1910* (Metuchen, NJ: Scarecrow Press, 1988), 147.

31. "Ernest Hogan's Minstrels Perform in Honolulu," *Pacific Commercial Advertiser* (Honolulu), March 27, 1899, quoted in Sampson, *Ghost Walks*, 206–7.

32. "Review of Ernest Hogan's Company," *Pacific Commercial Advertiser*, May 14, 1900, quoted in Sampson, *Ghost Walks*, 215.

33. Billy E. Jones, "New York News," *Freeman*, June 24, 1916, and *Freeman*, May 22, 1915. See also "Rucker and Winifred in 'The Chinaman and the Coon,' 'The Merchant Prince,' 'The Cabby' and Other Acts," *Philadelphia Evening Ledger*, August 5, 1916; and "Pantages Vaudeville at the Grand Opera House," *Great Falls (MT) Daily Tribune*, April 29, 1919.

34. Bernard L. Peterson Jr., *Profiles of African American Stage Performers and Theatre People* (Westport, CT: Greenwood Press, 2001), 276.

35. References appear in the *Norwich (CT) Bulletin*, September 23, 1914; January 29, 1914; January 31, 1914; and September 21, 1914.

36. "At the Palace," *Evening Star* (Washington, DC), April 15, 1928.

37. Sampson, *Blacks in Blackface*, 1382.

38. Program for Richards and Pringle's Georgia Minstrels, New Los Angeles Theatre, March 23, 1894, quoted in Sampson, *Ghost Walks*, 97.

39. Sampson, *Blacks in Blackface*, 1382.

40. "Ernest Hogan's Rufus Rastus Co.," *Freeman*, April 13, 1907.

41. Sampson, *Blacks in Blackface*, 1382.

42. Lester A. Walton, "Bert Williams Makes a Hit," *New York Age*, September 9, 1909.

43. "Bradford," "Bert Williams' Mr. Lode of Koal Co. at the Majestic Theatre, New York City," *Freeman*, November 20, 1909.

44. Lynn Abbott and Doug Seroff, *Ragged but Right: Black Traveling Shows, "Coon Songs," and the Dark Pathway to Blues and Jazz* (Jackson: University Press of Mississippi, 2007), 356.

45. "Darkest America," *Parsons (KS) Weekly Blade*, January 4, 1896; *Freeman*, February 1, 1896; "The Stage," *Freeman*, November 14, 1896.

46. "The Stage," *Freeman*, January 30, 1897. For a photograph of "Fiddler and Shelton as themselves," see Sampson, *Blacks in Blackface*, 381.

47. "Fiddler and Shelton," *Freeman*, September 12, 1908.

48. "Fiddler and Shelton," *Freeman*, April 10, 1915.

49. "Fiddler and Shelton," *Freeman*, April 10, 1915.

50. "Fiddler Is Playing in Omaha, Neb.," *Chicago Defender*, December 17, 1938.

51. "A Trip to Coontown," *Topeka Plaindealer*, January 6, 1899.

52. "Jules McGarr Ragtime Steppers Combined with 'Slim' Austin Jazz Orchestra, at the Vendome Theatre, Hot Springs, Arkansas, November 27," *Billboard*, December 13, 1924.

53. "Fiddler and Shelton," *Freeman*, September 12, 1908.

54. "Fiddler and Shelton at the Grand Opera House," *Freeman*, October 30, 1909.

55. J. D. Howard, "Cook and Stevens," *Freeman*, October 23, 1909.

56. Howard.

57. Moon, *Yellowface*, 136.

58. *Pittsburgh Courier*, December 21, 1929, quoted in Bernard L. Peterson Jr., *A Century of Musicals in Black and White: An Encyclopedia of Musical Stage Works by, about, or Involving African Americans* (Westport, CT: Greenwood Press, 1993), 307.

59. Salem Tutt Whitney, "Seen and Heard While Passing," *Freeman*, July 3, 1915.

60. Sampson, *Blacks in Blackface*, 928, 1031. Walker is not listed among the *Plantation Days* cast in Peterson's *Century of Musicals*, 270–71.

61. J. D. Howard, "Pinkey and Walker," *Freeman*, October 7, 1911.

62. "'Chinee' Walker, 12 Minutes in 'One,' Singing and Impersonations," *Freeman*, March 11, 1911.

63. "*Trip to Chinatown*—Darktown Follies Company, Reviewed at the Avenue Theatre, Chicago."

64. J. Harry Jackson, "The Stage," *Freeman*, June 17, 1899.

65. Advertisement for Lafayette Theatre, week of March 24, *New York Age*, March 22, 1919.

66. Salem Tutt Whitney, "Seen and Heard While Passing," *Freeman*, May 22, 1915.

67. J. H. Gray, "Gibson's New Standard Theatre, Philadelphia," *Freeman*, October 21, 1916.

68. "America's Comedians! Bert Williams Came from the Bermuda Islands, and Is Irresistibly Funny," *Topeka Plaindealer*, January 12, 1900.

69. "The Policy Players," *Topeka Plaindealer*, January 12, 1900.

70. "*Policy Players*, Reviewed at the Park Theatre, Indianapolis, Indianapolis," *Freeman*, February 17, 1901.

71. "*Sons of Ham*, Reviewed by Chicot, Bijou Theatre, New York City," reprinted from the *New York Telegraph*, *Freeman*, October 12, 1901.

72. William H. Ferris, *Negro World* (New York), May 13, 1922, quoted in Tony Martin, *Literary Garveyism: Garvey, Black Arts, and the Harlem Renaissance* (Dover, MA: Majority Press, 1983), 115.

73. V. L. McPherson, "'Tallaboo' Scores a Huge Success," *Negro World*, January 21, 1922.

74. Sabine Haenni, *The Immigrant Scene: Ethnic Amusements in New York, 1880–1920* (Minneapolis: University of Minnesota Press, 2008), 153.

75. Sampson, *Blacks in Blackface*, 929.

76. Sylvester Russell, "Address to Song Publishers," *Freeman*, April 2, 1904.

77. "Coon Songs Must Go," *Freeman*, January 2, 1909.

78. "Y.W.C.A. Puts Ban on Obnoxious Terms," *New York Age*, March 15, 1919.

79. Beatrice M. Murphy, "Think It Over," *Washington Tribune*, February 1, 1934.

80. "Fiddler and Shelton: Those Two Clever Boys," *Freeman*, February 26, 1910.

81. "Woodbine," "Stage," *Freeman*, August 25, 1900.

CHAPTER SEVEN

1. "Queen Dora, Who Does the Serpentine Fire Dance," *Freeman*, November 22, 1913. Dora also was noted as wearing a colorful "harem costume" with "pale-blue bloomers and purple chiffon dress" in an appearance at the American Theatre, *Variety*, February 5, 1915, quoted in Jayna Brown, *Babylon Girls: Black Women Performers and the Shaping of the Modern* (Durham, NC: Duke University Press, 2008), 154.

2. Caroline H. Yang, *The Peculiar Afterlife of Slavery: The Chinese Worker and the Minstrel Form* (Stanford: Stanford University Press, 2020), 167.

3. Cary B. Lewis, "At the Chicago Theaters," *Freeman*, October 8, 1910.

4. "The New Crown Garden Theater," *Freeman*, April 26, 1913.

5. See Anne Cheng, *Ornamentalism: A Feminist Theory for the Yellow Woman* (New York: Oxford University Press, 2019), chap. 1.

6. Peter C. Muir, *Long Lost Blues: Popular Blues in America, 1850–1920* (Urbana: University of Illinois Press, 2010), 18.

7. Oscar Gardner (music) and Fred D. Moore (lyrics), "Chinese Blues" (New York: Tell Taylor Music Publisher, 1915), Historical Popular Sheet Music Collection, SUNY College at Fredonia. "Chinese Blues" not only sold well as sheet music but also was "prolifically recorded," with "nine disc recordings and ten piano rolls" known to be records between 1915 and 1917 (Muir, *Long Lost Blues*, 18).

8. "Babe (Baby) Brown, Reviewed at the Crown Garden Theatre, Indianapolis," *Freeman*, September 27, 1913.

9. "The Cake-Walkers," *Augusta (GA) Chronicle*, December 15, 1900; "Theatrical," *Fort Worth Register*, January 20, 1901; "At the Theatre," *Trenton (NJ) Evening Times*, May 12, 1901.

10. Errol Hill, "The Hyers Sisters: Pioneers in Black Musical Comedy," in *The American Stage: Social and Economic Issues from the Colonial Period to the Present*, ed. Ron Engle and Tice L. Miller (New York: Cambridge University Press, 1993), 115–30.

11. *New York Tribune*, October 28, 1871.

12. *New York Evening Telegram*, October 28, 1871.

13. Lynn Abbott and Doug Seroff, *Out of Sight: The Rise of African American Popular Music, 1889–1895* (Jackson: University Press of Mississippi, 2002), 49.

14. Peter Hudson, "Opera," in *Africana: The Encyclopedia of the African and African American Experience*, ed. Kwame Anthony Appiah and Henry Louise Gates Jr. (New York: Basic Civitas Books, 1999), 1460.

15. E. Hill, "Hyers Sisters," 120–21.

16. Getchell, a white writer from Augusta, Maine, wrote several light operas as well as other literary work. According to an obituary in the *New England Medical Gazette*, she later attended Boston University Medical School and practiced homeopathy in Boston before her death in 1888. *New England Medical Gazette* 24 (October 1889): 471.

17. *San Francisco Chronicle*, March 31, 1879.

18. Jocelyn L. Buckner, "'Spectacular Opacities': The Hyers Sisters' Performances of Respectability and Resistance," *African American Review* 45, no. 3 (Fall 2012): 318.

19. *Star Tribune* (Minneapolis), November 2, 1878; "Urlina, the African Princess," *The Colonist* (Victoria, BC), May 9, 1879.

20. "Hyers Sisters," *The Colonist*, April 30, 1879.

21. "Amusements," *Daily Astorian* (Astoria, OR), April 19, 1879.

22. "Urlina, the African Princess," *The Colonist*.

23. "Amusements," *Daily Astorian*.

24. There is some scholarly dispute about locations in the opera. Gabriela Cruz insists that the later action takes place in Madagascar and that Nelusko is a Malagasy slave (Gabriela Cruz, "Laughing at History: The Third Act of Meyerbeer's *L'Africaine*," *Cambridge Opera Journal* 11 (March 1999): 31–76, 31). Jean Andrews points out that the "ship is supposedly wrecked on reefs past the Cape of Good Hope; geographically, this would indicate their being of Madagascar and this as the place where the survivors land." But at the same time, Andrews and others conclude that "the culture into which they are all absorbed in the fourth act and in which Selika is accepted as queen is quintessentially Indian" (Jean Andrews, "Meyerbeer's *L'Africaine*: French Grand Opera and the Iberian Exotic," *Modern Language Review* 102, no. 1 [January 2007]: 108–24). John Roberts stresses the importance Meyerbeer laid on the Indian elements in his composition (John H. Roberts, "Meyerbeer: *Le Prophète* and *L'Africaine*," in *The Cambridge Companion to Grand Opera*, ed. David Charlton [Cambridge: Cambridge University Press, 2003], 226). Roberts's arguments are consistent with Robert Letellier's suggestion that the source for the opera is "an unidentified German tale and a 1770 play by Antoine Lemierre, *La veuve de Malabar*, in which a Hindu maiden loves a Portuguese navigator, a theme already treated by the German composer Louis Spohr in his 1822 opera *Jessonda* (Robert Ignatius Letellier, *The Operas of Giacomo Meyerbeer* [Madison, NJ: Fairleigh Dickinson University Press, 2006], 246).

25. Giacomo Meyerbeer, *L'Africaine: A Lyric Drama in Five Acts*, English version by Thomas J. Williams (London: Royal Italian Opera, Covent Garden, 1871), 17. In-text citations are to this work.

26. "Amusements," *Daily Astorian*.

27. "Amusements," *Daily Astorian*.

28. "Amusements," *San Francisco Bulletin*, published as *Daily Evening Bulletin* (San Francisco), April 1, 1879.

29. "Amusements," *Morning Oregonian* (Portland), May 19, 1879; "Persons and Things," *New Haven (CT) Evening Register*, June 11, 1879.

30. Henry Pleasants noted in 1991 that though no longer popular two centuries later, Meyerbeer was a regular staple of opera houses in the second part of the nineteenth century. Henry Pleasants, "The Tragedy of Meyerbeer," *Opera Quarterly* 8, no. 1 (Spring 1991): 28–38.

31. "Amusements," *Daily Astorian*.

32. See Carolyne Lamar Jordan, "Black Female Concert Singers of the Nineteenth Century," in *Feel the Spirit: Studies in Nineteenth-Century Afro-American Music*, ed. George R. Keck and Sherrill V. Martin (Westport, CT: Garland, 1988), 41–46.

33. There are frequent notices of "Madame Selika," who is lauded in the *Freeman* as "the peerless queen of classical arrangement" ("Three Colored Artists of New York: Mme. V. A. Montgomery, Miss Blanche D. Washington, and Mrs. Albert Wilson, Victoria Earle," *Freeman*, March 23, 1889). According to the Blackpast website, Marie Williams's husband, the baritone Sampson Williams, took on the stage name "Signor Velosko

(The Hawaiian Tenor)." See Michelle Zhong, "Marie Selika Williams (ca. 1849–1937)," BlackPast, September 26, 2007, https://web.archive.org/save/https://www.blackpast.org /african-american-history/williams-marie-selika-c-1849-1937/.

34. Maud Cuney-Hare, "Caterina Jarboro," in *Negro Musicians and Their Music*, 2nd ed. (Washington, DC: Associated Press, 1943), 362.

35. According to Rosalyn Story, "The idea of a black Butterfly in a white opera company was revolutionary"; however, "Williams' portrayal of Cio-Cio-San served to prove to opera-goers that a black diva could not only sing the role, but also look the part and act it convincingly. And notions that a black lead performer would be distracting to the viewer's eye were dispelled. The gracefully attractive soprano was trim, petite, and a good actress. With makeup she looked as much like a former Geisha as most singers who have played Butterfly" (Rosalyn M. Story, *And So I Sing* [New York: St. Martin's Press, 1990], 73).

36. See Josephine Lee, "Decorative Orientalism," in *Asian American Literature in Transition, 1850–1930*, ed. Josephine Lee and Julia H. Lee (Cambridge: Cambridge University Press, 2021), 187–203.

37. Donna Carlton, *Looking for Little Egypt* (Bloomington, IN: IDD Books, 1994), xi.

38. See Paul Greenhalgh, *Ephemeral Vistas* (Manchester, UK: Manchester University Press, 1988), 85; and Carlton, *Looking for Little Egypt*, 13, 35.

39. Carlton, *Looking for Little Egypt*, 59.

40. Sharyn R. Udall, *Dance and American Art: A Long Embrace* (Madison: University of Wisconsin Press, 2012), 158.

41. Zen's letter was reproduced by Venetian chronicler Marino Sanuto in *I Diarii Autografi di Marin[o] Sanuto*, Biblioteca Nazionale Marciana, Venice (microfiche) Carte 66–68, Carte 67, quoted in Belgin Turan Özkaya, "Theaters of Fear and Delight: Ottomans in the Serenissima," in *After Orientalism: Critical Entanglements, Productive Looks*, ed. Inge E. Boer (Amsterdam: Rodopi B. V., 2003), 49–50.

42. Priya Srinivasan, *Sweating Saris: Indian Dance as Transnational Labor* (Philadelphia: Temple University Press, 2011), 52–53.

43. See Srinivasan, chap. 2.

44. Srinivasan, 69.

45. For more on Kawakami Sadayakko, see Leslie Downer, *Madame Sadayakko: The Geisha Who Bewitched the West* (New York: Gotham, 2003).

46. Rana Kabbani, *Europe's Myths of Orient* (Houndsmill, UK: Macmillan, 1986), 69.

47. See Amy Koritz, "Dancing the Orient for England: Maud Allan's 'The Vision of Salome,'" *Theatre Journal* 46, no. 1 (March 1994): 63–78; and Judith R. Walkowitz, "The 'Vision of Salome': Cosmopolitanism and Erotic Dancing in Central London, 1908–1918," *The American Historical Review* 108, no. 2 (April 2003): 337–76.

48. "Madamoiselle Dazie" was Daisy Peterkin, a ballet dancer and vaudeville performer who also appeared in Ziegfeld's *Follies* and other revues. Elizabeth Kendall, *Where She Danced* (New York: Alfred A. Knopf, 1979), 57. For more on Allan, see Felix Cherniavsky, *The Salome Dancer: The Life and Times of Maud Allan* (Toronto: McClelland and Stewart, 1991).

49. Lucinda Jarrett, *Stripping in Time: A History of Erotic Dancing* (London: Harper-Collins, 1997), 82.

50. *Times Literary Supplement* (London), March 25, 1908, 102, quoted in J. Brown, *Babylon Girls*, 179.

51. "The Drama: The New Dancer," *Times Literary Supplement*, March 25, 1908.

52. Koritz, "Dancing the Orient," 69.

53. Walkowitz, "'Vision of Salome,'" 346, 340.

54. According to Srinivasan, in 1910 one of the Indian men whom St. Denis hired to travel with her while on tour filed a lawsuit against St. Denis. In his lawsuit, Mohammed Ismail claimed that he had choreographed the Indian-themed dances that St. Denis was performing. The lawsuit was thrown out on the basis that Ismail was not white and therefore could not sue St. Denis, who was a white woman (Srinivasan, *Sweating Saris*, 83–84).

55. Rhonda K. Garelick, *Electric Salome: Loie Fuller's Performance of Modernism* (Princeton: Princeton University Press, 2007), 25–27.

56. Carlton, *Looking for Little Egypt*, 57.

57. Quoted in Marshall Stearns and Jean Stearns, *Jazz Dance: The Story of American Vernacular Dance* (New York: Da Capo Press, 1994), 123.

58. *Robinson Locke Scrapbook Covering the Life and Career of Augustin Daly, 1870–1920*, Billy Rose Theatre Division, New York Public Library of the Performing Arts, quoted in Srinivasan, *Sweating Saris*, 56.

59. The *Illustrated American* quoted in Wendy Buonaventura, *Belly Dancing: The Serpent and the Sphinx* (London: Virago, 1893), 78, and in Carlton, *Looking for Little Egypt*, 47.

60. C. W. Kellogg, "The Great Fair," *Savannah Times*, August 10, 1893, quoted in Carlton, *Looking for Little Egypt*, 47.

61. "Questions and Answers," *The Etude Music Magazine*, December 1898, 349.

62. Ed Rogers, "The Oriental Coon" (New York: Jos. W. Stern and Co., 1899), Lester S. Levy Sheet Music Collection, Johns Hopkins University. The song is also included in the theater program for "Phil R. Miller's New Musical Comedy-Travesty *The Hottest Coon in Dixie*," as played at the Bijou Opera House on April 15, 1900, James K. Hosmer Special Collections, Hennepin County Library.

63. See chapter 4 of Larry Hamberlin's *Tin Pan Opera: Operatic Novelty Songs in the Ragtime Era* (New York: Oxford University Press, 2011).

64. Ben M. Jerome and Edward Madden, "The Dusky Salome" (New York: Trebuhs, 1908), Lester S. Levy Sheet Music Collection, Johns Hopkins University.

65. Stanley Murphy and Ed Wynn, "I'm Going to Get Myself a Black Salome" (New York: M. Shapiro, 1908), Lester S. Levy Sheet Music Collection, Johns Hopkins University.

66. J. Brown, *Babylon Girls*, 180.

67. Paula Marie Seniors, *Beyond "Lift Every Voice and Sing": The Culture of Uplift, Identity, and Politics in Black Musical Theater* (Columbus: Ohio State University Press, 2009), 177–83.

68. David Krasner, "Black *Salome*: Exoticism, Dance, and Racial Myths," in *African American Performance and Theater History: A Critical Reader*, ed. Harry J. Elam Jr. and David Krasner (New York: Oxford University Press, 2001), 198.

69. Undated clip, quoted in Krasner, "Black *Salome*," 201.

70. Hamberlin, *Tin Pan Opera*, 125.

71. "Palace Theatre Matinee Programme," quoted in Walkowitz, "'Vision of Salome,'" 357.

72. *Vanity Fair*, August 3, 1912, quoted in J. Brown, *Babylon Girls*, 182.

73. J. Brown, *Babylon Girls*, 182, 184.

74. Carle Browne Cooke, "Among the Colored Performers Abroad," *Freeman*, December 9, 1905; *Cleveland Gazette*, December 30, 1905.

75. *Variety*, July 17, 1909, quoted in J. Brown, *Babylon Girls*, 182.

76. "Dorothy," and "The Abyssinia Maids," *Freeman*, October 20, 1906, 5.

77. J. Brown, *Babylon Girls*, 186–87.

78. Daphne Brooks, *Bodies in Dissent: Spectacular Performances of Race and Freedom* (Durham, NC: Duke University Press, 2006), 341.

79. J. Brown, *Babylon Girls*, 188.

80. See "Richard Potter, the First American-Born Magician," in Jim Haskins and Kathleen Benson, *Conjure Times: Black Magicians in America* (New York: Walker and Co., 2001), 7–21.

81. Philip Deslippe, "The Hindu in Hoodoo: Fake Yogis, Pseudo-Swamis, and the Manufacture of African American Folk Magic," *Amerasia Journal* 40, no. 1 (January 2014): 40.

82. "J. T. McCaddon's Company—Al. E. Holman's Band and Serenaders," *Freeman*, May 6, 1905.

83. "Geo. Slaughter, Louisville, Ky," *Freeman*, November 20, 1912.

84. Tim Owsley, "Princess Sotanki," *Freeman*, October 26, 1912.

85. "Princess Sotanki—Hindu Magician," *Freeman*, April 4, 1914.

86. "Princess Sotanki," *Freeman*, January 2, 1915.

87. "Princess Sotanki," *Savannah Tribune*, May 17, 1913.

88. "Crown Garden, Paducah, Ky," *Freeman*, October 11, 1913.

89. This image is reproduced online as part of a collection for Jason S. Dorman's book *The Princess and the Prophet: The Secret History of Magic, Race, and Moorish Muslims in America* (Boston: Beacon Press, 2020), accessed August 20, 2021, www.princessandprophet.com/primary-sources-2/.

90. "Princess Sotanki," *Freeman*, January 2, 1915.

91. Robert O. Bartholomew, *Report of Censorship of Motion Pictures* (Chicago, 1913), 14, quoted in Marybeth Hamilton, *"When I'm Bad, I'm Better": Mae West, Sex, and American Entertainment* (New York: HarperCollins, 1995), 11.

92. Sylvester Russell, "Musical and Dramatic," *Freeman*, November 16, 1912.

93. This postcard is part of the online collection "#samsmagiccollection Instagram Posts," accessed August 20, 2021, https://gramho.com/media/1911064737148698608/.

94. "Princess Sotanki," *Freeman*, January 2, 1915.

95. See Dorman, *Princess and the Prophet*, chap. 7.

96. Alvira Hazzard, *Mother Liked It*, in *Lost Plays of the Harlem Renaissance, 1920–1940*, ed. James V. Hatch and Leo Hamalian (Detroit: Wayne State University Press, 1998), 63–72. Additional in-text citations are also to this work.

97. Susan Nance, *How the Arabian Nights Inspired the American Dream, 1790–1935* (Chapel Hill: University of North Carolina Press, 2009), 236–37. See also Haskins and Benson, *Conjure Times*, 76.

98. Jessie Redman Fauset, *Plum Bun: A Novel without a Moral* (repr., London: Pandora, 1985), 218.

99. Vijay Prashad, *The Karma of Black Folk* (Minneapolis: University of Minnesota Press, 2000), 39.

CHAPTER EIGHT

1. "Notes," *Freeman*, November 9, 1895. For discussion of *On the Mississippi: A Southern Comic Melodrama*, see Barbara L. Webb, "Authentic Possibilities: Plantation Performance of the 1890s," *Theatre Journal* 56, no. 1 (March 2004): 63–82.

2. "The Stage," *Freeman*, November 14, 1896.

3. "The Stage," *Freeman*, December 25, 1897.

4. Robert C. Toll, *Blacking Up: The Minstrel Show in Nineteenth-Century America* (New York: Oxford University Press, 1974), 223.

5. *Trenton Evening Times*, December 16, 1897.

6. "The Stage," *Freeman*, December 25, 1897.

7. Bill Reed, *Hot from Harlem: Profiles in Classic African American Entertainment* (Los Angeles: Cellar Door Press, 1998), 46; "Interview with Nate Salsbury," *Boston Transcript*, July 1895. Other commentary on *Black America* appears in Toll, *Blacking Up*, 262–63.

8. *Trenton Evening Times*, December 19, 1897.

9. Roger Allan Hall, "*Black America*: Nate Salsbury's 'Afro-American Exhibition,'" *Educational Theatre Journal* 29, no. 1 (March 1977): 49–60, 59.

10. Webb, "Authentic Possibilities," 77.

11. "The Play Bill for This Week," *Trenton Evening Times*, December 19, 1897.

12. *Colored American (Washington, DC)*, November 4, 1896, quoted in "The Stage," *Freeman*, November 14, 1896.

13. *New York Age*, February 28, 1891, quoted in Lynn Abbott and Doug Seroff, *Out of Sight: The Rise of African American Popular Music, 1889–1895* (Jackson: University Press of Mississippi, 2002), 147.

14. *New York Age*, February 28, 1891.

15. *New Yorker Clipper*, April 4, 1891, quoted in Abbott and Seroff, *Out of Sight*, 148.

16. W. L. M. Chaise, "Gossip of the Stage," *New York Age*, June 6, 1891.

17. Kevin Kelly Gaines, *Uplifting the Race: Black Leadership, Politics, and Culture in the Twentieth Century* (Chapel Hill: University of North Carolina Press, 1996), xv.

18. Gaines, 69.

19. "The Stage," *Freeman*, June 19, 1897.

20. Bernard L. Peterson Jr. gives the date range of *Darkest America* as 1896–99 (*A Century of Musicals in Black and White: An Encyclopedia of Musical Stage Works by, about, or Involving African Americans* [Westport, CT: Greenwood Press, 1993], 96), but there are earlier reviews found in the *Sioux City Journal* (August 9 and August 20, 1895) and the *Portland Oregonian* (November 10, November 14, and November 17, 1895). The show may well have extended its run after 1899, since an announcement in the *Freeman* on May 23, 1903, reads "Wanted for Season 1903–1904. Half-hundred People for the Big Spectacular Sensation 'Darkest America' (Under the Direction of Mr. Al G. Field)."

21. Jayna Brown, *Babylon Girls: Black Women Performers and the Shaping of the Modern* (Durham, NC: Duke University Press, 2008), 92.

22. Henry T. Sampson, *The Ghost Walks: A Chronological History of Blacks in Show Business, 1865–1910* (Metuchen, NJ: Scarecrow Press, 1988), 246. Dean met her husband, Charles Johnson, a fellow performer in *The Creole Show*, and they later left the show to perform their own vaudeville act throughout houses in the United States and on tour in England, France, and Germany.

23. Lucinda Jarrett, *Stripping in Time: A History of Erotic Dancing* (London: HarperCollins, 1997), 9.

24. Cynthia J. Miller, "'Glorifying the American Girl': Adapting an Icon," in *The Adaptation of History: Essays on Ways of Telling the Past*, ed. Lawrence Raw and Defne Ersin Tutan (Jefferson, NC: McFarland, 2014), 29.

25. James Weldon Johnson, *Black Manhattan* (1930; repr., New York: Arno, 1967), 95.

26. Cedric J. Robinson, *Forgeries of Memory and Meaning: Blacks and the Regimes of Race in American Theater and Film before World War II* (Chapel Hill: University of North Carolina Press, 2007), 268–69.

27. Jacqueline Foertsch, *American Drama in Dialogue, 1714–Present* (London: Palgrave Macmillan, 2017), 71.

28. "Grand Opera House," *Daily Alta California*, July 7, 1889.

29. *New York Clipper*, July 19, 1890, quoted in Abbott and Seroff, *Out of Sight*, 153–54.

30. Advertisements for "Creole Burlesque Co.," *New York Clipper*, April 26 and October 11, 1890.

31. Irving Zeidman, *The American Burlesque Show* (New York: Hawthorn Books, 1967), 43.

32. Abbott and Seroff, *Out of Sight*, 154.

33. Quoted in Thomas L. Riis, *Just before Jazz: Black Musical Theater in New York, 1890–1915* (Washington, DC: Smithsonian Institution Press, 1989), 137.

34. M. J. O'Neill, *How He Does It: Sam. T. Jack, Twenty Years a King in the Realm of Burlesque* (Chicago: M. J. O'Neill, 1895), 72–73.

35. M. O'Neill, 72–73.

36. John Graziano, "Images of African Americans: African-American Musical Theatre, *Show Boat*, and *Porgy and Bess*," in *The Cambridge Companion to the Musical*, ed. William A. Everett and Paul R. Laird (Cambridge: Cambridge University Press, 2002), 65.

37. Quoted in Abbott and Seroff, *Out of Sight*, 161.

38. *Freeman*, September 20, 1890, quoted in Abbott and Seroff, *Out of Sight*, 154.

39. W. L. M. Chaise, "The Gossip of the Stage," *New York Age*, June 6, 1891, quoted in Abbott and Seroff, *Out of Sight*, 154.

40. Frank Cullen, with Florence Hackman and Donald McNeilly, *Vaudeville Old and New: An Encyclopedia of Variety Performance in America* (New York: Routledge, 2007), 164.

41. J. Brown, *Babylon Girls*, 92.

42. M. O'Neill, *How He Does It*, 184.

43. M. O'Neill, 233.

44. M. O'Neill, 237–38.

45. M. O'Neill, 71.

46. M. O'Neill, 71–72.

47. *New York Clipper*, November 11, 1891, quoted in Abbott and Seroff, *Out of Sight*, 159.

48. *Freeman*, September 5, 1891, quoted in Abbott and Seroff, *Out of Sight*, 158.

49. J. Brown, *Babylon Girls*, 106.

50. Paula Marie Seniors, *Beyond "Lift Every Voice and Sing": The Culture of Uplift, Identity, and Politics in Black Musical Theater* (Columbus: Ohio State University Press, 2009), 82–83.

51. "The Stage," *Freeman*, September 26, 1896.

52. Leigh Whipper, "The Negro Actor's Guild Scoreboard," quoted in Seniors, *Beyond "Lift,"* 81.

53. Will Marion Cook, "Autobiographical Notes," quoted in Seniors, *Beyond "Lift,"* 81.

54. J. Johnson, *Black Manhattan*, 95.

55. Henry T. Sampson, *Blacks in Blackface: A Sourcebook on Early Black Musical Shows*, 2nd ed. (Lanham, MD: Scarecrow Press, 2014), 50.

56. "The Stage," *Freeman*, October 10, 1896.

57. Graziano, "Images of African Americans," 66–67.

58. *New York Clipper*, December 21, 1895, quoted in Abbott and Seroff, *Out of Sight*, 166–67.

59. *Brooklyn Daily Eagle*, December 11, 1898. After performing in the chorus of *The Creole Show* and in Isham's *Oriental America*, Davis made her career abroad, touring Great Britain and Europe. In an act billed as "Belle Davis and Her Pickaninnies," Davis would later share the London stage with Maud Allan's *Vision of Salome*.

60. *Era* (London), May 1, 1897, quoted in Thomas L. Riis, "The Experience and Impact of Black Entertainers in England, 1895–1920," *American Music* 4, no. 1 (Spring 1986): 52–53.

61. *Era*, May 1, 1897.

62. *Morning Times* (Washington, DC), November 9, 1896, quoted in "The Stage," *Freeman*, November 7, 1896.

63. Quoted in Toll, *Blacking Up*, 152.

64. Toll, 154.

65. *Morning Times*, November 9, 1896.

66. John W. Isham, "Oriental America at Mrs. Waldorf's Fifth Anniversary: A Spectacular Operatic Absurdity in One Act" (1896), Library of Congress Rare Book and Special Collections Division, accessed August 20, 2021, www.loc.gov/item/varsep.s48875/.

67. "Amusements: The Oriental America," *Washington (DC) Bee*, October 31, 1896.

68. *Morning Times*, November 9, 1896.

69. "The Stage," *Freeman*, November 14, 1896.

70. "Amusements: The Oriental America," *Washington Bee*, November 28, 1896.

71. "Perry 'Mule' Bradford ('Musician-Composer-Comedian'), 'Earliest History of Negro in Show Business Dates to Philly in 1812,'" *New York Age*, August 22, 1953.

72. "Amusements," *Washington Bee*, October 31, 1896.

73. "John W. Isham's Famous Octoroons," *Washington Bee*, February 26, 1898.

74. Sampson, *The Ghost Walks*, 108.

75. "Bradford, 'Earliest History,'" *New York Age*, August 22, 1953.

76. "Black Patti's Troubadours," *Freeman*, December 19, 1896.

77. Peterson, *Century of Musicals*, 19.

78. After Cole was sued for ownership rights to his musical and won the case, a new version of "At Jolly Coon-ey Island" (also called "At Gay Coon-ey Island") was written for the Black Patti Troubadours by Ernest Hogan. Peterson, *Century of Musicals*, 20.

79. Quoted in William Foster, "Pioneers of the Stage: Memoirs of William Foster," *The Official Theatrical World of Colored Artists National Directory and Guide* 1, no. 1, April 1928, 48–49, Black Culture Collection Reel, UCSD Geisel Library.

80. Unidentified reviewer, February 6, 1900, Harvard Theatre Collection, Houghton Library, Harvard University, quoted in Riis, *Just before Jazz*, 77–78.

81. Advertisement for *A Trip to Coontown*, *Philadelphia Times*, October 8, 1899.

82. Percy Gaunt, "Push Dem Clouds Away, an African Cantata" (New York: T. B. Harms and Co, 1892), Library of Congress, accessed August 20, 2021, www.loc.gov/resource /ihas.200004922.0?st=gallery/.

83. For historical commentary on *A Trip to Coontown* and an excerpt of the play, see Krystyn R. Moon, David Krasner, and Thomas L. Riis, "Forgotten Manuscripts: A Trip to Coontown," *African American Review* 44, nos. 1–2 (Spring/Summer 2011): 7–8. I am

indebted to Krystyn R. Moon for sharing the typescript version of *A Trip to Coontown* with me. All quotations are taken from this unpaginated typescript.

84. David Krasner, *Resistance, Parody, and Double Consciousness in African American Theatre, 1895–1910* (New York: St. Martin's Press, 1997), 32, 33.

85. J. Harry Jackson, "The Stage," *Freeman*, April 16, 1898. Powers was a vaudeville and musical theater actor who played a prominent Chinese character in Sidney Jones's *The Geisha*. Jackson also notes that "another Negro, Mr. Bill Binkerton, gives an Italian act which is capital," without mentioning Tom Brown in the role of Binkerton.

86. "A Trip to Coontown," *Illinois Record* (Springfield), March 11, 1899.

87. "A Trip to Coontown," *Topeka Plaindealer*, January 6, 1899.

88. Jackson, "The Stage."

89. Lynn Abbott and Doug Seroff, *Ragged but Right: Black Traveling Shows, "Coon Songs," and the Dark Pathway to Blues and Jazz* (Jackson: University Press of Mississippi, 2007), 15.

90. Billy Johnson (lyrics), Bob Cole (music), and Theodore F. Morse (arranger), "The Wedding of the Chinee and the Coon" (New York: Howley, Haviland and Co., 1897), Music Division, New York Public Library.

91. Julia H. Lee, *Interracial Encounters: Reciprocal Representations in African and Asian American Literatures, 1896–1937* (New York: New York University Press, 2011), 24–25.

92. Julia Lee, 24.

CHAPTER NINE

1. "The Stage Negro," *Variety*, December 14, 1907, 30.

2. Henry T. Sampson, *Blacks in Blackface: A Sourcebook on Early Black Musical Shows*, 2nd ed. (Lanham, MD: Scarecrow Press, 2014), 58.

3. Camille F. Forbes, *Introducing Bert Williams: Burnt Cork, Broadway, and the Story of America's First Black Star* (New York: Basic Books, 2008), 21, 25.

4. Karen Sotiropoulous, *Staging Race: Black Performers in Turn of the Century America* (Cambridge, MA: Harvard University Press, 2006), 9.

5. W. E. B. Du Bois, "Krigwa Players Little Negro Theatre," *The Crisis* 32 (July 1926), 134.

6. Will Marion Cook, Jesse A. Shipp, and Paul Laurence Dunbar, *The Music and Scripts of "In Dahomey,"* ed. Thomas L. Riis, American Musicological Society (Madison, WI: A-R Editions, 1996). In-text citations are to this edition, which uses roman numerals for the introductions and scripts, and arabic numerals for the music. Riis points out that in the American script, Dahomey is often referred to as the French diminutive "Dahome" (see *The Music and Scripts of "In Dahomey,"* 111).

7. Daphne Brooks, *Bodies in Dissent: Spectacular Performances of Race and Freedom* (Durham, NC: Duke University Press, 2006), 265.

8. George W. Walker, "The Real 'Coon' on the American Stage," *Theatre Magazine*, August 1906, reprinted in liner notes to Bert Williams, *The Early Years, 1901–1909*, audio recording (Champaign, IL: Archophone Records, 2004), 18.

9. Monica White Ndounou, "Early Black Americans on Broadway," in *The Cambridge Companion to African American Theatre*, ed. Harvey Young (New York: Cambridge University Press, 2013), 69.

10. "At the Grand Next Week," *Rising Son* (Kansas City, MO), November 11, 1904.

11. Brooks, *Bodies in Dissent*, 265.

12. Sylvester Russell, "The Stage," *Freeman*, September 27, 1902.

13. Sylvester Russell, "'In Dahomey,' a Howling Success," *Freeman*, October 25, 1902.

14. This British script continuation of act 2, scene 3, through act 3 is included in Cook, Shipp, and Dunbar, *Music and Scripts of "In Dahomey,"* lxxiv–lxxvii.

15. Unidentified London review, October 23, 1903, *In Dahomey* folder, Harvard Theater Collection, Houghton Library, Harvard University; quoted in Riis, *Just before Jazz*, 103.

16. Program for Jesse A. Shipp and Alex Rogers, *Abyssinia*, Globe Theatre, Boston, for the week of March 18, 1907, from Black Drama, Third Edition database, Alexander Street, accessed November 30, 2021, https://search.alexanderstreet.com/view/work/bibliographic_entity%7Cbibliographic_details%7C3605665/.

17. According to John Potvin, images of violent punishment under Islamic law published in the *London Illustrated News* in the 1890s fostered associations of "oriental" countries such as Morocco with despotism and fanaticism. See John Potvin, "Warriors, Slave Traders and Islamic Fanatics: 'Reporting' the Spectacle of Oriental Male Bodies in the *Illustrated London News*, 1890–1900," in *After Orientalism: Critical Entanglements, Productive Looks*, ed. Inge E. Boer (Amsterdam: Rodopi B. V. 2003).

18. Will Marion Cook, Jesse A. Shipp, and Alexander Rogers, *Abyssinia*, libretto. The copyright was 1905, but the show did not make it to the stage until 1906. All quotations are taken from this unpaginated typescript, housed at the Music Division, Library of Congress, Washington, DC.

19. *Freeman*, October 20, 1906.

20. Brooks, *Bodies in Dissent*, 250–63.

21. George Wells Parker, *The Children of the Sun* (Hamitic League of the World, 1918; repr., Baltimore: Black Classic Press, 1981), 4. For an extended critical discussion of pan-Africanism and other theories of black roots, see Yaacov Shavit, *History in Black: African-Americans in Search of an Ancient Past* (London: Frank Cass, 2001).

22. Parker, *Children of the Sun*, 25.

23. Parker, 11.

24. Parker, 4–5.

25. Parker, 11. Bible quote is from the King James Version.

26. Parker, 30, 6.

27. Marc Gallicchio, *The African American Encounter with Japan and China: Black Internationalism in Asia, 1895–1945* (Chapel Hill: University of North Carolina Press, 2000), 2.

28. Gallicchio, 2–3.

29. W. E. B. Du Bois, "The African Roots of the War," *Atlantic Monthly*, May 1915, quoted in Gallicchio, *African American Encounter*, 18.

30. Reginald Kearney, *African American Views of the Japanese: Solidarity of Sedition* (Albany: State University of New York Press, 1998).

31. Thomas Riis, appendix I, in Cook, Shipp, and Dunbar, *Music and Scripts of "In Dahomey."* The program is reproduced in Allen Woll, *Black Musical Theatre from Coontown to Dreamgirls* (New York: Da Capo, 1989), 41.

32. In act 2 of Meyerbeer's opera, Selika sings the song while watching over a sleeping Vasco, whom she calls a "child of the sun."

33. Bernard L. Peterson Jr., *Profiles of African American Stage Performers and Theatre People, 1816–1960* (Westport, CT: Greenwood 2001), 266–69.

34. Comments on scenery and costumes from a review at the Majestic in Peoria,

Illinois, in advance of a performance at the Metropolitan Opera House in St. Paul beginning January 12, quoted in "The Smarter Set," *The Appeal* (St. Paul, MN), December 28, 1918; chorus and music described in J. H. Gray, "Auspicious Opening of the Fall and Winter Season of 1918 and 1919 by Whitney and Tutt 'Smarter Set' Company in 'Darkest Americans,'" *Washington Bee*, August 31, 1918.

35. The songs are listed in "'The Smarter Set' Coming to Howard Theatre," *Washington Bee*, August 24, 1918.

36. Quoted in "The Smarter Set," *The Appeal*.

37. Advertisement, *New York Age*, April 5, 1919; *Washington Bee*, August 24, 1918.

38. John Graziano, "Images of African Americans: African-American Musical Theatre, *Show Boat*, and *Porgy and Bess*," in *The Cambridge Companion to the Musical*, ed. William A. Everett and Paul R. Laird (Cambridge: Cambridge University Press, 2002), 70.

39. "Cole and Johnson," *Washington Bee*, August 25, 1906.

40. Herbert Aptheker, *Afro-American History: The Modern Era* (New York: Citadel Press, 1971, 1992), 175, quoted in David Krasner, *A Beautiful Pageant: African American Theatre, Drama, and Performance in the Harlem Renaissance, 1910–1927* (New York: Palgrave Macmillan, 2002), 133.

41. "Howard University and Its Lesson," *New York Age*, March 4, 1915, quoted in Krasner, *Beautiful Pageant*, 133.

42. *Washington Bee*, July 6, 1918.

43. *Washington Bee*, July 6, 1918.

44. "'The Smarter Set' Coming to Howard Theatre," *Washington Bee*, August 24, 1918, quoted from "The Smarter Set," *The Appeal*.

45. "Smarter Set Next Week," *New York Age*, September 20, 1919.

46. Lester A. Walton, "'The Children of the Sun' Most Pretentious of All Smarter Set Offerings," *New York Age*, September 27, 1919.

47. Lester A. Walton, "'Children of the Sun' Is Very Pleasing," *New York Age*, June 26, 1920.

48. For instance, an ad for a Howard Theatre performance reads, "Adapted from the Historical Book by George Wells Parker of the Same title," *Washington Bee*, October 18, 1919.

49. Parker, *Children of the Sun*, 3, quoted in "The Smarter Set Presents 'The Children of the Sun,'" *Sun-Dial* (Wilberforce, OH), reprinted in the *Kansas City (KS) Advocate*, January 2, 1920.

50. Advertisement, *Kansas City Advocate*, December 5, 1919; "The Smarter Set," *Kansas City Advocate*, December 5, 1919.

51. *Baltimore Evening Sun*, September 30, 1919, reprinted in "Merit in Negro Play at Albaugh's Theatre," *Washington Bee*, October 25, 1919.

52. From the *Sun-Dial*, quoted in "The Smarter Set Presents 'The Children of the Sun,'" *Kansas City Advocate*, January 2, 1920.

53. Parker, *Children of the Sun*, 22.

54. Parker, 29, 30.

55. *Baltimore Evening Sun*, September 30, 1919, reprinted in "Merit in Negro Play at Albaugh's Theatre," *Washington Bee*.

56. "Smarter Set Next Week," *New York Age*.

57. Zora Neale Hurston, *The First One*, in *Collected Plays*, ed. Jean Lee Cole and Charles Mitchell (New Brunswick, NJ: Rutgers University Press, 2008), 63–74, 65.

58. Sampson, *Blacks in Blackface*, 909.

59. *Amsterdam News*, March 14, 1923, quoted in Krasner, *Beautiful Pageant*, 265.

60. Noble Sissle and Eubie Blake, *Shuffle Along*, ed. Lyn Schenbeck and Lawrence Schenbeck, American Musicological Society (Middleton, WI: A-R Editions, 2018). In-text citations are to this edition.

61. Al Rose, *Eubie Blake* (New York: Schirmer, 1979), 78.

62. Lyn Schenbeck and Lawrence Schenbeck, introduction to Sissle and Blake, *Shuffle Along*, lxxiv.

63. Lester A. Walton, "'Shuffle Along' Latest Musical Gem to Invade Broadway," *New York Age*, June 4, 1921.

64. Robert Kimball and Williams Bolcom, *Reminiscing with Sissle and Blake* (New York: Viking, 1973), 88.

65. Zora Neale Hurston, "Characteristics of Negro Expression," in *Negro: An Anthology*, ed. Nancy Cunard (London: Wishart, 1934), 55.

66. Hurston, 55–56.

67. Gerald Bordman, *American Musical Theatre: A Chronicle*, 3rd ed. (New York: Oxford University Press, 2000), 369.

68. Bordman, 378.

69. Krasner, *Beautiful Pageant*, 240.

70. Krasner, 253.

71. Walton, "'Shuffle Along' Latest Musical Gem to Invade Broadway."

72. Lyn Schenbeck and Lawrence Schenbeck, introduction to *Shuffle Along*, xxv.

73. Alan Dale, "'Shuffle Along' Full of Pep and Real Melody," *New York American*, May 25, 1921, quoted in Kimball and Bolcom, *Reminiscing with Sissle and Blake*, 99.

74. Review of "Shuffle Along," *New York Herald*, May 24, 1921.

75. Sianne Ngai, *Ugly Feelings* (Cambridge, MA: Harvard University Press, 2005), 15.

76. "Shuffle Along," *Kansas City Advocate*, March 30, 1923.

77. Jayna Brown, *Babylon Girls: Black Women Performers and the Shaping of the Modern* (Durham, NC: Duke University Press, 2008), 191.

78. Lester A. Walton's commentary in *New York Age* notes his particular attention to white audience responses: "I attended a performance last week at the Sixty-third Street Theatre, for the express purpose of paying particular attention to the manner in which the white patrons received the show." "'Shuffle Along' Latest Musical Gem to Invade Broadway."

79. Lucien H. White, "Revival of Cake Walk by 'Shuffle Along' Artists," *New York Age*, November 12, 1921.

80. For discussion of Japanese acrobats, see Robert Toll, *Blacking Up: The Minstrel Show in Nineteenth-Century America* (New York: Oxford University Press, 1974), 171–73; and Krystyn R. Moon, "Paper Butterflies: Japanese Acrobats in Mid-nineteenth Century New England," in *Asian Americans in New England: Culture and Community*, ed. Monica Chiu (Durham, NH: University Press of New England, 2009), 66–90. For "Arab" acrobatic troupes, see Susan Nance, *How the Arabian Nights Inspired the American Dream, 1790–1935* (Chapel Hill: University of North Carolina Press, 2009), chap. 4; and Linda K. Jacobs,

"'Playing East': Arabs Play Arabs in Nineteenth Century America," *Mashriq and Mahjar* 2, no. 2 (2014): 79–110.

81. Nance, *Arabian Nights*, 131.

82. "Actors-Composers-Producers," *Savannah Tribune*, May 4, 1922.

CHAPTER TEN

1. Gerald Bordman, *American Musical Theatre: A Chronicle*, 3rd ed. (New York: Oxford University Press, 2000), 243.

2. Bordman, 140–41.

3. Frank Dumont, *The Witmark Amateur Minstrel Guide and Burnt Cork Encyclopedia* (Chicago: M. Witmark and Sons, 1899), 128–32.

4. Program for Black Patti Troubadours at the Los Angeles Theatre, January 14, 1902, in Henry T. Sampson, *The Ghost Walks: A Chronological History of Blacks in Show Business, 1865–1910* (Metuchen, NJ: Scarecrow Press, 1988), 242–43.

5. James Fisher and Felicia Hardison Londré, *Historical Dictionary of American Theater: Modernism* (London: Rowman and Littlefield, 2017), 89. The novel and reviews of *Across the Pacific* suggest many similarities to McCloskey's *Across the Continent*, and McCloskey is also listed as coauthor in "Across the Pacific," *Washington Post*, December 17, 1901; and in a program from the Bijou Theatre in Minneapolis dated October 28, 1900 (James K. Hosmer Special Collections Library, Hennepin County Libraries).

6. Charles E. Blaney, *Across the Pacific: A Novel; Founded upon the Melodrama of the Same Title* (New York: J. S. Ogilvie, 1904), 13. In-text citations are to this work.

7. See Caroline Levander, "Confederate Cuba," *American Literature* 78, no. 4 (2006): 832; and Jennifer C. James, *A Freedom Bought with Blood: African American War Literature from the Civil War to World War II* (Chapel Hill: University of North Carolina Press, 2007), 151.

8. John Cullen Gruesser, *The Empire Abroad and the Empire at Home: African American Literature and the Era of Overseas Expansion* (Athens: University of Georgia Press, 2012), 14.

9. "'Across the Pacific' at the Academy of Music," *Washington Post*, April 7, 1901.

10. "Harry Clay Blaney, in 'Across the Pacific,' at the Academy," *Washington Post*, January 10, 1904.

11. "Harry Blaney, in 'Across the Pacific,' at the Academy of Music," *Washington Post*, December 9, 1902.

12. Amy Kaplan, "Black and Blue on San Juan Hill," in *Cultures of United States Imperialism*, ed. Amy Kaplan and Donald E. Pease (Durham, NC: Duke University Press, 1993), 219.

13. "Harry Blaney, in 'Across the Pacific,' at the Academy of Music," *Washington Post*, December 9, 1902.

14. "Harry Clay Blaney, in 'Across the Pacific,' at the Academy," *Washington Post*, January 10, 1904.

15. Paula Marie Seniors, *Beyond "Lift Every Voice and Sing": The Culture of Uplift, Identity, and Politics in Black Musical Theater* (Columbus: Ohio State University Press, 2009), 52–53.

16. "Harry Clay Blaney, in 'Across the Pacific,' at the Academy," *Washington Post*, January 10, 1904.

17. Clyde Fitch, *Her Own Way: A Play in Four Acts* (New York: Macmillan, 1907). In-text citations are to this work.

18. William McKinley, Executive Order, December 21, 1898, The American Presidency Project, accessed August 20, 2021, www.presidency.ucsb.edu/ws/index.php?pid=69309/.

19. George Ade, *The Sultan of Sulu: An Original Satire in Two Acts* (New York: R. H. Russell, 1903). The music was written by Alfred G. Wathall. In-text citations are to this work.

20. Victor Román Mendoza, *Metroimperial Intimacies: Fantasy, Racial-Sexual Governance, and the Philippines in U.S. Imperialism, 1899–1913* (Durham, NC: Duke University Press, 2015), 51, 132.

21. "Many Places of Amusement Changed Bills Last Night," *St. Louis Republic*, September 8, 1902, quoted in Mendoza, *Metroimperial Intimacies*, 145.

22. George Ade, *George Ade's Stories of Benevolent Assimilation*, ed. Perry E. Gianakos (Quezon City, RP: New Day Publishers, 1985), 1.

23. Dean C. Worcester, *The Philippine Islands and Their People* (New York: Macmillan, 1901), 33.

24. Christine Bold, "Where Did the Black Rough Riders Go?," *Canadian Review of American Studies* 39, no. 3 (2009): 274.

25. Booker T. Washington, N. B. Wood, and Fannie Barrier Williams, *A New Negro for a New Century* (New York: Arno, 1900), 51–2, quoted in Bold, "Where Did the Black Rough Riders Go?," 277.

26. "The Cavalry at Santiago," *Scribner's Magazine*, 435, 436, quoted in Bold, "Where Did the Black Rough Riders Go?," 277.

27. Sylvester Russell, "Position and Place Where Colored Actors Actually Figure," *Freeman*, February 29, 1908.

28. Juli Jones, "Why There Are No Colored Playwriters," *Freeman*, April 10, 1909.

29. Ted Watson, "Composer's Sister Reveals the History of an Old Song," *Chicago Defender*, June 1, 1974.

30. Gruesser, *Empire Abroad*, 20.

31. "Cole and Johnson Show," *Freeman*, March 23, 1907.

32. "The Pekin," *Broad Ax*, July 6, 1907.

33. Sylvester Russell, "The Stage: The Pekin Stock Company in Captain Rufus," *Freeman*, September 7, 1907.

34. "'Captain Rufus' a Great Success," *Chicago Defender*, June 13, 1914.

35. Seniors, *Beyond "Lift,"* 61.

36. "Cole and Johnson," *Broad Ax*, December 15, 1906.

37. "Jerry Mills," *Broad Ax*, June 13, 1914.

38. Gruesser, *Empire Abroad*, 14.

39. Scot Ngozi-Brown, "African-American Soldiers and Filipinos: Racial Imperialism, Jim Crow, and Social Relations," *Journal of Negro History* 82, no. 1 (1997): 44, 46.

40. Sylvester Russell commented that *Captain Rufus* was a "manufactory of plagiarized scenes and transported music, lithely played by J. Ed Green" ("Russell's Annual Review. The Seventh Revival of the Actors' Work," *Freeman*, December 28, 1907). After Green's death, Russell defended these charges against criticism in the *New York Age* (March 24, 1910) and, later in reviewing the 1914 revival, credited the idea for the play to Cole and Johnson ("Chicago Weekly Review," *Freeman*, June 20, 1914).

41. James Weldon Johnson, *Along This Way: The Autobiography of James Weldon Johnson* (New York: Viking, 1933), 222–23.

42. The initial character and cast list appears in "Cole and Johnson," *Washington Bee*, August 25, 1906; a plot summary of the 1907 version appears in "Cole and Johnson on Broadway," *New York Age*, August 1, 1907.

43. "Abyssinia's Star Actress," *Freeman*, October 6, 1906.

44. "Cole and Johnson's 'Shoo-Fly Regiment,'" *Freeman*, February 8, 1908.

45. "Woodbine," "The Stage," *Freeman*, October 13, 1906; "Cole and Johnson Show," *Freeman*, March 23, 1907.

46. "Cole and Johnson on Broadway," *New York Age*, August 1, 1907.

47. See, for instance, Philip J. Kowalski, "No Excuses for Our Dirt: Booker T. Washington and a 'New Negro' Middle Class," in *Post-bellum, Pre-Harlem: African American Literature and Culture, 1877–1919*, ed. Barbara McCaskill and Caroline Gebhard (New York: New York University Press, 2006), 181–96.

48. James Weldon Johnson, "Shoo-Fly Regiment," typescript carbon, 1904–5. All quotations are taken from this incomplete version, which is housed at the Beinecke Rare Book and Manuscript Library, Yale University.

49. "Cole and Johnson," *Washington Bee*.

50. Seniors, *Beyond "Lift,"* 103.

51. J. D. Howard, "Cole and Johnson's Red Moon Co. at Park Theatre, Indianapolis," *Freeman*, November 21, 1908.

52. "News of the Theater," *Chicago Daily Tribune*, July 3, 1907. Brief plot summaries are also provided in *Variety*, August 24, 1907, 13; "Captain Rufus Coming," *Chicago Defender*, June 6, 1914; and "The Stage," *Freeman*, October 12, 1907.

53. "'Captain Rufus' a Great Success," *Chicago Defender*.

54. "News of the Theater," *Chicago Daily Tribune*, July 3, 1907.

55. Lester A. Walton, "Two Theatrical Sacrifices," *New York Age*, August 22, 1907.

56. Russell, "The Stage: The Pekin Stock Company in Captain Rufus."

57. "Captain Rufus Makes 'Em Laugh," *New York Age*, August 15, 1907.

58. "'Captain Rufus' a Great Success," *Chicago Defender*.

59. *Variety*, August 24, 1907, 13.

60. "The Pekin," *Broad Ax*, July 6, 1907.

61. Russell, "The Stage. The Pekin Stock Company in Captain Rufus."

62. "'Captain Rufus' a Great Success," *Chicago Defender*.

63. "Cole and Johnson," *Washington Bee*.

64. Emmett J. Scott mentions the songs "The Gay Lunetta" and "La Philippa" [*sic*] in "We May Forget the Singer but We Can't Forget the Song," *New York Age*, June 13, 1907; Sylvester Russell comments that "'La Philipena [*sic*],'" which opened the second act, was even richly interpreted both by the singer and chorus" ("The Stage: Cole and Johnson in the 'Shoo-Fly Regiment,'" *Freeman*, October 5, 1907).

65. Bob Cole (lyrics) and James Reese Europe (music), "On the Gay Luneta," in James Reese Europe, *The Music of James Reese Europe: Complete Works* (New York: Edward Marks, 2012), 155–57.

66. This effect is furthered, as Thomas Riis describes, by the tune's "habañera rhythm in the bass line of the verse." Thomas L. Riis, *Just before Jazz: Black Musical Theater in New York, 1890–1915* (Washington, DC: Smithsonian Institution Press, 1989), 131.

67. The *Broad Ax* features a picture of Navarro (spelled Sirea Navarra) as "Grizzelle, A Filipino dancer," with the caption, "Only Colored toe dancer in the world with Cole and Johnson in the *Shoo-Fly Regiment* at the Columbus Theatre" ("Cole and Johnson," *Broad Ax*, December 15, 1906). The *Dallas News* mentions "a little good dancing, some of it by 'Siren Navarro' in the show" ("'The Stage' by Woodbine," *Freeman*, October 13, 1906), and "Grizzelle, A Filipino dancer, played by Siren Nevarro" is listed in the cast for the show in "Cole and Johnson," *Washington Bee.*

68. "The Shoo-Fly Regiment," *Freeman*, March 9, 1907; "Dorothy," "Women of the Shoo-Fly Regiment," *Freeman*, March 30, 1907.

69. Seniors, *Beyond "Lift,"* 67.

70. Lucy Mae San Pablo Burns, *Puro Arte: Filipinos on the Stages of Empire* (New York: New York University Press, 2013), 42–43.

71. Ngozi-Brown, "African-American Soldiers," 47, 49.

72. T. Thomas Fortune, "The Filipino: A Social Study in Three Parts," *Voice of the Negro*, vol. 1, May 1904, 201, quoted in Ngozi-Brown, "African-American Soldiers," 47.

73. *New York Age*, August 1, 1907. The "Spanish" chorus also evidently was used in a subsequent production of *The Red Moon*, much to the puzzlement of Lester Walton: "Just why girls dressed in Spanish costumes should be brought on the stage to take part in an Indian dance, etc. is a little too inconsistent." "'Red Moon' Improves with Age," *New York Age*, September 2, 1909.

74. Seniors, *Beyond "Lift,"* 80–81.

75. Henry T. Sampson, *Blacks in Blackface: A Sourcebook on Early Black Musical Shows*, 2nd ed. (Lanham, MD: Scarecrow Press, 2014), 1372.

76. "The Shoo-Fly Regiment," *Freeman.*

77. Russell, "The Stage: Cole and Johnson in the 'Shoo-Fly Regiment.'"

78. Lester A. Walton, "Shoo Fly Regiment," *New York Age*, October 31, 1907.

79. Seniors, *Beyond Lift*, 79, 81.

80. "Dorothy," "Women of the Shoo-Fly Regiment."

81. "The Story of the Teddy Bear," National Park Service, July 28, 2019, accessed August 20, 2021, www.nps.gov/thrb/learn/historyculture/storyofteddybear.htm/.

82. "Stage: Before the Stage Mirror," *Freeman*, April 6, 1907.

83. Russell, "The Stage: Cole and Johnson in the 'Shoo-Fly Regiment.'"

84. Walton, "Shoo Fly Regiment."

85. "Captain Rufus Makes 'Em Laugh: Harrison Stewart, Funny Comedian, with the Pekin Stock Company," *New York Age*, August 15, 1907.

86. Russell, "The Stage. The Pekin Stock Company in Captain Rufus."

87. "Captain Rufus Costume from the East," *Freeman*, June 13, 1914.

88. "'Captain Rufus' a Great Success," *Chicago Defender.*

89. "Jerry Mills," *Broad Ax.*

90. Maureen D. Lee, *Sissieretta Jones: "The Greatest Singer of Her Race," 1868–1933* (Columbia: University of South Carolina Press, 2012), 219. The *Freeman* announced its opening as August 26, 1912, in Billy E. Jones, "Eastern Theatrical Notes," *Freeman*, August 17, 1912.

91. Lee's biography of Sissieretta Jones says that *Captain Jasper* was originally "written by the late J. Ed. Green in 1907 but never produced on stage during his lifetime" and then revised by Will A. Cooke in the summer of 1912 (M. Lee, *Sissieretta Jones*, 219).

92. "The Stage," *Freeman*, August 8, 1903.

93. "The Black Patti Co. Went Big in Little Rock, Ark," *Freeman*, October 19, 1912.

94. The settings and song list for *Captain Jasper* appear in "Black Patti. The Great Ovation Ever Accorded the Prima Don[n] a-Standing Room at a Premium," *Washington Bee*, February 8, 1913, 5; similar plot summaries found in "Black Patti," *Savannah Tribune*, January 4, 1913, 1; "Captain Jasper as Presented by The Black Patti Musical Company at the Globe Theater on Sunday," *Broad Ax*, March 22, 1913, 3; and "Black Patti at the Walnut Theater, Louisville, Ky.," *Freeman*, April 5, 1913.

95. Sylvester Russell, "Black Patti at the Globe Theater Chicago Gives the Famous Diva a Rousing Reception," *Freeman*, April 12, 1913.

96. Published on August 5, 1912, by M. Witmark and Sons, New York; listed in the *Catalog of Copyright Entries*, part 3, volume 7, issue 1 (Washington, DC: Library of Congress Copyright Office), 993.

97. "The Owl," "New York News," *Freeman*, May 31, 1913.

98. "At the Theatres, Black Patti at the Byers," *Fort Worth Star-Telegram*, October 12, 1912, quoted in M. Lee, *Sissieretta Jones*, 220.

99. Russell, "Black Patti at the Globe Theater Chicago."

100. *Washington Bee*, February 8, 1913, 5.

101. Frederic J. Haskin, "Faults of Black Man Being Laid Bare," *Freeman*, February 2, 1907.

102. Burns, *Puro Arte*, 25–26.

103. There were several performers with this name. The *New York Clipper* listed a Prince Mungo as a "Morean chieftain" (March 11, 1893), and the *Freeman* mentioned that "Prince Mungo, the Zulu glass dancer is finishing a two-weeks engagement at London Dime museum, Chicago" ("The Stage," April 3, 1897).

104. "Prince Mungo, Descendent of the Bhogirattes," *Freeman*, September 16, 1911.

105. "Looking Sells-Floto Over," *Freeman*, September 26, 1914.

106. "Prince Mungo, Descendent of the Bhogirattes," *Freeman*. There is a stylistic resemblance to the headpiece worn in a photograph taken by Dean Worcester. The "Old Bukidnon Chief" appears in a selection of photos in his collection published in *National Geographic* in 1913 with the caption "Datos who have killed large numbers of enemies wear a most remarkable head ornament fashioned from cloth of gold, with elaborate scarlet, blue, or white tassels. . . . No other Phillipine [*sic*] tribe has anything in the least like it." Dean C. Worcester, *National Geographic Magazine*, November 27, 1913, 1164.

107. "Hagenbeck-Wallace Shows in Indianapolis," *Freeman*, August 5, 1916.

108. "Notes from P. G. Lowery's Band with Hagenbeck & Wallace Circus," *Freeman*, September 2, 1915.

109. "Local," *Topeka Plaindealer*, April 24, 1903.

CONCLUSION

1. W. E. B. Du Bois, *The Souls of Black Folk* (Chicago: A. C. McClerg and Co., 1903; repr., New Haven: Yale University Press, 2015), 12. A more sustained discussion of writings on the subject of interracial alliance by Du Bois and other African Americans can be found in Marc Gallicchio, *The African American Encounter with Japan and China: Black*

Internationalism in Asia, 1895–1945 (Chapel Hill: University of North Carolina Press, 2000); and Yuichiro Onishi's *Transpacific Antiracism: Afro-Asian Solidarity in 20th-Century Black America, Japan, and Okinawa* (New York: New York University Press, 2013).

2. "Gibson's New Standard Theater [Philadelphia]," *Freeman*, June 27, 1914.

3. Krystyn R. Moon, *Yellowface: Creating the Chinese in American Popular Music and Performance, 1850s–1920s* (New Brunswick, NJ: Rutgers University Press, 2005), 146–47, 161, 151, 159–60.

4. "This Week's Vaudeville Reviews," *Billboard*, December 21, 1912, 10.

5. "New Acts This Week," *Variety*, January 27, 1922, 21.

6. Many newspaper accounts of Yuen's life and career can be found on a blog post by Alex Jay, *Chinese American Eyes*, published December 20, 2013, at http://chimericaneyes .blogspot.com/2013/12/lily-yuen.html/. The Lily Yuen Papers 1926–1992 at the New York Public Library Archives and Manuscripts Division also provide documents recording some of the details of her professional and performance life.

7. Henry T. Sampson, *Blacks in Blackface: A Sourcebook on Early Black Musical Shows*, 2nd ed. (Lanham, MD: Scarecrow Press, 2014), 1391.

8. "Interesting Show Pekin Theatre," *Savannah Tribune*, December 15, 1921.

9. "Theatres," *Kansas City Advocate*, February 19, 1926; "Lyric Midnight Frolic," *Times-Picayune*, February 13, 1925; "At the Lincoln," *Inter-State Tattler* (New York), April 19, 1929.

10. "Next Week," *New York Age*, June 13, 1931; "Alhambra Theatre," *New York Age*, June 20, 1931.

11. "At the Alhambra," *New York Age*, June 8, 1929.

12. "At the Alhambra," *New York Age*, April 26, 1930.

13. V. E. J. (Vere E. Johns), "Yeah! Man?," *New York Age*, June 4, 1932.

14. "Artist Here from Savannah Had Chinese Father," *Afro-American*, June 20, 1925.

15. "Artist Here from Savannah," *Afro-American*.

16. Sampson, *Blacks in Blackface*, 1014.

17. Al Johns, "In Far Off Mandalay," Frances G. Spencer Collection of American Popular Sheet Music, Crouch Fine Arts Library, Baylor University, accessed August 20, 2021, https://digitalcollections-baylor.quartexcollections.com/Documents/Detail /in-far-off-mandalay/39824/.

18. "Bradford," "Bert Williams' Mr. Lode of Koal Co. at the Majestic Theatre, New York City," *Freeman*, November 20, 1909.

19. Will Marion Cook (music) and Alexander Rogers (lyrics), "Chink Chink Chinaman" (Chicago: Will Rossiter, 1909), Frances G. Spencer Collection of American Popular Sheet Music.

20. Sampson, *Blacks in Blackface*, 1427. Most famously, Rogers had penned the despairing words to "Nobody," a number in *Abyssinia* that became Bert William's signature song.

21. Caroline H. Yang, *The Peculiar Afterlife of Slavery: The Chinese Worker and the Minstrel Form* (Stanford: Stanford University Press, 2020), 197–98.

22. "Pinkey and Walker," *Freeman*, April 26, 1913.

23. "Fifty-Ninth St. Theater," *Freeman*, November 29, 1913; advertisement for Lafayette Theatre, *New York Age*, May 8, 1920.

24. Sherman Boone, "A Coon with the Raglan Craze," *Freeman*, April 13, 1901.

25. "Chinese Restaurants," *New York Tribune*, February 3, 1901, quoted in Yong Chen, *Chop Suey USA: The Story of Chinese Food in America* (New York: Columbia University Press, 2014), 107.

26. "Restaurant Business in Harlem Is Largely Controlled by Chinese to the Exclusion of Negro Caterers. More Than Twenty Chop Suey Places Sell Both Chinese and American Food, at Lower Rates and with Better Quality of Food," *New York Age*, April 21, 1928.

27. "Restaurant Business in Harlem Is Largely Controlled by Chinese to the Exclusion of Negro Caterers," *New York Age*.

28. "Washington Letter," *New York Age*, April 26, 1917.

29. "To the Negroes of Harlem," *Negro World*, January 8, 1927.

30. "Lady Nicotine," "Between Puffs," *Inter-State Tattler*, February 17, 1928.

31. Jimmy Durante and Jack Kofoed, *Nightclubs* (New York: Knopf, 1931), 12.

32. James Weldon Johnson, *The Autobiography of an Ex-Colored Man* (New York: Alfred A. Knopf, 1927), edited by Jacqueline Goldsby (repr. New York: W. W. Norton Company, 2015), 55.

33. Sylvester Russell, "Jesse Shipp's Second Production," *Freeman*, April 17, 1910.

34. J. D. Howard, "A Slumming Party Visits a Chinese Restaurant. Go on a Sight-Seeing Expedition in the 'Mound City,'" *Freeman*, August 8, 1902.

35. See Chen, *Chop Suey USA*, chap. 1.

36. "American Chop Suey" (using veal and bananas), *Broad Ax*, October 23, 1915; "Chop Suey Made with Rabbit," *Washington Tribune*, April 22, 1932.

37. Miss G. B. Maxfield, "Paragraphic News: Important News Happenings of the Week Devoted to General Interest," *Washington Bee*, October 26, 1912.

38. "The Cameraman," "Colorful News Movies," *Broad Ax*, September 18, 1926.

39. Christina Klein, *Cold War Orientalism: Asia in the Middlebrow Imagination, 1945–1961.* (Berkeley: University of California Press, 2003).

40. See Robert G. Lee, *Orientals: Asian Americans in Popular Culture* (Philadelphia: Temple University Press, 1999), chap. 5; and Heidi Kim, *Illegal Immigrants/Model Minorities: The Cold War of Chinese American Narrative* (Philadelphia: Temple University Press, 2020), chap. 2.

41. "Chop Suey," in Richard Rodgers, Oscar Hammerstein II, and Joseph Fields, *Flower Drum Song* (New York, Farrar, Straus, and Cudahy, 1959), 61–63.

42. After her Tony Award, Hall was the focus of a short article in *Time*, "After 21 Years," which discussed her solo performances at Manhattan's Café Society after the success in *South Pacific* and described her transformation from, "at 14, a fat, bright-eyed little Negro girl from Keyport, N.J. [who] rolled into Manhattan with a high-school diploma in her hand, and an idea in her head that she would become a 'high dramatic soprano' to her success at age 35: she padded onto a Broadway stage as Bloody Mary, the betel-chewing Tonkinese mama in South Pacific . . . and stole a considerable piece of that smash hit from Mary Martin and Ezio Pinza." *Time*, June 6, 1948, 76.

43. "Show Business: Broadway. The Girls on Grant Avenue," *Time*, December 22, 1958, 42.

44. "Show Business: Broadway."

45. Rodgers says that the song was written in "five minutes over after-dinner coffee in a crowded room" ("Show Business: Broadway," 47).

Notes to Pages 260–66

46. Kathryn Edney, "'Integration through the Wide Open Back Door': African Americans Respond to *Flower Drum Song* (1958)," *Studies in Musical Theatre* 4, no. 3 (2010): 261–72, 262–63.

47. "Broadway 'Oriental': Juanita Hall Scores her Second Stage Hit in Eastern Role," *Ebony*, March 1, 1959, 128.

48. "Broadway 'Oriental.'"

49. "Cook and Steven," *The Star*, quoted by J. D. Howard, *Freeman*, October 23, 1909.

50. "Boston, Mass., Theatrical Notes," *Freeman*, January 22, 1916, 6.

51. "Gibson's New Standard Theater [Philadelphia]," *Freeman*, 6.

52. "Broadway 'Oriental,'" 128–29.

53. "Broadway 'Oriental,'" 130.

54. "Broadway 'Oriental,'" 130.

55. "Broadway 'Oriental,'" 128.

56. Harry F. Lorraine, "Nigger versus Chinese" (St. Louis, MO: Balmer and Weber, 1870), quoted in Yang, *Peculiar Afterlife of Slavery*, 3.

Selected Bibliography

NEWSPAPERS AND PERIODICALS

Amsterdam News
The Appeal (St. Paul, MN)
Augusta (GA) Chronicle
Ayr Observer (Scotland)
Baltimore Afro-American
Baltimore Evening Sun
Billboard
Bristol Times and Mirror (England)
British Press
Broad Ax (Chicago, IL)
Brooklyn Daily Eagle
Carmarthen Journal (Wales)
Chicago Daily Tribune
Chicago Defender
Cleveland Gazette
The Colonist (Victoria, BC)
Colored American (Washington, DC)
Cork Evening Herald
Cork Weekly Times and Commercial
    Economist
The Crisis Magazine
Daily Alta California
Daily Astorian (Astoria, OR)
Denver Daily Rocky Mountain News
Derby Mercury (England)
Doncaster Chronicle and Farmer's Journal
    (England)
Drogheda Journal (Ireland)
Ebony
Elevator Constructor
Era (London)
Etude Music Magazine

Evening Star (Washington, DC)
Fort Worth Register
Freeman (Indianapolis, IN)
Daily Tribune (MT)
Harper's Weekly
Huntsville (AL) Gazette
Illinois Record (Springfield)
Illustrated American
Illustrated London News
Illustrated Sporting and Dramatic News
Inter-state Tattler (New York)
Jasper (IN) Weekly Courier
Kansas City (KS) Advocate
Kilkenny Moderator (Ireland)
Los Angeles Times
Manchester Guardian
Minneapolis Tribune
Morning Times (Washington, DC)
Musical Courier
Negro World (New York)
New Haven (CT) Evening Register
New Orleans Herald
New York Age
New York American
New York Clipper
New York Daily Times
New York Evening Post
New York Evening Telegram
New York Herald
New York Sun
New York Times
New York Tribune

New York World
Norwich (CT) Bulletin
Oregonian and Morning Oregonian
    (Portland)
Pacific Commercial Advertiser
    (Honolulu, HI)
Parsons (KS) Weekly Blade
People's Voice (New York)
Philadelphia Evening Ledger
Philadelphia Inquirer
Philadelphia Times
Philadelphia Tribune
Pittsburgh Courier
The Playgoer
Publishers Weekly
Punch
Rising Son (Kansas City, MO)
San Francisco Bulletin
San Francisco Call
San Francisco Chronicle
San Francisco Daily Evening Bulletin
Savannah Times

Savannah Tribune
Scribner's Magazine
Sioux City (IA) Journal
Spirit of the Times (New York)
Stanraer Advertiser (Scotland)
Star Tribune (Minneapolis, MN)
St. Louis Globe-Democrat
St. Louis Republic
St. Mary's Chimes (Notre Dame, IN)
Time Magazine
Times (London)
Times Literary Supplement (London)
Times-Picayune (New Orleans, LA)
Topeka Plaindealer
Trenton (NJ) Evening Times
Vanity Fair
Variety
Washington (DC) Bee
Washington (DC) Post
Washington (DC) Tribune
Westmeath Guardian and Longford
    News-letter (Ireland)

BOOKS AND JOURNAL ARTICLES

Abbott, Lynn, and Doug Seroff. *Out of Sight: The Rise of African American Popular Music, 1889–1895.* Jackson: University Press of Mississippi, 2002.

———. *Ragged but Right: Black Traveling Shows, "Coon Songs," and the Dark Pathway to Blues and Jazz.* Jackson: University Press of Mississippi, 2007.

Adams, Bluford. *E Pluribus Barnum: The Great Showman and the Making of U.S. Popular Culture.* Minneapolis: University of Minnesota Press, 1997.

Ade, George. *George Ade's Stories of Benevolent Assimilation.* Edited by Perry E. Gianakos. Quezon City, RP: New Day Publishers, 1985.

———. *The Sultan of Sulu: An Original Satire in Two Acts.* New York: R. H. Russell, 1903.

Aladdin, or The Wonderful Lamp: A Drama in Three Acts as Performed at the Chestnut St. Theatre, Philadelphia. In *Alexander's Modern Acting Drama: Consisting of the Most Popular Plays Produced at the Philadelphia Theatres and Elsewhere, Vol. VI.* Philadelphia: Carey and Hart, C. Alexander, and W. Marshall and Co., 1835.

Aladdin: or, The Wonderful Lamp, a Drama, in Three Acts, with Original Casts, Costumes, and the Whole of the Stage Business Correctly Marked and Arranged by J. B. Wright, Assistant Manager of the Boston Theatre. Boston: William V. Spencer, 1857–58.

Andrews, Jean. "Meyerbeer's *L'Africaine*: French Grand Opera and the Iberian Exotic." *Modern Language Review* 102, no. 1 (January 2007): 108–24.

Bank, Rosemary K. "Frontier Melodrama." *Dutch Quarterly Review of Anglo-American Letters* 19, no. 2 (1989): 136–45.

Bartlett, John Russell. *Dictionary of Americanisms*. 4th ed. Boston: Little, Brown, 1877.

Beadle's Dime Dialogues, no. 41, 82–86. New York: Beadle and Adams, 1894.

Bean, Annemarie. "Double Inversion and Black Minstrelsy, circa 1890." In *African American Performance and Theater History: A Critical Reader*, edited by Harry J. Elam Jr. and David Krasner, 171–91. New York: Oxford University Press, 2001.

Bean, Annemarie, James V. Hatch, and Brooks McNamara, eds. *Inside the Minstrel Mask: Readings in Nineteenth-Century Blackface Minstrelsy*. Hanover, NH: Wesleyan University Press, 1996.

Bernard, William Bayle. *The Mummy: A Farce in One Act*. Boston: W. V. Spencer, 1856.

Bickerstaff, Isaac John. *The Padlock* (1768). Reprinted in *Slavery, Abolition and Emancipation: Writings in the British Romantic Period, Volume 5*, edited by Jeffrey N. Cox, 73–107. London: Pickering and Chatto, 1999.

Blanchard, Edward Litt Leman. *Aladdin; or Harlequin and the Wonderful Lamp, a Grand Comic Christmas Pantomime* (1874). In *English Plays of the Nineteenth Century, Volume 5*, edited by Michael Booth, 337–77. Oxford: Clarendon Press/Oxford University Press, 1976.

Blaney, Charles E. *Across the Pacific: A Novel; Founded upon the Melodrama of the Same Title*. New York: J. S. Ogilvie, 1904.

Bold, Christine. "Where Did the Black Rough Riders Go?" *Canadian Review of American Studies* 39, no. 3 (2009): 273–97.

Bordman, Gerald. *American Musical Theatre: A Chronicle*. 3rd ed. New York: Oxford University Press, 2000.

Boskin, Joseph. *Sambo: The Rise and Demise of an American Jester*. New York: Oxford University Press, 1986.

Bourdieu, Pierre. "Habitus." In *Habitus: A Sense of Place*, edited by Jean Hillier and Emma Rooksby, 27–34. Aldershot, UK: Ashgate, 2002.

———. *Outline of a Theory of Practice*. Translated by Richard Nice. Cambridge: Cambridge University Press, 1977.

Brooks, Daphne. *Bodies in Dissent: Spectacular Performances of Race and Freedom*. Durham, NC: Duke University Press, 2006.

Brown, Jayna. *Babylon Girls: Black Women Performers and the Shaping of the Modern*. Durham, NC: Duke University Press, 2008.

Brown, Thomas Allston. *A History of the New York Stage from the First Performance in 1732 to 1901, Volume One*. New York: Dodd, Mead, 1903.

Buckner, Jocelyn L. "'Spectacular Opacities': The Hyers Sisters' Performances of Respectability and Resistance." *African American Review* 45, no. 3 (Fall 2012): 309–23.

Buonaventura, Wendy. *Belly Dancing: The Serpent and the Sphinx*. London: Virago, 1893.

Burns, Lucy Mae San Pablo. *Puro Arte: Filipinos on the Stages of Empire*. New York: New York University Press, 2013.

Burwick, Frederick. *Romantic Drama: Acting and Reacting*. Cambridge: Cambridge University Press, 2009.

Byron, Henry J. *Aladdin: or, The Wonderful Scamp! An Original Burlesque Extravaganza, in One Act*. London: Samuel French, 1861.

Carlton, Donna. *Looking for Little Egypt*. Bloomington, IN: IDD Books, 1994.

Carter, Walter. *The Coon and the Chink: A Vaudeville Sketch in One Act*. New York: Dick and Fitzgerald, 1912.

Cerniglia, Kenneth J. "Negotiating American Identity through Ethnic Stereotypes in J. J. McCloskey's *Across the Continent* (1870) and Edward Harrigan's *The Mulligan Guard Ball* (1879)." *Theatre Annual* 61 (2008): 23–56.

Chen, Yong. *Chop Suey USA: The Story of Chinese Food in America.* New York: Columbia University Press, 2014.

Cheng, Anne. *Ornamentalism: A Feminist Theory for the Yellow Woman.* New York: Oxford University Press, 2019.

Cherniavsky, Felix. *The Salome Dancer: The Life and Times of Maud Allan.* Toronto: McClelland and Stewart, 1991.

Christy, E. Byron, and William E. Christy. *Christy's New Songster and Black Joker Containing All the Most Popular and Original Songs, Choruses, Stump Speeches, Witticisms, Jokes, Conundrums, etc., etc., as Sung and Delivered by the World-Renowned Christy's Minstrels at Their Opera Houses.* New York: Dick and Fitzgerald, 1863.

Cockrell, Dale. *Demons of Disorder: Early Blackface Minstrels and Their World.* Cambridge: Cambridge University Press, 1997.

Coleman, John. *Fifty Years of an Actor's Life.* London: Hutchinson, 1904.

Cook, Will Marion, Jesse A. Shipp, and Paul Laurence Dunbar. *The Music and Scripts of "In Dahomey."* Edited by Thomas L. Riis. American Musicological Society. Madison, WI: A-R Editions, 1996.

Cook, Will Marion, Jesse A. Shipp, and Alexander Rogers. *Abyssinia.* Libretto. 1905. Music Division, Library of Congress, Washington, DC. Not paginated.

Courtright, William. *The Complete Minstrel Guide.* Chicago: Dramatic Publishing Co., 1901.

Cruz, Gabriela. "Laughing at History: The Third Act of Meyerbeer's *L'Africaine*." *Cambridge Opera Journal* 11 (March 1999): 31–76.

Cullen, Frank, with Florence Hackman and Donald McNeilly. *Vaudeville Old and New: An Encyclopedia of Variety Performance in America.* New York: Routledge, 2007.

Cuney-Hare, Maud. *Negro Musicians and Their Music.* 2nd ed. Washington, DC: Associated Press, 1943.

Davis, David Brion. *The Problem of Slavery in Western Culture.* Ithaca: Cornell University Press, 1966.

Davis, Nancy. *The Chinese Lady: Afong Moy in Early America.* New York: Oxford University Press, 2019.

Deslippe, Philip. "The Hindu in Hoodoo: Fake Yogis, Pseudo-Swamis, and the Manufacture of African American Folk Magic." *Amerasia Journal* 40, no. 1 (January 2014): 34–56.

Desmet, Christy. "Confessions; or, the Blind Heart: An Antebellum Othello." *Borrowers and Lenders: The Journal of Shakespeare and Appropriation* 1, no. 1 (2005): 1–24.

Dickens, Charles. *Pictures from Italy, and American Notes for General Circulation.* Boston: Houghton, Osgood, 1880.

Dorman, Jason S. *The Princess and the Prophet: The Secret History of Magic, Race, and Moorish Muslims in America.* Boston: Beacon Press, 2020.

Downer, Leslie. *Madame Sadayakko: The Geisha Who Bewitched the West.* New York: Gotham, 2003.

Drake, St. Claire. *Black Folk Here and There: An Essay in History and Anthropology.* Los Angeles: University of California Center for Afro-American Studies, 1991.

Du Bois, W. E. B. "Egypt and India." *The Crisis* 18, no. 2 (June 1919): 62.

———. *The Souls of Black Folk*. Chicago: A. C. McClerg and Co., 1903. Reprint, New Haven, CT: Yale University Press, 2015.

Dumont, Frank. *The Witmark Amateur Minstrel Guide and Burnt Cork Encyclopedia*. Chicago: M. Witmark and Sons, 1899.

Dunbar, Paul Laurence. "We Wear the Mask." In *Lyrics of Lowly Life*. New York: Dodd, Mead, 1896. Reprinted in *The Collected Poetry of Paul Laurence Dunbar*, edited by Joanne M. Braxton, 71. Charlottesville: University Press of Virginia, 1993.

Dunlap, William. *A History of the American Theatre*. New York: J. and J. Harper, 1832.

Dunson, Stephanie. "The Minstrel in the Parlor: Nineteenth-Century Sheet Music and the Domestication of Blackface Minstrelsy." *American Transcendental Quarterly* 16, no. 4 (2002): 241–56.

Durante, Jimmy, and Jack Kofoed. *Nightclubs*. New York: Knopf, 1931.

Dwyer, Richard A., and Richard E. Lingenfelter. *The Songs of the Gold Rush*. Berkeley: University of California Press, 1963.

Edney, Kathryn. "'Integration through the Wide Open Back Door': African Americans Respond to *Flower Drum Song* (1958)." *Studies in Musical Theatre* 4, no. 3 (2010): 261–72.

Europe, James Reese. *The Music of James Reese Europe: Complete Works*. Forewords by Reid Badger and Rick Benjamin. New York: Edward Marks, 2012.

Fauset, Jessie Redman. *Plum Bun: A Novel without a Moral*. Reprint, London: Pandora, 1985.

Fisher, James, and Felicia Hardison Londré. *Historical Dictionary of American Theater: Modernism*. London: Rowman and Littlefield, 2017.

Fitch, Clyde. *Her Own Way: A Play in Four Acts*. New York: Macmillan, 1907.

Foertsch, Jacqueline. *American Drama in Dialogue, 1714–Present*. London: Palgrave Macmillan, 2017.

Forbes, Camille F. *Introducing Bert Williams: Burnt Cork, Broadway, and the Story of America's First Black Star*. New York: Basic Books, 2008.

Forman, Ross. *China and the Victorian Imagination: Empires Entwined*. Cambridge: Cambridge University Press, 2013.

Foster, William. "Pioneers of the Stage: Memoirs of William Foster." In *The Official Theatrical World of Colored Artists National Directory and Guide* 1, no. 1, April 1928, 48–49. Black Culture Collection Reel, UCSD Geisel Library.

Gaines, Kevin Kelly. *Uplifting the Race: Black Leadership, Politics, and Culture in the Twentieth Century*. Chapel Hill: University of North Carolina Press, 1996.

Galland, Antoine, trans. *Arabian Nights Entertainments. Consisting of One Thousand and One Stories*. 12 vols. London: W. Taylor, W. Chetwood, and S. Chapmar, 1721–22.

Gallicchio, Marc. *The African American Encounter with Japan and China: Black Internationalism in Asia, 1895–1945*. Chapel Hill: University of North Carolina Press, 2000.

Garelick, Rhonda K. *Electric Salome: Loie Fuller's Performance of Modernism*. Princeton: Princeton University Press, 2007.

Gautier, Théophile. *Voyage en Russie*. Paris: Charpentier, 1867.

Gest, Morris. "The Famous Freaks of Hammerstein's." *Green Book Magazine* 12 (September 1914): 551–57.

Gevingson, Alan, ed. *Within Our Gates: Ethnicity in American Feature Films, 1911–1960*. American Film Institute Catalog. Berkeley: University of California Press, 1997.

Gibbs, Jenna M. *Performing the Temple of Liberty: Slavery, Theater, and Popular Culture in London and Philadelphia, 1760–1850*. Baltimore: Johns Hopkins University Press, 2014.

Gilbert, William Schwenk, and Arthur Sullivan. *The Mikado; or, The Town of Titipu*. In *The Compete Annotated Gilbert and Sullivan*. Introduced and edited by Ian Bradley. Oxford: Oxford University Press, 1996.

Glaude, Eddie S., Jr. *Democracy in Black: How Race Still Enslaves the American Soul*. New York: Crown, 2016.

Graziano, John. "Images of African Americans: African-American Musical Theatre, *Show Boat*, and *Porgy and Bess*." In *The Cambridge Companion to the Musical*, edited by William A. Everett and Paul R. Laird, 63–76. Cambridge: Cambridge University Press, 2002.

Greenhalgh, Paul. *Ephemeral Vistas: The Expositions Universelles, Great Exhibitions and World's Fairs, 1851–1939*. Manchester, UK: Manchester University Press, 1988.

Grimaldi, Joseph. *Memoirs of Joseph Grimaldi*. London: George Routledge and Sons, 1853.

Gruesser, John Cullen. *The Empire Abroad and the Empire at Home: African American Literature and the Era of Overseas Expansion*. Athens: University of Georgia Press, 2012.

Haenni, Sabine. *The Immigrant Scene: Ethnic Amusements in New York, 1880–1920*. Minneapolis: University of Minnesota Press, 2008.

Hall, Roger Allan. "*Black America*: Nate Salsbury's 'Afro-American Exhibition.'" *Educational Theatre Journal* 29, no. 1 (March 1977): 49–60.

———. *Performing the American Frontier, 1870–1906*. Cambridge: Cambridge University Press, 2001.

Hamberlin, Larry. *Tin Pan Opera: Operatic Novelty Songs in the Ragtime Era*. New York: Oxford University Press, 2011.

Hamilton, Marybeth. "*When I'm Bad, I'm Better*": *Mae West, Sex, and American Entertainment*. New York: HarperCollins, 1995.

Hare, Walter Ben. *Abbu San of Old Japan: Comedy-Drama in Two Acts for Fifteen Girls*. Chicago: T. S. Denison, 1916.

Harte, Bret. *Bret Harte's California: Letters to the "Springfield Republican" and "Christian Register," 1866–67*. Edited by Gary Scharnhorst. Albuquerque: University of New Mexico Press, 1990.

———. "Plain Language from Truthful James." *Overland Monthly* 5, no. 3 (1870): 287–88.

———. *Two Men of Sandy Bar. A Drama*. Boston: Houghton, Mifflin, 1888.

Harte, Bret, and Mark Twain. *Ah Sin*. In *The Chinese Other, 1850–1925: An Anthology of Plays*, edited by Dave Williams, 39–95. Lanham, MD: University Press of America, 1997.

Haskins, Jim, and Kathleen Benson. *Conjure Times: Black Magicians in America*. New York: Walker and Co., 2001.

Hazzard, Alvira. *Mother Liked It*. In *Lost Plays of the Harlem Renaissance, 1920–1940*, edited by James V. Hatch and Leo Hamalian, 63–72. Detroit: Wayne State University Press, 1998.

Hill, Constance Valis. *Tap Dancing America: A Cultural History*. New York: Oxford University Press, 2009.

Hill, Errol. "The Hyers Sisters: Pioneers in Black Musical Comedy." In *The American Stage: Social and Economic Issues from the Colonial Period to the Present*, edited by Ron Engle and Tice L. Miller, 115–30. New York: Cambridge University Press, 1993.

Hornback, Robert. *Racism and Early Blackface Comic Traditions*. Cham, Switz.: Palgrave Macmillan, 2018.

Hudson, Peter. "Opera." In *Africana: The Encyclopedia of the African and African American Experience*, edited by Kwame Anthony Appiah and Henry Louise Gates Jr., 1460–61. New York: Basic Civitas Books, 1999.

Hughes, Langston, and Milton Meltzer. *Black Magic: A Pictorial History of the Negro in American Entertainment*. Englewood Cliffs, NJ: Prentice-Hall, 1967.

Hunter, Tera W. *To 'Joy My Freedom: Southern Black Women's Lives and Labors after the Civil War*. Cambridge, MA: Harvard University Press, 1997.

Hurston, Zora Neale. "Characteristics of Negro Expression." In *Negro: An Anthology*, edited by Nancy Cunard, 49–68. London: Wishart, 1934.

———. *The First One*. In *Collected Plays*, edited by Jean Lee Cole and Charles Mitchell, 63–74. New Brunswick, NJ: Rutgers University Press, 2008.

Hutton, Lawrence. *Curiosities of the American Stage*. New York: Harper and Bros., 1890.

Hyde, Stuart W. "The Chinese Stereotype in American Melodrama." *California Historical Society Quarterly* 34 (December 1955): 357–65.

Isaac, Allan Punzalan. "Displacing Filipinos, Dislocating America: Carlos Bulosan's *America Is in the Heart*." In *Racially Writing the Republic*, edited by Bruce Baum and Duchess Harris, 231–46. Durham, NC: Duke University Press, 2009.

Isham, John W. "Oriental America at Mrs. Waldorf's Fifth Anniversary: A Spectacular Operatic Absurdity in One Act" (1896). Library of Congress Rare Book and Special Collections Division.

Jacobs, Linda K. "'Playing East': Arabs Play Arabs in Nineteenth Century America." *Mashriq and Mahjar* 2, no. 2 (2014): 79–110.

James, Jennifer C. *A Freedom Bought with Blood: African American War Literature from the Civil War to World War II*. Chapel Hill: University of North Carolina Press, 2007.

Jarrett, Lucinda. *Stripping in Time: A History of Erotic Dancing*. London: HarperCollins, 1997.

Johnson, James Weldon. *Along This Way: The Autobiography of James Weldon Johnson*. New York: Viking, 1933.

———. *The Autobiography of an Ex-Colored Man*. New York: Alfred A. Knopf, 1927. Reprint edited by Jacqueline Goldsby. New York: W. W. Norton, 2015.

———. *Black Manhattan*. 1930. Reprint, New York: Arno, 1967.

———. "Shoo-Fly Regiment." Typescript carbon. 1904–5. Beinecke Rare Book and Manuscript Library, Yale University.

Johnson, Stephen. "Gender Trumps Race? Cross-Dressing Juba in Early Blackface Minstrelsy." In *When Men Dance: Choreographing Masculinities across Borders*, edited by Jennifer Fisher and Anthony Shay, 221–39. New York: Oxford University Press, 2009.

Jones, J. Wilton. *The Entirely New and Strictly Original Comic Grand Christmas Pantomime, Aladdin and the Wonderful Lamp; or, Harlequin and the Fairies of the Jewel Cavern*. Overture, incidental, and ballet music specially composed and arranged by D. Gribbin. Leeds: F. R. Spark, 1880.

Jordan, Carolyne Lamar. "Black Female Concert Singers of the Nineteenth Century." In *Feel the Spirit: Studies in Nineteenth-Century Afro-American Music*, edited by George R. Keck and Sherrill V. Martin, 35–48. Westport, CT: Garland, 1988.

Jun, Helen H. *Race for Citizenship: Black Orientalism and Asian Uplift from Pre-emancipation to Neoliberal America*. New York: New York University Press, 2011.

Jung, Moon-Ho. "Coolie." In *Keywords for American Cultural Studies*, edited by Bruce Burgett and Glenn Hendler, 64–66. New York: New York University Press, 2007.

———. "Outlawing 'Coolies': Race, Nation, and Empire in the Age of Emancipation." *American Quarterly* 57, no. 3 (2005): 677–701.

Kabbani, Rana. *Europe's Myths of Orient*. Houndsmill, UK: Macmillan, 1986.

Kaplan, Amy. "Black and Blue on San Juan Hill." In *Cultures of United States Imperialism*, edited by Amy Kaplan and Donald E. Pease, 219–36. Durham, NC: Duke University Press, 1993.

Kearney, Reginald. *African American Views of the Japanese: Solidarity of Sedition*. Albany: State University of New York Press, 1998.

Kendall, Elizabeth. *Where She Danced*. New York: Alfred A. Knopf, 1979.

Kim, Heidi. *Invisible Subjects: Asian America in Postwar Culture*. New York: Oxford University Press, 2016.

Kimball, Robert, and William Bolcom. *Reminiscing with Sissle and Blake*. New York: Viking, 1973.

Klein, Christina. *Cold War Orientalism: Asia in the Middlebrow Imagination, 1945–1961*. Berkeley: University of California Press, 2003.

Knowles, Mark. *Tap Roots: The Early History of Tap Dancing*. New York: McFarland, 2002.

Koritz, Amy. "Dancing the Orient for England: Maud Allan's 'The Vision of Salome.'" *Theatre Journal* 46, no. 1 (March 1994): 63–78.

Kowalski, Philip J. "No Excuses for Our Dirt: Booker T. Washington and a 'New Negro' Middle Class." In *Post-bellum, Pre-Harlem: African American Literature and Culture, 1877–1919*, edited by Barbara McCaskill and Caroline Gebhard, 181–96. New York: New York University Press, 2006.

Krasner, David. *A Beautiful Pageant: African American Theatre, Drama, and Performance in the Harlem Renaissance, 1910–1927*. New York: Palgrave Macmillan, 2002.

———. "Black *Salome*: Exoticism, Dance, and Racial Myths." In *African American Performance and Theater History: A Critical Reader*, edited by Harry J. Elam Jr. and David Krasner, 192–211. New York: Oxford University Press, 2001.

———. *Resistance, Parody, and Double Consciousness in African American Theatre, 1895–1910*. New York: St. Martin's Press, 1997.

Kunhardt, Philip B. *P. T. Barnum: America's Greatest Showman*. New York: Knopf, 1995.

Lee, Esther Kim. *Made-Up Asians: Yellowface during the Exclusion Era*. Ann Arbor: University of Michigan Press, 2022.

Lee, Josephine. "Decorative Orientalism." In *Asian American Literature in Transition: 1850–1930*, edited by Josephine Lee and Julia H. Lee, 187–203. Cambridge: Cambridge University Press, 2021.

———. *The Japan of Pure Invention: Gilbert and Sullivan's "The Mikado."* Minneapolis: University of Minnesota Press, 2010.

———. "Yellowface: Historical and Contemporary Contexts." In *The Oxford Encyclopedia of Asian American Literature and Culture*, edited by Josephine Lee, Floyd Cheung, Jennifer Ann Ho, Anita Mannur, and Cathy Schlund-Vials, 1205–23. New York: Oxford University Press, 2020.

Lee, Julia H. *Interracial Encounters: Reciprocal Representations in African and Asian American Literatures, 1896–1937*. New York: New York University Press, 2011.

Lee, Maureen D. *Sissieretta Jones: "The Greatest Singer of Her Race," 1868–1933*. Columbia: University of South Carolina Press, 2012.

Lee, Robert G. *Orientals: Asian Americans in Popular Culture*. Philadelphia: Temple University Press, 1999.

Letellier, Robert Ignatius. *The Operas of Giacomo Meyerbeer*. Madison, NJ: Fairleigh Dickinson University Press, 2006.

Levander, Caroline. "Confederate Cuba." *American Literature* 78, no. 4 (2006): 821–45.

Lhamon, W. T. *Jump Jim Crow: Lost Plays, Lyrics, and Street Prose of the First Atlantic Popular Culture*. Cambridge, MA: Harvard University Press, 2003.

Lindfors, Bernth. *Ira Aldridge: Performing Shakespeare in Europe, 1852–1855*. Rochester, NY: University of Rochester Press, 2013.

———. "Ira Aldridge's London Debut." *Theatre Notebook* 60, no. 1 (2006): 30–44.

———. *Ira Aldridge: The Vagabond Years, 1833–1852*. Rochester, NY: University of Rochester Press, 2011.

Lindsay, Nicholas Vachel. "The Golden-Faced People: A Story of the Chinese Conquest of America." *The Crisis* 9, no. 1 (November 1917): 36–42.

Locke, Alain. "Steps toward the Negro Theatre." In *The Works of Alain Locke*, edited by Charles Molesworth, 93. New York: Oxford University Press, 2012.

Lott, Eric. *Love and Theft: Blackface Minstrelsy and the American Working Class*. New York: Oxford University Press, 1993.

Lowe, Lisa. *The Intimacies of Four Continents*. Durham, NC: Duke University Press, 2015.

Magarshack, David. "Stanislavsky." In *The Theory of the Modern Stage*, edited by Eric Bentley, 215–74. 1968. Reprint, New York: Penguin, 1980.

Mahar, William J. *Behind the Burnt Cork Mask: Early Blackface Minstrelsy and Antebellum American Popular Culture*. Urbana: University of Illinois Press, 1999.

Makonnen, Atesede. "'Our Blackamoor or Negro Othello': Rejecting the Affective Power of Blackness." *European Romantic Review* 29, no. 3 (2018): 347–55.

Manring, Maurice M. "Aunt Jemima Explained: The Old South, the Absent Mistress, and the Slave in a Box." *Southern Cultures* 2, no. 1 (Fall 1995): 19–44.

Marshall, Herbert, and Mildred Stock. *Ira Aldridge: The Negro Tragedian*. New York: Macmillan, 1958. Reprint, Washington, DC: Howard University Press, 1993.

Martin, Tony. *Literary Garveyism: Garvey, Black Arts, and the Harlem Renaissance*. Dover, MA: Majority Press, 1983.

Matsukawa, Yuko. "Representing the Oriental in Nineteenth-Century Trade Cards." In *Re/collecting Early Asian America*, edited by Josephine Lee, Imogene Lim, and Yuko Matsukawa, 200–217. Philadelphia: Temple University Press, 2002.

Mayer, David. *Harlequin in His Element: The English Pantomime, 1806–1836*. Cambridge, MA: Harvard University Press, 1969.

McAllister, Marvin. *Whiting Up: Whiteface Minstrels and Stage Europeans in African American Performance*. Chapel Hill: University of North Carolina Press, 2011.

McCloskey, James J. *Across the Continent; or, Scenes from New York Life and the Pacific Railroad*. In *Davy Crockett and Other Plays*, edited by Isaac Goldberg and Hubert Heffner, 23–56. Princeton: Princeton University Press, 1940.

McCoy, Sharon D. "'The Trouble Begins at Eight': Mark Twain, the San Francisco Minstrels, and the Unsettling Legacy of Blackface Minstrelsy." *American Literary Realism* 41, no. 3 (Spring 2009): 232–48.

McKahan, Jason Grant. "Substance Abuse Film and the Gothic: Typology, Narrative, and Hallucination." In *Monsters in and among Us: Towards a Gothic Criminology*, edited by Caroline Joan (Kay) Picart and Cecil E. Greek, 117–41. Madison, NJ: Fairleigh Dickinson University Press, 2007.

Meers, Sarah. *Uncle Tom Mania: Slavery, Minstrelsy, and Transatlantic Culture in the 1850s*. Athens: University of Georgia Press, 2005.

Mendoza, Victor Román. *Metroimperial Intimacies: Fantasy, Racial-Sexual Governance, and the Philippines in U.S. Imperialism, 1899–1913*. Durham, NC: Duke University Press, 2015.

Metzger, Sean. *Chinese Looks: Fashion, Performance, Race*. Bloomington: Indiana University Press, 2014.

Meyerbeer, Giacomo. *L'Africaine: A Lyric Drama in Five Acts*. English version by Thomas J. Williams. London: Royal Italian Opera, Covent Garden, 1871.

Mieder, Wolfgang. "'No Tickee, No Washee': Subtleties of a Proverbial Slur." *Western Folklore* 55 (Winter 1996): 1–40.

Miller, Cynthia J. "'Glorifying the American Girl': Adapting an Icon." In *The Adaptation of History: Essays on Ways of Telling the Past*, edited by Lawrence Raw and Defne Ersin Tutan, 25–41. Jefferson, NC: McFarland, 2014.

Miyoshi, Masao. *As We Saw Them: The First Japanese Embassy to the United States (1860)*. Berkeley: University of California Press, 1979.

Moon, Krystyn R. "Paper Butterflies: Japanese Acrobats in Mid-nineteenth Century New England." In *Asian Americans in New England: Culture and Community*, edited by Monica Chiu, 66–90. Durham, NH: University Press of New England, 2009.

———. *Yellowface: Creating the Chinese in American Popular Music and Performance, 1850s–1920s*. New Brunswick, NJ: Rutgers University Press, 2005.

Moon, Krystyn R., David Krasner, and Thomas L. Riis. "Forgotten Manuscripts: A Trip to Coontown." *African American Review* 44, nos. 1–2 (Spring/Summer 2011): 7–24.

Mooney, Jennifer. *Irish Stereotypes in Vaudeville, 1865–1905*. New York: Palgrave Macmillan, 2015.

Muir, Peter C. *Long Lost Blues: Popular Blues in America, 1850–1920*. Urbana: University of Illinois Press, 2010.

Mullen, Bill V. *Afro-Orientalism*. Minneapolis: University of Minnesota Press, 2004.

Nance, Susan. *How the Arabian Nights Inspired the American Dream, 1790–1935*. Chapel Hill: University of North Carolina Press, 2009.

Ndounou, Monica White. "Early Black Americans on Broadway." In *The Cambridge Companion to African American Theatre*, edited by Harvey Young, 59–84. New York: Cambridge University Press, 2013.

Ngai, Sianne. *Our Aesthetic Categories: Zany, Cute, Interesting*. Cambridge, MA: Harvard University Press, 2012.

———. *Ugly Feelings*. Cambridge, MA: Harvard University Press, 2005.

Ngo, Helen. *The Habits of Racism: A Phenomenology of Racism and Racialized Embodiment*. Lanham, MD: Lexington Books, 2017.

Ngozi-Brown, Scot. "African-American Soldiers and Filipinos: Racial Imperialism, Jim Crow, and Social Relations." *Journal of Negro History* 82, no. 1 (1997): 42–53.

Nussbaum, Felicity A. "The Theatre of Empire: Racial Counterfeit; Racial Realism." In *A New Imperial History: Culture, Identity and Modernity in Britain and the Empire, 1660–1840*, edited by Kathleen Wilson, 71–90. Cambridge: Cambridge University Press, 2004.

Odell, George C. D. *Annals of the New York Stage*. New York: Columbia University Press, 1931.

O'Keeffe, John. *The Recitatives, Airs, Choruses, &c. in Aladin; or, The Wonderful Lamp. A Pantomime Entertainment Performed at the Theatre-Royal, Covent-Garden*. London: T. Cadell, 1788.

O'Neill, John Robert. *Aladdin, or The Wonderful Lamp: A Piece of Oriental Extravaganze in One Act*. London: G. H. Davidson, 1855.

O'Neill, M. J. *How He Does It: Sam. T. Jack, Twenty Years a King in the Realm of Burlesque*. Chicago: M. J. O'Neill, 1895.

Onishi, Yuichiro. *Transpacific Antiracism: Afro-Asian Solidarity in 20th-Century Black America, Japan, and Okinawa*. New York: New York University Press, 2013.

Ou, Hsin-yun. "Mark Twain's Racial Ideologies and His Portrayal of the Chinese." *Concentric* 36, no. 2 (September 2010): 33–59.

Özkaya, Belgin Turan. "Theaters of Fear and Delight: Ottomans in the Serenissima." In *After Orientalism: Critical Entanglements, Productive Looks*, edited by Inge E. Boer, 45–62. Amsterdam: Rodopi B. V., 2003.

Palmer, Sheldon. *Fun in a Chinese Laundry*. Chicago: T. S. Denison, 1920.

Pan, Yusha. "Intention versus Reception: The Representation of the Chinese in *Ah Sin*." In *Constructing Identities: The Interaction of National, Gender and Racial Borders*, edited by Antonio Medina-Rivera and Lee Wilberschied, 48–60. Newcastle upon Tyne: Cambridge Scholars Publishing, 2013.

Parker, George Wells. *The Children of the Sun*. Hamitic League of the World, 1918. Reprint, Baltimore: Black Classic Press, 1981.

Peress, Maurice. *Dvorak to Duke Ellington: A Conductor Explores America's Music and Its African American Roots*. New York: Oxford University Press, 2004.

Peterson, Bernard L., Jr. *A Century of Musicals in Black and White: An Encyclopedia of Musical Stage Works by, about, or Involving African Americans*. Westport, CT: Greenwood Press, 1993.

———. *Profiles of African American Stage Performers and Theatre People, 1816–1960*. Westport, CT: Greenwood Press, 2001.

Pickering, Michael. *Blackface Minstrelsy in Britain*. Aldershot, UK: Ashgate, 2008.

Potvin, John. "Warriors, Slave Traders and Islamic Fanatics: 'Reporting' the Spectacle of Oriental Male Bodies in the *Illustrated London News*, 1890–1900." In *After Orientalism: Critical Entanglements, Productive Looks*, edited by Inge E. Boer, 81–103. Amsterdam: Rodopi B. V., 2003.

Prashad, Vijay. *Everybody Was Kung Fu Fighting: Afro-Asian Connections and the Myth of Cultural Purity*. Boston: Beacon Press, 2002.

———. *The Karma of Black Folk*. Minneapolis: University of Minnesota Press, 2000.

Price, Edward Le Roy. *Monarchs of Minstrelsy, from "Daddy" Rice to Date*. New York: Kenny Publishing, 1911.

Reed, Bill. *Hot from Harlem: Profiles in Classic African American Entertainment*. Los Angeles: Cellar Door Press, 1998.

Reynolds, Harry. *Minstrel Memories: The Story of Burnt Cork Minstrelsy in Great Britain from 1836–1927*. London: Alston Rivers, 1928.

Richards, Jeffrey. *The Golden Age of Pantomime: Slapstick, Spectacle, and Subversion in Victorian England*. London: I. B. Tauris, 2015.

Riis, Thomas L. "The Experience and Impact of Black Entertainers in England, 1895–1920." *American Music* 4, no. 1 (Spring 1986): 50–58.

———. *Just before Jazz: Black Musical Theater in New York, 1890–1915*. Washington, DC: Smithsonian Institution Press, 1989.

Roberts, John H. "Meyerbeer: *Le Prophète* and *L'Africaine*." In *The Cambridge Companion to Grand Opera*, edited by David Charlton, 208–33. Cambridge: Cambridge University Press, 2003.

Robinson, Cedric J. *Forgeries of Memory and Meaning: Blacks and the Regimes of Race in American Theater and Film before World War II*. Chapel Hill: University of North Carolina Press, 2007.

Rodgers, Richard, Oscar Hammerstein II, and Joseph Fields. *Flower Drum Song*. New York: Farrar, Straus, and Cudahy, 1959.

Roediger, David R. *The Wages of Whiteness: Race and the Making of the American Working Class*. London: Verso, 1999.

Romeo, Jacqueline L. "Comic Coolie: Charles T. Parsloe and Nineteenth-Century American Frontier Melodrama." PhD diss., Tufts University, 2008.

Rose, Al. *Eubie Blake*. New York: Schirmer, 1979.

Said, Edward W. *Orientalism*. New York: Random House, 1978.

———. "Orientalism Reconsidered." In *Reflections on Exile and Other Literary and Cultural Essays*, 197–215. London: Granta Books, 2000.

Sampson, Henry T. *Blacks in Blackface: A Sourcebook on Early Black Musical Shows*. 2nd ed. Lanham, MD: Scarecrow Press, 2014.

———. *The Ghost Walks: A Chronological History of Blacks in Show Business, 1865–1910*. Metuchen, NJ: Scarecrow Press, 1988.

Saxton, Alexander. "Blackface Minstrelsy and Jacksonian Ideology." *American Quarterly* 27, no. 1 (March 1975): 3–28.

Scharnhorst, Gary. *Bret Harte: Opening the American Literary West*. Norman: University of Oklahoma Press, 2000.

———. "'Ways That Are Dark': Appropriations of Bret Harte's 'Plain Language from Truthful James.'" *Nineteenth-Century Literature* 51, no. 3 (December 1996): 377–99.

Schironi, Francesca. "The Trickster Onstage: The Cunning Slave from Plautus to Commedia dell'Arte." In *Ancient Comedy and Reception: Essays in Honor of Jeffrey Henderson*, edited by S. Douglas Olson, 447–78. New York: De Gruyter, 2013.

Schulman, Barbara. "Blackface Minstrelsy: Instructional Handbooks for the Amateur, 1899–1921." PhD diss., University of Minnesota, 2018.

Senelick, Lawrence. *Jacques Offenbach and the Making of Modern Culture*. Cambridge: Cambridge University Press, 2017.

Seniors, Paula Marie. *Beyond "Lift Every Voice and Sing": The Culture of Uplift, Identity, and Politics in Black Musical Theater*. Columbus: Ohio State University Press, 2009.

Shavit, Yaacov. *History in Black: African-Americans in Search of an Ancient Past*. London: Frank Cass, 2001.

Sheppard, W. Anthony. *Extreme Exoticism: Japan in the American Musical Imagination*. New York: Oxford University Press, 2019.

Sissle, Noble, and Eubie Blake. *Shuffle Along*. Edited by Lyn Schenbeck and Lawrence Schenbeck. American Musicological Society. Middleton, WI: A-R Editions, 2018.

Songs, Choruses, &c, in the Grand Melo Dramatic Romance Called Aladdin; or, The Wonderful Lamp: as Performed at the Philadelphia Theatre. Philadelphia: T. Desilver, 1816.

Sotiropoulous, Karen. *Staging Race: Black Performers in Turn of the Century America*. Cambridge, MA: Harvard University Press, 2006.

Southern, Eileen. "The Georgia Minstrels: The Early Years." In *Inside the Minstrel Mask: Readings in Nineteenth-Century Blackface Minstrelsy*, edited by Annemarie Bean, James V. Hatch, and Brooks McNamara, 163–75. Hanover, NH: University Press of New England, 1996.

Spenser, Willard. *The Little Tycoon: A Comic Opera in Two Acts*. New York: William S. Gottsberger, 1882.

Srinivasan, Priya. *Sweating Saris: Indian Dance as Transnational Labor*. Philadelphia: Temple University Press, 2011.

Starks, Michael. *Cocaine Fiends and Reefer Madness: An Illustrated History of Drugs in the Movies, 1894–1978*. Berkeley: Ronin, 2015.

Stearns, Marshall, and Jean Stearns. *Jazz Dance: The Story of American Vernacular Dance*. New York: Da Capo Press, 1994.

Stephenson, Myra Lynn. "Ira Aldridge: A Black Othello on the Nineteenth-Century English Stage." MA thesis, Shakespeare Institute, University of Birmingham, 1977.

Stone, Fred. *Rolling Stone*. New York: McGraw-Hill, 1945.

Story, Rosalyn M. *And So I Sing: African-American Divas of Opera and Concert*. New York: St. Martin's Press, 1990.

Takaki, Ronald. *Iron Cages: Race and Culture in 19th-Century America*. Oxford: Oxford University Press, 1978.

Tchen, John Kuo Wei. *New York before Chinatown*. Baltimore: Johns Hopkins University Press, 1999.

Toll, Robert C. *Blacking Up: The Minstrel Show in Nineteenth-Century America*. New York: Oxford University Press, 1974.

Trumble, Alfred. *The Heathen Chinee at Home and Abroad*. New York: Fox, 1882.

Twain, Mark. *Roughing It*. Hartford, CT: American Publishing Co., 1872.

Udall, Sharyn R. *Dance and American Art: A Long Embrace*. Madison: University of Wisconsin Press, 2012.

Waldo, Terry. *This Is Ragtime*. New York: Hawthorn Books, 1976. Reprint, New York: Da Capo Press, 1991.

Walkowitz, Judith R. "The 'Vision of Salome': Cosmopolitanism and Erotic Dancing in Central London, 1908–1918." *American Historical Review* 108, no. 2 (April 2003): 337–76.

Warner, Marina. *Stranger Magic: Charmed States and the Arabian Nights*. Cambridge, MA: Harvard University Press, 2012.

Washington, Booker T., N. B. Wood, and Fannie Barrier Williams. *A New Negro for a New Century*. New York: Arno, 1900.

Webb, Barbara L. "Authentic Possibilities: Plantation Performance of the 1890s." *Theatre Journal* 56, no. 1 (March 2004): 63–82.

White, C. *The Virginia Mummy. Dick's Standard Plays.* Vol. 14, No. 25. London: John Dicks, 1840–49?

Wilkerson, Isabel. *Caste: The Origins of Our Discontents.* New York: Random House, 2020.

Williams, Dave. *The Chinese Other, 1850–1925.* Lanham, MD: University Press of America, 1997.

Williams, Henry Llewellyn. *Waxworks at Play.* Chicago: T. S. Denison, 1894.

Winter, Marian Hannah. "Juba and American Minstrelsy." *Dance Index* 6, no. 2 (February 1947): 28–47.

Witchard, Anne Veronica. *Thomas Burke's Dark Chinoiserie: Limehouse Nights and the Queer Spell of Chinatown.* London: Routledge, 2009.

Wong, Edlie L. *Racial Reconstruction: Black Inclusion, Chinese Exclusion, and the Fictions of Citizenship.* New York: New York University Press, 2015.

Worcester, Dean C. *The Philippine Islands and Their People.* New York: Macmillan, 1901.

Worrall, David. *Harlequin Empire: Race, Ethnicity, and the Drama of the Popular Enlightenment.* New York: Routledge, 2015.

Wycherley, William. *The Country Wife.* Edited by Thomas Hikaru Fujimura. Lincoln: University of Nebraska Press, 1965.

Yang, Caroline H. *The Peculiar Afterlife of Slavery: The Chinese Worker and the Minstrel Form.* Stanford: Stanford University Press, 2020.

Yoshihara, Mari. *Embracing the East: White Women and American Orientalism.* New York: Oxford University Press, 2002.

Young, Harvey. *Embodying Black Experience: Stillness, Critical Memory, and the Black Body.* Ann Arbor: University of Michigan Press, 2010.

Zeidman, Irving. *The American Burlesque Show.* New York: Hawthorn Books, 1967.

Index

Abbu San of Old Japan (Hare), 16, 62–63,
  73–78, 200, 283n72, 283n73
Abyssinia (Cook, Shipp, Rogers, and
  Williams), 18, 191, 194–95, 200,
  202–6, 207, 208, 255, 259, 301n16,
  301n18; Aida Overton Walker, 157; Bert
  Williams, 309n20
Across the Continent (McCloskey), 16,
  86–91, 92, 285
Across the Pacific (Blaney), 225, 226–28,
  229, 304n5
Ade, George, 225, 230–32, 305; *The Sultan
  of Sulu*, 229–34, 243
African Grove Theatre, 10, 44, 51
Ah Sin (Harte and Twain), 16, 83, 86, 89,
  91–99
Aladdin (Disney film), 21–22, 36, 42–43,
  275n12
Aldridge, Ira, 5, 15–16, 17, 36, 44–59, 119,
  125, 278n1
Alexander, Eva (Princess Sotanki), 158–62,
  163, 254
Allan, Maud, 149, 155
Allee Samee 'Mellican Man, 102–3
Allen, Irving, 210, 238
Anderson, Alfred, 239

Backus, Charles, 102
Bandanna Land, 121, 153, 155, 158, 191,
  195, 214
Barnum, P. T. (Phineas Taylor), 12, 13, 25,
  64, 68, 148
Ba-ta-clan (Ching Chow Hi) (Offenbach), 3

Bickerstaff, Isaac John, 16, 47; *The
  Padlock*, 16, 45, 47–52, 81–82, 251
*Black Beard the Pirate; or, The Captive
  Princess* (Cross), 46–47
Black Patti Troubadours, 123–24, 127, 140,
  183–84, 225, 235; *Captain Jasper*, 18,
  245–49
Blake, Eubie, 18, 32, 195, 215, 220, 221,
  222, 223; "If You've Never Been
  Vamped by a Brownskin," 217–18; "I'm
  Just Simply Full of Jazz," 218; "I'm Just
  Wild about Harry," 215
Blanchard, E. L. L., 24, 26, 29, 32, 38, 41
Blaney, Charles E., 225, 226–28, 229
Bourdieu, Pierre, 9
Brown, Tom, 17, 107, 125–31, 137, 176, 254,
  261; *Mr. Lode of Koal*, 258–59; *Oriental
  America*, 181–82; *A Trip to Coontown*,
  130, 187–88
Brown, William Alexander, 10, 44
Burnside, R. H., 33; *Chin-Chin; or A
  Modern Aladdin*, 33–36, 109, 219
Byron, Henry J., 26

Caldwell, Anne, 33; *Chin-Chin; or A
  Modern Aladdin*, 33–36, 109, 219; "Go
  Gat Sig Gong-Jue" ("The High Cost of
  Living"), 34
Captain Jasper, 18, 225, 233–35, 245–49,
  308n94
Captain Rufus, 14, 18, 225, 233–36, 239–41,
  243–46, 305n40
Carter, Walter, 110, 112–14, 116

Catlin, George, 17, 125–27, 132–33, 137, 254; *In Dahomey*, 199, 200–202, 205, 259

"Characteristics of Negro Expression" (Hurston), 119, 218

The Children of the Sun (Whitney and Tutt), 195, 209, 211–14, 253

Chin-Chin; or A Modern Aladdin (O'Dea, Caldwell, and Burnside), 33–36, 109, 219

"The Chinee Laundryman" (song), 95–96, 102, 205, 286n46

"Chinese Blues" (Moore and Gardner), 139

"The Chinese Washerman" (song), 102

Chop suey recipes, 262, 310n36

Christy's Minstrels, 29, 53, 61, 63, 64, 65, 72, 77, 100, 280n8

Clorindy, or The Origin of the Cake Walk (Cook and Dunbar), 13, 195

Clough, Inez, 236, 244

Cole, Robert Allen "Bob," 1, 2, 123, 124, 271n2; *The Red Moon* (Cole and Johnson), 128, 238–39; *The Shoo-Fly Regiment*, 14, 18, 210, 225, 233, 236; *A Trip to Coontown*, 5, 17, 165, 183–90, 196

commedia dell'arte, 81–82, 91

Cook-Pankey, Anna, 243

Cook, Sam, 17, 108, 114–15, 127, 130–31, 137, 254, 267

Cook, Will Marion, 175, 183; *Clorindy, or The Origin of the Cake Walk*, 13, 195

The Coon and the Chink (Carter), 110, 112–14, 116

Courtright, William, 83–86, 284n15

Crane, Walter, 29

The Creole Show (Jack), 17, 137, 166, 170–76, 180, 183, 198, 216

Cross, John Cartwright, 46

Daly, Augustin, 150; *Zanina*, 148, 151

Darkest America (Fields), 30, 129, 165–69, 177, 188

Darkest Americans (Whitney and Tutt), 209–11

Dean, Dora, 137, 170

Dibdin, Charles, 16, 47, 48, 279n12; *The Padlock*, 16, 45, 47–52, 81–82, 251

Dickens, Charles, 69, 70

Dilward, Thomas, 16, 17, 62–73, 100, 125, 254, 281n28

Djemille, Fatima, 147

Du Bois, W. E. B., 18, 19, 117, 120, 193, 208, 210, 237, 254

Dumont, Frank, 30, 68, 73–75, 169, 224–25

Dunbar, Paul Laurence, 120; *Clorindy, or The Origin of the Cake Walk*, 13, 195

"The Dusky Salome" (song), 153–54

Europe, James Reese, 241

Fiddler, Harry Jacob, 17, 107, 125, 127–31, 135–37, 176, 181, 254, 257, 260

Field, Al G., 129, 166, 167; *Darkest America*, 30, 129, 165–69, 177, 188

Fields, Joseph, 263

Fitch, Clyde, 225, 228–29, 243

Florodora (Owen), 13, 224, 230

Flower Drum Song (Rodgers and Hammerstein), 18, 253, 254, 263–69

Foo, Lee Tung, 14, 255, 273n45

Fun in a Chinese Laundry (Palmer), 105–6

Galland, Antoine, 23, 25, 32, 33, 38

Gardner, Oscar, 138; "Chinese Blues," 139

Gautier, Théophile, 44–45, 278n2

Getchell, Ellen S., 126, 141, 292n16

Glenn, Nettie, 241

"Go Gat Sig Gong-Jue" ("The High Cost of Living") (Caldwell and O'Dea), 34

"The Golden-Faced People" (Lindsay), 101, 115–17

Goodwin, J. Cheever, 94; *Panjandrum*, 224

Grady, Lottie, 245, 246

Grimaldi, Joseph, 38, 39, 41, 277n59

habitus, 9

Hall, Juanita Long, 18, 253, 254, 263–69, 310n42

Hall, Owen, 224; *Florodora*, 13, 230

Hammerstein, Oscar II, 14, 263; *Flower Drum Song*, 18, 253, 254, 263–69
Hare, Walter Ben, 16, 62–63, 75–78, 200
Harte, Bret, 16, 79, 83, 86, 89, 91–92, 94, 97–98, 205; *Ah Sin*, 91–99
"The Heathen Chinee" ("Plain Language from Truthful James"), 89, 92, 97, 255
Her Own Way (Fitch), 225, 228–29, 243
Hewlett, James, 10, 44
House-Rent Party (film), 107
Howard University, 210–11
Hurston, Zora Neale, 119, 214, 218–19
Hyers, Anna Madah, 5, 17, 126, 140–46, 160
Hyers, Emma Louise, 5, 126, 140–42, 146

"If You've Never Been Vamped by a Brownskin" (Blake and Sissle), 217–18
"I'm Going to Get Myself a Black Salome" (Murphy and Wynn), 153–54
"I'm Just Simply Full of Jazz" (Blake and Sissle), 218
"I'm Just Wild about Harry" (Blake and Sissle), 215
In Dahomey (Cook, Shipp, and Dunbar), 1, 18, 191, 194–203, 205, 208, 255, 259; "For Florida" (Cook), 209
Isham, John W., 5, 17, 129, 165, 166, 175–83; *Isham's Octoroons*, 129, 166, 176, 180
Isham's Octoroons (Isham), 129, 166, 176, 180; *Oriental America* (Isham), 5, 17, 129, 165, 166, 175–83

Jack, Sam T., 17, 137, 166, 170–75, 183; *The Creole Show*, 170–76, 180, 198, 216
Johnson, Billy, 5, 17, 165, 183–84, 189, 196
Johnson, Edward (Black Carl), 222
Johnson, James Weldon, 1, 118, 170, 175, 261; *The Red Moon*, 128; *The Shoo-Fly Regiment*, 14, 210, 225, 236
Johnson, John Rosamond, 1, 2, 124, 238, 239, 258; *Mr. Lode of Koal*, 32, 158–59; *The Red Moon*, 128, 238–39; *The Shoo-Fly Regiment*, 14, 18, 210, 225, 234, 236

Johnson, William Henry, 68
Jones, Sissieretta ("Black Patti"), 5, 17, 140, 248–49
Jones, Wilton, 26, 29, 41
Juba (Master Juba, William Henry Lane), 69–71, 282n45

Kawakami, Sadayakko, 148, 202, 294n45
Kersands, Billy, 5, 77, 107, 126, 131, 142–43, 146
Kim-Ka! or the Misfortunes of a Ventilator, 11

L'Africaine (Meyerbeer), 143–47, 208–9, 293n24
Le Bourgeois Gentilhomme, 3–4, 54, 164, 186
Lindsay, Vachel, 101, 115–17
"Little Egypt" (dancer), 12, 147, 171, 172
Loving, Walter, 249–50
Lucas, Sam, 11, 172, 210, 238
Lyles, Aubrey, 215, 220, 223

McCloskey, James, 16, 86–91, 92; *Across the Continent*, 285
Meyerbeer, Giacomo, 143–47, 208–9; *L'Africaine*, 293n24
Miller, Flournoy E., 215, 220, 223
Mills, Jerry, 240, 261
Molière, 3–4, 54, 91, 164
Montgomery, Dave, 33–36, 109, 219
Moore, Fred D., 138; "Chinese Blues," 139
Moore, Tim, 122–23
Morse, Woolson: *Panjandrum*, 224
Moy, Afong, 12
Mr. Lode of Koal (Shipp, Rogers, and Johnson), 32, 128, 158–59
The Mummy (Bernard), 54–56
Murphy, Stanley, 153–54, 200
"My Castle on the Nile" (song), 1–3
"My Dahomian Queen" (song), 197–98

Navarro, Siren, 128, 241, 258

O'Dea, James, 33; *Chin-Chin; or A Modern Aladdin*, 33–36, 109, 219; "Go Gat

Sig Gong-Jue" ("The High Cost of Living"), 34

Offenbach, Jacques, 3–4

O'Keeffe, John, 15, 22, 24, 25

"The Old Flag Never Touched the Ground" (song), 233–34

O'Neill, John Robert, 32, 172

On Jolly Coon-ey Island, 127, 183–85, 248

Onojirō Noriyuko, Tateishi ("Japanese Tommy"), 65–69, 71

"On the Gay Luneta" (song), 241–42

Oriental America (Isham), 5, 17, 129, 165, 166, 175–83

"Oriental Blues" (song), 215–16, 220, 221

"The Oriental Coon" (song), 151–53

The Padlock (Bickerstaff and Dibdin), 16, 45, 47–52, 81–82, 251

Palmer, Sheldon, 105; Fun in a Chinese Laundry, 105–6

Panjandrum (Goodwin and Morse), 224

Parker, George Wells, 207–9, 211, 212, 213

Plautus, 81, 91

"Possum up a Gum Tree" (song), 51, 59

Prince Mungo, 249–51, 254

"Ragtime Temple Bells" (song), 35

The Red Moon (Cole and Johnson), 128, 238–39

Rice, Thomas Dartmouth, 16, 45, 53, 57, 58, 60

Robinson Crusoe (play), 41, 61, 171

Rodgers, Richard, 254, 263, 266; Flower Drum Song, 18, 253, 263–69

Rogers, Alexander Claude "Alex," 259; Mr. Lode of Koal, 32, 128, 158–59

Ross, Albert, 191–94

Russell, Sylvester, 121, 124, 133, 134, 161, 198, 261; Captain Rufus, 234, 235, 240, 248; The Shoo-Fly Regiment, 233, 243, 244, 245

Said, Edward, 3, 4, 14, 50

"The Sheik of Araby" (song), 5–7

Shipp, Jesse A., 195, 198, 258, 261; Mr. Lode of Koal, 32, 128, 158–59

The Shoo-Fly Regiment (Cole, Johnson, and Johnson), 14, 18, 128, 209, 210, 225, 233–39, 241–45

Shuffle Along (Blake and Sissle), 18, 32, 195, 214–23

Sissle, Noble, 18, 32, 195, 215–17, 220–23; "If You've Never Been Vamped by a Brownskin," 217–18; "I'm Just Simply Full of Jazz," 218; "I'm Just Wild about Harry," 215

Spyropoulos, Fahreda Mahzar, 147

Stanislavski, Konstantin, 8

Stevens, Gus, 108–9, 254, 260, 267

Stewart, Cal, 104

Stone, Fred, 33–36, 109, 219

The Sultan of Sulu (Ade), 225, 229–34, 243

Tin Pan Alley (film), 5–7

Tribble, Andrew, 236

A Trip to Coontown (Cole and Johnson), 5, 17, 165–66, 183–90, 194, 195, 196, 207; Tom Brown, 127–28, 130

Tuskegee Institute, 236, 238, 239

Tutt, J. Homer, 18, 121–22, 195, 209, 211–15, 253; Darkest Americans, 209–11

Twain, Mark (Samuel Clemens), 16, 83, 86, 91, 92, 94–97, 106, 182, 205; Ah Sin, 89, 91–99

"Uncle Josh in a Chinese Laundry" (sound recording), 104

"Uncle Snow" (song), 64, 100

Uncle Tom's Cabin (play), 11, 35, 60, 74, 117, 122, 123, 141, 221

"Under the Bamboo Tree" (song), 2

Virginia Minstrels, 10, 60

The Virginia Mummy, 16, 45, 47, 52–59, 279nn27–28

Wabe, Ashea, 147

Walker, Aida Overton, 5, 17, 153, 155–57, 203, 208, 236, 242

Walker, Frank, 17, 125, 127, 131–32, 137, 138, 261

Walker, George, 1, 5, 13, 18, 191–94, 200,

210, 213, 285, 259; *Abyssinia*, 203–4;
Bandanna Land, 121, 155; *In Dahomey*,
195–97
Wallace, Lizzie, 246
Walton, Lester, 76, 82, 125, 128, 211, 216,
220, 239
Washington, Booker T., 236, 239, 305
Waxworks at Play (Williams), 110–13
"The Wedding of the Chinee and the
Coon" (song), 188–90
Whitney, Salem Tutt, 18, 121–22, 131,
132, 195, 209, 211–15, 253; *Darkest
Americans*, 209–11
Williams, Bert, 1, 5, 13, 18, 19, 191–94,
210, 213, 214, 219, 259; *Abyssinia*,

203–4; *Bandanna Land*, 121, 155, 158;
In Dahomey, 191–97, 199; *Mr. Lode of
Koal*, 32, 128, 258
Williams, Henry Llewellyn, 110–13
Williams, Marie, 146, 293–94n33
Williams, Robin, 22, 36
Wise, Fanny, 239, 244, 245
Wynn, Ed, 108; "I'm Going to Get Myself
a Black Salome," 153–54, 200

Yuen, Lily, 18, 254–58, 309n6

Zanina (Daly), 148, 151
Ziegfeld, Florenz, Jr., 140, 170, 219
Ziegfeld Follies (Ziegfeld), 149, 170, 219, 294